THE WORLD
AND THE
INDIVIDUAL

THE WORLD
AND THE
INDIVIDUAL

JOSIAH ROYCE

First Series

The Four Historical Conceptions

of Being

with an Introduction by

Professor John E. Smith, Yale University

GLOUCESTER, MASS.

PETER SMITH

1976

Library of Congress Catalog Card Number: 59-14226

Manufactured in the United States of America

Reprinted, 1976, by
Peter Smith Publisher, Inc.
ISBN 0-8446-2842-5

INTRODUCTION TO DOVER EDITION

THE past decade has witnessed a marked revival of interest in Royce's philosophy and this is as it should be. Regardless of current fashions and the most variable winds of doctrine, no thinker who has grappled with major issues can long remain in the shade. We may criticize and we may modify his doctrine, but we cannot neglect the philosophical and religious problems that formed the basis and driving force of his thought.

The World and the Individual, the Gifford Lectures delivered by Royce in the University of Aberdeen during the years 1899 and 1900, represents his most sustained metaphysical effort. It is not, as we are now very much aware, the final form of his philosophy. The doctrines of interpretation and community as expressed in *The Problem of Christianity* bring his thought to completion. But the main doctrines of his positive theory of Being are to be found in these Gifford Lectures. For in them he sought to answer the fundamental philosophical question: What does it mean *to be?* And his reply in the form of an absolute voluntarism — what he often called his "absolute pragmatism" — remains one of the original and profound solutions to the problem.

The singular fact about these lectures is that they constitute the only sustained effort by an American philosopher to interpret the nature of things in a systematic and comprehensive manner. Whereas Charles Peirce had inclusive and basic ideas he never succeeded in bringing them to systematic form, and James was too wary of the "block universe" to feel at home in any philosophical system. Dewey alone came close to Royce's systematic interest. Royce would not have been at home amidst the current fashion of minute philosophy set forth in collected essays; he belonged to that company for whom philosophy and systematic comprehension always belong together.

In considering *The World and the Individual* we must not overlook the intimate connection Royce envisaged between the problems raised by religion and the classical metaphysical problems. For him, the proper criticism of religion could be carried out only by developing a general theory of Being. The relations between philosophy and religion are not adequately symbolized, according to his view, by a one-way street; the two contribute to each other's life at the same time that they engage in mutual criticism. There is, or should be, constant interaction between them.

Basic to Royce's thought is the approach to the nature of things through analysis of the nature of knowing. Unlike essentially critical philosophers for whom the theory of knowledge is an end in itself, Royce studied the relation of an idea to an object for the purpose of discovering in that relationship a clue to the general nature of Being. He was, in this regard, closer to the post-Kantians than to Kant. He did not, on the other hand, approach metaphysical problems directly as a pre-Kantian might have done; the critical hand of Kant was always upon him. Before it is possible to say what it is to be, one must first settle the problem of what it is to be known.

A proper understanding of Royce's own position — the thoroughly teleological view of reality described by him as the Fourth Conception of Being — forces us to lay hold of the other positions he regarded as inadequate. We need to follow him through his ingenious — at times too ingenious — criticisms of realism, mysticism and critical rationalism. We must see why he could not accept as sufficient unto themselves the three theses that to be is *to be independent;* to be is *to be immediate;* and to be is *to be valid,* even though he attempted to incorporate in his own view the dominant element of truth in each.

To master the central thesis that Being is what fulfills intended meaning and furnishes the goal of a purpose, we need to pay close attention to the crucial chapter, "The Internal and External Meaning of Ideas." There is found expressed the basic notion of a teleological relationship between an idea or meaning and the object which it intends to qualify. For Royce all depends upon the realization of a purpose and the reaching of what is genuinely individual. Unlike other thinkers in the tradition of absolute idealism, Royce would not rest content with the idea that the individual is a construction from universals or a product resulting from some process of specifying universals. He demanded something more and that is found in his voluntarism. Instead of locating all features of individuality in the system of internal relations within the whole of thought, Royce held that the proper uniqueness of the individual is the *interest* he personally takes in his dependence upon the whole and the active *deeds* and decisions through which he responds to that interest. Being an individual becomes a matter of freedom; as a moral achievement it has more to do with the active process of *dominating* through will than with the intellectual process of *determining* through logic.

Royce's somewhat ponderous metaphysical approach has led many to criticize his philosophy as unrepre-

sentative of American thought and experience. George
Herbert Mead, it will be recalled, was most definite in
his judgment on this point. It is a curious fact, however, that Royce's theory of the individual illustrates
better than that of either Peirce or Dewey the widely
accepted doctrine that the American genius is in its
will power and not in its theory. Only James came close
to Royce in finding the essence of the individual in the
unique, voluntary response he made to his situation. It
is hard to believe that any thinker who, like Royce,
finds the human will at the center of the human self
can be seriously out of step with the dominant pattern
of American life.

Santayana teased Royce for writing huge books and
then putting what he really wanted to say in an appendix. *The World and the Individual* has such an appendix
in the form of the "Supplementary Essay" about the
problem of the actual infinite. It occupies a most important place in the argument. For one thing, it is an excel-
lent example of the use made by Royce of the tools of
modern logic for treating metaphysical problems. Its
size might have been less, but its main point is not one
that can safely be ignored. Whether or not we are ready
to go all the way with Royce in his logical method or his
extended argument is not as important as being clear
about the central thesis of the essay. Its main point is
to provide an effective answer to the scepticism of F. H.
Bradley and to show that he was mistaken in denying
to the human mind genuine knowledge of the individual. In reply Royce took on the formidable task of
defending the actual infinite and thus of attempting to
show how genuine individuals can be the subject of a
metaphysical dialectic. The argument aimed at pointing out how a formula that expresses a general purpose
and requires an infinite series of terms for its complete
expression is the model of the actual infinite. The entire

discussion forms an essential link between the two volumes, for the second set of lectures seeks to apply the Fourth Conception of Being to the actual world of nature and to the self as individual reality. Royce could not leave unchallenged Bradley's doctrine that the unity of the one and the many — of the absolute individual and finite individuals — cannot be grasped by the human mind without contradictions. Royce had to show that his program could be carried out despite the formidable scepticism of so acute a metaphysical thinker.

It is to be hoped that the reappearance of *The World and the Individual* will act as a stimulus not only to the further pondering of Royce's thought, but that through it we may recover a concern for those large metaphysical questions that are the life blood of philosophy.

JOHN E. SMITH

Professor of Philosophy
Yale University

New Haven, Connecticut
June, 1959

PREFACE

THE Lectures upon which this volume is based were
delivered before the University of Aberdeen between
January 11 and February 1, 1899. They appear in a
decidedly more extended form than that in which they
were delivered; and they have been subject to some
revision. Lecture VII, in particular, has been much
lengthened in the final preparation for publication.
These differences between the lectures as read and the
printed volume have seemed to me necessary, in order
to complete my statement of the problems at issue, and
of the solution that I offer.

The plan of the whole course is explained more at
length in the opening lecture. Lord Gifford's Will calls
upon his lecturers for a serious treatment of some aspect
of the problems of Natural Religion. These problems
themselves are of the most fundamental sort; and in
this first Series I have not seen my way clear to attempting anything less than a philosophical inquiry into first
principles. The second Series, especially in its later
lectures, will contain the more detailed application of
these first principles to problems that directly concern
religion. But the reader of the present lectures will not
fail to discover how I define, in general terms, God, the

World, the finite Individual, and the most fundamental relations that link them together. But these, as I suppose, are the essential problems of the Philosophy of Religion.

The philosophy here set forth is the result of a good many years of reflection. As to the most essential argument regarding the true relations between our finite ideas and the ultimate nature of things, I have never varied, in spirit, from the view maintained in Chapter XI of my first book, *The Religious Aspect of Philosophy*.[1] That chapter was entitled *The Possibility of Error*, and was intended to show that the very conditions which make finite error possible concerning objective truth, can be consistently expressed only by means of an idealistic theory of the Absolute, — a theory whose outlines I there sketched. The argument in question has since been restated, and set into relations with other matters, without fundamental alteration of its character, and in several forms;[2] once in my *Spirit of Modern Philosophy* (in a shape intended for a popular audience, but with an extended discussion of the historic background of this argument); again, in the book called *The Conception of God*, where my own statement of the argument has .the

---

[1] Published in 1885 at Boston, Mass., by Houghton, Mifflin & Co.

[2] I may here set down the titles of the other books that I have printed, dealing with philosophical problems : *The Spirit of Modern Philosophy* (Boston, Houghton, Mifflin & Co., 1892) ; *The Conception of God* (a discussion in which three colleagues, Professor Howison, Professor LeConte, and Professor Mezes, took part with me, while I was kindly allowed, by the indulgence of my friends, by far the most of the time and the space ; New York, The Macmillan Co., 1897) ; *Studies of Good and Evil* (a collection of essays upon various applications of idealistic doctrine and upon related topics ; New York, Appleton & Co., 1898).

further advantages of Professor Howison's kindly exposition and keen criticism ; and still again, in the paper
called *The Implications of Self-consciousness*, published in
the *Studies of Good and Evil*.   In the present lectures
this argument assumes a decidedly new form, not because
I am in the least disposed to abandon the validity of the
former statements, but because, in the present setting,
the whole matter appears in new relations to other philosophical problems, and becomes, as I hope, deepened in
its significance by these relations.   The new statement,
indicated already in the opening Lecture, is especially
developed in Lecture VII, and is defended against objections in Lecture VIII.

While this central matter regarding the definition of
Truth, and of our relation to truth, has not essentially
changed its place in my mind, I have been doing what
I could, since my first book was written, to come to clearness as to the relations of Idealism to the special problems
of human life and destiny.   In my first book the conception of the Absolute was defined in such wise as led me
then to prefer, quite deliberately, the use of the term
Thought as the best name for the final unity of the
Absolute.   While this term was there so defined as to
make Thought inclusive of Will and of Experience, these
latter terms were not emphasized prominently enough,
and the aspects of the Absolute Life which they denote
have since become more central in my own interests.
The present is a deliberate effort to bring into synthesis,
more fully than I have ever done before, the relations of
Knowledge and of Will in our conception of God.   The
centre of the present discussion is, for this very reason,

the true meaning and place of the concept of Individuality, in regard to which the present discussion carries out a little more fully considerations which appear, in a very different form of statement, in the *Supplementary Essay*, published at the close of *The Conception of God*. As for the term *Thought*, I now agree that the inclusive use which I gave to it in my first book is not wholly convenient; and in these lectures I use this term *Thought* as a name for the process by which we define or describe objects viewed as *beyond* or as *other than* the process whereby they are defined or described, while, in my *Religious Aspect of Philosophy*, the term, as applied to the Absolute, referred not only to finite processes of thinking, but also, and expressly, to the inclusive Whole of Insight, *in* which both truth and value are attained, not as objects beyond Thought's ideas, but as appreciated and immanent fulfilment or expression of all the purposes of finite Thought. This usage seems to be less effective for purposes of exposition than that which I have tried to employ in this book. Besides, I now more emphasize the distinctions there already implied, while I surrender in no whit my assurance of the unity of God and the World.

As for the present discussion, it is useless to defend its methods to people who by nature or by training are opposed to all thoroughgoing philosophical inquiry. Such are nowadays accustomed to say that they are already well aware of the limits of human thinking, and that they confine themselves wholly to "the realm of experience." It is useless to tell them that this book also is an inquiry regarding just this realm of experience. For such critics, after a fashion not unknown amongst people who think themselves to be "pure" empiricists, will of course know, quite *a priori* and absolutely, that there is nothing absolute to be known. Not for such critics, who may be left where God has placed them, but for still open-hearted inquirers, I may as well say, however, that, to my mind, the only demonstrable truths of an ultimate philosophy relate to the constitution of the actual realm of Experience, and to so much only about the constitution of this realm as cannot be denied without self-contradiction. Whenever, in dealing with Experience, we try to find out what, on the whole, it is and means, we philosophize. Our goal is reached, so far as the demonstrable truth is concerned, whenever we have found a series of propositions relating to the constitution of the realm of experience, and such that, as soon as you try to deny these propositions, you implicitly reaffirm them by your very attempt at denial. After you have found these propositions, you have, of course, a right to use them, more or less effectively, as a partial basis for special applications and results which will indeed remain, like all our human knowledge of particulars, more or less hypothetical. But your hypotheses about particular problems must be judged by themselves. Your body of central truth is subject only to the test just mentioned. And you call this truth "absolute" merely because you conceive that it bears this test. Whether it does so is a question of fact, not of authority. And every man must, in such a matter, look for himself before judging about what is offered to him.

As to the principal special features of this discussion,

they are : (1) The definition and comparison of what I have called the Four Historical Concepts of Being. I believe this aspect of these lectures to be, in many respects, a novelty in discussion. (2) The form here given to the criticism of Realism in the Third Lecture. (3) The use made of the parallelism between the realistic and the mystical concepts of Being in the Fourth and Fifth Lectures. (4) The transition, in the Sixth and Seventh Lectures, from the concept of the Real as the Valid to that concrete conception of Being which, to my mind, constitutes Idealism. (5) The statement of the finite contrast and the final unity of the External and Internal Meaning of Ideas. (6) The concept of Individuality which is expounded in the Seventh and in the later lectures, and the reconciliation of the One and the Many proposed here and in my *Supplementary Essay*.

This *Supplementary Essay* itself, which my publisher has very self-sacrificingly allowed me to add to the present volume, contains my defence against the objections which Mr. Bradley's *Appearance and Reality* seems to render so serious as obstacles in the way of any such account as mine of our concrete relations to the Absolute. My defence is itself but a very poor expression of the very deep and positive obligations which I owe to Mr. Bradley's book, — a book without which much of what appears in my Lectures themselves could never have received anything like the present form. As a part of this defence, I have been led into a discussion of the concept of the quantitative Infinite; and in this portion of my investigation my obligations are indeed numerous, and are, in part, recognized in the notes to the *Supple-*

mentary Essay. In particular, however, I have now to mention what there can only appear in a very inadequate fashion, viz. my special obligation to Mr. Charles Peirce, not only for the stimulus gained from his various published comments and discussions bearing upon the concept of the Infinite, but for the guidance and the suggestions due to some unpublished lectures of his which I had the good fortune to hear. I need not say that I do not intend, by this acknowledgment, to make him appear responsible for my particular opinions. My own present study of the concept of the Infinite may be justified by its effort to bring into connection a number of apparently unrelated tendencies of recent discussion, and to review the whole issue in the light of my own conception of what constitutes an Individual. The result, as I hope, may serve to justify some of the essential bases of my thesis as to the relations of God and Man.

I regret that Professor Ladd's *Theory of Reality* appeared too late for me to take account of this important contribution to the problems of the present volume.

My thanks are due to my colleague, Professor Charles R. Lanman, for his translations of the passages from the *Upanishads* which appear in the lecture on Mysticism. I have also to thank my other colleagues, Professor Maxime Bôcher and Professor William F. Osgood, for kind suggestions as to the remarks concerning specifically mathematical topics in the *Supplementary Essay* and in the lectures on Validity. And my especial thanks also are owed to my wife, for invaluable aid in preparing my lectures for publication. That, after all, quite apart from the problematic issues discussed, plain errors doubtless remain visible in text and in matters of fact, is something for which I alone am responsible. An index to both series of lectures is intended to accompany the Second Series, which will probably appear within a year.

CAMBRIDGE, MASSACHUSETTS,
    October 30, 1899.

CONTENTS

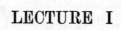

LECTURE I

THE WORLD AND THE INDIVIDUAL

FIRST SERIES: *THE FOUR HISTORICAL CON-*
CEPTIONS OF BEING

LECTURE I

INTRODUCTION: THE RELIGIOUS PROBLEMS AND THE THEORY OF BEING

In the literature of Natural Religion at least three different conceptions of the subject are represented. The first of these conceptions regards Natural Religion as a search for what a well-known phrase has called "the way through Nature to God." If we accept this conception, we begin by recognizing both the existence of the physical world and the validity of the ordinary methods and conceptions of the special sciences of nature. We undertake to investigate what light, if any, the broader generalizations of natural science, when once accepted as statements about external reality, throw upon the problems of religion. It belongs, for instance, to this sort of inquiry to ask: What countenance does the present state of science give to the traditional argument from Design?

The second of our three conceptions views Religion less as a doctrine to be proved or disproved through a study of the external world than as a kind of consciousness whose justification lies in its rank amongst the various inner manifestations of our human nature.   Man, so this conception holds, is essentially a religious being. He has religion because his own inmost nature craves it. If you wish, then, to justify religion, or even to comprehend it, you must view it, not as a theory to be proved or disproved by an appeal to external reality, but rather as a faith to be estimated through reference to the inner consciousness of those who need, who create, and who enjoy religion.   From this point of view the study of Natural Religion concerns itself less with proof than with confession, with a taxing of interior values, and with a description of the religious experience of mankind.   A somewhat extended interpretation of this point of view treats the purely historical study of the various religions of mankind as a contribution to our comprehension of Natural Religion.

But a third conception of the study of Natural Religion remains.   This third view identifies the doctrine in question with the fundamental Philosophy of Religion.   It is the Nature of Things, viewed in the light of the most critical examination of our reason, that is now the object of an inquiry into Natural Religion. The problems at issue are, for this view, those of Aristotle's *Metaphysics*, of Fichte's *Wissenschaftslehre*, of Hegel's *Logik*, — of all the undertakings that, in the history of thought, have most directly attempted the contemplation of Being as Being.   For our first conception the student of Natural Religion, having accepted the natural knowledge of his time as valid, and not having attempted to delve beneath the foundations of that knowledge, seeks to interpret external nature in the light of religious interests. For our second conception Natural Religion is viewed simply as the voice of human nature itself, whose faith is to be expressed, whose ideals are to be recorded, whose will and whose needs are to be, above all, consulted and portrayed, since, for this view, the consciousness of those who believe in religious truth is, when once made articulate, its own apology. But, for our third conception, the office of the student of Natural Religion is to deal with the most fundamental metaphysical problems. He is for this view a thorough-going critic of the foundations of our faith, and of the means of our insight into the true nature of Reality.

All these three conceptions, however much they may differ, have in common what makes it proper enough to view them as conceptions of the study of Natural Religion. For they are all three concerned with religion; they can all alike be pursued without explicit dependence upon any creed as to a revealed religion; and finally, they are busied about some relation between the natural order of truth and the contents of religious doctrine. They differ in the sort of natural truth that forms their starting-point, or that limits the scope of the investigation which they propose. I suppose that no one of these various lines of inquiry will ever come to be wholly neglected. But their office is distinct. And I mention them here in order all the more clearly to say, at the outset, that our own business, in these lectures, is with the most neglected and arduous of the methods of studying the relations between religion and the ultimate problems of the Theory of Being. From the first, to be sure, we shall be concerned, in one sense, with human nature, as every philosophy has to be concerned.   And in the latter half of this course the Philosophy of Nature will play a part in our investigation.   But the central problem of our discussion will be the question: What is Reality ?

I

In thus stating, in the opening words, the plan of these lectures, I do so with a full sense of the shadow that such a programme may, at the first glimpse, seem to cast upon the prospects of our whole undertaking.   It is true that, in calling the fundamental problems of the Metaphysic of Religion relatively neglected, I do not fail to recognize that they are both ancient and celebrated, and that some of us may think them even hackneyed.   It is certainly not uncommon to call them antiquated.   But what I have meant by the phrase " relatively neglected " is that, compared with the more easily accessible fashions of dealing with Natural Religion, the strictly metaphysical treatment less frequently involves that sort of ardent hand-to-hand struggle with the genuine issues themselves that goes on when men are hopefully interested in a study for its own sake.   It is one thing to expound, or even to assail, the theology of Hegel or of St. Thomas, or to report any of those various quaint opinions of philosophers in which even the popular mind often delights.   It is another thing to grapple with the issues of life for one's self.   The wiser religions have always told us that we cannot be saved through the piety of our neighbors, but have to work out our own salvation with fear and trembling.   Well, just so the theoretical student of Natural

Religion has to learn that he cannot comprehend ultimate philosophical truth merely by reading the reports of other people's reasonings, but must do his thinking for himself, not indeed without due instruction, but certainly without depending wholly upon his text-books. And if this be true, then the final issues of religious philosophy may be said to be relatively neglected, so long as students are not constantly afresh grappling with the ancient problems, and giving them renderings due to direct personal contact with their intricacies. It is not a question of any needed originality of opinion, but it is rather a matter of our individual intimacy with these issues.

And now, in recognizing the fact of the comparative neglect of the Theory of Being in the discussions of Natural Religion, I recognize also the motives that tend to make such an inquiry seem, at the first glimpse, un-promising. These motives may be expressed in the forms of three objections, namely, first, that such undertakings are pretentious, by reason of the dignity and the mystery of the topic; secondly, that they are dreary, by reason of the subtle distinctions and the airy abstractions involved in every such research; and thirdly, that they are op-posed, in spirit, to the sort of study for which in our day the sciences of experience have given the only worthy model.

Such objections are as inevitable as they are, to lovers of philosophy, harmless. Philosophy necessarily involves a good deal of courage; but so does life in general. It is pretentious to wrestle with angels; but there are some blessings that you cannot win in any other way. Philos-ophy is an old affair in human history; but that does not make the effort at individuality in one's fashion of thinking a less worthy ideal for every new mind. As to the dreariness of metaphysics, it is always the case, both in religion, and in thinking about religion, that, just as the letter killeth, and the spirit giveth life, so the mere report of tradition is dreary, but the inward life of thinking for one's self the meaning within or behind the tradition constitutes the very coming of the Spirit of Truth himself into our own spirits ; and that coming of the Spirit, in so far as it occurs at all, never seems to any of us dreary. As for the fine-drawn distinctions and airy abstractions, no distinction is ever too subtle for you, at the moment when it occurs to you to make that distinction for yourself, and not merely to hear that somebody else has made it. And no abstraction seems to you too airy in the hour when you rise upon your own wings to the region where just that abstraction happens to be an element in the concrete fulness of your thoughtful life. Now it chances to be a truth of metaphysics, as it is an experience of religion, that just when you are most individual, most alone, as it were, in your personal thinking, about ultimate and divine matters, you are most completely one with that universal Spirit of Truth of which we just spoke. It is then your personal process of thinking that both gives interest to the subject and secures your relation to the Reality. Hence not the universality nor yet the ultimate character of the principles of which we think, but rather our own sluggishness in thinking, is responsible for the supposed dreariness of the Theory of Being. As Aristotle observed, that Theory itself is what all men most desire. You may in these regions either think or not think the truth; but you cannot think the truth without loving it; and the dreariness which men often impute to Metaphysics, is merely the dreariness of not understanding the subject, — a sort of dreariness for which indeed there is no help except learning to understand. In fact, nobody can ever regret seeing ultimate truth. That we shall hereafter find to be, so to speak, one of the immediate implications of our very definition of Being. When people complain of philosophy as a dreary enterprise, they are then merely complaining of their own lack of philosophical insight. The lover of philosophy can only offer them his sincerest agreement, and sympathy, so far as concerns the ground of their own complaint. He too shares their complaint, for he is human, and finds his own unwisdom dreary. But he is at least looking lovingly toward yonder shining light, while they walk wearily with their backs to the Celestial City.

As to the supposed opposition between the methods of philosophy and those of the special sciences of experience, — it exists, but it does not mean any real opposition of spirit. Here are two ways of getting insight, not two opposed creeds. The very wealth and the growth of modern empirical research furnish especially strong reasons for supposing that the time is near when the central problems of the Theory of Being shall be ready for restatement. Our life does not grow long and healthily in one region, without being ready for new growth in other regions. The indirect influence of special science upon philosophy is sure, but does not always mean a logical dependence of philosophy upon the empirical results of science. Just so, pure mathematical science has no logical dependence upon physics. Yet we have all heard how largely physical science has influenced the lines of investigation followed by the modern mathematicians. Within the mathematical realm itself, pure Algebra, when once abstractly defined, is not logically dependent upon Geometry for its principles or for its theories, yet some theories of modern Algebra have actually developed largely under the spell, as it were, of ideas of an unquestionable geometrical origin. Now a similar relation, I think, will in future find the development of pure Philosophy, and in particular of Rational Theology, to the progress of the special sciences, both mathematical and empirical. I do not think it right to regard philosophy merely as a compendium of the results of special science. Philosophy has its own field. But on the other hand, to reflect upon the meaning of life and of science (and in such thorough-going Reflection philosophy consists), is a process whose seriousness and wealth must grow as our human life and science progress. And hence every great new advance of science demands a fresh consideration of philosophic issues, and will insure in the end a power to grasp, more critically and more deeply, the central problem of Being itself. Hence the more we possess of special science, the more hope we ought to have for pure Philosophy.

II

So much then for the most general definition and justification of the proposed scope of these lectures.

I cannot forbear to point out the easily recognizable
fact that, in thus defining the plan before us, I have
merely tried to adhere, so far as I can, to the programme explicitly laid down by Lord Gifford. A study
of religion is required of your lecturer, and Lord Gifford, as appears from the words of his Will, would
himself have thought, above all, of studying religion
not only as a matter of purely natural and rational
knowledge, but primarily as a body of Ontological
problems and opinions, in other words as, in its theory,
a branch of the Theory of Being.   It is of " God, the
only Substance," that your lecturer, if his Ontology so
far agrees with Lord Gifford's, will principally speak.
Well then, I can best work in the spirit of Lord Gifford's requirements if I explicitly devote our principal
attention to the ultimate problems of Ontology, laying
due stress upon their relations to Religion.

And now let me venture to sketch, in outline, the
particular discussions by which I propose to contribute
my fragment towards a study of the inexhaustible problems propounded by Lord Gifford's Will. Programmes
in philosophy, as Hegel used to say, mean far less
than in other enterprises. But even here some sort of
programme is needed to fix in advance our attention.

My precise undertaking then, in the following lectures, is to show what we mean by Being in general,
and by the special sorts of Reality that we attribute to
God, to the World, and to the Human Individual.
These I regard as the problems of the ontology of religion.   In every step of this undertaking I shall actually be, in a psychological and in an historical sense,

dependent, both for my ideas and for their organization, upon this or that philosophical or theological tradition (well known to every student of philosophy); and therefore I must early introduce into my work a sketch of certain philosophical traditions in which we are to be especially interested. Here, of course, you might expect to find, as such an historical introduction to our later critical enterprises, either a summary of the history of the principal religious ideas, or some account of the technical history of the Philosophy of Religion itself. Yet for neither of these two very natural enterprises shall I have time. My very fragmentary historical discussions will be limited to an attempt to depict some of the principal conceptions concerning the ultimate nature of Being, in other words to sketch the history of what one might call the ontological predicate of the expression *to be*, or *to be real*, used as a means of asserting that something exists. I shall dwell upon the nature of Being, because to assert that God is, or that the World is, or even, with Descartes, that I am, implies that one knows what it is to be, or in other words, what the so-called existential predicate itself involves. Now it is true that the existential predicate, the word *is* used to assert the real Being of any object, is often viewed as something of an absolutely simple, ultimate, and indescribable meaning. Yet even if this view were sound, the ultimate and the simple are, in philosophy, as truly and as much topics for reflective study as are the most complex and derived ideas of our minds. Moreover, a great deal of popular religion seems to involve the notion that it is both easier and more important to know *that* God is, than to know, with any sort of articulation, *What* God is, so that if you express even a total ignorance of the Divine nature and attribute, there are some very traditionally minded people who will hardly dare to disagree with you, while if you express the least doubt of the assertion that God is, the same people will at once view you with horror as an atheist. Now this preference in much popular religious thinking for the ontological predicate in its purity is not an altogether rational preference.   Yet we shall find that it is based upon very deep and even very worthy, if vague, instincts.   It is true that if I pretend to know no attributes whatever, characterizing a given object X, I seem to have won very little by believing that X nevertheless exists.   Yet the fondness for the Unknowable in theology has been to some extent supported by the dim feeling that even in asserting the bare existence of a being, and especially of God, I am already committed to extremely important attributes, whose definition, even if not yet overt, is already, however darkly, implied in my abstract statement.   It is interesting, therefore, to study historically what men have supposed themselves to mean by the ontological predicate.

The basis having been thus laid in the history of the subject, our lectures, at various points in the historical summary, will have at some length to undertake a critical comparison and analysis of the various meanings of the ontological predicate.   Such an analysis will constantly show us unexpected connections of these meanings with the concrete interests of religion.   We shall find it with ontology, as it certainly is with ethics.   People often regard moral philosophy as a topic very abstract and dry. And yet wherever two or three are gathered together indulging in gossip about the doings of their neighbors, their speech, even if it involves out-and-out scandal, is devoted to a more or less critical discussion, to an illustration, and even to a sort of analysis of what are really very deep ethical problems, — problems about what men ought to do, and about the intricate relations between law and passion in human life.   Well, as even the most frivolous or scandalous gossip really manifests an intense, if rude concern, for the primal questions of moral philosophy, so our children and all our most simple and devout souls constantly talk ontology, discourse of being, face the central issues of reality, but know it not.   Yet once face the true connection of abstract theory and daily life, and then one easily sees that life means theory, and that you deal constantly, and decisively, with the problems of the Theory of Being whenever you utter a serious word. This then is the reason why our ontological studies will bear directly upon the daily concerns of religion.

Our discussion of the general meaning and of the relative value of the various ontological predicates will, moreover, throw light, as we go, upon some of the best known of the special issues of the history of theology.   We shall see, for instance, what has been the real motive that has made the doctrine of the speculative Mystics so important a factor in the life of the more complex religious faiths. We shall see too, in the great historical conflicts between the Realistic and the Mystical conceptions of the nature of Reality, the source of some of the most important con-

troversies concerning the being and attributes of God,
the existence of the physical world, and the nature of
human individuality. Thus we shall gradually approach
a position where we shall learn the inevitableness of a certain final conception of the meaning of our ontological
predicates ; and the result of our critical study will be a
light that we may not wholly have anticipated, both upon
the conception of God, and upon our notion of the relations between God, the World, and the Human Individual. With the development of these fundamental
conceptions, the first of my two series of lectures will
close. We shall herewith have stated the bases of
religion.

The second series I intend first to devote to the application of our fundamental conceptions to the more special
problems of the nature of the human Ego, the meaning of
the finite realm called the Physical World, and the interpretation of Evolution. The vast extent of the discussions
thus suggested will be limited, in our own case, by the
very fact that we shall here be attempting merely the
application of a single very general ontological idea to a
few problems which we shall view rather as illustrations
of our central thesis concerning Reality, than as matters
to be exhaustively considered for their own sake. Having thus sketched our Cosmology, if I may call it such,
we shall then conclude the whole undertaking by a summary discussion of the problems of Good and Evil, of
Freedom, of Immortality, and of the destiny of the Individual, still reviewing our problems in the light of our
general conception of Being. The title that I shall have
given to the whole course of lectures, " The World and

the Individual " will thus, I hope, prove to be justified by the scope of our discussion in the two divisions of this course.

III

The plan of the proposed investigation has now been set before you in outline.   May I next undertake to indicate a little more precisely not merely what problems we are to attempt, but the sort of positive argument that we are to use, and the kind of result that we may hope to reach?   A philosophy must indeed be judged not by its theses, but by its methods ; and not upon the basis of mere summaries, but after a consideration of the details of its argument.   Yet it helps to make clearer the way through an intricate realm of inquiry if one first surveys, as it were, from above, the country through which, in such an enterprise, the road is to pass.   I propose then, to indicate at once, and in the rest of this lecture, where the central problem of the Theory of Being lies, and by what method I think that this problem is, in a general sense, to be solved.   To state the proposed solution, however, even in the most abstract and necessarily unconvincing fashion, is to arouse comments as to the meaning of this thesis, as to its consequences, and, above all, in a discussion like the present, as to its bearing upon the more practical interests of religion.   I think that we may be helped to an understanding hereafter, if I attempt at once to call out, and, by anticipation, to answer, a few such comments.

I am one of those who hold that when you ask the question : What is an Idea ? and : How can Ideas stand in any true relation to Reality ? you attack the world-knot in the way that promises most for the untying of its meshes. This way is, of course, very ancient. It is the way of Plato, and, in a sense, already the way of his Master. It is, in a different sense, the way of Kant. If you view philosophy in this fashion, you subordinate the study of the World as Fact to a reflection upon the World as Idea. Begin by accepting, upon faith and tradition, the mere brute Reality of the World as Fact, and there you are, sunk deep in an ocean of mysteries. The further you then proceed in the study of that world, the longer seems the way to God or to clearness, unless you from the start carry with you some sort of faith, perhaps a very blind and immediate faith, that God reigns, or that the facts in themselves are somehow clear. The World as Fact surprises you with all sorts of strange contrasts. Now it reveals to you, in the mechanics and physics of the stars or in the processes of living beings, vast realms of marvellous reasonableness; now it bewilders you, in the endless diversities of natural facts, by a chaos of unintelligible fragments and of scattered events; now it lifts up your heart with wondrous glimpses of ineffable goodness; and now it arouses your wrath by frightful signs of cruelty and baseness. Conceive it as a realm for pure scientific theory; and, so far as your knowledge reaches, it is full at once of the show of a noble order, and of hints of a vain chance. On the other hand, conceive it as a realm of values, attempt to estimate its worth, and it baffles you with caprices, like a charming and yet hopelessly wayward child, or like a bad fairy. That is the world of brute natural fact as you, with your present form of consciousness, are forced to observe it, if you try to get any total impression of its behavior. And so, this World of Fact daily announces itself to you as a defiant mystery — a mystery such as Job faced, and such as the latest agnostic summary of empirical results, in their bearing upon our largest human interests, or such as even the latest pessimistic novel will no doubt any day present afresh to you, in all the ancient unkindliness that belongs to human fortune.

The World as Fact is, then, for all of us, persistently baffling, unless we find somewhere else the key to it. The philosophers of the Platonic type have, however, long ago told us that this defect of our world of fact is due, at bottom, simply to the fault of our human type of consciousness. And hence a whole realm of philosophical inquiry has been devoted, in the best ages of speculative thinking, to a criticism of this human type of consciousness itself. Upon such a criticism, Plato founded his conception of the Ideal World. By such criticism, Plotinus sought to find the way upwards, through Soul to the realm of the Intellect, and beyond the Intellect to his Absolute " One." Through a similar criticism, Scholastic doctrine attempted to purify our human type of consciousness, until it should reach the realm of genuine spirituality, and attain an insight but a little lower than that of the conceived angelic type of intelligence. For all such thinkers, the raising of our type of consciousness to some higher level meant not only the winning of insight into Reality, but also the attainment of an inner and distinctly religious ideal. To a later and less technically pious form of thinking, one sees the transition in Spinoza, who was at once, as we now know, a child of Scholasti-

cism, and a student of the more modern physical conceptions of his day,—at once a mystic, a realist, and a partisan
of nature.   For Spinoza too, it is our type of finite consciousness that makes our daily world of fact, or, as he
prefers to say, of imagination, seem chaotic ; and the way
to truth still is to be found through an inner and reflective purification of experience.   A widely different interpretation is given to the same fundamental conception, by
Kant.   But in Kant's case also, remote from his interests
as is anything savoring of mysticism, the end of philosophical insight is again the vindication of a higher form of
consciousness.   For Kant, however, this is the consciousness of the Moral Reason, which recognizes no facts as
worthy of its form of assurance, except the facts implied
by the Good Will, and by the Law of the good will.   All
these ways then of asserting the primacy of the World as
Idea over the World as Fact, agree in dealing with the
problem of Reality from the side of the means through
which we are supposed to be able to attain reality, that is,
from the side of the Ideas.

IV

But if this is to be the general nature of our own
inquiry also, then everything for us will depend upon
the fundamental questions, already stated, viz. first :
What is an Idea ? and second : How can an Idea be
related to Reality ?   In the treatment of both these
questions, however, various methods and theories at
once come into sight.   And, to begin with one of the
favorite issues, namely the fundamental definition of the

word "idea" itself, there is a well-known tendency in a good deal of philosophy, both ancient and modern, either to define an idea, as an Image, destined to picture facts external to the idea, or else, in some other way, to lay stress upon the *externally* cognitive or "representative" value of an idea as its immediately obvious and its most essential aspect. From this point of view, men have conceived that the power of ideas to know a Reality external to themselves, was indeed either something too obvious to excite inquiry, or else an ultimate and inexplicable power. "Ideas exist," says this view, "and they exist as knowing facts external to themselves. And this is their fundamental character." Now I myself shall, in these lectures, regard this power of ideas to cognize facts external to themselves not as a primal fact of existence but as an aspect of ideas which decidedly needs reflective consideration, and a very critical restatement. Hence I cannot here begin by saying : "Ideas are states of mind that image facts external to themselves." That would be useful enough as a definition of ideas in a Psychology of Cognition. For such a Psychology would presuppose what we are here critically to consider, namely, the very possibility of a cognition of Being. But, for the purpose of our present theory, the definition of the term "idea" must be made in such wise as not formally to presuppose the power of ideas to have cognitive relations to outer objects.

Moreover, in attempting a definition of the general term "idea," while I shall not be attempting a psychology of cognition, I shall myself be guided by certain psy-

chological analyses of the mere contents of our consciousness, — analyses which have become prominent
in recent discussion. What is often called the active
and sometimes also the motor aspect of our mental
life, has been much dwelt upon of late. This is no
place, and at present we have no need, for a psychological theory of the origin or of the causes of what
is called activity, but as a fact, you have in your mental life a sort of consciousness accompanying the processes by which, as the psychologists are accustomed to
say, you adjust your organism to its environment; and
this sort of consciousness differs, in some notable features, from what takes place in your mind in so far as
the mere excitation of your sense organs by the outer
world is regarded apart from the experiences that you
have when you are said to react upon your impressions. The difference between merely seeing your
friend, or hearing his voice, and consciously or actively
regarding him as your friend, and behaving towards
him in a friendly way, is a difference obvious to consciousness, whatever your theory of the sources of mental activity. Now this difference between outer sense
impressions, or images derived from such impressions,
and active responses to sense impressions, or ideas
founded upon such responses, is not merely a difference
between what is sometimes called the intellect, and
what is called the will. For, as a fact, the intellectual
life is as much bound up with our consciousness of our
acts as is the will. There is no purely intellectual life,
just as there is no purely voluntary life. The difference between knowledge and will, so far as it has a

metaphysical meaning, will concern us much later. For the present, it is enough to note that your intelligent ideas of things never consist of mere images of the things, but always involve a consciousness of how you propose to act towards the things of which you have ideas. A sword is an object that you would propose to use, or to regard in one way, while a pen is to be used in another; your idea of the object involves the memory of the appropriate act. Your idea of your friend differs from your idea of your enemy by virtue of your consciousness of your different attitude and intended behaviour towards these objects. Complex scientific ideas, viewed as to their conscious significance, are, as Professor Stout[1] has well said, plans of action, ways of constructing the objects of your scientific consciousness. Intelligent ideas then, belong, so to speak, to the motor side of your life rather than to the merely sensory. This was what Kant meant by the spontaneity of the understanding. To be sure, a true scientific idea is a mental construction supposed to correspond with an outer object, or to imitate that object. But when we try to define the idea in itself, as a conscious fact, our best means is to lay stress upon the sort of will, or active meaning, which any idea involves for the mind that forms the idea.

By the word "Idea," then, as we shall use it when, after having criticised opposing theories, we come to state, in these lectures, our own thesis, I shall mean in the end any state of consciousness, whether simple or complex, which, when present, is then and there viewed as at least the par-

[1] Stout, *Analytic Psychology*, Vol. II, Chap. VIII, especially pp. 114, 124.

tial expression or embodiment of a single conscious purpose. I shall indeed say nothing for the present as to what
causes an idea. But I shall assert that an idea appears in
consciousness as having the significance of an act of will.
I shall also dwell upon the inner purpose, and not upon
the external relations, as the primary and essential feature
of an idea. For instance, you sing to yourself a melody,
you are then and there conscious that the melody as you
hear yourself singing it, partially fulfils and embodies a
purpose. Well, in this sense, your melody, at the moment when you sing it, or even when you silently listen
to its imagined presence, constitutes a musical idea, and is
often so called. You may so regard the melody without
yet explicitly dwelling upon the externally cognitive
value of the musical idea, as the representative of a melody
sung or composed by somebody else. You may even suppose the melody original with yourself, unique, and sung
now for the first time. Even so, it would remain just as
truly a musical idea, however partial or fragmentary ; for
it would then and there, when sung, or even when inwardly heard, partly embody your own conscious purpose.
In the same sense, any conscious act, at the moment when
you perform it, not merely expresses, but is, in my present
sense, an idea. To count ten is thus also an idea, if the
counting fulfils and embodies, in however incomplete and
fragmentary a way, your conscious purpose, and that
quite apart from the fact that counting ten also may
enable you to cognize the numerical character of facts external to the conscious idea of ten itself. In brief, an
idea, in my present definition may, and, as a fact always
does, if you please, appear to be representative of a fact

existent beyond itself. But the primary character, which
makes it an idea, is not this its representative character,
is not its vicarious assumption of the responsibility of
standing for a being beyond itself, but is its inner character as relatively fulfilling the purpose (that is, as presenting the partial fulfilment of the purpose), which is in the
consciousness of the moment wherein the idea takes place.
It is in this sense that we speak of any artistic idea, as
present in the creative mind of the artist. I propose, in
stating my own view hereafter, to use the word "idea" in
this general sense.

Well, this definition of the primary character of an
idea, enables me at once to deal with a conception which
will play no small part in our later discussions. I refer
to the very conception of the Meaning of an idea. One
very fair way to define an idea, had we chosen to use that
way, might have been to say : An Idea is any state of
mind that has a conscious meaning. Thus, according to
my present usage of the word "idea," a color, when merely
seen, is in so far, for consciousness, no idea. A brute
noise, merely heard, is no idea. But a melody, when
sung, a picture, when in its wholeness actively appreciated, or the inner memory of your friend now in your
mind, is an idea. For each of these latter states means
something to you at the instant when you get it present
to consciousness. But now, what is this meaning of any
idea? What does one mean by a meaning? To this
question, I give, for the instant, an intentionally partial
answer. I have just said that an idea is any state of
mind, or complex of states, that, when present, is consciously viewed as the relatively completed embodiment,

and therefore already as the partial fulfilment of a purpose. Now this purpose, just in so far as it gets a present conscious embodiment in the contents and in the form of the complex state called the idea, constitutes what I shall hereafter call the Internal Meaning of the Idea. Or, to repeat, the state or complex of states called the idea, presents to consciousness the expressed although in general the incomplete fulfilment of a purpose. In presence of this fulfilment, one could, as it were, consciously say: "That is what I want, and just in so far I have it. The purpose of singing or of imagining the melody is what I want fulfilled ; and, in this musical idea, I have it at least partially fulfilled." Well, this purpose, when viewed as fulfilled through the state called the idea, is the internal meaning of the idea. Or yet once more, — to distinguish our terms a little more sharply, — in advance of the presence of the idea in consciousness, one could abstractly speak of the purpose as somewhat not yet fulfilled. Hereupon let there come the idea as the complex of conscious states, the so-called act wherein this purpose gets, as it were, embodied, and relatively speaking, accomplished. Then, finally, we shall have the internal meaning of the idea, and this internal meaning of the completed idea is the purpose viewed as so far embodied in the idea, the soul, as it were, which the idea gives body. Any idea then, viewed as a collection of states, must have its internal meaning, since, being an idea, it does in some degree embody its purpose. And our two terms, "purpose embodied in the idea," and "internal meaning of the idea," represent the same subject-matter viewed in two aspects. The purpose which the idea, when it comes, is to fulfil, may first be viewed apart from the fulfilment. Then it remains, so far, mere purpose. Or it may be viewed as expressed and so far partially accomplished by means of the complex state called the idea, and then it is termed " the present internal meaning of this state."

V

So now we have defined what we mean by an idea, and what we mean by the internal meaning of an idea. But ideas often seem to have a meaning, yes, as one must add, finite ideas always undertake or appear to have a meaning, that is not exhausted by this conscious internal meaning presented and relatively fulfilled at the moment when the idea is there for our finite view. The melody sung, the artist's idea, the thought of your absent friend —a thought on which you love to dwell : all these not merely have their obvious internal meaning, as meeting a conscious purpose by their very presence, but also they at least appear to have that other sort of meaning, that reference beyond themselves to objects, that cognitive relation to outer facts, that attempted correspondence with outer facts, which many accounts of our ideas regard as their primary, inexplicable, and ultimate character. I call this second, and, for me, still problematic and derived aspect of the nature of ideas, their apparently External Meaning. In this sense it is that I say, " The melody sung by me not only is an idea internally meaning the embodiment of my purpose at the instant when I sing it, but also is an idea that means, and that in this sense externally means, the object called, say, a certain theme which Beethoven composed." In this same sense, your idea of your absent friend, is, for my definition, an idea primarily, because you now fulfil some of your love for dwelling upon your inner affection for your friend by getting the idea present to mind. But you also regard it as an idea which, in the external sense, is said to mean the real being called your friend, in so far as the idea is said to refer to that real friend, and to resemble him. This external meaning, I say, appears to be very different from the internal meaning, and wholly to transcend the latter.

By thus first distinguishing sharply between the conscious internal meaning of an idea and its apparently external meaning, we get before us an important way of stating the problem of knowledge or, in other words, the problem of the whole relation between Idea and Being. We shall find this not only a very general, but a very fundamental, and, as I believe, despite numerous philosophical discussions, still a comparatively neglected way. And in problems of this kind so much turns upon the statement of the issue, that I must be excused for thus dwelling at length, at this early stage, upon the precise sense in which we are to employ our terms.

Plainly, then, whoever studies either a special science, or a problem of general metaphysics, is indeed concerned with what he then and there views as the external meaning of certain ideas. And an idea, when thus viewed, appears as if it were essentially a sort of imitation or image of a being, and this being, the external object of our thoughtful imitation, appears to be, in so far, quite separate from these our ideas that imitate its characters or that attempt to correspond to them. From such a point of view, our ideas seemed destined to perform a task which is externally set for them by the real world. I count, but I count, in ordinary life, what I take to be real objects, existent quite apart from my counting. Suppose that I count ships seen from the shore. There, says common sense, are the ships, sailing by themselves, and quite indifferent to whether anybody counts them or not. In advance of the counting, the ships, in so far as they are a real collection, have their number. This common sense also presupposes. Let there be seen, yonder, on the sea, nine ships or ten ; this number of the real ships is in itself determinate. It does not result from my counting, but is the standard for the latter to follow. The numerical ideas of anybody who counts the ships must either repeat the preëxistent facts, or else fail to report those facts accurately. That alternative seems absolute and final. The question how anybody ever comes to count ships at all, is a question for psychology. But there remains for the seeker after metaphysical truth, just as much as for the man of common sense, the apparently sharp alternative : Either actual ships, whose multitude is just what it happens to be, whose number preëxists, in advance of any counting, are correctly represented by the ideas of one who happens to be able to count, or else these ships are incorrectly counted. In the latter case we seem to be forced to say that the counting process misses its external aim. In the former case we say that the ideas expressed by the one who counts are true. But in both cases alike the ideas in question thus appear to be true or false by virtue of their external meaning, by virtue of the fact that they either correspond or do not correspond to facts which are themselves no part of the ideas. This simple instance of the ships and of the ideas of a man who sits watching and counting the ships, is obviously typical of all instances of the familiar relation of ideas to Being, as the metaphysic of common sense views Being, or of the relation of ideas to what we have here called the objects of their external meaning. That ideas have such external meanings, that they do refer to facts existent wholly apart from themselves, that their relation to these facts is one of successful correspondence or of error-producing non-correspondence, that the ideas in so far aim, not merely to embody, like the musical ideas just exemplified, an internal purpose, but also to imitate, in the form of their conscious structure and in the relationship of their own elements, the structure and relationship of a world of independent facts, — what could possibly seem, from such a common-sense point of view, more obvious than all this ? And if common sense presupposes that ideas have such external meanings, how much more does not natural science appear to involve the recognition of this essentially imitative function of ideas ?

In any special natural science, a scientific description appears as an adjustment, express, conscious, exact, of the internal structure of a system of ideas to the external structure of a world of preëxistent facts ; and the business of science has been repeatedly defined, of late years, as simply and wholly taken up with the exact description of the facts of nature. Now the world of Being, when viewed in this light, appears to mean simply the same as the fact world, the external object of our ideas, the object that ideas must imitate, whatever their internal purpose, unless they want to be false. But for this very reason, no study of the inner structure of ideas, of their conscious conformity to their internal purpose, can so far promise to throw any direct light upon their success in fulfilling their external purpose. Or, as people usually say, you cannot make out the truth about facts by studying your "mere ideas." And so, as people constantly insist, no devotion to the elaboration of the internal meaning of your own ideas can get you in presence of the truth about Being. The world of Being is whatever it happens to be, as the collection of ships is what it is, before you count. Internal purposes cannot predetermine external conformity to truth. You cannot evolve facts out of your inner consciousness. Ideas about Being are not to be justified like melodies, by their internal conformity to the purpose of the moment when they consciously live. They must submit to standards that they themselves in no sense create. Such is the burden of common sense, and of special science, when they tell us about this aspect of the meaning of our ideas.

I state thus explicitly a very familiar view as to the whole externally cognitive function and value of ideas. I mean thus to emphasize the primary appearance of hopeless contrast between the internal purpose and the external validity of ideas. In fact, nothing could seem sharper than the contrast thus indicated between the melody on the one hand, the musical idea, as it comes to mind and is enjoyed for its beauty while it passes before consciousness, and the counting of the ships, on the other hand, — a process whose whole success depends upon its conformity to what seem to be absolutely indifferent and independent outer facts. In the one case we have the embodiment of a conscious inner purpose, — a purpose which is won through the very act of the moment, and by virtue of the mere presence of a certain series of mental contents. In the other case we have a conformity to outer truth, — a conformity that no inner clearness, no well-wrought network of cunning ideal contrivance, can secure, unless the idea first submits to the authority of external existence.

And yet, sharp as is this apparent contrast, every student of philosophy knows how profound are also the motives that have led some philosophers to doubt whether such contrast can really be as ultimate as it seems. After all, the counting of the ships is valid or invalid *not* alone because of the supposed independent being of the ships, but also because of the conscious act whereby just this collection of ships was first consciously selected for counting. After all, then, no idea is true or is false except with reference to the object that this very idea first means to select as its own object. Apart from what the idea itself thus somehow assigns as its own task, even that independent being yonder, if you assume such being, cannot determine the success or failure of the idea. It is the idea then that first says : "I mean this or that object. That is for my object. Of that I am thinking. To that I want to conform." And apart from such conscious selection, apart from such ideal predetermination of the object on the part of the idea, apart from such free voluntary submission of the idea to its self-imposed task, the object itself, the fact world, in its independence, can do nothing either to confirm or refute the idea. Now in this extremely elementary consideration, namely, in the consideration that unless ideas first voluntarily bind themselves to a given task, and so, by their internal purpose, already commit themselves to a certain selection of its object, they are neither true nor false, — in this consideration, I say, there may be hidden consequences that we shall later find momentous for the whole theory of Being and of truth. This consideration, that despite the seemingly hopeless contrast between internal and external meaning, ideas really possess truth or falsity only by virtue of their own selection of their task as ideas, is essentially the same as the consideration that led Kant to regard the understanding as the creator of the phenomenal nature over which science gradually wins conscious control, and that led Hegel to call the world the embodied Idea. This consideration, then, is not novel, but I believe it to be fundamental and of inexhaustible importance. I believe also that some of its aspects are still far too much neglected. And I propose to devote these lectures to its elaboration, and to a study of its relations to the various conceptions of Reality which have determined the scientific and religious life of humanity.

In any case I say, then, at the outset, that the whole problem of the nature of Being will for us, in the end, reduce to the question: How is the internal meaning of ideas consistent with their apparently external meaning? Or again: How is it possible that an idea, which is an idea essentially and primarily because of the inner purpose that it consciously fulfils by its presence, also possesses a meaning that in any sense appears to go beyond this internal purpose? We shall, in dealing with this problem, first find, by a development of the consideration just barely indicated, that the external meaning must itself be interpreted, not primarily in the sense of mere dependence upon the brute facts, but in terms of the inner purpose of the idea itself. We shall, perhaps to our surprise, reach the seemingly paradoxical and essentially idealistic thesis that no being in heaven or in earth, or in the waters under the earth, has power to give to an idea any purpose unless, the idea itself, as idea, as a fragment of life, as a conscious thrill, so to speak, of inner meaning, first somehow truly learns so to develope its internal meaning as to assign to itself just that specific purpose. In other words, we shall find that while, for our purposes, we, the critics, must first sharply distinguish the apparently external purpose that, as it were, from without, we assign to the idea, from the internal meaning of the idea, as present to a passing conscious instant, still, this our assignment of the external purpose, this our assertion that the idea knows or resembles, or imitates, or corresponds to, fact wholly beyond itself, must in the end be justified, if at all, by appeal to the truth, *i.e.* to the adequate expression and development of the internal meaning of the idea itself. In other words, we shall find either that the external meaning is genuinely continuous with the internal meaning, and is inwardly involved in the latter, or else that the idea has no external meaning at all. In brief, our abstract sundering of the apparently external from the consciously internal meaning of the idea must be first made very sharp, as we have just deliberately made it, only in order that later, when we learn the true relations, we may come to see the genuine and final unity of internal and external meaning. Our first definition of the idea seems to make, yes, in its abstract statement deliberately tries to make, as you see, the external meaning something sharply contrasted with the internal meaning. Our final result will simply reabsorb the secondary aspect, the external meaning, into the completed primary aspect, — the completely embodied internal meaning of the idea. We shall assert, in the end, that the final meaning of every complete idea, when fully developed, must be viewed as wholly an internal meaning, and that all apparently external meanings become consistent with internal meanings only by virtue of thus coming to be viewed as aspects of the true internal meaning.

To illustrate this thesis by the cases already used : The melody sung or internally but voluntarily heard, in the moment of memory, is, for the singer's or hearer's consciousness, a musical idea. It has so far its internal meaning. And to say so much first means simply that to the singer, as he sings, or to the silent memory of a musical imagination, the present melody imperfectly and partially fulfils a conscious purpose, the purpose of the flying moment. On the other hand, the melody may be viewed by a critic as an idea corresponding to external facts. The singer or hearer too may himself say as he sings or remembers: " This is the song my beloved sang," or " This is the theme that Beethoven composed in his Fidelio." In such a case, the idea is said to have its apparently external meaning, and this, its reference to facts not now and here given, is the idea's general rela-

tion to what we call true Being.   And such reference not
only seems at first very sharply different from the internal meaning, but must, for our purposes, at first be sundered by definition from that internal meaning even more
sharply than common sense distinguishes the two.   For
abstract sundering is, in us mortals, the necessary preliminary to grasping the unity of truth.   The internal meaning is a purpose present in the passing moment, but here
imperfectly embodied.   Common sense calls it, as such,
an expression of transient living intent, an affair of Will.
Psychology explains the presence and the partial present
efficacy of this purpose by the laws of motor processes, of
Habit, or of what is often called association.   Ethical
doctrine finds in such winning of inner purposes the
region where Conscience itself, and the pure moral Intention, are most concerned.   On the other hand, the apparently external meaning of the idea is at first said to be an
affair of the externally cognitive intellect, and of the hard
facts of an independently real world.   Not purpose, but
the unchangeable laws of the Reality, not the inner life,
but the Universe, thus at first seems from without to assign to the idea whatever external meaning it is to obtain.
Subject and Object are here supposed to meet, — to meet
in this fact that ideas have their external meaning, — but
to meet as foreign powers.

Now we are first to recognize, even more clearly, I
say, than common sense, the sharpness of this apparent
antithesis between the conscious internal and the seemingly external meaning.   Here, as I have said, is indeed
the world-knot.   We are to recognize the problem, but
we are, nevertheless, to answer it in the end (when we

get behind the appearances, and supplement the abstractions), by the thesis that at bottom, the external meaning is only apparently external, and, in very truth, is
but an aspect of the completely developed internal meaning. We are to assert that just what the internal
meaning already imperfectly but consciously is, namely,
purpose relatively fulfilled, just that, and nothing else,
the apparently external meaning when truly comprehended also proves to be, namely, the entire expression
of the very Will that is fragmentarily embodied in the
life of the flying conscious idea, — the fulfilment of the
very aim that is hinted in the instant. Or, in other
words, we are to assert that, in the case mentioned, the
artist who composed, the beloved who sang the melody,
are in verity present, as truly implied aspects of meaning,
and as fulfilling a purpose, in the completely developed
internal meaning of the very idea that now, in its finitude, seems to view them merely as absent. I deliberately choose, in this way, a paradoxical illustration. The
argument must hereafter justify the thesis. I can here
only indicate what we hereafter propose to develope as
our theory of the true relation of Idea and Being. It
will also be a theory, as you see, of the unity of the
whole very World Life itself.

In brief, by considerations of this type, we propose to
answer the question : What is to be? by the assertion
that : To be means simply to express, to embody the
complete internal meaning of a certain absolute system
of ideas, — a system, moreover, which is genuinely implied in the true internal meaning or purpose of every
finite idea, however fragmentary.

VI

You may observe already, even in this wholly preliminary sketch of the particular form of Idealism to
be developed in these lectures, two principal features.
First, Our account of the nature of Being, and of the
relation between Idea and Being, is to be founded
explicitly upon a theory of the way in which Ideas
possess their own meaning.   Secondly, Our theory of
the nature of Meaning is to be founded upon a definition in terms of Will and Purpose.   We do not indeed
say, Our will causes our ideas.   But we do say, Our
ideas now imperfectly embody our will.   And the real
world is just our whole will embodied.

I may add, at once, two further remarks concerning
the more technical aspects of the argument by which we
shall develope our thesis.   The first remark is, that the
process by which we shall pass from a study of the first
or fragmentary internal meaning of finite ideas to that
conception of their completed internal meaning in terms
of which our theory of Being is to be defined, is a
process analogous to that by which modern mathematical
speculation has undertaken to deal with its own concepts
of the type called by the Germans *Grenzbegriffe*, or
Limiting Concepts, or better, Concepts of Limits.   As a
fact, one of the first things to be noted about our conception of Being is that, as a matter of Logic, it is the
concept of a limit, namely of that limit to which the
internal meaning or purpose of an idea tends as it grows
consciously determinate.   Our Being resembles the concept of the so-called irrational numbers.   Somewhat

as they are related to the various so-called "fundamental series" of rational numbers, somewhat in that
way is Being related to the various thinking processes
that approach it, as it were, from without, and undertake to define it as at once their external meaning, and
their unattainable goal. That which is, is for thought,
at once the fulfilment and the limit of the thinking
process. The thinking process itself is a process
whereby at once meanings tend to become determinate,
and external objects tend to become internal meanings. Let my process of determining my own internal
meaning simply proceed to its own limit, and then I
shall face Being. I shall not only imitate my object as
another, and correspond to it from without: I shall
become one with it, and so internally possess it. This
is a very technical statement of our present thesis, and
of our form of Idealism, — a statement which only our
later study can justify. But in making that statement
here, I merely call attention to the fact that the process
of defining limits is one which mathematical science
has not only developed, but in large measure, at the
present time, prepared for philosophical adaptation, so
that to view the concept of Being in this light is to
approach it with an interest for which recent research
has decidedly smoothed the way. We shall meet both
with false ways of defining the limit, and with true
ways.

My second remark is closely related to the first, but
is somewhat less technical, and involves a return to the
practical aspects of our intended theory. I have just
said that the development of the conception of an idea

whose internal meaning is fully completed, and whose relation to Being is even thereby defined, will involve a discussion of the way in which our internal, our fragmentary finite meanings, as they appear in our flying moments, are to attain a determined character or are to become, as Hegel would say, *bestimmt,* so as to pass from vagueness to precision.   Our theory, as you already see, will identify finite ignorance of Reality with finite vagueness of meaning, will assert that the very Absolute, in all its fulness of life, is even now the object that you really mean by your fragmentary passing ideas, and that the defect of your present human form of momentary consciousness lies in the fact that you just now do not know precisely what you mean.   Increase of knowledge, therefore, would really involve increase of determination in your present meaning.   The universe you have always with you, as your true internal meaning.   Only this, your meaning, you now, in view of the defect of your momentary form of consciousness, realize vaguely, abstractly, without determination.   And, as we have further asserted, this indetermination of your ideas also involves a hesitant indeterminateness of your momentary will, a vagueness of conscious ideal as well as of idea, a failure not only to possess, but wholly to know what you want.   To pass to your real and completed meaning, to the meaning implied in this very moment's vagueness, would be a passage to absolute determinateness.   So to pass would therefore be to know with full determination truths of an often desired type, truths such as: What you yourself are; and, who you are, as this individual; what this individual physical fact now before you is.

Yes, it would be to know what the whole individual Being called the World is; and who the Individual of Individuals, namely the Absolute, or God himself, is. Just such final determinateness, just such precision, definiteness, finality of meaning, constitutes that limit of your own internal meaning which our theory will hereafter seek to characterize. And so my present remark hereupon is that, in following our enterprise of defining Being, we shall not be looking for mere abstract principles, but we shall be seeking for the most concrete objects in the world, namely for Individual Beings, and for the system that links them in one Individual Whole, — for Individuals viewed as the limits towards which all ideas of universal meanings tend, and for the Absolute as himself simply the highest fulfilment of the very category of Individuality, the Individual of Individuals.

Will, meaning, individuality, these will prove to be the constant accompaniments and the outcome of our whole theory of ideas, of thought, and of being. And in the light of these remarks we may now be able to anticipate more precisely the form of doctrine to which these lectures are to be devoted.

Idealism in some sense is indeed familiar in modern doctrine. And familiar also to readers of idealistic literature is some such assertion, as that the whole of Reality is the expression of a single system of thought, the fulfilment of a single conscious Purpose, or the realm of one internally harmonized Experience. But what the interested learners ask of idealistic teachers to-day is, as you are all aware, a more explicit statement as to just how Thought and Purpose, Idea and Will, and above all finite thought and will, and absolute thought and will, are, by any idealist, to be conceived as related to each other. My definitions in the foregoing have been deliberately intended to prepare the way for our later direct dealing with just these issues. An idea, in the present discussion, is first of all to be defined in terms of the internal purpose, or, if you choose, in terms of the Will, that it expresses consciously, if imperfectly, at the instant when it comes to mind. Its external meaning, its externally cognitive function as a knower of outer Reality, is thus in these lectures to be treated as explicitly secondary to this its internal value, this its character as meaning the conscious fulfilment of an end, the conscious expression of an interest, of a desire, of a volition. To be sure, thus to define, as we shall see, is not to separate knowing from willing, but it is rather to lay stress, from the outset, upon the unity of knowledge and will, first in our finite consciousness, and later, as we shall see, in the Absolute. Our present statement of our doctrine is therefore not to be accused, at any point, of neglecting the aspect of value, the teleological, the volitional aspect, which consciousness everywhere possesses. We shall reach indeed in the end the conception of an Absolute Thought, but this conception will be in explicit unity with the conception of an Absolute Purpose. Furthermore, as we have just asserted, we shall find that the defect of our momentary internal purposes, as they come to our passing consciousness, is that they imply an individuality, both in ourselves and in our facts of experience, which we do not wholly get presented to ourselves at any one instant. Or in other words, we finite beings live in the search for individuality, of life, of will, of experience, in brief, of meaning. The whole meaning, which is the world, the Reality, will prove to be, for this very reason, not a barren Absolute, which devours individuals, not a wilderness such as Meister Eckhart found in God, a *Stille Wüste, da Nieman heime ist*, a place where there is no definite life, nor yet a whole that absorbs definition, but a whole that is just to the finite aspect of every flying moment, and of every transient or permanent form of finite selfhood, — a whole that is an individual system of rationally linked and determinate, but for that very reason not externally determined, ethically free individuals, who are nevertheless One in God. It is just because all meanings, in the end, will prove to be internal meanings, that this which the internal meaning most loves, namely the presence of concrete fulfilment, of life, of pulsating and originative will, of freedom, and of individuality, will prove, for our view, to be of the very essence of the Absolute Meaning of the world. This, I say, will prove to be the sense of our central thesis; and here will be a contrast between our form of Idealism and some other forms.

And thus, in this wholly preliminary statement, I have outlined our task, have indicated its relation to the problems of religion, have suggested its historical affiliations, and have, in a measure, predicted its course. I have defined in general the problem of the relation of the World as Idea to the World as Fact, and have stated our issue as precisely this relation between Ideas and Reality. In order to assist in clarifying our undertaking, I have also

given a general definition of what an idea is, and have
stated the logical contrast between the consciously internal and the apparently external meaning of any finite idea.
And finally I have asserted that, in dealing with the problem as to how internal and external meaning can be
reduced to a consistent whole, we shall be especially
guided to fruitful reflection upon the final relation of the
World and the Individual. This, then, is our programme.
The rest must be the actual task.

I am not unaware how valueless, in philosophy, are
mere promises. All, in this field, must turn upon the
method of work. The question in philosophy is not about
the interest or the hopefulness of your creed, but about
your rational grounds for holding your convictions. I
accept the decidedly strict limitations imposed by this
consideration, and shall try, when we come to the heart of
our critical and constructive task, to be as explicit as the
allotted time permits, both in expounding the precise sense
of the doctrine now loosely and dogmatically sketched in
the foregoing statement, and in explaining the grounds
that lead me to prefer it, as a solution both of logical and
of empirical problems, to its rivals. But the way of detailed
argument is long, and the outlook of the whole enterprise
may often seem, as we proceed with our difficulties, dark
and perplexing. Introductions also have their rights ;
and I have meant in these opening words merely to re-
count the dream of which what follows must furnish both
the interpretation and, in a measure, the justification.

LECTURE II

LECTURE II

In our opening lecture the general plan of these discussions was sketched. Of this former lecture we now need recall but a single feature. We are to found our view of the Philosophy of Religion upon a treatment of the most fundamental problems of the Theory of Being. Without a further apology for our plan, and without further preliminary statement of its prospects and methods, we now proceed directly to our task itself.

I

We express in language, by means of verbs, adjectives, and equivalent expressions, *what*, as to their qualities, things are, what they do, and in what relation they stand. But in addition to such expressions, by which we qualify, describe, compare, and distinguish the various objects that we observe and think about, we have certain other expressions by means of which we assert *that* given objects are, or are real, rather than are not, or are unreal. Now, in technical phrase, we shall hereafter call the expressions of the latter type the ontological vocabulary of our language. Hard as it is to grasp or to render articulate the conception of Being, the vocabulary used, at least in the language of the Indo-European family, for the purpose of asserting that a thing is, is so rich, so living, so flexible

47

a vocabulary, as to remind us at every turn how familiar in the concrete is the idea of Real Being even to the most unlearned mind. Let us forthwith exemplify. It is for common sense one thing to have, as they say, an idea " in your head," and quite another thing to believe steadfastly that this idea corresponds to a "real outer fact." It is one thing to read a "rumor " in a current newspaper. It is quite another thing to be sure that, in truth, as they say, the rumor is "so." Now, in all these cases, the contrast between any plan and its actual fulfilment, between the so-called "mere idea " and the same conceived object when believed in as a "real outer fact," between the newspaper "rumor " and the same story if viewed as that which is "so," — this contrast, I say, is precisely the contrast between what *is not* and what *is*. The contrast in question, as I insist, is thus extremely familiar, and of the utmost practical importance. You may observe of course at once that this contrast is closely related to the one made at the last time between the internal meaning of ideas, plans, and the like, and their external meaning, or their relation to that which fulfils or realizes them. In the grasping of just this contrast, and upon fidelity to this distinction, the whole of the everyday virtue of truthfulness appears, in the world of common sense, to depend. The liar is a man who deliberately misplaces his ontological predicates. He says the thing that is not. His internal meaning is one affair; his external expression of his meaning is another, and contradicts the internal meaning. Upon a similarly clear sense of this same contrast, the life of all our external volition seems to depend. A plan involves an idea of what some possible object may sometime be. The execution of the plan, the voluntary act of one charged with the fulfilment of the idea, involves a process whereby one can come truthfully to say: "The fact is accomplished : the plan is no longer a mere plan : that which was the object of the plan once was not, but now it is. The 'mere idea' has turned into reality."

All these are familiar distinctions of common sense. Our language is thus indeed full of expressions founded upon the contrast between what is and what is not. Our task is to make a beginning at grasping the precise sense of this contrast. And here you may already permit me a brief excursion into the realm of more technical language.

For the next remark which our study of even our popular vocabulary here suggests has already been implied in the foregoing words. Whatever the contrast between being and non-being ultimately involves, we all observe that we express the existence or reality of an object by saying *that* it is, while when we tell merely *what* a given object is, we do not, in so far, appear to throw any light upon the truth of the assertion that the object in question is real. Thus I can tell you what a fairy is; but in so far I do not yet tell you whether a fairy is in any given sense real or unreal. Now the distinction thus expressed is very naturally stated, in a familiar technical phrase, by calling it, as many metaphysicians do, the difference between the *that* and the *what*, or between the *existence* and the *essence* of a fairy. In this phraseology of the philosophers, the *that* refers to the assertion of the onto-logical predicate itself. The *what*, also sometimes called the essence, refers to the ideal description of the object of which we may later assert, or learn, whether it is or is not. Kant, who much insisted upon this abstraction of the *what* from the *that*, maintained the view that the predicate *is*, or *is real*, or *exists*, never, properly, makes any difference to the *what* of the object in question, or adds anything to the essence of this object. For a fairy, once fully conceived as a possible live creature, would change in no whit the *what*, the characterizing predicates which now belong to fairies, if such a fairy came, by a creative act, or by an evolutionary process, into real existence. Just so too, the *what*, to use Aristotle's favorite example, is common to the planned house, and to the real house later built in conformity to the plan. The *that* of the house is what the builder's work effects.

I give this most elementary of the metaphysical abstractions its place here at the outset of our discussions merely to remark, at once, first that, as said, the contrast in question corresponds to the contrast between the internal and external meaning of ideas, and then that we are not bound to suppose this abstraction final. As a fact, my own view of Being will in the end turn upon supplementing and transforming the abstraction, which is itself a mere stage on the way to insight. But for the first we borrow its phraseology from language, as the philosophers since Aristotle have done, and we make its true meaning our problem. The ontological predicate thus appears to us as, in Kant's phrase, no true predicate at all, since the ontological predicate shall make no difference whatever to the conceivable characters of the object to which it is applied. And, to add Kant's own famous example, a hundred real dollars, according to Kant, differ in no nameable essential or logical characters from a hundred ideal or possible dollars. It is my actual wealth that differs according as I do or do not own the real dollars. Yet, on the other hand, this so abstract ontological predicate, otherwise viewed, does indeed also appear as if it were the most momentous of all predicates, since precisely the *is* and the *is not* somehow are to express all the difference between the true story and the false rumor, between the sound witness and the liar, between waking life and dream, between history and myth, — yes, between the whole world and nothing at all.[1]

[1] Human thought must first sunder, in order perhaps later to reunite. One historical result of the present mode of abstractly contrasting the ontological predicate with all the other predicates of objects, was that first, Aristotle, and later the scholastic text-books, sometimes attempted a sort of external union, under one abstractly common name, of the very aspects thus first so carefully divided. In consequence the term "Being" often gets a usage that in passing I have merely to mention. The scholastic text-books, namely, as for instance the *Disputations of Suarez*, employ our terms much as follows. *Being* (*ens*), taken quite in the abstract, such writers said, is a word that shall equally apply *both* to the *what* and to the *that*. Thus if I speak of the being of a man, I may, according to this usage, mean either the ideal nature of a man, apart from man's existence, or the existence of a man. The term "Being" is so far indifferent to both of the sharply sundered senses. In this sense Being may be viewed as of two sorts. As the *what* it means the Essence of things, or the *Esse Essentiæ*. In this sense, by the Being of a man, you mean simply the definition of what a man as an idea means. As the *that*, Being means the Existent Being, or *Esse Existentiæ*. The *Esse Existentiæ* of a man, or its existent being, would be what it would possess only if it existed. And so the scholastic writers in question always have to point out whether by the term Ens, or Being, they in any particular passage are referring to the *what* or to the *that*, to the Esse Essentiæ or to the Esse Existentiæ. On occasion, Scholastic usage also distinguishes Reality from Existence, by saying that the essence of a not yet existing, but genuine future fact can be called in some sense Real, apart

This fragmentary technical digression as to our terms thus ended, we return for a moment to popular speech.

Language, as commonly used, does not leave us altogether to the mercy of the perplexing separation of the ontological predicate from all the other, from what Kant called the true predicates of objects. The abstraction of the *what* and the *that* grew up slowly in men's minds : it is seldom even now consciously completed in the minds of any but technical thinkers. As a fact, very many words and phrases which have an obvious reference to the *what* have gradually come to be used, in the popular ontological vocabulary, as means of indicating that an object is real. Of these many popular ways of expressing reality, three classes, just here, especially interest us, because they are preliminary hints, so to speak, of our various more technical conceptions of Being.

And first, then, in various tongues, we find used for

from Existence, and that in general one can distinguish Real Essences from mere figments.

But I have to mention this technical usage only to say at once that we ourselves shall be little troubled by it. In these lectures I shall always mean by Being the Real Being of things, the *that*. Nor shall I try to make any systematic difference in usage between Reality and Existence, or the adjectives real and existent. So long as the *what* and the *that* remain abstractly sundered in our investigation we shall call the *what* the *essence*, or again, the *idea* taken abstractly in its internal meaning. By contrast, the *that*, the Real Being of things, will at this stage appear to us as corresponding to what we at the last time called the External Meaning of our ideas. But by and by we shall indeed learn that this whole sundering of the *what* and the *that* is a false abstraction, — a mere necessary stage on the way to insight. We shall also find that objects can be Real in various degrees ; but we shall not try, as many writers do, to speak only of certain grades of Reality as Existent. We shall use the latter terms interchangeably.

declaring the reality of objects certain forms of speech whose notable feature lies in their telling us that their object is *to be seen*, or is *at hand*, or can be *found*, or is *marked*, or is *plain*, or *stands out*, or is *there*, or, as the Germans also say, is *vorhanden;* while the unreal has *no standing*, or *is not at hand*, or is *not to be found*, or is *not there*. These expressions bring the real being of an object into close relations with the sharpness, nearness, clearness, or mere presence, of our experience of this object. They accordingly often imply that the object seems more or less *accidental*. It *haps*, it *chances*, — these are phrases thus frequently employed as the means of telling that an object is. "You may think that there is no hereafter, but there happens to be one," — so a preacher may say to a scoffer. The common feature of these popular expressions is that they lay stress upon what the philosophers call the immediacy of real facts, as the most marked sign of their reality. For the immediate, such as light or sound or pain, just happens to be found, or is given as a fact.

A second class of expressions, however, in very strong contrast to the first class, declares that an object is real, not by virtue of its mere presence or obviousness, but in so far as it is *deeper* than what is visible, or in so far as it has *foundation*, *solidity*, *permanence*, *interior constitution*, *profundity* of meaning. Much of the language here in question takes the form of metaphors. What merely seems is a *rind* or *husk;* what is real is the *core* or *kernel* of things. "These but seem," says Hamlet, "for these are tokens that a man might feign, but I have that within which passeth show." Other metaphors, in ancient tongues of our Indo-European family, indentify *to be* with *to breathe* or *to dwell*. The real also in general *lives;* for it is internally self-sustaining, as, to a more primitive mind, natural life may seem to be. And *breathing* is a well-known token of life. So *to breathe* is to be. The unreal again is like a wanderer or a stranger. But the real *abides* in its own house. So to be real is *to dwell*. Or again the real is the *result* of principles, it is what *has grown*. It is the *outcome* and *goal* of processes. It is both necessary and abiding. All such notions are easy to illustrate by the ontological phraseology of various tongues.

A third type of popular expressions gives us still another view of what it is to be. According to this portion, as it were, of the mere folk-lore of being, to be real means above all to be *genuine* or to be *true*. One sees this meaning, by contrast, in the very many popular names for objects whose unreality and illusoriness has once been detected. Such an unreal object may be called, if it is better than the objects believed to be real, an *Ideal;* but most of the numerous appellatives for the unreal objects are terms of reproach : such an unreality is an *appearance*, a *delusion*, a *sham*, a *myth*, a *fraud*, a *phantasm*, an *imitation*, a *lie*. By contrast the real is what you can *depend upon*. It is *genuine*, no mere imitation. It is *true*.

II

And thus we have indicated, although by no means exhausted, the scope of the ontological speech of the people. *To be immediate*, or, on the other hand, *to be well founded* in what is not immediate, and, thirdly, *to be genuine and true*, — these seem to be the three principal conceptions of what it is to be real in the popular ontology. Technical metaphysic, like all other learned enterprises, has its foundations in just such linguistic folk-lore, so to speak, as the foregoing; and one easily misapprehends the philosophers if one fails to observe whence they got their vocabulary. As Teichmüller, in the introduction to his own essay on metaphysics well says, the Aristotelian theory of Being is founded in part upon a series of grammatical and lexicographical comments upon the forms of speech used in Greek language. All the more philosophical conceptions of being are due, in part, to an attempt to take note of the same aspects of human experience which the three classes of popular ontological predicates have from an early stage recognized. And, as a fact, the ontological concepts are limited in their range of variation by a situation in which we all find ourselves, and of which the foregoing variations of the popular vocabulary have already reminded us. It is necessary, as we pass to the more technical realm, to sketch, in outline, what this familiar situation is. For the problem about Being is, like all other human problems, first of all a problem of experience, and of distinctly practical needs.

We all of us, from moment to moment, have experience. This experience comes to us, in part, as brute fact : light and shade, sound and silence, pain and grief and joy, — all these, in part, *i.e.* in one of their universal aspects, are just data of sense, of emotion, of inner life in general. These given facts flow by ; and, were they all, our world would be too much of a blind problem for us even to be puzzled by its meaningless presence. Now, in so far, we have what is called merely immediate experience, that is, experience just present, apart from definition, articulation, and in general from any insight into its relationships. But that is not all. In addition, we all, when awake and thoughtful, find present what one might call more or less richly *idealized* experience, experience that, in addition to its mere presence, possesses Meaning. On this side of our lives we are aware of the series of mental processes called Ideas. These ideas have the character of presenting, in a more or less incomplete but never perfect way, what, at the last time, we called the fulfilment of purpose, the embodied inner meaning present to us at any instant. In so far as these ideas fill our moments, the life within is thus lighted up with meaning. But now, in any one of these our flying present moments, such meaning is never fully possessed. Whatever our business or our doctrine, we all endlessly war against the essential narrowness of our conscious field. We live looking for the whole of our meaning. And this looking constitutes the process called thinking.

In general, this process is involved in a curious conflict with these brute facts which constitute the mere immediacy aforesaid. These facts themselves, in so far as they remain merely immediate, are an obstacle to the idealizing process. We say that they confuse or puzzle us. On the other hand, these very facts, on occasion, may arise in consciousness only to fuse at once or very quickly with our ideas. This is, for instance, the case whenever we accomplish a voluntary act, and at the same time approvingly perceive, through our senses, the outer

results of our act.   It is also the case wherever we look
for an expected object, and looking find the object.   In
such instances the realm of the ideal appears to us constantly to extend.   We then say either that we control
facts by our will, or else that we confirm our intellectual
expectations as we go.   Or again, we may succeed in
recognizing and interpreting the immediate data in terms
of our ideas.   In such cases we feel at home in our world.
But when the data, as so often happens, remain obdurate,
decline to be recognized, disappoint expectations, or refuse
our voluntary control, then, whatever our theory of the
universe, and whatever our practical business may be, we
have on our hands some instance of the endless finite conflict of mere experience and mere idea.   These two aspects of our lives, the immediate aspect and the ideal
aspect, then show themselves in sharp contrast.   Ideal
meditation and brute immediacy stand in opposition to
each other.   We then know our finitude, and we are
inwardly disquieted thereby.   Such disquietude is our
almost normal experience as finite wanderers.   The situation may be one of private toil or of public controversy,
of practical struggle or of theoretical uncertainty; but
in any such case, amid the endless variety of our lives,
the conflict retains essentially and profoundly similar
features, — purpose at war with fortune, idea with datum,
meaning with chaos, — such is the life of our narrow
flickering moments, and in so far as we are indeed
finite, in so far as our will wins not yet its whole battle, our intellect grasps not the truth that it seeks.

Practically, this conflict has other names; but viewing
it theoretically, namely, with reference to the contents

and relationships involved, we call this conflict the effort
of Thought to comprehend Being. By Thought we here
mean the sum total of the ideas, this whole life of inner
meanings, *in so far as* it is precisely the effort to comprehend and interpret the data, the brute facts of immediacy,
in terms of the ideas themselves — the effort to win over
facts to ideas, or to adjust ideas to facts. Were the facts
wholly interpreted, they would fuse with the ideas; and
the conflict of Thought and Being would cease. But
now, — Thought it is which attempts to recognize the
given facts. Thought it is which goes on when, our
present ideas failing to light up sufficiently the chaos
of immediacy, we look for other ideas, in terms of which
to interpret our problems. Thought it is which we may
regard as possessing the countless ideal weapons, the
storehouse of what we call memories of our past, the
arsenal of what we call general principles for the interpretation of fact, the vast collection of traditional ideas
with which our whole education has supplied us.
Thought possesses, — nay, thought rather is, this whole
collection of ideas taken as in contrast with facts. The
ideas are our resources in the warfare with immediacy,
just as from moment to moment they come to mind.

So much then, at this stage, for Thought. But what
do we mean by Being? The effort to give answer to
this question brings to light several possible alternatives. These we are even now trying to define more
exactly. Yet all the alternatives involve a common character. Being, in this warfare, that which is real, as opposed and contrasted to that which just now is merely
suggested to us by our momentary ideas as they fly, and

which is not yet confirmed by facts, — Being, I say, always appears in the conflict and in the incompleteness of our human thinking, as that which we first regard as real in advance of more special definition, in so far as we call it Other than our merely transient and finite thinking of the moment. Our situation, as finite thinkers, is, as we just said, disquieting. We want some other situation in place of this one. Our ideas, while partial embodiments of meaning, are never complete embodiments. We are never quite at home with our world. The Other, then, which we seek, would involve, if completely found, a situation where thought and fact were no longer at war, as now they are, and where thought had finished its ideal task as now it is not finished. To define in advance this situation, we must then form some more or less precise notion as to the question: Wherein lies the defect of our present thoughts, both in themselves, and in their relation to facts?

It follows that, in defining this defect of our present situation, in predicting the character of the Other that we seek, of the needed supplement, whose presence, once observed, would end the now insistent conflict, — in thus defining and predicting, I say, we are limited, as to our choice of alternatives, by the exigencies of the finite conscious situation herewith summed up. We can define the Other, the true Being, as that which, if present to us in this moment, would *end our conflict*. In so far it seems something desirable and desired, — an object of longing. On the other hand, we may, and often do, regard Being as that in terms of which our ideas are to be *controlled*, *set right*, or, if necessary, wholly *set aside* as useless. In so far Being appears as a sort of fate, or perhaps as a supreme authority, which judges our ideas and which may thwart them. On this side, what is, is often the *un*desired, and may seem the hopelessly evil. Meanwhile, there remain many ways in which we can define Being either more in terms of Immediacy or else more in terms of Ideas. But Fact and Idea, Immediacy and Thought, these are the factors whose contrast and whose conflict must determine what notion we can form of what it is to be. Some conceived union of elements furnished by these two factors that enter into our finite conflict constitutes, for any theory, the notion of reality.

And now at last we are ready, having summarized the vaguer popular views, and having seen what situation determines the whole effort to define Being, — we are ready, I say, to pass directly to the alternative conceptions of what it is to be real which have appeared in the course of the history of philosophy.

I say, these fundamental conceptions, as they gradually become differentiated in the course of the history of thought, are four in number. In this lecture I shall at some length define two of them. The others I shall not expound until later lectures, after a critical study of the first two has prepared the way.

But first let me name all the four. The mere list will not be very enlightening, but it will serve to furnish titles for our immediately subsequent inquiries. The first conception I shall call the technically Realistic definition of what it is to be. The second I shall call the Mystical conception. The third I cannot so easily name. I shall sometimes call it the typical view of modern Criti-

cal Rationalism.   Just now I prefer to name it by its
formulation, the conception of the real as the Truth, or,
in the present day, usually, as the Empirically verifiable
Truth.   The fourth I shall call the Synthetic, or the constructively Idealistic conception of what it is to be.   For
the first conception, that is real which is simply *Independent* of the mere ideas that relate or that may relate to it.
For this view, what is, is not only external to our ideas
of it, but absolutely and independently decides as to the
validity of such ideas.   It controls or determines the
worth of ideas, and that wholly apart from their or our
desire or will.   What we "merely think" makes "no
difference" to fact.   For the second conception, that is
real which is absolutely and finally *Immediate*, so that
when it is found, *i.e.* felt, it altogether ends any effort
at ideal definition, and in this sense *satisfies* ideas as
well as constitutes the fact.   For this view, therefore,
Being is the longed-for goal of our desire.   For the
third conception, that is real which is purely and simply
Valid or True.   Above all, according to the modern
form of this view, that is real which Experience, in
verifying our ideas, shows to be valid about these ideas.
Or the real is the valid "Possibility of Experience."
But for the fourth conception, that is real which finally
presents in a completed experience the whole meaning
of a System of Ideas.

I proceed at once to a statement of the first two conceptions.   These two are the polar opposite each of the other.
Their warfare is very ancient.   The history of Theology
has been, above all, determined by their conflict.

III

The first of the four is the best known of all. According to this conception, I repeat, to be real means to be independent of an idea or experience through which the real being is, from without, felt, or thought, or known. And this, I say, is the view best known as metaphysical Realism, the view which, recognizing independent beings as real, lays explicit stress upon their independence as the very essence of their reality.

To comprehend what this conception of Reality implies, I must first point out that, of all our four views, this first one most sharply and abstractly undertakes to distinguish the *what* from the *that*, in case of every real object, and to hold the two aspects asunder. What objects are in this sense real, the realistic definition does not undertake in the least to predetermine. But by virtue of the definition, you are to know, as far as that is knowable at all, wherein consists the determining feature that distinguishes real from unreal objects. Unreal objects, centaurs, or other fictions, ideals, delusions, may be what they please. Real objects may in their turn possess any *what* that experience or demonstration proves to belong to them. But the difference between real and unreal objects is an unique difference, and is not properly to be called a difference as to the *what* of the real and unreal objects themselves. This difference, relating wholly to the *that*, is a difference expressible by saying that fictitious objects are dependent wholly upon ideas, the hopes, dreams, and fancies, which conceive them ; while real objects are *wholly independent of any ideas which may have them as objects, just in so far as these ideas are different from their objects.*

To countless and to endlessly various objects this first form of the ontological predicate has accordingly been applied by the thinkers who have used it. Both matter and mind have equally been called real in this first sense. Realism has, of course, no necessary tendency towards Materialism, although the materialists are realists. Since all here turns upon the ontological predicate, and not upon the *what* of the subject to which a given realistic philosopher applies this ontological predicate, you never know in advance but that a realist's world may prove to be full of minds. By way of illustration of the varieties of Realism, I may refer at once to typical entities of realistic type which have appeared in the course of the history of philosophy. The Eleatic One, and the Many of Empedocles or of Democritus ; the Platonic Ideas, in the form in which Plato defines them in his most typi-cal accounts of their supreme and absolute dignity as real beings; and the Aristotelian individual beings of all grades, from God to matter ; the Stoic Nature and the Epicurean atoms; the whole world of created en-tities in the Scholastic theology, whenever viewed apart from its dependence upon God; the Substance of Spinoza ; the Monads of Leibniz; the Things in Themselves of Kant; the Reals of Herbart ; The Mind Stuff of Clif-ford ; the Unknowable of Mr. Spencer ; and even the moral agents of most modern ethical systems of meta-physics : — all these endlessly varied types of conceived objects, differing in value and in description almost without limit, have been declared real in what their authors have more or less clearly identified with this our first sense of the word real. All these thinkers were in so far realists.

Plainly, therefore, this idea of what it is to be real is not identical with any of the foregoing simpler and popular definitions of reality. The atoms, as we have now learned to define them, are invisible; the Eleatic One is only to be known by thinking; the Platonic Ideas are above all, incorporeal. On the other hand, a portion (although by no means all) of the ordinary realistic metaphysics which one meets with in many text-books of special science, deals with visible and tangible objects. The Monads of Leibniz are Souls. Kant's Things in Themselves and Herbart's Reals, are as unknowable as the Power of which Mr. Spencer tells us. Yet to all these different sorts of objects, our first form of the ontological predicate has been applied by thinkers who have had it more or less clearly in mind. Hence neither visibility, nor any other of the forms in which the popular metaphysic conceives immediacy, is adequate to express the present conception. Yet it is true that real Being implies, for this our first notion, that what is real is in a certain sense *given*, and is so far a *brute fact*. Much nearer to the present notion is that second popular view, according to which to be real means to be the deeper basis, that furnishes the ground for what is given, or that is somehow beneath the surface of immediate presentation. In some measure, moreover, our present form of technical doctrine is a development out of the third of the foregoing popular conceptions, according to which whatever is real thereby renders ideas about itself either true or false. In brief, then, the present ontological definition is a Synthesis of the three popular conceptions, with stress laid upon the second, that is, upon the idea that the real, as such, is behind or beyond the merely immediate facts of our experience.

As to its relation to that warfare of thought and immediacy in our passing finite moments of consciousness, to that disquieting conflict of which I before spoke, — our present form of the ontological predicate defines the Other precisely as a realm *wholly* other than the inner states whereby we know it. What is, is thus independent of our inner conflict, just because this realm of true Being is wholly sundered from the defects of our imperfect apprehension. The Real is that which you would know if you should wholly escape from the limits imposed upon you by the merely inner life of your consciousness. As monks forsake the world to win an abstract peace, so Realism bids you forsake what depends upon your mere finite inner apprehension, if you want to get at the independent truth. As to the way of escape, as to how to forsake the inner conflict, and to find the independent reality, — that, indeed, is another matter. We are here concerned only with the realistic definition of the Real, not with the realistic Theory of Knowledge. A realist may or may not believe that he can thus escape. What interests us here is that he believes that he ought to escape if he is ever to know the final truth.

But I must still explain a little the sort of independence to which the realistic view refers. You have an idea or an experience, — say a perception. You declare that this experience or idea is cognitive, and that hereby you know something real. Now the first of our four conceptions of what it is to be real, essentially declares that if you thus know a real object, and if thereupon your knowledge vanishes from the world, that vanishing of your knowledge makes no difference, except by accident, or indirectly, to the real object that you know. For example, you look at a real mountain. You see it. That is a case of knowing something real. Now look away. Your seeing ceases; but the mountain, according to this view, remains just as real, and real in the very sense in which it before was real. This, I say, is what any genuinely realistic view presupposes. Now our first conception of reality asserts that just this independence of your knowing processes, and *of all such knowing processes*, as is your seeing, *i.e.* of all actual or possible external knowing processes whatever, is not only a universal character of real objects, but also constitutes the very definition of the reality of the known object itself, so that to be, is to be such that an external knower's knowledge, whether it occurs or does not occur, can make no difference, as mere knowledge, to the inner reality of the known object.

A real object, in this view, may then be a known *or* an unknown object, or it may be sometimes known, and sometimes unknown, or, above all, it may be known now by one person and again by another, the two knowing it simultaneously or separately. All that makes no sort of difference to the object, if, in this first sense, it is real. To use this supposed independence as a means of defining reality, is the essence of our first conception of being.

Let us look back for an instant at our three popular ontological predicates, and see for ourselves afresh how they are related to this new predicate. And first, Is the real, in this new sense, a given or immediate fact? The realistic philosopher answers that in a sense it is given, although he often answers that the way in which it is given may go far beyond anything that can be merely felt. The real, he says, is in one sense given, or immediate, just because no knowing process, in us who know the object, creates, affects, or otherwise mediates the known real object. There it is, the real. You may "struggle as you like." It is a *datum*. In this sense of being mediated by nobody's knowing, the Platonic Ideas were given as real, although they could not be felt. Hence, they are so far as much realistic beings as were Herbart's Reals. Yet Realism often makes little of this *given* character of being, although some forms of realism dwell more upon it, especially when in controversy with sceptics and mystics. But secondly, Is the real, in our present sense, also *deeper* than what is merely immediate? Yes, in a sense it is, if you mean by the given, merely the felt, or the observed, facts of sense, or of other experience. The real, as the independent, is as careless of your immediate feelings as it is of the mediation of your thinking processes. It is beyond what you see, feel, touch. For seeing, feeling, touch, vanish; but reality remains when unseen, unfelt, untouched by any external observer. Now realists usually lay great stress upon the substantiality of the real, and the classic doctrine of substance was developed upon the basis of this notion of the independently real. And thirdly, Does the real make ideas true or false? Yes, answers the realist, because ideas, in trying to be true, in trying to shun falsity, seek to express what is independent of themselves, in other words seek to escape from the bondage of their own processes.

So, then, Realism is, as we said, a synthesis of the three popular ontological predicates, although, as history shows, with a preference for the second predicate. Realism is fond of substances, of "inner" or of "deeper" fundamental facts, and of inaccessible universes. Yet sometimes it loves an ostentatious, although never a very thoroughgoing empiricism. As to many other matters, however, Realism, as an ontological doctrine about what it is to be, is neutral. Almost any content you please might belong, as we have already said, to an object real in this first sense. Real in this sense might be, for instance, even a state of feeling, or even the very act of knowledge itself, if only one asserted that this state of feeling, or this act of knowledge, could be anyhow externally known, as an object, by another knowing process. For even an act of knowing would then be independent of the external knowing that knew this act. In this sense, most psychologists prefer, in their usual discussions, realistic views as to the Being of mental processes. These processes are then viewed as knowable, but are also viewed as independent of the knowledge that is supposed to be able to know them, so that it makes no direct difference to them whether they are known from without or not. Hence the objects of realistic ontology are objects not necessarily outside of *any* knowledge whatever, but only *independent of any knowing that is external to themselves*. A world of conscious monads might be, in this sense, independently real. Nevertheless, any realistic world must contain *some objects* that are outside of any knowing process whatever, since the relations between the various knowing processes and their objects, even in a world of conscious minds, would have to be external relations, in order to save the realistic type of independence. Hence no realistic world can be through and through a conscious world. It must have some aspects lying outside of any possible knowledge.

As to the relation which Realism assumes between knowledge and its real object, this is a curious relation, — a relation whose obviously practical import at once tends to throw light on the meaning of the whole situation. It is a relation that shall make "no difference" whatever to one of the related terms, namely, to the real object, which is totally indifferent to being known or not known; although this same relation, while inevitably leaving the other term of the relation, namely, the knowing consciousness, itself a fact independently existing, makes all the difference possible to the value of this other term, namely, to the truth or accuracy of the knowing consciousness, since a knowledge without a real object, independent of it, is supposed by the hypothesis to be utterly vain. The real object, in its independence, is not even related to the truth or value of the poor knowing process, as is the sedate big dog to the little dog when the latter barks. For the big dog at least presumably hears the barking. The realistic relation of the knowing being to its object is more like the relation of a horse to a hitching post, only that even here the horse can strain at the post when he pulls, while realistic knowing is absolutely naught to its object. By doctrines about the Will, to be sure, the more ethical amongst the realists generally try to correct the externality of the relation between knower and object. Knowledge, they say, moves will, or sets it moving itself, and hereupon will often alters independent object. But these volitional relations are another story, although, as I may add, they are fatal to the consistency of the realistic conception.

IV

And now for some hint of the historical fortunes of Realism. I have pointed out how wide-spread is this realistic conception of Being in the history of philosophy. I may now add that I think that this conception has never been held wholly alone, and apart from other conceptions of reality, by any first-rate thinker. The general rule is that any great system of philosophy has some objects in it which are earnestly insisted upon as real, but which are yet obviously, even explicitly, not real in the realistic sense, or which have a reality only in part definable in a realistic sense. Thus Aristotle's God, as viewed from the side of the world, looks at first like another real object, whose reality is wholly of the independent type. Yet if you examine closer the self-centred purity of Being that Aristotle's lonely God possesses, you find that, although in regard to formal truth omniscient, and thus fully knowing what reality is, the God of Aristotle cannot regard his own reality as of any independent type. For if he did so regard himself, he would then have to observe that his reality is independent of our knowledge of him; and in that case he would be taking account of us, and would view our world as another than himself. But such views, according to Aristotle, would be unworthy of God. So God, who is formally omniscient, still knows of no reality that is independent of the knowledge which refers to this reality. For God, as Aristotle says, knows only himself. Just so Plato's Ideas, although for us now independent realities, were once, in our previous state of being, according to a half true myth, immediately and fully known by a direct intuition. And this character of the ideal world, if consistently developed at the expense of the other characters, transforms the reality of the Ideas of Plato into the form which the doctrine later assumed in Plotinus; but that is in part a mystical form. Nor are there lacking other tendencies, in Plato, to ascribe to the Ideas a Being that is not of the realistic type. Kant was a realist; but he invented, in the world of *Mögliche Erfahrung*, a new realm of objects which he regards as real, and yet as not at all possessed of the independent type of reality. Spinoza's Substance is not only an independent reality, but is also a mystical Absolute. Notoriously, it keeps two sets of accounts, or even an infinite number. And hence it is like a defaulting cashier. You never quite know with what sort of reality you are dealing when you consult its books. Herbart's world has in it, in addition to its independent Reals, " *Zufällige Ansichten* " and forms of " *Zusammen* " without number. These are for our knowledge "*wirklich*," but they have no realistic, that is, for Herbart, no ultimate, no simply independent being. I regard this series of episodes in the history of Realism as profoundly instructive. Any realistic world, if well thought out, contains objects that either are not real in the realist's sense, or else are real, not only in that sense, but also in quite another sense. This is what a student easily overlooks. But it is a fact extremely ominous for Realism.

As to the historical and practical significance of realistic metaphysics in the history of life and of religion, one must say at once that, like all human conceptions, these various fundamental metaphysical conceptions also are, in one aspect, distinctly active and practical attitudes towards that Other which finite thought seeks. For Realism, the true meaning of our ideas is to be wholly external. Yet the internal meaning of the ideas stubbornly remains. The realist actually believes his doctrine because he finds it simple, or rational, or otherwise contenting to his inner interests. We never think without also acting, or tending to act. When we think we will. We have then internal meanings. So far as we have ideas really present to us, they embody purposes. Accordingly we shall find that all of our four various definitions of the ontological predicate are expressions of distinctly universal and human interests in life and the universe. Man confesses his practical ideals when he defines his philosophical notions.

And so, in particular, Realism, in addition to being an effort to meet the general problem of Being, is also the product and expression of essentially Social motives and interests. It is socially convenient, for purely practical reasons, to regard my fellow as a being whose mind shall be wholly independent, as to its inner being, of my own knowledge about my fellow. This view of the social relation is indeed suggested by well-known experiences, but in its ideally extreme forms, it is warranted by no experience, and is actually contradicted by every case of the communication of mind with mind. But we also find it socially convenient to view the common objects of our human and social knowledge as independent both of my fellow and myself, even while we still view these objects as the same for both of us, and for all other actual and possible human observers And so, in the end, we conceive these common objects, abstractly, as independent of all knowing processes whatever. When, to these social motives, we add that interest in escape from our private and finite disquietude of incomplete insight of which we before spoke, the special motives for the more abstract forms of Realism are in substance stated. It is true that there is a deeper and a very general motive at the heart of Realism, — a motive which we shall only later learn to appreciate. This is the interest in viewing the Real as the absolutely and finally Determinate or Individual fact. But this motive is present for Realism in a very abstract and problematic form. And even this motive, as we shall later see, is a practical one. We believe in the determinate individuality of things because we need and love individuality. We can justify this belief, in the end, only upon other than realistic grounds.

In consequence we may say that Realism is, in its special contrast with other views, an interpretation of the folk-lore of being in the interests of a social conservatism. Accordingly, in the history of thought, Realism is the metaphysic of the party of good order, when good order is viewed merely as something to be preserved. Hence the typical conservatives, the extreme Right wing of any elaborate social order, will generally be realistic in their metaphysics. So too are the conservative theologians, so long as they teach the people. Amongst themselves, these conservatives, if deeply religious souls, may use quite other, namely, mystical speech. Realistic, too, are those plain men, whose only metaphysic is the blind belief in "established facts." Realistic also are the tyrants. Realism has lighted the fires for the martyrs, and has set up the scaffolds for the reformers. As to its most familiar cases of real objects, Realism is fond of socially important objects. Property in general, technical objects, money, mechanism, instruments, whatever can be passed from hand to hand, the solid earth on which we all alike appear to walk, — these are the typical and exemplary instances of realistic metaphysics. If you question Realism, the realist asks you whether you do not believe in these objects, as facts independent of your ideas. With these instances, then, the realist is ready to confute the objector. The realist is fond of insisting upon the "sanity" of his views. By sanity he means social convenience. Now reflective thinking is often socially inconvenient. When it is, the realist loves to talk of "wholesome " belief in reality, and to hurl pathological epithets at opponents. It is thus often amusing to find the same thinker who declares that reality is quite independent of all merely human or mental interests, in the next breath offering as proof of his thesis the practical and interesting "wholesomeness" of this very conviction.

But you will ask, Have no realists then been reformers, liberals, atheists? Yes, I answer, the pure materialists have been realists. But these more unorthodox realists are still what Kant called Dogmatists, partisans of a tradition preached as authoritative, — conservatives as to certain conceptions of a distinctly social, even if unorthodox origin.

Yet Realism, if indeed strictly sane, as sanity goes amongst us men, is a view as falsely abstract as it is convenient. This sundering of external and internal meaning is precisely what our later study will show to be impossible. As a shorthand statement of the situation of the finite being, Realism, laying stress as it does upon our vast and disquieting inadequacy to win union with the Other that we seek, is a good beginning of metaphysics. As an effort to define determinateness and finality, it is a stage on the way to a true conception of Individuality and of Individual Beings. As a summary indication of the nature of our social consciousness, and of our social world, Realism is indeed the bulwark of good order. For good order, in us men, practically depends, from moment to moment, upon abstractions, since we have at any one instant to think narrowly in order to act vigorously. But viewed as an ultimate and complete metaphysical doctrine, and not as a convenient half-truth, Realism, as we shall find hereafter, upon a closer examination, needs indeed no external opposition. It rends its own world to pieces even as it creates it. It contradicts its own conceptions in uttering them. It asserts the mutual dependence of knowing and of Being in the very act of declaring Being independent. In brief, realism never opens its mouth without expounding an antinomy.

Its central technical difficulty, as we shall later more particularly see, and as Aristotle's Metaphysics already laboriously shows you, is that wondrous problem of the nature of individuality and as to the meaning of universals. The independent realities must be individuals, for they are fixed data, finished and unique in advance of any knowing. And in a realistic world, as we shall find, there must be at least two individuals, independent of each other. But there cannot be such individuals; for the individuals of a realistic world are essentially Noumena, objects defined, even for the realist, by a thinking process. And mere thinking, when taken as in opposition to facts, merely abstract thinking, as Plato well and irrefutably observed, — can define only universals, and only linked systems of fact. Herein lies the doom of Realism. Its laws, as universals, contradict its facts, which have to be independent individuals. Whatever is said to be true of its reals is a conceived, and hence an universal truth, linking many in one. But its reals are not universal, and are not to be linked. Their essence excludes universality, and demands mutual independence. Hence, in the end, nothing whatever proves to be true of them. History shows many examples of this consequence. The troubled darkness of the Herbartian realm of the Reals is one such historical example. In Herbart's world, in an uncanny and impossible way, these Reals, which can have nothing to do with one another, still, according to the philosopher come *" Zusammen "*; and while nothing can happen to them, they preserve themselves changeless amidst unreal disturbances, by crawling, as it were, like worms, and so producing a *" wirkliches Geschehen."* [1] Well, this strange metaphysical scene, in the distracted globe of Herbart's system, is only one instance of the sort of thing that has to be found in any realistic world, if one confesses the truth, as Herbart nobly confessed it.

V

But we must leave this great problem of the Realistic Ontology for a later and more detailed study. I must proceed, as I close the present lecture, to a sketch of the second of our four forms of the ontological predicate. Realism, despite its prevalence, has long had a very ancient historical foe. This foe was originally not Idealism, in its modern form, but something very different, namely, Mysticism. And so the second conception of what it is to be real is characteristic of that most remarkable group of teachers, the philosophical Mystics. Mysticism as a mere doctrine for edification, is indeed no philosophy. Yet a philosophy has been based upon it.

While this second conception appears to me to have been very generally misunderstood by most of the critics

---

[1] See Mr. Bradley's observation in *Appearance and Reality*, p. 30.

of philosophical Mysticism, its historical significance, as I must insist, is of the very greatest. Again and again it appears, as marking a transition stage in human civilization. It has had an enormous influence on literature. It has been responsible for a very large share in the development of all the great religions. You cannot understand the history of religion, without appreciating the mystical definition of Being.

As to the history of Mysticism, it began in India, with the Upanishads and the Vedânta. It early passed to Europe, and perhaps was independently rediscovered there. Even Plato's dialogues contain some hints of its spirit. Even Aristotle's account of God's inner life has relation to its motives. In a marvellous combination with realistic and even with more concretely idealistic conceptions, it forms an element in the doctrine of Plotinus. Through the Neo-Platonic school it passed over into Christian theology. Throughout the Middle Ages it formed a motive in the speculations of the philosophers of the School. St. Thomas Aquinas sought to deal justly with its merits, without endangering the interests of orthodoxy. Meister Eckhart, who was by training a follower of St. Thomas, but who gradually grew more independent of the master as he taught, helped to introduce mystic conceptions into German thinking. The German mystics deeply influenced later Protestant theology. The favorite devotional books of all the churches, and some of the best known of the religious poets and hymns, have continued to extend the mystical influence amongst the laity even until to-day. The unorthodox forms of Mysticism are almost countless. Schopenhauer is a marked modern instance in a part of his doctrine, of one result of mystical influence.

Any fair-minded student ought, therefore, to want to comprehend what philosophical Mysticism has meant to those who have held it, and especially how it stands opposed to Realism. But the mystical conception of Being is one peculiarly liable to be misunderstood. It is usually not rightly distinguished from the realistic view of Being. A student often, after a brief study of this or that mystical treatise, accordingly comes away displeased. " Mere sentimentality," such a student often says. " This mystical view seems to hold that the only real object is some voiceless and incomprehensible Absolute, and further, that when you feel uncommonly entranced or enraptured, you get some strange revelation as to the nature of the real, and so become one with the Absolute. Now it is plain," he continues, " that such views have nothing to do with common sense, or with the physical world, or with matter, or with the facts of daily life. For can one say that this wall, and yonder stars, and my neighbors, and even my own daily self, are the Atmân of the Hindoos, or are the Mystic Absolute, or are anything else that you feel when you are in a trance? Now these objects yonder are well known to be real. Reality means for everybody a character that they possess. Hence the mystic needs no further notice. He substitutes his feelings for the solid facts. He is simply a man who prefers not to think about reality, but merely to revel in his own feelings."

This criticism is obvious, but it is the external view of a realistic metaphysic. It leaves the matter uncomprehended. And nobody, I must hold, can understand a large part of human nature without understanding Mysticism. The true historical importance of Mysticism lies not in the subject to which it applied the predicate real, but in the view it holds of the fundamental meaning of that very ontological predicate itself. No matter what subject the mystic seems to call real. That might be from your point of view any subject you please ; yourself, or God, or the wall. The interest of Mysticism lies wholly in the predicate. Mysticism consists in asserting that to be means, simply and wholly, to be *immediate*, as what we call pure color, pure sound, pure emotion, are already in us partly and imperfectly immediate. Mysticism asserts that this aspect of Being, which common sense already, as we have seen, recognizes and names in the popular ontological vocabulary, must be kept quite pure, must be wholly and abstractly isolated from all other aspects, must be exclusively emphasized. And the mystic further holds that your eternal salvation depends on just such an abstract purifying of your ontological predicate. Purer than color or than music or the purest love must the absolute immediate be. Now why the mystic says this, is a matter for further study. But this is what he says. He certainly does not assert, if you are an ordinary realist, that his Absolute is real in your sense, say real as money is real. The true issue for him is whether the fundamental ontological predicate, reality, ought not itself to be altered, altered namely by a certain purification, so as to be another predicate than what ordinary metaphysic confusedly takes it to be. That the mystic is dealing with experience, and trying to get experience quite pure and then to make it the means of defining the real, is what we need to observe.

That meanwhile the mystic is a very abstract sort of person, I well admit. But he is usually a keen thinker. Only he uses his thinking sceptically, to make naught of other thinkers. He gets his reality not by thinking, but by consulting the data of experience. He is not stupid. And he is trying, very skilfully, to be a pure empiricist. Indeed, I should maintain that the mystics are the only thorough-going empiricists in the history of philosophy.

In its origin, and in its greatest representatives, Mysticism appears in history as the conception of men whose piety has been won after long conflict, whose thoughts have been dissected by a very keen inner scepticism, whose single-minded devotion to an abstraction has resulted from a vast experience of the painful complications of life, and whose utter empiricism is the outcome of a severe discipline, whereby they have learned to distrust ideas. The technical philosophical mystics are the men who, in general, began by being realists. They learned to doubt. They have doubted through and through. Whenever they choose to appear as discursive thinkers, they are keen and merciless dialecticians. Their thinking as such is negative. What they discover is that Realism is infected, so to speak, by profound contradictions. Hereby they are led to a new view of what it is to be. This view asserts, first, that of course the real is what makes ideas true or false. But, as the mystic continues, owing to certain essential defects of the process of ideation, experience shows that explicit ideas, of human, perhaps of any type, are always profoundly false, just in so far as they are always partial, fleeting, contradictory, dialectical, disunited. The thinking process, just because it looks to another as its guide, is always a dissatisfied process, — like the finite search for happiness. And now, secondly, the mystics admit that true Being is something deeper than what usually is seen or felt or thought by men. But they add that this is just because ordinary thinking, like Realism, like money getting, like pleasure seeking, like mortal love making, always looks beyond the truly complete immediate, looks to false ideas, to fleeting states that die as they pass, and so indeed looks to what the mystic regards as the contradictory and consequently superficial aspect of experience. "Look deeper," he says, "but not deeper into illusory ideas. Look deeper into the interior of experience itself. There, if you only look deeper than all ordinary and partial immediacy, deeper than colors and sounds, and deeper than mortal love, then when once rightly prepared, you shall find a fact, an immediate and ineffable fact, such that it wholly satisfies every longing, answers every inquiry, and fulfils the aim of every thought. And this it will do for you just because it will be at last the pure immediate, with no beyond to be sought. You talk of reality as fact. Well," insists the mystic, "here shall be your fact, your datum, an absolutely pure datum. As pure it will fulfil the purpose of thinking, which always desires its own Other, or in other words always really desires just the cessation of all its strife in peace. Only in the immediate that has no beyond, is such peace. Now that is the Reality, that is the Soul. Or, to repeat the Hindoo phrase: *That art thou.* That is the World. That is the Absolute. That, as Meister Eckhart loved to say, is the " *stille Wüste der Gottheit.*"

Now the essence of this view of the mystic is that to be real means to be felt as the absolute goal and consequent quietus of all thinking, and so of all striving. Or in other words, Reality is that which you immediately feel when, thought satisfied, you cease to think. The mystic is, as I said before, the only thoroughgoing empiricist. We owe to him an illustration of what an absolutely pure empiricism, devoid of conventions, and alone with immediacy, would mean. Ordinary empiricism only half loves the facts of experience, as facts; for it no sooner gets them than it gets outside of them, makes endless hypotheses about them, restlessly tries to explain them by ideal constructions, and, if realistic, forsakes them altogether to talk of independent beings. The mystic loves the simple fact, just so far as it is simple and unmediated, the absolute datum, with no questions to be asked. That alone, for him, is worthy of the name real. If it takes a trance to find such a fact, that is the fault of our human ignorance and baseness. The fact in question is always in you, is under your eyes. The ineffably immediate is always present. Only, in your blindness, you refuse to look at it, and prefer to think instead of illusions. The ineffably immediate is also, if you like, far above knowledge, but that is because knowledge ordinarily means contamination with ideas.

So much for the mystic's conceptions of what it is to be. If you ask what to think of this conception, in comparison with the first, I answer at once that, as a more detailed study will show us, it is precisely as much and precisely as little a logically defensible conception as the former conception, that of Realism. Both are abstractions; both, if analyzed, go to pieces upon their own inner contradictions; both have had a long history; both express a fragment of the whole truth about Being; both stand for perfectly human and common-sense tendencies, merely pushed to technical extremes. Both can only be judged by means of their dialectic. No Theory of Knowledge can prove either of them sound or unsound except by undertaking directly an ontological analysis and criticism of what each one of them means. Our present purpose, however, is simply to understand their general drift and their historical importance.

The realistic predicate, independence of any external knowing process, could be applied to very various conceived objects, to souls, to matter, to God, etc. On the contrary, the mystic meaning of what it is to be implies the absolute and immediate inner finality and simplicity of the object to which the predicate real can be directly given. Yet, on the other hand, this reality of the mystic, if viewed from without and taken as a subject, to which this predicate is given (in other words, if viewed in a way that the mystic himself calls a false way) — this reality appears to you, while you look on, to be only this or that state of the mystic's mind, his sensations when he fasts or takes ether, his feelings in a trance, or the feelings that he usually has towards God, or towards life. Hence, as you, from without, view the mystics, and their faiths and feelings, they seem diverse enough. And what the mystics talk about as the Absolute, the subjects to which they apply their predicate real, will appear to you, thus seen from without, as very various

facts, named in many tongues.   Hence the mystics may
be of any human creed.   Their doctrine passes " Like
night from land to land" and "has strange power of
speech."   It says, like the Ancient Mariner: —

> "The moment that his face I see,
>   I know the man that must hear me:
>   To him my tale I teach."

And the mystic always thus appeals, in the ordinary
world, to the individual man.   Hence, in history, the
mystics have been great awakeners of the very spirit
that they have most condemned, namely of individuality.
The great and stormy individuals, like St. Augustine,
or like Luther, have loved them, and have learned from
them, although in a sense that indeed soon transformed
the mystic conception of Being, for such men, into quite
another.   Mysticism has been the ferment of the faiths,
the forerunner of spiritual liberty, the inaccessible refuge
of the nobler heretics, the inspirer, through poetry, of
countless youth who know no metaphysics, the teacher,
through the devotional books, of the despairing, the
comforter of those who are weary of finitude.   It has
determined, directly or indirectly, more than half of the
technical theology of the Church.   The scholastic philosophy endeavored in vain to give it a subordinate place.
In the doctrine of St. Thomas, the faithful, in this life,
are permitted only a moderate though respectful use of
mystical notions.   Yet it is plain that the God of St.
Thomas's theology is himself a mystic, and even a pan-
theistic mystic, since the Being of the world, although
for us real in the formal or realistic sense, makes abso-

lutely no real difference to God, who was just as complete before he created it as afterwards. And God's perfection is, for himself, a perfectly immediate fact.

So much, then, for a preliminary glance at the meaning of the mystical conception of reality.

And thus, after a discussion, at the outset of the present lecture, of the general nature of the ontological predicate, we have proceeded, first, to sketch three different meanings that the popular use of language seems to have especially had in mind in asserting that any object is real. We have seen, of course, that these three meanings were fragmentary, and more or less conflicting. We have turned from popular usage to study the more elaborate efforts of the philosophers to purify or to harmonize the ontological concepts. Of the four resulting forms of the ontological predicate which, as we asserted, are prominent in the history of philosophy, we have now briefly outlined two. As a result, we have before us definitions of Being which are the polar opposites of each other. These are the realistic and the mystical definitions. Realism defines Real Being as a total Independence of any idea whose external object any given Being is. Mysticism defines Real Being as wholly within Immediate Feeling. These two concepts, both of them, as I must hold, false abstractions, are still both of them fragmentary views, as I also hold, of the truth, — hints towards a final definition of the Other, of that fulfilment which our finite thinking restlessly seeks. But any fair criticism of either of the two conceptions so far before us, demands a separate lecture; and the third and fourth conceptions of Real Being will be considered only after these two have first been examined.

In the present discussion I have tried, then, merely to open the way towards the point where we shall for the first time rightly see how profoundly a definition of Being must influence, and in fact predetermine, the issues of life, and, in particular, of Religion.

LECTURE III

LECTURE III

THE INDEPENDENT BEINGS: A CRITICAL EXAMINATION
OF REALISM

In the foregoing lecture, after naming four historical conceptions of Being, we undertook an exposition and comparison of two of these four conceptions. We indicated the general attitude towards life and towards the universe which is assumed on the one hand by Realism, on the other hand by Mysticism. Before proceeding with our list of the historical conceptions of what it is to be real, we may well pause to examine still further these two; both as to their inner consistency, and as to their adequacy to their task of expressing the problems which beset our finite thought.

The present lecture I shall devote to a critical study of the realistic conception of what it is to be. The next lecture will similarly be concerned with a study of Mysticism. Then only shall we be prepared to go still further in the effort to define true Being.

I

The realistic conception of Being is, as we saw, extremely familiar in metaphysical doctrine. It has won no small favor in popular discussion. It is the typical notion of socially respectable conservatism, whenever such conservatism begins to use the speech of technical philosophy.

But the task of critically analyzing Realism, to get at the essential meaning, is austere and intricate. Realism easily assumes its vast metaphysical responsibilities; yet an examination of the true state of its accounts with the truth proves to be a very baffling enterprise. The preparation of a balance sheet of these accounts, the definite presentation of the assets and the liabilities of Realism, has been repeatedly attempted by philosophers ever since Plato, and even before his time. Of the difficulty of the work let the proverbial obscurity of metaphysical treatises bear witness; for very much of that obscurity is due to just this problem. As a fact, all here depends upon finally simplifying the issue, upon leaving out countless non-essential problems, which have been discussed by this or that realistic system of doctrine, and upon reducing the central question of every realistic view of the universe to its lowest terms. Once thus separated from its historical setting, the mere intricacy of this problem indeed vanishes; and you find yourself at last in presence of a very precise issue. But then your difficulty only changes its shape; for hereupon the issue brought to light by Realism proves to be highly abstract; and the austerity of which I just spoke comes to be felt all the more as the crisis of the enterprise approaches. Nowhere in these lectures shall we have to undertake, in fact, a more abstract investigation than the one here immediately before us. May the magnitude of the interests at stake justify the inevitable hardships of just this day of our voyage!

Realism asserts, as I have said, that to be real means to be independent of ideas which, while other than a given real being, still relate to that being. If you suppose a realist to be addressing yourself, what he asserts may then be put into very much the following words: " The world of Fact," he tells you, " is independent of your knowledge of that world. This independence, and the very reality itself of the world of Fact, are one. Were all knowledge of facts to cease, the only direct and logically necessary change thereby produced in the real world, would consist in the consequence that the particular real fact known as the existence of knowledge, would, by hypothesis, have vanished. Since we men are not only knowers, but voluntary agents as well, it is true that the vanishing of our own knowledge would indirectly alter the fact-world in a negative and perhaps in a very important way, since all the real results that our will, in view of our knowledge, might have brought to pass, would be prevented from taking place. But this is a secondary matter. Primarily, the vanishing of our knowledge would make no difference in the being of the independent facts that now we know."

In brief, to sum up this whole view in a phrase, Realism asserts that the mere knowledge of any Being by any one who is not himself the Being known, " makes no difference whatever " to that known Being.

Otherwise stated, Realism involves, as its consequence, a characteristic mental attitude towards the truth, — an attitude celebrated in one of the best-known stanzas of Fitzgerald's *Omar Khayyám*. Realism, at least in so far as it considers knowledge and does not add a special hypothesis to explain the active deeds of voluntary agents, submits. It accepts its realities as facts to which its own knowledge makes "no difference," and so any group of so-called "merely knowing" beings, or of "pure ideas," can say to one another, concerning the whole world of facts beyond themselves, viewed precisely in its whole-ness : —

> "When you and I behind the Veil are past,
> Oh, but the long, long while the World shall last,
> Which of our Coming and Departure heeds,
> As the seven seas should heed a pebble cast."

To be sure, as I have indicated, any individual realist may chance to deny altogether that in all this he himself means to be at all practically fatalistic. But in that case he needs a special hypothesis to explain how voluntary agents, according to his system, can use their knowledge to alter the independent facts. Primarily, knowledge shall make precisely what the characteristic phrase of Realism describes as "no difference" to fact. And so the realm of realistic Being that is real beyond your ideas or mine, is, in its wholeness, indeed like a sea, into which any of our ideas about its waves fall like pebbles. Wave and pebble are primarily to be viewed as mutually foreign facts. If the pebble itself creates new waves, that is at first sight something wholly non-essential. The sea is the sea, and Being is indifferent to our mere ideas.

This statement of the general realistic definition of what it is to be real may be set in a clearer light by a comparison with other more or less frequent efforts to state the same historical view. Sometimes Realism is defined as the doctrine that reality is "extra-mental" or is "out-side of the mind." But this mode of definition involves a space-metaphor, and arouses the question as to what the world "outside" is here literally to mean. Space, too, in its wholeness, may be viewed by a realist as "extra-mental." But space as a whole is obviously not in any literal and spatial sense "outside" of anything whatever; so that to call space "extra-mental" is to use a phrase that *ipso facto* needs further interpretation. Accordingly, "extra-mental" is often interpreted as meaning merely "other than" the knowing mind. From this point of view Realism would mean only that an object known is other than the idea, or thought, or person, that knows the object. But in this very general sense, any and every effort to get at truth involves the admission that what one seeks is in some way more or less other than one's ideas while one is seeking; and herewith no difference would be established between Realism and any opposing meta-physical view. Idealism, and even the extremest philo-sophical Scepticism, both recognize in some form, that our goal in knowledge is other than our effort to reach the the goal. Still, then, the realistic meaning of the phrase "outside of the knowing mind" would need an explana-tion.

But if this phrase is next taken to mean "different from or apart from the contents of *any or of all* minds," the phrase is inadequate to express what Realism has historically meant by the reality of the world. It is indeed true that in any realistic system there must be at least some real facts that find no place amongst the con-tents of any mind whatever. This is true, for any realistic view, at least, with regard to those supposed facts called the real relations between knowing beings and the "out-side" objects which they know. For those real relations, in any realistic system, are directly present to no consciousness whatever, and are thus absolutely different from the contents of any mind. But, on the other hand, it is not true that Realism need regard only such unconscious facts or beings as real in its sense of the word real. You, for instance, as a conscious mind, might be viewed by a realist as a being that he would call real in his sense. That assertion, if made by a typical realist, would simply mean that the contents of your mind, although present within your own consciousness, are real without regard to whether anybody else knows of your existence or not. It is true that some realists, namely, the extreme materialists, have in their systems declared only matter to be real. It is also true that such a realist as Herbart, who was no materialist, still defined the real beings as in themselves absolutely simple, and therefore not conscious beings. But, on the other hand, many realistic systems have regarded conscious beings as in the realistic sense real; and it is historically possible for a realist to maintain that his world consists wholly of conscious beings, or even of mere states of mind, when taken together with the unconsciously real relationships existent amongst these beings. Whether such a theory can be consistently worked out, with a purely realistic sense of what it is to be real, is indeed another question. But one could be a realist in his definition of Being, and still insist that all Being is in its nature entirely psychological.

All these various interpretations of the phrase "outside of the mind," prove, then, inadequate to express the meaning of the realist. There remains as the one essential idea conveyed by the phrase "outside of the mind" and

as the one mark of the realistic type of Being, the indifference of any real being to what you may, as knower,
think about it, so long as you yourself are not the
being that is known. The being, known by you, may
be in itself a mere state of consciousness in the mental
life of your neighbor. But it is a realistic being so long
as it is supposed to be quite independent of your knowledge, and so undetermined by your knowledge. If
you think the truth, so much the better for your
knowledge. But if you or any other knower chance to
think error, or chance even to vanish from the universe,
the realistic realm is thereby modified only in respect of
so much of its reality as you intelligent beings carry
away with you when you blunder or vanish. To say
just that, is to be realistic. This then is a general statement of the Realism which I mean in the present lecture
to examine. This definition still needs, however, some
further historical exemplification, to make sure that we
have stated it not unfairly.

II

Historically speaking, this general realistic conception
of what it is to be has been held with various degrees
of consciousness and definiteness of conception. The
early Greek thinkers soon learn to make a sharp distinction between what existed, as they said, "by nature,"
and what was merely believed from the point of view
of human and of false "opinion." These two realms,
the real and the false, they erelong not only distinguished, but sundered. It was this sundering that

made them realists, and not the particular sort of nature which they regarded as real. The changeless, although sensuous and materialistic Being of the Eleatics, is only one case of such sharp sundering of the real from the seeming. That true Being is, in some essential way, independent of false opinion, thus comes early to be regarded as a sort of obvious maxim. When Protagoras attacks this maxim, his extreme form of expression is a natural reaction from another extreme. Plato's theory of the incorporeal Ideas, in its more extreme form, rests upon the presupposition, that unless knowledge is founded upon the absolutely independent reality, nothing is known.[1] Aristotle, in his *Metaphysics*, spends a long time in trying to define what makes any real object, or substance, just *itself*, — a being logically independent of other beings. That the definition of this essence or of any being also implies that a real substance is independent of the accident that it is known by another is, for Aristotle, rather a tacitly assumed and self-evident matter than a topic of frequent overt argument. But when, in

---

[1] Any summary statement of the significance of the Platonic Ideas has to be, in a measure, unjust. I here follow what is, on the whole, Zeller's interpretation ; and I lay stress upon the extremer form of the Platonic theory. Plato himself sometimes saw much deeper. Independence, in the abstract sense hereafter to be defined, seems indeed certainly to be implied in the famous expression (Sympos. p. 211, A and B): αὐτὸ καθ' αὑτὸ μεθ' αὑτοῦ μονοειδές ἀεὶ ὄν, taken in its context as the climax of an effort to define the complete indifference of the Ideas to all beyond. But that the Plato of the *Philebus* and the *Sophist* recognizes other aspects of the situation is true. The argument (Sophist, p. 248) that our knowledge of Being is one of the proofs that the Real is both active and passive, and enters into relations, is identical in spirit with the criticism of Realism here to be given.

the fourth book of the *Metaphysics*, he has to deal with Protagorean scepticism, Aristotle uses, as one *reductio ad absurdum*, the consideration that, were this Protagorean doctrine true, " There would exist nothing in case beings with souls vanished from the world. For then," he says, " sense-perceptions would cease." " That," he continues, " perceivable objects and sense-percepts would then vanish, is perhaps true, for all this latter existence (*i.e.* as we should say, the existence of color, odors, etc.) is a state of a sentient being ; but that the substrata upon which sense is based, should not persist, even were there no sense-perception, is impossible. For sense-perception is not a perception of itself, but there is some other over and above perception ; and this other must necessarily be prior to perception. For what moves, is prior in nature to what is moved. And if one says that these two principles (subject and object, moved and mover) are related to each other, the same result still holds true." That in all this Aristotle admits interrelation, and recognizes no independence as absolute, is true, but here is one of the central difficulties of Aristotle's system.

Later Realism only makes this sundering of knowledge and object more express, as scepticism has to be faced, and as the idea of the individual Self gets more sharply contrasted with all ideas of outer things. The Cartesian dualism of extended and of thinking substance derives its extreme character from considerations with which the problem of knowledge has not a little to do. Occasionalism is an instance of the translation of a logical independence of essence into the assertion of a real causal independence.

Locke states the realistic definition briefly when he says, of his primary qualities: "The particular bulk, number, etc., of the parts of fire, or snow, are really in them, *whether any one's senses perceive them or no;* and therefore they may be called real qualities, because they really exist in those bodies." As to the secondary qualities, as he goes on to say: "*Take away the sensation of them* . . . and all colors, tastes, odors, and sounds, as they are such particular ideas, vanish and cease." Here then is the realistic touchstone, the test of reality. Does the object stay when the knowledge vanishes? The converse of this test, however, also holds true for any realism. For erroneous ideas are possible. Hence, whether the object is or is not, any given idea may be held by anybody that you please. The idea might then persist when the object vanishes, or remain changeless when the object changes. [1]

It is of service to compare these familiar expressions of the classical realistic view with the speech used by an ancient Hindoo system of philosophy, the Sânkhya. The Sânkhya was a realistic doctrine, and very sharply dualistic. Its world consisted of matter and of soul, each of these sorts of realities being, in ultimate nature, totally different from the other. In fact, the salvation of the wise man depends, for the Sânkhya, upon his absolutely distinguishing himself as soul from all material objects,

[1] Kant, in his criticism of the Ontological Proof for God's existence, emphasizes this expression of the realistic test of being. The being of fact, he says, never follows from any mere idea. The *that* never follows from the *what*. In other words, whether or no any object exists, your ideas about that supposed being may be whatever they happen to be.

states, and possessions. In a Sânkhya treatise translated by Garbe (a commentary upon the text called the Kârikâ), I find a statement of the realistic definition of Being, in a form abstract enough, but illustrated in characteristic Hindoo fashion.[1] I may first quote the statement of the commented Sânkhya text in question concerning the two types of Being of which this extreme dualism makes the world consist. On the one side, as this text tells us, there is the material world. On the other side, however, there is the soul, which the Sânkhya doctrine makes absolutely immaterial. Now both the matter and the soul are real beings. The text here describes them as to their essential metaphysical characters very briefly, and side by side. " The formed matter," it says, — i.e., the matter of the physical world, "is composed of three constituents, — is object, is common object for all knowers, is of non-mental character, and is productive. The *materia prima* also possesses these same characters. The soul is opposed to both; yet (being real) it has certain features in common with them."

The commentator explains this text at some length. " The word 'object,'" he says, " is used in opposition to those who say (as the Buddhistic metaphysicians had asserted) that there are only states of mind, such as joy, sorrow, confusion, tones, and the like. An object," he continues, " is that which is known as outside one's ideas. Therefore is the term 'common object' also used. For this term implies that material objects, such as pottery, for

---

[1] See *Der Mondschein der Sânkhya-Wahrheit*, in deutscher Uebersetzung von Richard Garbe, Abhandl. der Bayer. Akad. der Wiss. I. Cl., *Bd.* XIX, *Abth.* III, p. 567.

instance, are known independently by many different souls. But if the objects were only the soul's state of mind, then, since states of mind are affections of one individual only, the objects would be similarly limited, precisely as one man cannot observe another man's ideas, since the interior organ is invisible. That is what the text means. And so," continues the commentator, "it becomes comprehensible how very many men can bethink themselves of a single (*i.e.* of the same) coquettish glance of a dancing girl, while that otherwise (namely, upon the basis of subjective idealism) would not be possible." So much then for independent beings of the material sort. You see, Their independence implies that these beings are out of all mind, and yet can become common objects for many minds at once.

The commentator then indicates, what he elsewhere developes more at length, namely, the features that the souls, as real beings, have in common even with their extreme opposite, matter. They too, he points out, are eternal; they are independent; and they are not the product of anything else. To be sure, unlike matter, they are not perceivable from without through sense. But they are utterly separate in being from matter, and, as thus separate, they are independent individuals. As we just saw, salvation, for the Sânkhya philosophy, depends upon coming to know precisely this utter independence of the true soul and the material world. In fact the soul is not only separated by a chasm from matter; it is even really unaffected by matter. What seem to be affections of the soul are, according to the Sânkhya psycho-physical theory, material states, which merely appear to be in the soul, as, according to a favorite Sânkhya similitude, the red Hibiscus flower is reflected in a crystal that all the while remains inwardly unaltered by the presence of the flower. The result is a theory of a sort of psycho-physical parallelism, founded, to be sure, according to the Sânkhya, upon an illusion.

While the commentary just cited belongs, according to Garbe, to the twelfth century of our era, and the commented text of the Kârikâ itself is known to have existed not much before the fifth century, the metaphysical views here in question are no doubt of a very ancient date, and may well be quite independent of any but Hindoo origins. In any case the passage just quoted serves to give us, from a remote source, two or three very characteristic and universal features of realistic doctrines, — features whose meaning becomes all the clearer for our attention by reason of their foreign dress. The whole may be summed up in a phrase: This realistic world is a world of Independent Beings.

Any real being, as you see, has to be essentially, and if possible absolutely, independent. The nature of the gulf that divides the independent beings from one another is peculiarly indicated, and in fact is typically exemplified, by a certain separation that is discoverable between knowledge and its material objects. What is known, if it is a physical thing, is outside of the knower. To this sundering of knower and physical object common sense bears witness. Moreover, a certain proof of the fact of the sundering, and at all events an explanation of what the sundering means, is furnished by the further fact that many knowers, while notoriously isolated from one another, as our failure to read the ideas of our neighbors proves, can still know the same outer object. The sameness of the physical fact for all souls, is only explicable, in view of the mutual isolation of the souls, by the supposition of an equal isolation of the physical fact from the inner life of all who know it. Finally, if the material objects are independently real, the souls that know are also independently real. All is now independence and isolation. This is a world of chasms. The independence meant is intended to be a mutual relation.

So much for our Sânkhya authors. They bring again to mind what I earlier mentioned about the social motives of realism. Our acceptance of our physical objects as topics of common knowledge for all men, stands side by side with an equally social assurance on our part that any man's knowledge is primarily a secret from all his neighbors. The mutual independence of the knowers requires their common separation from all their common objects. The independence of the objects makes possible their community for all the independent knowers. These social presuppositions have a great deal to do with the development of the whole realistic world, — a world where an abstract reduction of the reality to a mysterious unity, such as the Eleatic One, has alternated with a tendency to create numerous gaps and separations. In this world, thought, as you see, first declares certain barriers absolute; and then proceeds, by immediate assurance, or by elaborate devices of reasoning, to transcend in knowledge these barriers, and to join in insight what Being is first said to have put forever asunder. The result is a struggle in which the unity sometimes completely triumphs; but then the One becomes a mystery, or the many survive, and then where are the links?

Two features, frequent, but by no means universal, in realistic systems, I have in this whole summary deliberately kept in the background. Reality has often been regarded, by the realists who are of a more or less Eleatic type, as implying, essentially, the permanence and unchangeableness of the reals. So it was with Plato's Ideas; so it was with Herbart's Reals; and Spinoza's Substance was eternal. A similar eternity the Sânkhya knew, although that doctrine also recognized a realm of real changes. Reality has also often been made, by these or by other Realists, to imply essentially the causal efficacy, the active potency, of the real entities. These two views, of course, cannot easily be harmonized. But regarding both these features of many realistic systems, I can here only observe that they are, to my mind, secondary features.

Historically, they are indeed not unimportant in the development of Realism. Permanence, in the first place, has always been regarded, — and especially by the older forms of Realism, — as a peculiarly strong evidence of independence; and often it has been conceived as, in the second place, a necessary condition of such independence. So it was, for instance, for Herbart. What lasts forever, wholly unchanged by anything, must of course be unchanged by the coming and going of knowledge. Hence the concept of the real as the absolutely Abiding, has played a great part, not only in the Eleatic doctrine, in Plato, and in Atomism, but also in modern, scientifically colored, speculations. And just so, too, Power, Efficacy, Activity, seem to be evidences of independence. Plato associates them in the *Sophist*, with Reality. Yet, I insist, none of these predicates are essential to Realism.

Realism especially tends to sunder the *what* from the *that*, the essence from its existence. But permanence properly belongs to the *what* and not to the *that* of any being in a realistic world. And the same is true of activity, potency, effectiveness. One can define a mythical being, say Achilles, conceiving him as yellow-haired. To be yellow-haired belongs to the *what* of Achilles; to his essence, not to his existence. One can so conceive him while not asserting that he is, but while defining him as a myth. But just as easily one can conceive him as active, as pursuing Hector; and still one need not conceive him as anything but a myth. Activity and realistic existence are then certainly different ideas, just as much as yellow-haired and existence. Just so it is with permanence. Not all realists have asserted that permanence holds true of the Real. A world of events could be independently real for any Heraclitean thinker. The flashes of moonlight upon water may as well stand for independent realities as any other facts of experience. With the arguments used in special realistic systems, for the permanence of the reals, we have here nothing to do. Our concern is with the definition.

So there remains one more as the one essential historical mark of the realistic type of Being, its ontological independence of knowledge that refers to it from without.

III

I have thus defined the realistic view (and have tried by historical examples both to elucidate and to justify the definition given at the outset) and above all I have tried to separate the one essential feature that lies at the basis of every realistic system from the countless accidental features, and from the more or less controversial consequences that, in this realistic system, or in that, distract our attention from the most fundamental issue. This issue is simply the problem whether any realistic definition whatever can be self-consistent, or can be adequate to what we seek when we look for true Being. Our problem, you see, is not here whether the real world contains one or another special type of beings, whether only states of consciousness and their real relations really exist, or whether only atoms have being, whether colors are real, or whether space has genuine being, or whether souls or angels are to be found in the outer universe. Our only present problem relates to the sense in which anything whatever can be called real at all. We wish to know whether this abstract sundering of the *what* and the *that* can be consistently carried out.

But when the issue is thus simplified, the realistic definition stands before you as something that is on the one hand very plausible and familiar, and on the other hand very baffling and mysterious. As for its plausibility and familiarity, we hardly need here further dwell upon them. Is it not perfectly obvious that the very life of ordinary, socially colored common sense depends

upon tacitly admitting, or on occasion vigorously asserting that "whether or no" this or that observer, or this
or that pupil at school, or a given doubter in faith, or a
particular philosophical thinker, knows certain facts, those
facts, whether physical or mental, whether God, or matter, or moonbeams, are what they are? This "whether
or no" of ordinary common sense seems to be simply
crystallized in a technically abstract expression in the
fundamental definition of systematic realism as so far
stated. On the other hand, so soon as one undertakes
to formulate an exact account of the way in which Being
is independent of knowledge, one discovers that nothing
seems harder to carry out to its ultimate logical consequences than the definition of precisely that type of
independence which is here in mind. Common sense
knows, in the ordinary world of experience, very various
grades and instances of relative independence amongst
objects; but common sense also knows that often empirical objects which have been called mutually and
even totally independent turn out to be, in other aspects,
very closely linked. Yet the independence which Realism has in mind as characterizing the ultimate Being
of things, must be something of a very fundamental and
exact meaning and consequence. For it defines just
what gives to things their whole Reality. Nevertheless
realistic systems usually find it very much easier to
assert or tacitly to assume the general definition of independent being just stated, than to give any precise
account of the logical consequences to which the definition leads. As soon, however, as these consequences
themselves are directly faced, they often become fairly

startling in their strangeness. And in what sense this
last observation is true, a very moderate knowledge of
the history of Realism will show. For the paradox of
this history is that while the realistic metaphysic begins
as the very voice of common sense, the more developed
and thoroughgoing realistic systems show a character
which has made realism, from the Sânkhya to Herbart,
or to Herbert Spencer, the breeding place of a wholly
marvellous race of metaphysical paradoxes. The Atoms
and the Monads, the Ideas of Plato, the isolated Souls
of the Sânkhya, the unknowable Things in Themselves
of Kant, the transcendent Reals of Herbart, the Eleatic
One, the Substance of Spinoza, and the Unknowable of
Spencer, are beings far more remote from our ordinary
experience and from common sense than are many views
such as Realism vigorously opposes. Yet all these types
of hypothetical realistic beings were invented in the very
effort to make a realistic definition of what it is to be,
consistent with itself, and adequate to the demands of
life and of experience.

A definition whose union with common sense is at
first so close, but whose consequences are subject to
such remarkable and rapid transformations, is not indeed
thereby discredited, but is at all events properly subject to
a close scrutiny, to see whether we may not find out the
reason of this tendency towards unexpected interpretations of Being. But if we indeed look yet more narrowly
at the history of Realism, we find obvious motives run-
ning through the whole which make it seem in still other
ways paradoxical. For upon such closer scrutiny we find
that Realism has, as it were, vibrated between two histori-

cal extremes, extremes suggested by the well-known question whether the real world contains One independently real Being, or Many such beings, all equally independent of any knowledge that, not belonging to their own nature, refers to them from without. It is just the problem of the One and the Many which, when it arises in a world defined in the realistic way, is the deeper source of those marvellous metaphysical hypotheses of which we just spoke. And it is when we consider this aspect of the history of Realism that we become at length fully awake to the gravity of the problems in hand.

Realistic systems have frequently, like the Sânkhya, taught that many different beings are real. The historical fate of such pluralistic forms of Realism is well known, and has already been mentioned. Again and again, with an uniformity that seems characteristic, such types of Realism, in order to assure the true multiplicity of their real beings, have defined these beings as in ultimate nature quite independent of one another, as essentially out of all mutual relations, as isolated. The result one sees in the Monads of Leibniz, or in the Reals of Herbart, or in the souls of the Sânkhya itself. Then, necessarily, there has arisen the question why, despite the isolation of the real Beings, this, our own world of experience, seems so full of interrelationships, of mutual connections, of laws that bind soul to soul, and sun to planet, and all things to space, to time, or to God. To meet such demands, Realism has in just such pluralistic systems resorted to various paradoxical secondary explanations. Preëstablished harmonies, illusory forms of unreal linkage, or assumptions of intermediating principles,

— assumptions such as lead the philosopher into a hopeless, because unreasonable, complexity, — such are the
devices whereby Realism has in such cases sought to
join again the sundered fragments of its disintegrated
universe, like a careless child tearfully trying to mend a
shattered crystal.

Or, on the other hand, some historical systems of
Realism have been simply monistic, as the Eleatic doctrine was, or as, upon the realistic side of his ambiguous
system, Spinoza's teaching appears. But in such cases,
not only has common sense often revolted at the thought
of making all the independently real beings into a single
Being, but the realist's own logic has been easily turned
against him. For, as an objector may then briefly sum
up the case, addressing the merely monistic realists:
" Our so-called false opinions, when we believe that the
realities of the world are many, and are not One Being,
— are not these opinions themselves, viewed merely as
opinions, still also psychical facts, as real in the mental
world as is your One Being in its world. For you cannot even say that the opinions are false without admitting that, even as mere psychical facts, the opinions are
in existence. But our false opinions, as you yourself
also say, are many. Hence there is a real manifoldness
in the world, and your simple One cannot be the whole
truth." And this statement is, of course, conclusive as
against any absolutely simple oneness about the independent reality.

Paradox has faced the realist, therefore, whenever he
has attempted, during the history of thought, seriously
to apply that idea of the fundamental definition of Being

which lies at the basis of his whole doctrine, to the development of a positive. conception of a world that shall contain either One Being or Many Realities. Either all Unity, or else no linkages : such has been his historical alternative. Now is this fate of Realism a mere accident, due to the defects of individual realistic thinkers ? Or is it somehow founded in the very nature of the realistic definition of what it is to be?

This question deserves to be considered more carefully, and upon its own merits. We have perhaps exhausted the aid that a merely historical survey can just at present give us. We must turn back to our realistic definition itself, and must directly consider, first, how best to state its exact logical force, and then how to test it by applying it to that famous problem as to whether the universe contains One real Being or Many real Beings. For, as I must insist, it is precisely the problem of the One and the Many which will prove to be the great test problem of realistic metaphysics.

IV

And so we turn from the perplexing and varied history of the fortunes of realistic doctrine, to the even more forbidding task of reflecting upon the first principles of Realism. We lay aside for the time all thought of whether God, or the souls, or permanent matter, or the flashes of moonlight upon water, or the coquettish glances of our Sânkhya commentator's world of Oriental courts and splendors, are to be regarded as real beings. We ask only as to the most general theory of the constitution of any realistic world. And here we shall restate the precise sense of the realistic definition, and next shall develope, in a series of formal propositions, its inevitable consequences, until we see to what end they lead, both the realist himself, and all whose faith, whether in the world of science or in the realm of religion, depends upon realistic philosophical formulas.

As to the meaning of the realistic definition, we must take our realist seriously. He declares that whenever you know any being not yourself, your object is primarily and logically quite independent of your knowledge, so that whether your knowledge comes or goes, is true or is false, your object so far may remain whatever it was. He asserts, also, that in knowing the rest of the universe, you do, on the whole, know a being that is not your knowledge, and that is consequently independent of your knowledge. He asserts that this independence is the very means of defining the Being of any real object, when viewed in relation to any knowledge of this real object that is not itself a part of the object known. Now this definition turns upon the conception of independence. In just what sense is the reality to be independent of the knowing process?

In the Mathematical Theory of Probabilities, the conception of events that are said to be mutually independent is familiar. Two chance throws of dice, two drawings of a lottery, are such independent events. But the definition of such independence in the theory in question is always relative, and is limited to special aspects of the objects in question. One sometimes means, in such cases, that while both events, say both throws of the dice, are indeed supposed to be connected in the general causal order of the universe, and so are not wholly independent, we happen not to know what this causal connection is. Or again, even if one talks of pure chance, and ignores causal linkage, one has indeed to observe that any two physical events are viewed as occurring in the same space, and in the same time, or perhaps in the case of the same dice. One has also to admit that all parts of space, and all moments of time, are, in a sense, conceptually interdependent. For you cannot conceive a cubic foot of space destroyed, without abstracting from all space; nor can you suppose this hour to vanish wholly from the time stream without abolishing all time. But if space and time are thus Wholes of conceptually linked and mathematically interdependent parts, of course one has to admit that, in a sense, no two objects, no two events, in space and in time, can be defined as through and through logically or essentially independent of each other; since in defining each as to its time and space relations, one has to take account of facts which can be recognized only as mathematically linked with the space and time aspects of the other object or event. Yet, nevertheless, in the theory of probabilities, one still calls two events that occur in the same space and time, or even in the repeated throwing of the same dice, independent events. Plainly then, one merely means that while these events are not wholly independent, there is an aspect in which they may be called independent, either because one does not know what the interdependence is, or because knowing, one ignores some aspect of the interdependence as insignificant.

Now Realism usually also admits, even while it speaks

of the object as independent of the knowledge, that various causal connections, nevertheless, bind this or that object to this or that state of knowledge. On the other hand, the independence here in question seems to mean something much more nearly absolute than the independence which the Theory of Probabilities has in mind when it speaks of the two throws of the dice as independent events. For the "whether or no" of customary realistic phraseology means to sunder knowledge and object, taken in their deepest truth, more completely than any adjacent physical events, or even than any two merely physical facts can be sundered. For it is the very *that* of the object which is to be essentially and wholly sundered from the *what* of the object, in so far as the latter is expressed in any idea.

The only way to deal with a possibly ambiguous conception like this, is to view it first in its most extreme form, and to observe its consequences. Then later, if the conception is proposed in some modified form, the possibility of such modification may be considered. In this lecture, then, I shall henceforth take the realistic type of independence literally, and as a *total* independence. How alone a modified Realism can be stated, we shall see in connection with our Third Conception of Being. For the time, our realist shall be supposed to say, as many do, " Knowledge makes no difference to its real outer Object." What follows?

In brief, then, this realistic definition seems to imply two assertions : First, that even if your knowledge and its object are facts which when examined, say by a psychologist, appear to him to be causally connected, or which, when externally observed, seem to agree, still any such linkage, where it exists, is no part of the essential nature, *i.e.* of the mere definition, either of your object in so far as it is real, or of your knowledge in so far as it consists of mere ideas. If your knowledge is true, is sound, is valid, it is indeed such as somehow to agree with the object. In other words, ideas depend for their truth upon objects. But then false opinion is just as possible in a realistic world as is truth. You cannot tell by examining a "mere idea" as an idea in a realistic world, whether its real object is or is not, any more than you can tell by merely considering an object, whether any particular idea external to that object does or does not rightly represent it. That is why a realist has to reject with Kant the well-known ontological proof for God's existence. God's existence cannot be proved from any mere idea about God. No "mere idea" is, as such, essentially linked to its independent object. The *that* in a realistic world never follows from the mere *what*. Nothing has real being merely by virtue of the fact that it is conceived by any knower. Conversely, nothing is conceived in idea merely by virtue of the mere fact that it is real. If, then, idea and object are linked, by ties of causation, or by the mere fact that the idea happens to be true, then such linkage, for a realist, is another fact, namely, just the fact that the causal connection itself exists, or that the idea, by good fortune, is true of its object. A cat may look at a king; and hereupon both cat and king may be viewed by a student of psychology or physics as facts in the interdependent world of space and time. But the cat's looking, viewed as knowledge, makes "no difference" to the king; it is no part of the definition of the king's real being that he should be known or observed by a cat. On the other hand, the cat's idea of the king may be as false as you please. The "mere idea" in the cat's mind in no wise essentially determines the existence of the king. Just so, Realism asserts that existent causal or other linkage between any knower and what he knows is no part of the definition of the object known, or of its real being, or of the essence of the knowing idea if viewed in itself alone as a "mere idea."

In the second place, however, Realism, taken in its unmodified form, asserts that the independence here in question, namely, the logical or essential independence of object over against knowledge, is, indeed, in its own realm, absolute. For it is the whole Being of the object, spatial, temporal, inner, and outer, and all that is really true of it, that is independent of the fact that anybody knows this truth.

This view of Being may, for the sake of precision, receive still a little further development, and we may now afresh state the matter in the most general terms thus: —

Let there first be conceived any possible object, let us call it *o*. We want to know what would happen if this possible object *o* were real. To this end let there be conceived a second object, other than the first; and let this second object be called somebody's knowledge or idea or opinion, true or false, about the first object *o*. For brevity, let us simply name this second member of our pair "the idea of *o*." We shall first view it merely as a knowing process. We care in no whit whose idea this is, or how good or poor a representative of the first object it seems to be.

Next let us define the relation of the idea of *o* to its object *o*, the other member of the pair, — the relation, namely, which unmodified Realism regards as essential. The definition in question is now, as a mere abstract statement, easy. Simply suppose the idea of *o* to change, in any way, becoming a good idea where it was formerly bad, or dim where it formerly was clear, or altering in the reverse of these ways, or in any other way. Let the idea of *o* be first one man's idea, and then another man's idea of *o*, or finally, let the idea of *o*, for the time, vanish altogether from the scene. Having tried all such changes in the idea of *o*, then arbitrarily define *o* as such an object that, as far as the nature of *o* and that of the idea of *o* are alone considered, there is no logical necessity that any change in *o*, or in the whole Being of *o* so far as *o* is real, need correspond to or follow from any of these variations of the idea of *o*. In other words, if *o* is later to be viewed as causally linked to the idea, some third and wholly external power, say somebody's will, must be also real, and must be supposed, if that be still possible, to cooperate with the idea and to induce such changes in the knowing object. This definition of *o* as such an object that by the definition of *o* itself no change in *o* logically need correspond to any variation in the idea of *o*, or even to the total vanishing of that idea, — this definition, I say, will hereupon be the more fully developed statement of the proposition that the object *o* is independent of the idea or opinion of knowledge which refers to it, or that essence and existence are mutually independent. Any causal or other linkage between *o* and the idea will have to be later added as a third fact, involved neither in the mere essence of *o* nor in that of the idea, in case any such linkage is to be found.

Moreover, the essential independence of object and " mere idea," in so far as each is first viewed by itself alone, will have to be a mutual independence. The idea will have to be, in its own separate essence, independent of the object. Otherwise, by merely examining the idea, taken by itself, you could prove something about the existence of its object. But, if so, then the *that* would follow from the *what*, and the independent existence of a thing from the presence of some mere idea of the thing. That, however, is forbidden by the whole spirit of realism. For *that* anything is, is a mere fact, to be wholly sundered from *what* anybody thinks it to be. So we can accordingly add that the object *o* also, when viewed in itself, might be supposed to change or to vanish without any change occurring in the idea of *o*. Of course *if* the idea is to remain *true*, it will indeed change when *o* changes, and so will be in that way dependent upon *o*. But then an idea might be false. That any given idea is true, or agrees with its object, is itself a further fact in a realistic world, a *tertium quid*. But this fact, like any other, may either be or not be. Mention to me a mere idea, define it as you will, and in a realistic world I have to say that this idea might be all that it now is whether or no any corresponding object exists in the real world.

And now suppose that *o* stands for any real object that you please, whether an angel, or a worm, or a Spencerian Unknowable ; and that *o* is, precisely thus, independent of any idea that you please, so long as this idea is not itself a part of *o*. Suppose, too, that the object *o* is consequently also independent even of the very ideas by which we just now declared it to be independent. Suppose just so that the ideas are, as mere ideas, definable independently of their objects. Then, finally, we have before us the unmodified realistic definition of the sense in which the object *o* is real. For Realism asserts simply that the real being of *o* is adequately defined by the supposed law that no change in either *o* or the mere idea of *o* primarily or essentially corresponds to any change or variation or vanishing of the other member of this pair, so long as that idea is not itself a part of *o*, and that any causal connection, or truthful agreement, or other such mutual dependence of *o* and the idea, if it ever came to exist, would be a third fact, external both to the primary nature of *o* and to that of the idea.

This abstract development of the sense of that "whether or no" which common sense so lightly utters when it speaks of an object as real "whether or no" you are aware of the fact, — this development, I say, already serves to bring more clearly before us the extreme subtlety of the considerations upon which the realistic view depends. But the definition is now complete. Let us at once set it to work. It has defined a world. Let us enter that world, and see what is there.

V

And so next I ask the formal question: In the realistic world whose Being is thus defined, could there exist Many different beings? And if they existed, in what relation to one another would they stand? Or again, could a realistic world contain only One sole Being, to the exclusion of many beings?

These questions at once raise another question, viz., What are we now to mean by the term "One real Being," and what by the term "Many real Beings"? Some realistic systems have answered this question by saying at once that by calling a real Being One, we mean that this being is perfectly simple, having no parts or passions, no internal variety of nature, no complexity about it. This is what Herbart declares about each one of the many real beings of which his world is composed. A realist of Herbart's type would insist that wherever there is real variety, there must be many real beings, so that to assert that there is only one reality in the world, would be to assert that all variety is illusory. Since Herbart holds that variety is real, he has to say that the world consists of many different beings, while each separate being for him is absolutely simple.

The arguments used for such views by realists like Herbart need not here concern us. In this general examination of Realism we may avoid altogether that issue, and may leave it a wholly open question, by arbitrarily defining the sort of difference between two beings which, if it were certainly known to be present, would be great enough to suffice to assure us that these beings were really two, and were not mere parts or aspects of any single being. This characteristic difference which would suffice to assure us that two beings were different realities, may be defined without in the least attempting to pass upon the question whether any variety could afterwards be found, in a realistic world, within the bounds of a single being.

Accordingly, I shall here not at all either assert or deny that a single realistic being, if found, would be a simple being. For all that I now know, a single realistic entity may be as simple as Herbart wished, or as complex as the whole arch of the heavens. I shall only say that if, in the realistic world, we were to find two objects that were as independent of each other as, in our definition of the general realistic conception of what it is to be, the object of knowledge was independent of any knowledge of that object, then, and then only, we should call those objects two real beings, really different from each other. If, however, on the other hand, we should find that, within the realistic world, all the real objects there present were in any way linked together, so as not to be mutually independent, we should so far have, according to just the present definition, to regard them as parts or aspects of One real being.

This way of stating our present meaning for the terms " One " and " Many," as applied to the realistic world, is of course, if you please, an arbitrary way. But it has the advantage of leaving open all the questions as to whether any single being would also, upon examination, prove to be a simple being; and this definition of unity and multiplicity has also the advantage of exhaustively stating a perfectly definite alternative.   Let me restate then, in exact form, just this definition of the One and the Many.

Suppose then that, in the realistic world, we should find two real objects, *a* and *b*.   Suppose that they were found to be such that if either of them changed in any way whatever, or vanished, the other of them might still consistently be conceived as undergoing no change whatever.   That is, suppose that the presence or the absence, or any alteration of either of them, logically speaking, need make "no difference" to the other, in precisely the same sense in which Realism says that it now makes "no difference" to your object whether you know it or not.   Suppose, in brief, the universal law that, so far as the nature of *a* and *b* is alone considered, no change in either *a* or *b* need correspond to any change in the other member of this pair.   Then, by my present definition, *a* and *b* would be two different real beings; while if any less mutual independence than this existed, my present definition would regard *a* and *b* as parts of one complete Being.   Upon this basis we could once more ask the realist: "Does your world contain in just this sense Many different, that is mutually independent beings, or does it contain only One real being, whose inner structure, perhaps simple, perhaps infinitely complex, still permits of no mutual independence of parts.

Two answers are, logically speaking, now open to the realist.   He can decide for the One ; he can decide for the Many.   For the argument's sake, I suppose him first to decide for the Many.   His world shall now contain various mutually independent beings — beings such that, as they at first are defined, the existence and the nature of any one of them is essentially indifferent to the presence, or absence, or alteration of any of the others. So far as the primary definition of any one of them goes, no change in that one need correspond to any change in the others. This is my realist's present hypothesis. I ask at once, what further consequences follow from this hypothesis? And in particular I want to know whether, when once the realist has defined his many beings as logically independent and as all in his sense real, he can ever afterwards define any way in which they can come to be linked, say by causation or space or time? In brief, I want to see him mend the broken crystal of the world of the Many, and make one world of it. In answer, I suppose that the realist may here at once counsel me to consult experience. What is more familiar than the existence of really independent beings? Yonder in the ocean there are drops of water. Here on the land is my desk. Both are real. Does any change in one of these beings just now need to correspond to any change in the other. If either were supposed to vanish, would the other thereby be changed? The unseen meteors in interplanetary spaces, are they not beings that are real, and that yet just now make no difference to your being or to mine? If we change or die, do they not move on unheeding? If their swarms disintegrate, do we therefore suffer? What then is more familiar than the empirical fact that the real world contains many mutually independent beings? In fact there are men in China or in Lapland who are beings utterly independent of me. They know me not, nor I them; and our lives make "no difference" to one another. Is this not the verdict of experience?

But as to the consequences of such independence, why is not experience also again our guide? Beings, thus primarily independent, may later come to be linked by actual ties. These ties are then new facts in the world. But they are possible. The drop of water in the ocean, evaporated, may enter into the atmospheric circulation, may be carried, as moisture, to my desk, and may there help to warp the wood. The meteors, reaching the earth's neighborhood, may be seen and perhaps heard as they explode. The men in China or in Lapland may become my business correspondents, my enemies, or my neighbors. So then independence, first real, may later change to mutual dependence, and what were strangers may become linked. Is not all this obvious?

But if one thus urges upon me such considerations, I reply at once that all this is simply not obvious as any case of true independence or of its possible consequences. I have just abstractly defined an absolute type of mutual independence supposed to exist amongst many real beings. This independence, I suppose a realist hypothetically to assert as the truth about this world. I ask for the consequences of this hypothesis. But now I distinctly decline to admit that, in our concrete human experience, you can ever show me any two physically real objects which are so independent of each other that no change in one of them need correspond to any change of the other. On the contrary, the very cases mentioned are cases of objects such that certain changes of one do very really correspond to very precise changes in the other, and the very beings of each can only be defined by admitting the possibility of just such a change. The water, once absorbed by the wood of the desk, changes the desk. But the absorption itself is due to certain changes occurring in the temperature, movement, density of the water or of its vapor. The man in China who may become my enemy or my neighbor is already such that certain changes in him, if they occurred, would not be indifferent to me. This possibility already makes part of his being. Furthermore, in our ordinary world of experience, beings like meteors and planets, water and wood, men and other men, viz. beings that on occasion may come into a very obvious connection, are already, even before their so-called actual linkage, truly related, yes, linked to one another, by space, by time, by physical and moral ties. What happens when we say that they pass from mutual independence to linkage, is really that we find them, in our experience, passing from relations whose importance is merely to us less obvious, into relations of more obvious human interest. But now the relations of an object in ordinary experience make parts of the object itself. A change in these relations would result from the change of other objects. Hence these empirical objects are never known as independent. If I am already related to the drops of water now in the ocean, to the meteors that might become visible to me, to men whom I might come to know, then you can never say that experience proves me to be independent of the existence of those as yet unobserved relations. What experience can show is only that a certain mutual dependence of objects may long remain unobserved by us men, until this or that meteor-flash in the heavens, or consequence of the damp weather, or meeting with a man from far lands, shows us how important even the remotest and heretofore least obvious empirical relation may at any moment become.

Our human experience, then, never shows us how beings would behave if they were mutually independent, in the ideal sense of our exact definition. Unhampered, therefore, by empirical guidance, we turn back to the chill realm of the hypothetical many beings of our realist's hypothesis. These many beings are so far the creatures of an exact definition, whose consequences, purely hypothetical so far, we want to predetermine. We must do so solely upon the basis of our realist's supposed present assumption. And hereupon, assuming the real world now before us to contain many mutually independent beings, I will prove at once two theses: (1) The many different real beings once thus defined can never come to acquire or later to be conceived as possessing any possible real linkages or connections, binding these different beings together; and so these beings will remain forever wholly sundered, as if in different worlds. (2) The many real beings thus defined can have no common characters; they are wholly different from one another. Only nominally can any common characters be asserted of them.

As to the first thesis: If I am defining mere ideas, apart from reality, I can of course first define two objects as independent, and can later add a definition of something that then comes to link them together. But if first I define two objects as so far quite independent of one another in essence, and if I next define each of them severally as real, apart from and inde-

pendently of all ideas, I have, once for all, in my real
world of objects, two beings, each so far quite separate
from the other, and each, by hypothesis, a complete
instance of a reality, so far as concerns its independence
of the other. If hereupon there is later to appear in
my real world any so-called link or tie between the
two, — any so-called causal linkage, or spatial connection,
or temporal relation, then this so-called linkage will be
a new fact, not logically involved in the definition of
either of these real beings, in so far as they were first
declared to be real. For, by hypothesis, neither of the
two, as first defined and as then declared to be independently real, possessed, as far as the definition yet went,
any character already involving a tie with the other.
For each, consistently with its definite nature, might
so far remain unchanged if the other wholly vanished.
But then at once it follows, that the new real being,
the so-called link, when it comes to light, is as truly
and as much *another* being as the two beings were
originally diverse from each other. For if before the
link came to light the completely defined beings were
real but not yet defined as linked together, the link,
when it comes, will be another new being. Furthermore,
the link will be a fact, logically independent of both
of the original beings. For as another being, a new
fact, it will be, by the very definition of what constitutes
another being, as independent of them, as each of them
is essentially independent of the other. It follows that
the so-called link is no link except in name, and can
never come to be one; it is simply a third being, independent of both of them, and not yet linked to either

of the two. This analysis holds of every possible link
that is secondarily to bind together any two of the many
beings that were declared to be primarily independent.
Thus the many cannot be linked as even the most widely
sundered empirical objects are always found to be linked,
even at the very moment when you first observe their
relations. The realist's many beings, as defined, are
defined as wholly disconnected, and they must remain
so. You cannot first say of them, for instance, that they
are logically independent, and then truly add that nevertheless they are really and causally linked. No two of
them are in the same space; for space would be a link.
And just so, no two are in the same time; no two are
in any physical connection; no two are parts of any
really same whole. The mutual independence, if once
real, and real as defined, cannot later be changed to any
form of mutual dependence.

And now for the second thesis. In our ordinary experience we often, as a fact, observe that two objects have
some character, as we say, "in common." We call this
the "same" character, quality or feature, present in both
of them. Thus in experience, what is called the same
redness can appear in two cherries. The old controversy
about universals has made familiar the question whether
that which is truly the *same* can ever really form part of
two different beings. How this question is to be answered
when it concerns the structure of that organic whole,
that realm of mutual interdependence called our concrete experience, we shall later see. For the moment we
have only to consider such a question as applying solely
to the independent beings which the realist has defined.

Take any two such independent beings. Then, as I observe, these two beings can have no real quality or feature whatever that is actually common to both of them, or that is, apart from name and from seeming, the same in both of them, beyond the mere fact that each exists.

For suppose that they are first said to possess in common a quality. Suppose, namely, that, to an onlooker, they both seem red, or round, like two cherries, but that as a fact they are independent beings. Call this apparently common quality Q. Then let one of the two beings be destroyed. By hypothesis, *no change whatever* need occur in the other being. And this means, as we now know, that no character or relation, visible or invisible, which is in any wise *essential* to the first definition of the being that is supposed to remain, is in the least altered when its fellow vanishes. Q, then, the quality supposed to be the same in both beings, survives unchanged in the being that does not vanish.

But now, if one man survived a shipwreck in which another was drowned, could you then call the survivor the same as the drowned man? But by hypothesis, the quality Q, together with all relationships essential into its reality, survives unchanged in the being that remains, while what is called the same quality in the other being has passed away.

But our realist, unwilling to concede this last consequence, may hereupon say that what he meant was that the quality Q in the two beings was *partly* the same, and *partly* not the same. This way of escape I meet, however, with the simple challenge: Leave aside that which is in part. Come to the ultimate fact. If something is only partly the same in your two independent beings, then some part of the part, some aspect of the aspect, must be really and ultimately quite the same. Name me any feature whatever in one of these two beings, — any character sensuous or supersensuous of which you will say: It is a common feature, really the same in these two beings. Then in my turn I will show you that just that feature is *not* the same, for I will suppose one of the two objects destroyed, as by hypothesis I have a right to do. I will then find the other in all its features quite unchanged, as by hypothesis I can do. And so I will show that what was destroyed in the one object cannot be the same as what survives unchanged in the other, precisely as the survivors of a shipwreck cannot be the same as the drowned. All this, you must remember, I assert upon the one basis of the realistic hypothesis about the many independent beings as stated above.

It follows that, as was to be proved, the many entities of this realistic world have no features in common. If they appear to have, this is seeming, is " mere name and form," as the Hindoo philosophers would say. In brief, such sameness is not at all real. The appearance called "similarity" has no real basis except when we are dealing with the aspects or functions that may exist within what our present arbitrary definition would call a single real being.

I sum up the results of these two inquiries concerning the world of the many independent reals by asserting simply: The real beings, if in the present sense many, namely, if real beings thus logically independent of one another, have no common features, no ties, no true relations; they are sundered from one another by absolutely impassable chasms; they can never come to get either ties or community of nature; they are not in the same space, nor in the same time, nor in the same natural or spiritual order.

VI

The doctrine of the Many, upon a basis of the arbitrarily assumed definition of many, thus becomes, in seeming, paradoxical enough. Historically, Realism has more than once assumed, however, almost this uncanny form; and the mere seeming of paradox is in itself no refutation of a philosophical doctrine. Yet before we press this very paradox to its final extreme, we must first see whether the realist is in any way forced to persist in defining his real Beings as in this sense many at all. Have we not ourselves admitted the possibility that, in one real Being, unity and multiplicity, for all that yet we see, can be reconciled? The Many, if once irrevocably defined as real, and as essentially independent, can never again be linked by external ties. They indeed thenceforth remain strangers. "But surely," one may say, "the realist is not forced to remain in so scattered a world. He can still pass over to the other hypothesis. He can say: 'My world is One Being, a single, real, but perhaps an internally complex, yes an infinitely wealthy Being, whose various aspects and functions are not logically independent, but are linked in a system, so that fully to define one part or region would be to define something of the essence of all, and so that no portion can indefinitely alter or wholly vanish without some implied change, however minute, in all the other parts. Diversity there is in my world, but no sundering of entities.' Why may not a realist take refuge in this modified monism, — not in the Eleatic Being, or even in the Substance of Spinoza, but in the assurance that the All, however manifold and full of contrast, is still an interrelated whole ? ”

Why not, indeed ? Ah, — but just as we are about to enter, with the realist, to explore this harbor of refuge, we suddenly observe that the realist has long since carefully closed the channel of entrance with a wholly impassable blockade. For let us remember that, as we observed before, there are already at least Two genuinely and absolutely independent real Beings in the realistic world.

For now comes a single proposition to which I have already made reference. Consider that “idea of o,” of which any object o was to be independent. Let that idea be the realist's own idea, when he talks of any independent object. I ask the realist: “Is not your own idea itself a real being, or at least a part of one? Come let us reason together. If you, the realist, are a being independent of my idea of you, then are not your own ideas a part of your own independent being? Are not your ideas then real? If, therefore, your object o yonder is independent of your ideas, are not your ideas, in so far as they also are parts of an entity and so have being, independent of o itself? If o vanished, could not your idea consistently be conceived as remaining, as a psychical fact, just what it now is? Yes, ideas, even the most false ones, are facts in the mental world. The realist must call them real in his sense, or abandon his system. And by the very first hypothesis of the system, since independence is a mutual relation, the idea and its object o are mutually and typically a pair of independent beings. Now the thesis that, if reality means independence, the ideas too, of anybody you please, are themselves existent entities, or are parts of an entity existent and independent, constitutes what I may call the Forgotten Thesis of most realistic systems. The whole present argument depends upon simply declining to countenance that forgetfulness. An idea has Real Being if anything has Being. And whatever existence means, that an idea also possesses.

A knowing process and its independent object, constitute then the irreducible minimum of the realistic world. But herewith I propose a perfectly simple and final procedure. I propose to treat this pair of entities precisely as we have just treated any two independently real beings in general. For this pair are not only the so-called idea and object; they are also a pair of mutually independent entities. We must not forget this aspect. The two theses just proved are now merely to be applied to them. The crisis of the realist's destiny is reached. The doom of his world is at hand.

Object and idea, viewed as entities, are twain. Realism began by saying so. So much is nominated in the bond. The realist shall have his pound of flesh, although we can grant him indeed not one drop of blood for all his world. By the original hypothesis either any individual idea, or o, the object of that idea, could without contradiction be conceived as changing, or as vanishing, without any logically necessary change in the other member of the pair. Therefore, according to what we have now shown to be the case with any two independent realities, the idea of o and o, as real beings, not only have, as first defined, no connection with each other, but they can never get any possible linkage or relation. All their connections are nominal. As idea, the idea was said to have *o* for its object. But the idea is an entity. It can have nothing to do with the other entity *o*. These two are not in the same space, nor in the same time, nor in the same natural order, nor in the same spiritual order. They have nothing in common, neither quality nor worth, neither form nor content, neither truth or meaning. No causality links them. If you say so, you again use mere names. No will genuinely can relate them. That they appear to have connections is simply a matter of false seeming. Our original definition called the one of them an idea relating to the object *o*. We now know that such an expression was a mere name. The idea has assumed as idea an obligation that, as independent entity it cannot pay. It has no true relation with *o*, and *o* has no community with the idea. To speak of any being not *o* itself as if it were really an idea of *o*, is as if you spoke of the square root of an odor, or of the logarithm of an angel. For idea and object are two real beings. Their irrevocable sundering no new definition of their essence can now join again. For reality, in this doctrine, is independent of all definitions that could be made after the fact. Relations that could link the two entities would merely prove to be new independent beings other than either of them.

Nor is this all. The idea here in question is any idea or opinion. *o* is any object. Now a realist's own theory is an idea or opinion. And the world was to be

his object. Our perfectly general result, true of all
ideas, applies of course to the group of ideas called the
realistic theory. As an entity, the realist is an independent being. His ideas, as part of his being, can have
nothing to do with any object that exists independently
of himself or themselves. The realistic theory, then,
as we now know, by its own explicit consequences,
and just because its real objects are totally independent
of its ideas, has nothing to do with any independently real
object, and has no relation to the independent external
world that its own account defines. Nor can it ever come
to get such a relation. No realist, as he himself now must
consistently maintain, either knows any independent
being, or has ever, in idea, found himself related to one,
or has ever made any reference to such a being, or has
ever formed or expressed an opinion regarding one, or,
in his own sense of the word "real," really believes that
there is one.

VII

And thus, suddenly at one stroke, the entire realistic
fabric, with all those "suns and milky ways" to which
Schopenhauer, in a famous passage, so prettily referred,
vanishes, — leaving not a wrack, not even a single
lonely Unknowable, behind. For an Unknowable, too,
would be an independent real object. Our present idea
of it would have to refer to this object, if it were real;
and no idea, as we know, can refer to any independent
reality, since in order for such reference to be itself real,
two irrevocably sundered beings would have to destroy

the chasm whose presence is determined by their own very essence.

In brief, the realm of a consistent Realism is not the realm of One nor yet the realm of Many, it is the realm of absolutely Nothing. This judgment is not due to us. The consistent realist merely happens to remember that his ideas too are, by his own hypothesis, existences; that also, by his own hypothesis, the objects of his ideas are other existences independent of his ideas; that this independence is a mutual relation; and finally, that two beings once defined, in his way, as independent, are wholly without inner links, and can never afterwards be linked by any external ties. The consistent realist remembers all this. And then he at once observes that if this be true, his own theory, being an idea, and at the same time an independent entity, has no relation to any other entity, and so no relation to any real world of the sort that the theory itself defines. He observes then that his whole theory has defined precisely a realm of absolute void. Nothing can be real merely in his sense.

But what then is left us, if the realistic definition of Being simply and rigidly applied, destroys its own entire realm, denies its own presuppositions, and shows us as its one unquestionable domain the meaningless wilderness of absolute Nothingness. Where, then, is *our* real world?

There is left us, I reply, just this world of our daily experience, with precisely its stars and milky ways, with its human life and its linkages — this world, only given already a deeper meaning by this very study. For now

we already begin to see, as from afar, the realm of truth
that is not independent of, but the very heart and life
of this fragmentary finite experience of ours. We begin
to see what later we shall view nearer by, — the realm
of truth where indeed nothing, not the least idea, not
the most transient event, is absolutely independent of
the knowledge that relates to it, or of any other fact
in the entire universe. In this realm it does, then, in
the long run, make a difference to all objects, divine or
material, whether they are known or not, by any being.
That a relative independence, and that both individuality and freedom have their concrete meaning in this
truer realm, we shall indeed in due season learn. But
what we now learn is that any definition of absolutely
independent beings, beings that could change or vanish
without any result whatever for their fellows, is, in all
regions of the universe, natural or spiritual, a hopeless
contradiction. There are no such mutually indifferent
beings. But this other realm, where no fact, however
slight, transient, fleeting, is absolutely independent of
any of its fellow facts, this is the realm where when
one member suffers others suffer also, where no sparrow
falls to the ground without the insight of One who
knows, and where the vine and the branches eternally
flourish in a sacred unity. That is the city which hath
foundations, and thither our argument already, amidst
these very storms of negation, is carrying us over the
waves of doubt.

LECTURE IV

LECTURE IV

THE UNITY OF BEING, AND THE MYSTICAL INTER-PRETATION

OF the four historical conceptions of Being we have now expounded in a general way, and with reference to their history, two conceptions, that of Realism, and that of Mysticism; and of these two we have critically examined one, namely, the realistic conception. If any one remarks that the sole result of our foregoing discussion was a mere negation, a mere rejection of an extreme form of realistic dualism, and that such a result is not yet positively enlightening, then I myself so far agree with the observation. It is true that we ended the last lecture with an assertion of the unity of Being. But if it be here further objected that the mere fact of unity is of small importance unless one comes to learn of what nature the unity is, and how it bears itself towards the varieties of our wealthy life, towards the vast phenomenal diversities of physical facts, towards the contrasts and tragedies of existence, towards that relative independence of moral individuals upon whose recognition all modern civilization depends, — then I fully admit the force of this objection. In fact, the explicit outcome of our examination of Realism, at the last time, merely so far opposed one abstraction by another, and we ended, for the moment, in a denial of dualism, with a hint added of a coming theory of the genuine unity of Being. Before we proceed, however, to a closer study of the first historical rival of Realism, namely, to the Mystical definition of the ontological predicate, something is still needed by way of a reminder of our precise present position.

I

The genuine essence of Realism consists, as we saw, in defining any being as real precisely in so far as in essence it is wholly independent of ideas that, while other than itself, refer to it. We insisted, at the last time, that this thesis implies an absolute dualism within the world of real being, since an idea also is an existent fact, and is as *independently* real as is the supposed independent object. No realist can consistently reduce the world to one independently real Being, however complex and wealthy in inner structure this One Being might be permitted to become. At least two mutually independent Beings, such that either of them, by its changing or by its vanishing, would imply no correspondent change in the other, remain in the realist's world. Moreover, these two beings, once defined and real, would forbid us to speak afterwards of their having any real tie, or real fashion of coöperation, unless this so-called tie is really a new fact, independent of both the beings that are to be linked. Such a tie, however, is a tie only in name. If beings are, like the objects of our ordinary experience, already interdependent, they can indeed consistently assume new ties, as young people who are already members of the same social order or of the same human family can marry. But in the supposed, and distinctly not empirical realm, to which the consistent realist finds himself driven, the two independent beings of which his world, if reduced to its lowest terms, consists, have no ties, and can never get any. For a similar reason, they have no common characters, and can never get any. The inevitable result is that the very presupposition of the entire doctrine is contradicted by its outcome. For if idea and object have no ties and no common characters whatever, they simply cannot be related as idea and object. The consequence is that both the realistic definition, and the totally independent beings, prove to be contradictory, and vanish together, leaving us, as our result so far, the thesis that, if the Other which our finite thinking, in its disquietude, seeks to attain, is to be defined at all, it cannot be totally independent of the thought which defines it, or remain unchanged if that thought essentially alters or vanishes. The ultimate dualism of the realistic view is false and must be abandoned. This, so far, is all that we have definitely made out concerning the conditions of a consistent definition of real Being.

But hereupon we are brought face to face with that ancient rival of the realistic definition. And this is Mysticism. If the dualism is to be abandoned, must we instead define Being as an absolute and simple unity? Must we say, the phrase " to be real " means something that cannot be asserted of any object whatever, so long as this object is defined through ideas that refer to it, or so long as the ideas themselves, with their endless search for the Other, trouble our consciousness, emphasize differences, and by their very striving after something beyond, keep our knowledge from its true goal? Must we insist that only such an object as quenches thought through the presence of a single and absolutely immediate truth is an object whereof we can say : *It is?*

II

Just such a view is of the essence of philosophical, or of the truly significant historical Mysticism. By this term I now mean, as you know from our second lecture, not a vaguely applied name for superstition in general, or for beliefs in spirits, in special revelations, and in magic, but a perfectly recognizable speculative tendency, observable in very various ages and nations, and essentially characterized by the meaning that it gives to the ontological predicate.

For the mystic, according to the genuinely historical definition of what constitutes speculative Mysticism, to be real means to be in such wise Immediate that, in the presence of this immediacy, all thought and all ideas, absolutely satisfied, are quenched, so that the finite search ceases, and the Other is no longer another, but is absolutely found. The object which fulfils this definition, and which is therefore worthy to be called real, is of necessity in itself One and only One ; since variety, when consciously faced, calls forth thought, and arouses demands for characterization and explanation. In countless ways, however, this One real object of the mystic's quest may be approached, by those finite thinkers who, in their ignorance, still seek their Other, — in countless ways, whose only common character is that, the nearer you come to the goal, the less the varieties and oppositions of the world of ordinary thinking distract you, and the more you are in possession of something that is present, given, satisfying, peaceful. If a realist, viewing your progress from without, observes hereupon that you are simply ignoring the manifold realities of the finite world, you reply that those so-called realities, just because they are many, and because they pretend to be independent beings, are illusory, and that in forsaking such a world, you simply spare yourself errors. As, in the world of the supposed independent beings, nothing is real, you care nothing for that world. If the realist, hearing that you seek something called Unity, reminds you that realists also may undertake to be monistic in their view of reality, you reply that, for reasons now sufficiently set forth in our own discussion, what is One can never be independent of the insight that knows it, and that therefore the only place to look for unity is within, at the heart of experience, not without and beyond where the realist looks for Being. If a worldly critic, wondering at your pretensions, asks you how you dare to assert that just you, in your loneliness, can ever win an immediate relation to the final truth of all the universe, can ever find God within your poor self, you reply that just in so far as you have approached the goal most nearly, you, the supposed finite thinker, the private individual, have simply ceased to be known, even to yourself, so that not your private self, but the Absolute, alone, will remain when the goal is reached. For your very discovery of *that which is*, would involve the forgetting of your finite personality as an illusion, an error, an evil dream.

If now a Protagorean sceptic, asserting that *Man is the measure of all things*, hereupon observes that indeed Realism was false, and that nothing *is*, except what is felt, at the

moment when it is felt; and if such a sceptic, also talking of
the real as the present, now insists that, for this very reason,
your own search for the Mystic One is idle, since what empirically is felt, — now here and now there, — is not one, but
many, and since, as such a Protagorean sceptic will assert,
whoever feels anything whatever, has merely his own little
share or case of immediate Being present to himself, — then
even this apparently dangerous foe of the mystical faith
meets with an easy answer, if once you have won the genuinely mystical spirit.   For you in reply ask this critic
whence he gets the assurance of the being of his various men,
of his diverse experiences, of his many human feelings and
points of view.   Has he himself experienced immediately,
or felt at any one moment what the supposed other real
men and women feel?   Has he himself ever felt anything
purely immediate that involved two or more separate
points of view?   Is his direct experience that of many
men?   If he replies that common sense knows the many
men with many minds, the countless feelings and points
of view, to be real facts; then he has forsaken his own
form of scepticism, even by his very appeal to commonly
accepted truth.   He returns to his illusions; you let him
alone.   If he declares that the many points of view are
independently real facts of being, he is a realist, and is
now already refuted.   If he merely says that he is a sceptic because he feels that his feeling, although present, is
not absolute, and that it is to him just now *as if there were*
other points of view than his own, you reply, as a Mystic,
that in thus confessing his scepticism to be identical with
his dissatisfaction regarding his own present state, he confesses also that he is not lost in the presence of a satisfying

immediate fact. But a fact not satisfying, is not a pure fact. For, as you will here maintain, a fact not wholly immediate,—by reason of the very dissatisfaction mingled with it,—sends you elsewhere for a presentation that you do not possess, and thus declares itself not yet the real. In none of these ways, then, will you allow yourself to be distracted from your goal by the objectors.

And finally, if your critic asks, why then, since you believe in no variety of experiences or points of view as genuinely real, you still argue with your critics *as if* they were real, disagree with other points of view *as if* they existed, thoughtfully maintain your own case as if thoughts were valuable aids, and confess your own experiences *as if* you, too, the private finite self, were a fact in a genuine world, then for this objection also you are prepared. For you will now insist that while you know what true Being in general is, you have not yet won the presence of it, so that, like any other imperfect finite thinker, you are struggling with illusions. You yourself, as finite person, your critic as another, your ideas and glimpses as various seeming facts,—these are all alike illusions. You confess this. You lament it. You could be bounded in a nutshell and count yourself king of infinite space, were it not that you have just these bad dreams of ordinary error and finitude. Of the true seer, who should go home to the Immediate Presence, one could say, with Shelley :—

> "Peace, peace, he is not dead, he doth not sleep.
> He hath awakened from the dream of life.
> 'Tis we, who lost in stormy visions keep
> With phantoms an unprofitable strife,
> And in mad trance strike with our spirit's knife
> Invulnerable nothings."

Only, as mystic, you will add that your strife is made as little unprofitable as possible if steadfastly you *so* war with the invulnerable nothings that their inner illusoriness is dwelt upon, their contradictions are exposed, and their voices are thus gradually made to cease, until at last the lonely stillness of the Absolute alone shall be left. It is true that had you reached this perfect peace, we should no longer hear from you. For the mystic abode of Being is the silent land. They come not back who wander thither. For they, as mere finite thinkers, as seekers, are not at all, when once they have awakened to the truth. How should they return? "Believe not those prattlers," says one often-quoted mystical word, "who boast that they know God. Who knows him — is silent."

III

For us, who are here concerned with the mystic's predicate, and not yet with the subject to which it could be applied, the mystic's mere admission that he has not yet reached his goal, need of course so far arouse no objections against this definition. One can define what it is to be without asserting that he has yet faced the object which fulfils the definition. No realist supposes himself to have an exhaustive knowledge of the independent reality, just as no mathematician hopes, in any finite time, to see his science completed. Being is once for all, to a finite thinker, at least in part, the Other that he seeks. The case of the mystic must not stand or fall with his personal perfection, or with his winning of the Other, but with the inner consistency of his definition, and its adequacy to express the constitution of our search for truth.

In a general statement, this definition is now once more before you. Viewed as to its logical relations with its rival, the position of Mysticism should prove, from this starting point, readily comprehensible. You may remember our former sketch of the finite situation that sends us all alike looking for true Being. Data of experience, present facts, are on our hands,—colors, sounds, pains, passions. These are so far relatively immediate; in psychology we call them masses of sensation or of feeling; they are in general not wholly satisfactory, usually perplexing, often very tragic. The mystic would insist that for this very reason they are not wholly immediate. In our more clearly conscious moments they constantly stimulate us to think and to act. On the other hand, we have our ideas. These too are, in one aspect, masses of relatively immediate data; for they are present; the psychologists would find their mere contents, in general, to be of an obviously sensory type; they come and go in their own way. But then, the ideas too are explicitly and obviously facts that are not *merely* immediate. They are contents of thought as well as masses of feeling; and the peculiar way in which they are more than immediate is what makes them worthy to be called ideas. And as contents of thought, as ideas, they already present to us, however incompletely, that relative fulfilment of purpose, that partial embodiment of meaning, which sets them in contrast to those brute facts of the lower forms of immediacy, those meaningless accidents of sensation, which, in our case, always accompany them. The ideas thus constitute the relatively significant aspect, the uncomprehended brute facts present the relatively meaningless aspect, of our ordinary and momentary conscious life. In two ways, however, is the resulting form of finite consciousness unsatisfactory: first, in so far as its finite meanings, even where as nearly present as we ever get them, are viewed by ourselves as incompletely present; and, secondly, in so far as the seemingly accidental sensations of the instant are relatively opposed to even so much of our meaning as is now in sight, so that our sensations tend, as we say, to confuse or to puzzle us. This doubly unsatisfactory form of our finite consciousness is an universal character with us men as we are. Never do all the current sensory experiences completely fuse with our ideas, so as simply to aid in developing the meaning of our inner life. Never do our passing meanings get at any instant presented to us, in their own adequate wholeness, even as so-called "mere" ideas. We mean more than we find. We find also data foreign to those that we mean.

The advantage of this way of stating the universal form of our finite human consciousness lies in the fact that this, our fashion of statement, here presupposes no abstract sundering of the Intellect from the Will, but that it shows the actual unity of theoretical and practical processes, and is as valid for the consciousness of a wanderer struggling to reach a mountain top, or to find his way home, as it is for the conscious life of a mathematician seeking to solve an equation, of a chemist waiting for the results of the experiment which he all

the while controls, of a soldier in battle, of a lover com-
posing his woful sonnet, of a statesman planning his
nation's destiny, of an anchorite in the desert waiting
patiently for God. The endless varieties of the finite
situation depend partly upon the immediate contents
presented; partly upon the particular contrast between
current data and current ideas; partly upon the degree
to which fulfilment, never here consciously attained, is
approximated at any instant; and finally, upon the direction in which the special search is tending. Browning's
lover, in the *Last Ride Together*, when he has his universal vision of finitude, sees, in essence, precisely the
situation that we have been defining, precisely this
aspect of all our present form of conscious life when
he says: —

> " Fail I alone, in words and deeds?
> Why, all men strive, and who succeeds?
> We rode; it seemed my spirit flew,
> Saw other regions, cities new,
> As the world rushed by on either side.
> I thought, — All labor, yet no less
> Bear up beneath their unsuccess.
> Look at the end of work, contrast
> The petty done, the undone vast,
> This present of theirs with the hopeful past;
> I hoped she would love me; here we ride.
>
> " What hand and brain went ever paired?
> What heart alike conceived and dared?
> What act proved all its thought had been?
> What will but felt the fleshly screen?
> We ride, and I see her bosom heave.
> There's many a crown for who can reach,
> Ten lines, a statesman's life in each!
> The flag stuck on a heap of bones,

A soldier's doing ! What atones?
They scratch his name on the Abbey-stones.
My riding is better by their leave."

As statesman, soldier, poet, sculptor, musician thus in
succession pass before the lover's contemplation, he sees
the common problem of their labors, whether their task
be heroic or studious; and he sees this problem as identical with his own. It is the absolutely universal problem of being consciously finite. And the lover states
the case with an almost technical exactness, when he
asks: "What act proved all its thought had been?"
"What will but felt the fleshly screen?"

Thoughts, ideas, inner contents as far as they come
with a presented meaning, are, as you know from modern
psychology, already nascent deeds. To conceive clearly,
is to construct an object that is already, at the instant of
its construction, more or less fully present to your inner
observation as an embodiment of your meaning. But
this embodiment is so far partial. Hence what we call
outer acts, deeds that involve what the outer eyes can
see, and what, as you accomplish such deeds, warms
your muscles with the immediate glow of partially successful effort, — such outer deeds are, for your consciousness, at the instant, only more vivid thoughts,
more brilliantly clear ideal expressions of your longing,
so that in them, as they arise, you find what you also
comprehend, as well as win what you seek. Herein
lies the true unity of our thinking and our willing.
That all our thoughts are not at once thus presented
to our consciousness with the vividness of our external
deeds, this defect is due in part to the triviality of our

present materials for action, which often decline to furnish to us any data whatever that are at once vivid
with the clearness of our sense perceptions, and adequate to our inner aim. But the same frequent divorce
of inner aim and observable outward expression is also
in part due to the confusedness of our inward purposes
themselves, or to the fragmentariness with which we hold
to these purposes, — in brief, to our powerlessness to
retain before us the inner vision itself. And consequently we are accustomed to regard thought which
conceives, and will which executes, as two sundered
functions of our conscious life; because sometimes we
have relatively clear masses of ideas, to which we still
cannot give the vivid clothing of outer sense, and sometimes the defect seems to be that while outer sense is
plastic, ideas are halting, and we know not what to undertake. Yet all such diversity is so far only one of
the aspects. All our thinking is itself a process of willing; all our conscious deeds are merely immediately
visible and tangible ideas. And the truer contrast between the idea and its Other is the one upon which
Browning's lover has fixed his attention. This contrast
is between the inadequacy of all the expressions, whether
inner or outer, which we just now find ourselves able to
give to our finite purposes, — between this inadequacy
of expression, and just these purposes themselves. The
act never proves, for us, all that its thought had been.
And by the "fleshly screen" that hinders the will, our
lover in the poem means the same that we here more
technically mean by whatever proves to be uncontrollable
about the immediacy of our present conscious life.

IV

This universal, this actually commonplace character of our human form of consciousness, first appears, if you will, as just an arbitrary fact of life. But it gives rise, we have said, to the whole problem of Being, as we men face that problem, and to the various definitions of the ontological predicate. What for us is real, is viewed as an Other that, if in its wholeness completely present, would consciously end at least so much of the finite search as could by any possibility be ended. It is true that, in ordinary life, we learn to make a very sharp distinction between the wished for and the real. And this distinction is, indeed, in the world of common sense, a very unconquerable one. It is also true, that realism, in its abstract sundering of facts from desire, would seem often to have abandoned entirely any effort to win for our consciousness any final satisfaction in the presence of reality. But it is also true that such separation of what is real from what is desirable, is a secondary result, in the consciousness of every one of us. Primarily, in seeking Being, we seek what is to end our disquietude. But secondarily we do, indeed, usually learn by experience that, since not all finite desires can be satisfied, more is won, for our finite striving, by making the desire to know what we ordinarily call facts a primal motive in the more rational life of common sense; while our desire merely to gratify this or that momentary impulse becomes a secondary matter, which we learn to oppose to the general desire to know. In time we thus come to hold, in the world of finite common sense, that much is real and inevitable, that thwarts our desires. Yet it still remains true that what we usually call reason, namely, the search for the truth as such, gets placed at the head, in our wiser daily life, and gets even opposed to the search for ordinary satisfaction, just because there is, in the long run, more true satisfaction in being rational, *i.e.*, in our recognition of the facts of common sense, than there is in striving irrationally. And the real, although common sense thus often opposes it to the merely desirable, remains to the end that which, if present, would, as we say, satisfy reason, and thereby give us the greatest fulfilment possible to our type of consciousness.

We need not wonder, then, to find a view like Mysticism breaking altogether with ordinary thought, passing as it were to the limit, cutting the knot of the ultimate problems, casting down the usual distinctions, and insisting that the primal purpose of all our finite striving can be accomplished in presence of a form of Being which is at once the Real and the Good; the final Fact and the absolute Perfection. For the mystic, the common sense antitheses on the one hand, between the immediate and the ideal, and on the other hand, between the real and the desirable, are deliberately and consciously rejected, as something to be overcome. One overcomes them not, indeed, through an indulging of our fickle, momentary impulses, but through a transformation of these impulses. One wins the truth not through a cultivation of what we ordinarily call Reason, but through a quenching of Reason in the very presence of the absolute goal of all finite thought. And, finally, peace is attained not through a lapse into the ordinary, but always imperfect immediacy of the brute data of sense, but through a finding of a final and ideally perfect Immediate Fact.

Historically, as I have said, Mysticism first appears in India. Its early history is recorded in the Upanishads. But this early history contains already essentially the whole story of the Mystic faith. These half philosophical, half dogmatic treatises, compounded in a singular fashion of folk-lore, of legend, of edifying homily, and of reflective speculation, have for a number of years been best known to English readers through Professor Max Müller's Sacred Books of the East. They have lately been made more accessible than before, to the philosophical student, by the translations and comments of Professor Deussen, of Kiel, himself a learned representative of a modern philosophical Mysticism of the Schopenhauerian type. I venture upon no independent opinion as to the composition and chronology of these early Hindoo works. I take as simply as possible what upon their face they seem to contain. I read as well as I can Deussen's systematic interpretation of their general sense; and then, as I try to restate this sense in my own way, I find, amidst all the numerous doctrinal varieties of these various Hindoo Scriptures, this main thought concerning the ultimate definition of Being.

V

What is, is at all events somehow One. This thought came early to the Hindoo religious mind. For the sake of its illustration and defence, the thinkers of the Upanishads seize, at first, upon every legend, upon

every popular interpretation of nature, which may serve
to make the sense of this unity living in the reader's
or hearer's mind. For the writers of the greater Upanishads, this unity of Being is not so much a matter of
argument as it is an object of intuition. You first
look out upon the whole circle of the heavens, and
upon the multitudes of living forms, and you say of
the whole: It is One, because at first you merely feel
this to be true. Especially is the life of the body, or
the life of any animate creature, felt to be one. But
the Hindoo is animistic. His world is all alive. Hence
he easily feels all this life to be one.

But, as we saw at the last time, a metaphysical
realist also can attempt, however inconsistently, to call
all Being One. In this case there would result such
a doctrine as that of the Eleatic school. But to what
obvious objection any Eleatic doctrine is open, we also
saw. For if the Real is the Independent Being, existent wholly apart from your ideas about it, there is no
way of escape from the assertion that our false opinions
are themselves real in the same sense in which the One
is real. The realist is essentially a dualist. The Hindoo was early aware of this danger threatening every
monistic interpretation of the Real. He undertook to
escape the danger by a device which in the Upanishads
appears so constantly, and with such directness of expression, as to constitute a sort of axiom, to which the
thinker constantly appeals. The Hindoo seer of the
period of the Upanishads is keenly and reflectively self-
conscious. His own thinking process is constantly before him. He cannot view any reality as merely

independent of the idea that knows it, because he has a strong sense that he himself is feeling, beholding, thinking, this reality, which he therefore views as an object meant by himself, and so as having no meaning apart from his point of view. The axiom which our European idealists often state in the form: *No object without a subject*, is therefore always, in one shape or another, upon the Hindoo's lips. He states it less technically, but he holds it all the more intuitively. The world is One — why? *Because I feel it as one.* What then is its oneness? *My own oneness?* And who am I? I am Brahman; I myself, in my inmost heart, in my Soul, am the world-principle, the All. In this form the Hindoo's Monism becomes at once a subjective Idealism; and this subjective Idealism often appears almost in the epistemological form in which that doctrine has so often been discussed, of late, amongst ourselves. But the further process of the Hindoo's monistic philosophy leads beyond this mere beginning, and results in an elaborate series of reflections upon the mystery of the Self. The final product of these reflections transforms the merely epistemological Idealism, which, if abstractly stated, has with us often led to a rather trivial scepticism, into something very different from mere scepticism, namely into a doctrine not merely epistemological, but metaphysical. Let us follow a few steps of the process.[1]

"1. Verily the universe is Brahm. Let him whose soul is at peace, worship it, as that which he would fain know.

---

[1] The following passage, from the Chandogya Upanishad, III, 14, has been translated for me by my colleague, Professor C. R. Lanman.

" Of knowledge, verily, is man constituted. As is his knowledge in this world, so, when he hath gone hence, doth he become. After knowledge then let him strive.

" 2. Whose substance is spirit, whose body is life, whose form is light, whose purpose is truth, whose essence is infinity, — the all-working, all-wishing, all-smelling, all-tasting one, that embraceth the universe, that is silent, untroubled, —

" 3. That is my spirit within my heart, smaller than a grain of rice or a barley-corn, or a grain of mustard-seed; smaller than a grain of millet, or even than a husked grain of millet.

" This my spirit within my heart is greater than the earth, greater than the sky, greater than the heavens, greater than all the worlds.

" 4. The all-working, all-wishing, all-smelling, all-tasting one, that embraceth the universe, that is silent, untroubled, — that is my spirit within my heart; that is Brahm. Thereunto, when I go hence, shall I attain. Who knoweth this, he in sooth hath no more doubts.

" Thus spake Shandilya — spake Shandilya."

In such passages, which are very frequent in the Upanishads, an immediate sense of the unity of all things runs parallel with an equally strong sense that this unity is wholly in myself who know the truth, — in my heart, just because what for me is, is precisely what I know.

The famous and often quoted instruction given to the young disciple, called Shvetaketu, by his father Uddalaka, deserves closer analysis in this connection. This instruction begins with a statement of the general monistic

view of Being, uses arguments at first partly identical
with those of the Eleatic school, illustrates unity by
various observations of nature; but then, in the very
midst of what at first seems a merely realistic doctrine,
suddenly, and with a dramatic swiftness of transformation, identifies the world principle with the inmost soul
of the disciple himself, and with him, in so far as he is
the knower of the Unity.

The beginning of the argument, I repeat, appears, from
one side, realistic. The world, says Uddalaka, is, and
is one. The disciple is to note this fact and to bring
it home to himself by frequent empirical illustrations
taken from outer nature. Then he is to observe that
he, too, in so far as he is at all real, is for this very
reason one with the world principle. The teaching
seems at this state still a realism, only now a realism
that has become reflective, recognizing the observer of
the reality as also a real being, and therefore asserting
of him, as knower, whatever one also asserts of the
Being that he knows. But suddenly, even as one speaks,
one becomes aware that, through this very identification
of the essence of the knower and of the object known,
the inmost reality of the world has itself become transformed. It is no longer a world independent of knowledge. One never really has observed it as an external
world at all. It has no independent Being. It is a
world identical with the knower. It is a vision of his
soul. Its life is his life. It is in so far as he creates
it. Whatever he is as knower, that is his world.[1]

---

[1] I quote again from the Chandogya VI, 2–15, and again owe the translation to Professor Lanman.

"Being only, O gentle youth," says Uddalaka to his son, "was this [universe] in the beginning, one only, without a second.

"Now some indeed say, 'Non-being only was this [universe] in the beginning, one only, without a second. From this non-being, Being was born.'

"But how, O gentle youth, might it be so? — thus spake [his father]. How from non-being might Being be born?

"Rather, Being only, O gentle youth, was this [universe] in the beginning, one only, without a second."

And this One Being, so Uddalaka hereupon continues, somehow mysteriously resolved to become many. And immediately there follows in the text at some length, a cosmology, in which the various principles appear in an order obviously determined by tradition. This tradition, however, at first seems upon its face thoroughly realistic. But erelong this mere cosmology gives place to deeper inquiries. It is one thing to teach the tradition about how, in Nature, the Many came from the One. It is another thing to ask how the Many, now that they appear, are related to the One. As Uddalaka dwells upon this mysterious relation, he soon is led to explain that the Many are essentially illusory, and that not the false consciousness which seems to display to us their diversity, but rather even the unconsciousness of deep sleep itself must express the true relation of the false finite to the true absolute.

"As, O gentle youth, the honey-makers, when they make honey, gather the juices of manifold trees, and bring the [resulting] juice to unity [one-ness, *eka-tām*], —

"As those [juices] therein [in that unity] retain no distinction [so that one could say], 'I am the juice of such-and-such a tree' [and another], 'I am the juice of such-and-such a tree,' —

"Just so, O gentle youth, have all these creatures, when [in sleep] they merge in the [one] Being, no consciousness that they are merged in the [one] Being;

"They, whatsoever in the world they be, be it tiger or lion or wolf or boar or worm or moth or gadfly or midge, — that [on emerging] become they once more."

So far you see, the result is still like the Eleatic doctrine. In vain does any mere cosmology endeavor to explain how the Many came out of the One. As a fact, Uddálaka, in his cosmological speculations, has by this time exhausted the motives of the traditional lore. Through the experiences of a long fast, the disciple has been taught to observe how the psychical principle can be made to fade away, like a dying coal, until only a spark remains, and how, when food is again taken, the psychical principle flames once more like the spark that finds fuel. What is thus hinted is that the psychical principle is the one central coal of the world-fire. In a similar spirit the sequence of the physiological process has been discussed; the relations of body and soul to the universal world life have been illustrated, the meaning of growth and decay in nature has been brought into relation to the doctrine of the absolute One; but still the theory has not made clear in what sense the One can have decreed to itself: "I will be Many."

What way remains? Does it not become plain that the many must be indeed altogether illusory? And that is why one has now turned to the figure of the honey and the plant juices, and to the reflection that in sleep all the fierce hostilities of the jungle lapse, and the countless living beings are as one, even while their life-principle survives in all its central might. It is the process of the many that is then the falsity. The One really never resolved to be many at all. How could it thus resolve? In truth, the illusory universe sleeps in one central soul.

An Eleatic doctrine would at this point remain fast bound, dimly suggesting perhaps, as Parmenides did, that Being and Thought are somehow one, but not making anything definite of the suggestion, and meaning it, as no doubt Parmenides also did, in the purely realistic sense, as an assertion that thought knows Being, even while Being is independent of thought. But the Hindoo goes further. He, at just this stage, turns from the world directly to the disciple himself. This mystery, he says, this oneness of all Being, in this you too at all events share. In whatever sense the world is real, you are real. Is the world but One Being, then you, so far as you are real, are identical with that One.

Still the assertion, if understood in a realistic sense, appears only to make the self of the disciple one of the many juices that are really lost in the honey, one of the countless living creatures that roam the jungle in illusory mutual hatred, and that enter again into the truth only when they sleep. And still the mystery of the nature of the One Being has not been lighted up. But Uddalaka means his teaching to be taken, from this point on, in quite another sense. The variety is illusory. But *whose illusion is it?* The One Being exists. But how? As known Being, and also as One with the Knower. The very reflection that knowledge is real, — that reflection which Realism finds it so hard and so fatal to make, is now to furnish the solving word. The reality cannot be independent. Its life is the Knower's life and his alone. Its multiplicity is his illusion, and his only. The disciple has been taught by nature symbols. They were, in a way, to mediate the higher insight. But still their interpretation was itself intuitive and in so far unmediated, just because only unmediated intuition was from the outset really present. There was and is only the Knower. The disciple was the Knower. It was he who blindly resolved, " Let me become many." He shall now, in a final intuition, grasp the immediate fact that he is, and eternally was, but One. The parable of the honey and the juices is at once to be interpreted in this form. Another parable may assist: —

" These rivers, O gentle youth, flow eastward towards the sunrise, and westward towards the sunset. From ocean to ocean they flow, and become (again) mere ocean.

" And as they there know not that they are this or that river, so verily, O gentle youth, all these creatures know not when they issue from the One Being, that they issue from the One.

" What that hidden thing is, of whose essence is all the world, that is the Reality, that is the Soul, *that art thou*, O Shvetaketu." And now the nature allegories recur. But henceforth they have quite a new sense: —

" ' Bring me a fruit from that Nyagrodha tree.' ' Here

it is, venerable Sir.' 'Cut it open.' 'It is cut open, venerable Sir.' 'What seest thou in it?' 'Very small seeds, venerable Sir.' 'Cut open one of them.' 'It is cut open, venerable Sir.' 'What seest thou in it?' 'Nothing, venerable Sir.'

"Then spake he: 'That hidden thing, which thou seest not, O gentle youth, from that hidden thing verily has this mighty Nyagrodha tree grown.'

"Believe, O gentle youth, what that hidden thing is, of whose essence is all the world, — that is the Reality, that is the Soul, *that art thou*, O Shvetaketu.

"About a dying man sit his relatives, and ask: 'Dost thou know me? Dost thou know me?' So long as his speech does not merge in his mind, his mind in his life, his life in that central glimmer, and this in the highest divinity, so long he knows them.

"But when this has taken place, then he knows them no more.

"What this fine thing is, of whose essence is all the world, that is the Reality, that is the Soul, *that art thou*, O Shvetaketu."

VI

Our own difficulties in comprehending such passages as this teaching of Shvetaketu come from a failure to see easily at what point and why the allegorical and essentially exoteric cosmology passes over into that subjective idealism upon which the whole doctrine finally depends. Clearer becomes the nature of this doctrine when we compare such a scripture as the teaching of Shvetaketu with those passages, elsewhere in the

Upanishads, in which the teacher starts with an explicit idealism. In such passages the topic of inquiry is directly the problem: What is the Self? It is here assumed that the Self is the universe. But even here the Self appears in a twofold way. It is first one's life principle, typified by the breath, by the desire, or by the mere physical sense of being, which any one feels within him at any moment. As thus typified the Self or Atman seems finite, changes, grows old, longs, is disappointed, dies, transmigrates, is subject to fate. On the other hand, the Self is the Knower. As such it is the topic of an ingenious reflective process, which these Hindoo thinkers pursue through an endless dialectic, recorded in legendary dialogues and discourses of seers with learners. The purpose of the dialectic is always to make naught of every dualistic account, either of the relation between the Self and the universe, or of the inner structure and meaning of the Self. All the finite process of thinking and of desiring is now to be treated as a process of seeking the Self. Could the true Self be found, it would be found as the fulfilment of desire, as the perfection, as the finality, and as nothing but this. The contrast between the real and the desirable is itself a dualism. It must be cast off, together with the false realism that regards any truth as independently real. The finite world is simply the process of striving after self-knowledge. And in this process the seeker pursues only himself. But if he found himself, if all desires were fulfilled, if knowledge were complete — what would remain? Or rather, since this use of *if* and of *would* is itself a mere expression of finite illusion, since in very truth there is only the Self, since the finite process of striving after the Self is wholly illusory, and the Self in its perfection is alone real, what now remains as the Absolute? Well, in the first place the true Self does not strive. It has no idea of any other. It has no positive will. Object and Subject are in it no longer even different. It has no character. There is the murderer no longer murderer, nor the slave a slave, nor the traitor a traitor. Differences are illusory. The Self *merely* is. But now *is* in what sense? Not as the independent Other, not as the object of a thought, not as describable in terms of an idea, not as expressible in any way, and still less as mere nothing. For it is the All, the only Being. There remains to hint what the being of the Self is only what we now call the immediacy of present experience. Only henceforth we must regard the absolute immediacy not as the raw material of meaning, but as the restful goal of all meaning, — as beyond ideas, even because it is simpler than they are. It is at once nothing independent of knowledge and nothing that admits of diversity within knowledge. The Self is precisely the very Knower, not as a thing that first is real and then knows, but as the very act of seeing, hearing, thinking, in so far as the mediating presence of some Other, of some object that is known, seen, heard, thought, is simply removed, and in so far as the very diversity of the acts of knowing, seeing, hearing, thinking, is also removed.

Most obvious about the Self, from our finite point of view, is its perfection as a fulfilment of our striving. For us to win oneness with the Self means to attain a state of perfect finality, simplicity, peace. Upon this fulfilment of desire the Upanishads constantly insist. We therefore have to express the nature of the Self in terms of feeling, of states of mind. And the Hindoo expressly declines to go outside of the knowing Subject for the definition of the Reality. *That art thou*, is the whole story. But within the mind what comes nearest to simplicity and peace? Plainly, the most satisfying and ineffable experience, just in so far as it involves no diversity, and sends us in no wise abroad either for other experience, or for any ideal characterization of the *what* of this experience itself. The Self then is some final and wholly immediate fact within the very circle of what we now call consciousness, but apart from the restlessness from which consciousness suffers.

VII

But now comes indeed the hardest problem of Mysticism. Absolute Immediacy, perfect peace, fulfilment of meaning by a simple and final presence, — when do we finite beings come nearest to that? On the borderlands of unconsciousness, when we are closest to dreamless slumber. The Absolute, then, although the Knower, must be in truth Unconscious. Into Being all the fierce creatures, all the swarms of the jungle, enter, as we have seen, when they sleep. The dreamless sleeper is, for the Upanishads, the frequent type of the soul gone home to peace. It is so too with the dead, so far as they are really dead, although not so far as they return from death, to the bad dream of finite life, through the wretched fate of transmigration. But if this is so, wherein does the Absolute Being differ from pure Nothing?

The seers of the Upanishads are fully alive to this problem. It is a mistake to imagine that they ignore it. More than once they discuss it with the keenest dialectic. In one legend Indra, the god, learns from Prajapati, the highest god, the lore about the true Self, in the form of a series of parables. He first learns that the Self is not the material self, the mere "Me" (as some of our modern psychologists would call it), but that the Self is rather the Knower. A man dreaming is therefore a better type of the true Self, since the dream is the dreamer's own creation. But even the subjective idealism of the dreamer's world is an insufficient illustration of the truth, since to the dreamer *it still is as if* facts beyond himself were real. But the true Self does not dream. He knows the truth. And that truth is only himself. Of what beyond him should he therefore dream? That is what Aristotle himself says of God. But for the Hindoo this means that the dreamless sleeper must be a still better type of the Self. But, as Indra hereupon objects to this teacher: Has not the dreamless sleeper gone to mere nothingness? Is he real at all?

In a similar fashion, in another legend, the sage Yâjnavalkya teaches his wife Maitreyî, first that nothing in the universe is real or is desirable except the Absolute Self. But then the Self, he goes on to say, is in its immortality unconscious. For all consciousness involves partially dissatisfied ideas of a Beyond, and includes desires that seek another than what is now

wholly present. But in the true Self all is attained,
and therefore all is One; there is no Beyond, there is
no Other. There are then, in the true Self, no ideas,
no desires, just because he is the final attainment of
all that ideas and desires seek.

Yet Maitreyî objects. "The doctrine confuses me,"
she says. How, in fact, should the immortal One be
unconscious? Yâjnavalkya, in reply, can only give, as
reductio ad absurdum of every objection, the argument
that all dualism, involving the reality of objects outside the Knower, is illusory, while all consciousness implies just such dualism.

Absolute Immediacy is to be something better, you
see, than the only partially immediate sensations which,
in our present finite state, merely serve to set us thinking. It is also to be above ideas,—as the peace that
passeth understanding. But all our relative immediacy
actually does set us thinking. All our relative satis-
factions take the form of finite ideas. The Absolute
must then be ineffable, indescribable, *and yet not outside of the circle within which we at present are conscious*. It is no other than we are; consciousness
contains it just in so far as consciousness is a knowing.
Yet, when we speak of the Absolute, all our words
must be: "Neti, Neti," "It is not thus; it is not thus."
So the sage Yâjnavalkya himself, more than once in
these legends, teaches: To us, *it is as if* the Absolute,
in its immediacy, were identical with Nothing. But
once more:—Is the Absolute verily a *mere* nothing?

The Hindoo's answer to this last question is in one
sense precise enough. The Absolute is the very Oppo-

site of a mere Nothing. For it is fulfilment, attainment, peace, the goal of life, the object of desire, the end of knowledge. Why then does it stubbornly appear as indistinguishable from mere nothing? The answer is: *That is a part of our very illusion itself.* The light above the light is, to our deluded vision, darkness. It is our finite realm that is the falsity, the mere nothing. The Absolute is All Truth.

One sees, at last then, this mystic Absolute gets, for the Hindoo, its very perfection from a Contrast-Effect. Here is the really solving word as to the whole matter. It is by contrast with our finite seeking that the goal which quenches desires and ideas at once appears as all truth and all life. But to attribute to the goal a concrete life and a definite ideal content would be, for this view, to ruin this very contrast. For concreteness means variety and finitude, and consequently ignorance and imperfection. The Absolute home appears empty, just because, wherever definite content is to be found, the Hindoo feels not at home, but finite, striving, and deluded into a search for something beyond.

Yet just this very contrast-effect, whereby what is defined as having no definite characters, is even thereby conceived as the most perfect, — we all know this same feature well in our own religious literature. The mediæval poem of Bernard of Cluny concerning the Golden Jerusalem, — the poem called *De Contemptu Mundi*, — what is it, apart from its sensuous, and so far consciously false imagery, but a crowding of antitheses and of negations, to the end that by merely denying our illusions, and forsaking our world, we may contemplate an ineffable glory whose true names are all only negative. Addressing the Eternal, the poet says : —

> " Tu sine littore.
> Tu sine tempore."

Shoreless and timeless is the depth of true Being. Contrasting the present life with the perfect life, one has the wholly negative antithesis : —

> " Hic breve vivitur
> Hic breve plangitur
> Hic breve fletur ;
> Non breve vivere
> Non breve plangere
> Retribuetur."

To be sure, Bernard's hymn is a very treasure-house of brilliant sensuous characterizations of the joys of the home of peace; but just these characterizations, as we but now observed, are metaphorical, and are as such intended to be false. They hint at some final immediacy; and this justifies their use of sensuous language. They mean the ineffable, but their intended truth lies, above all, in the antitheses and in the negations that they merely illustrate : —

> " Nescio, nescio
> Quae jubilatio
> Lux tibi qualis."

The *Nescio, nescio* of Bernard, is identical in meaning with the *Neti, Neti ; it is not so ; it is not so*, of the sage Yâjnavalkya. In the very contrast of the finite with the ineffable this mysticism lives, whether it be Hindoo or Christian Mysticism : —

" Urbs Sion unica
Mansio mystica
Condita Caelo, —
Nunc tibi gaudeo
Nunc mihi lugeo
Tristor, anhelo."

And in view of this fact, that these infinite contrasts are
the only expressible aspect of the whole situation, the
Hindoo metaphor of the dreamless sleeper is, indeed, as
apt to suggest the perfect glory of the home of peace,
as are many of the metaphors of Bernard; as are, for
instance, the joys and delights, the sweet sounds and the
gay colors, with which his vision falsely fills the depths,
where, truly, as the poet himself believes, eye hath not
seen and ear hath not heard.

But if you ask why the Hindoo philosophical mystics
feel so sure that, despite this wholly negative expression
of the nature of their Absolute, they are still teaching a
truth that is not only indubitable, but positively significant and even portentous, then the answer for them
always lies in the *reductio ad absurdum* of opposing
efforts either to win final truth or to satisfy the practical
needs of life. For our conscious finitude, they insist,
means at once dissatisfaction, and the admission that the
truth is not present to us. Common-sense Realism, observing this very fact, makes the truth an independent
Being, that is beyond our striving, in the sense of being
wholly apart from every knowledge which refers to it.
But, in reply, the Hindoo in his own way observes, and
insists upon, that essentially contradictory character of
all ordinary Realism, — that very character which we at
the last time set forth, in our own way, in detail. What

the Hindoo finds, then, positively sure, is that *Nothing can be real that is independent of the Knower.* Here is indeed the centre, the moving principle, of this entire dialectical process which the sages of the Upanishads remorselessly pursue. The only alternative to their own view of Being that is known to them is simply Realism. But simple Realism they see to be self-contradictory, and so absurd. The truth cannot then be independent of the Knower. But if not independent of the Knower, and yet if not given to him by his finite experience and thought, what can the truth be except what one approaches, within one's own very heart, when one gradually casts off finitude, and wins unity and peace.

The process of accomplishing this end proves to consist of a series of stages whose terms lose finite definition and expressible qualities the farther you proceed in the series. The limit of this series of stages of purification and of simplification of life appears to the restless finite creature as zero. But, as the Hindoo now with assurance insists, this zero must be also the Absolute, the One sole Being, and must be so precisely because, even as the limit of the series, it is also the goal of the process, the wished for home of the soul, the expected object of perfect knowledge, — in brief, the Attainment. Now this contrast-effect, and this alone, gives the zero, that is the limit of the finite process, its value, its truth, its absoluteness. And if you waver at the gate of this heaven, half minded to turn back to error and to transmigration, wondering whether there be any true glory within, the Hindoo, reminding you of the hopelessness of every realistic definition of truth, and of the failure

of every finite effort to express the reality, can now only
ask you: For what else but this Absolute within the
gate, within the knowing heart, smaller than the mustard
seed, yet vaster than the heavens,— for what else can
you seek? He simply defies you to find other definition of Being than this. And herewith you have his
whole case presented.

VIII

I have dwelt so long upon the Upanishads, because,
as I have said, they contain already the entire story of
the mystic faith, so far as it had a philosophical basis.
The rest of its story is not any part of philosophy. End
lessly repeated in history, perhaps often independently
rediscovered elsewhere, the dialectic of Mysticism has
nowhere any essentially different tale to tell, nor any
other outcome to record. How in Europe Plotinus combined the mystical theory of the One with realistic, and
in some respects with still deeper and often more constructively idealistic, conceptions of the constitution of
the world from the Nous downward; how the Christian
faith took to its heart the stranger doctrine whose origi
nal home was in India, until the faith of the Middle
Ages became half a Mysticism; how the heretics used
the mysterious light of the same teaching to guide them
into forbidden paths; how the devotional books and the
poets have taught to the laity many of the formulas
that one first finds in the Upanishads — all this I have
already very vaguely sketched in a former lecture. But
to narrate the tale of the mere historical fortunes of
Mysticism would require volumes, but would introduce

no novelties except those involved in the profoundly interesting personal temperaments of individual mystics.

Our concern lies here in observing that the philosophical Mystic, whatever his personal type, and whatever his nation or tongue, always uses the same general metaphysical and dialectical devices. His theoretical weapon is some *reductio ad absurdum* of Realism. His polemic is against the sharp outlines of the world of Independent Beings, against the fallacies of all finite ideas, and against the possibility of worldly satisfaction. With the author of the Imitation of Christ, he reminds you that if you could see all created things together, it would be but a vain show, and hence he bids you forsake every creature. With Spinoza, he tells you that only in the Eternal is there joy alone, and that all else, being but imagination, perishes. With Eckhart he explains that the very creed of the Church, as ordinarily understood, is but allegory, and that even the Trinity is only, as it were, a superficial emanation from the Godhead, while the true Godhead, the Deitas, never "looked upon deed," never dreamed of diversity, but is a "simple stillness" that you can find within your heart whenever you have won the ultimate virtue, and have forsaken all things for the wilderness of Being.

In general, the mystic knows only Internal Meanings, precisely as the realist considers only External Meanings. But the mystic, nevertheless, condemns all finite ideas, just because they have no absolute internal meaning. He bids you look within; but he desires first wholly to transform your inner nature. He compares your heart to the Bethlehem, where God may at any

instant be born.   Nor in all this is the mystic, if he be
a thinker, devoid of reasons.   His thought is eager to
dwell : —

> " On doubts that drive the coward back,
> And keen through wordy snares to track
> Suggestion to her inmost cell."

His doubts are exposures of the fallacies of all ordinary
opinion.   He thinks, to the very end that he may destroy the vanity of mere thinking.   An Eckhart is
amongst the most learned of trained scholastic dis-
putants.   A Spinoza is the most merciless foe of the
illusions of common sense.   With ideas the mystic wars
against all mere ideas.   With the abstract weapons of
Realism he refutes Realism.   At last he believes himself to have won the right, by virtue of the very
breadth of his vision of finitude, to condemn, like
Browning's lover in the *Last Ride Together*, the whole
of finitude.

Nor, after all, is the mystic's result so unlike, in its
logic, the result reached by Browning's lover himself.
I have said, more than once, that the essence of Mysticism lies not in the definition of the subject to
which you attribute Being, but in the predicate Being
itself.   This predicate in case of Mysticism is such that,
as soon as you apply it, the subject indeed loses all
finite outlines, lapses into pure immediacy, quenches
thought, becomes ineffable, satisfies even by turning into
what ordinary Realism would call a mere naught.
Now you may call this subject by any name you please:
The Self of our Hindoo, or the Holy Grail, or Spinoza's

Eternal, or Eckhart's Stille Wüste, or the One of Plotinus, or the " Æonian music " of Tennyson's famous vision in the *In Memoriam*, or the unspeakable happiness which Browning's lover has vainly mourned. In any case, both your process and your result, if you are a Mystic, will be the same. First you look for the object in a realistic world. It is so far an Independent Being. In theory you define it. In life you try to win it. Then you become reflective. You observe that such a Being, just in so far as it is independent, is unknowable, inaccessible, indefinable, in fact, self-contradictory. You observe then that your Realistic definition was false. Moreover, you also see that the whole meaning of the search lies within yourself; that your theory of Being never had any but a practical sense; that the whole question is one of the search for a certain limiting state of your finite variable, for a state called Attainment. And hereupon you are prepared to come on *that which is* and to catch "the deep pulsations of the world." Your ideas, keenly observing all the paradoxes and failures of finitude, finally, through their dialectic, destroy one another and themselves as well. And the goal of the process is at least momentarily reached when you come to the conclusion of Browning's lover. For he, after his vision of the vanity of all finite striving, abandons at last the hope for the so-called lady, the Independent Being who rides so proudly beside him in the illusory world of ordinary life, — abandons that hope, only to take refuge in the ineffable immediacy of an experience that he takes for the instant to be the ultimate reality.

"And yet, she has not spoke so long!
What if heaven be that, fair and strong
At life's best, with our eyes upturned
Whither life's flower is first discerned,
We fixed so, ever should so abide?
What if we still ride on, we two,
With life forever old yet new,
Changed not in kind but in degree,
The instant made eternity,
And heaven just prove that I and she
Ride, ride together, forever ride."

The language is here not that of the mediæval or of the Hindoo mystics. But the ontology is in essence one with theirs.

In fine, mysticism is, as a conception of Being, the logically precise and symmetrical correspondent of realism. In its innermost conceptual constitution it is the mirror picture, so to speak, of its opponent. Each doctrine seeks an Absolute finality, — a limit which is conceived solely by virtue of its contrast with the process whereby our ideas tend towards that limit. Realism seeks this limiting object, this true Being, as somewhat Independent of Ideas. Mysticism, declaring that independent Being is self-contradictory and so impossible, seeks Being within the very life of the knowing process. Each doctrine is a conscious abstraction. Neither can tell what it means by its goal. Each is sure *that* its goal *is*. Practically, the two doctrines are related as are positive and negative quantities in mathematics. "*Submit to the facts*," says Realism. "*They are without. You can do nothing to make them different by merely knowing them.*" "*Know*," says Mysticism. "*The truth is nigh thee, even*

*in thy heart. Purify thyself. In thee is all truth. How
shall it be except as known and as one with the Knower?"*

Yet each doctrine, pursued to the end, culminates in a
passive abandonment of all our actual finite ideas about
Being as vain. Realism is often unwilling to observe
that, if it is true, ideas are also Beings; Mysticism undertakes explicitly to deny that ordinary ideas are at all
real. But both end in a *reductio ad absurdum* of every
definite finite idea of the Real.

In their logical outcome these two theories, polar opposites of each other as they are, must, nevertheless, in
consequence of this parallelism of their structures, precisely agree. Each in the end defines Nothing whatever. Only the realist does not intend this result, while
the mystic often seems to glory in it. He thus glories,
as we have seen, because in fact he is defining a very
fascinating and a highly conscious contrast-effect, — a
contrast-effect that, far from being itself anything absolute, or actually unknown and ineffable, is a constantly
present character of our human type of finite consciousness. As a fact, our thinking is a search for a goal that
is conceived at once as rationally satisfying and as theoretically true. And this goal we conceive as real precisely in so far as we consciously pursue it, and mean
something by the pursuit. But now this goal, since it
is not yet present to us, in our finite form of consciousness, is first conceived by contrast with the process of
the pursuit. So far indeed we conceive it negatively.
In this sense we can say of the goal, *Nescio, Nescio*, or
Neti, Neti, just as Bernard of Cluny, or as the Hindoo
sages, said. But the meaning of these very negatives

lies in the positive contrast-effect that they even now
actually present to us. Finite as we are, lost though we
seem to be in the woods, or in the "wide air's wildernesses," in this world of time and of chance, we have
still, like the strayed animals or like the migrating birds,
our homing instinct. It is this homing instinct that we
for the first merely articulate when we talk of true Being.
Being means something for us, however, because of the
positive presence, in finite consciousness, of this inner
meaning of even our poorest ideas. We seek. That is
a fact. We seek a city still out of sight. In the contrast with this goal, we live. But if this be so, then
already we actually possess something of Being even in
our finite seeking. For the readiness to seek is already
something of an attainment, even if a poor one. But
when the Mystic, defining his goal wholly in negative
terms, lays stress upon the contrast as simply absolute,
he finds that so far his Absolute is defined as nothing
but the absence of finitude, and so as apparently equivalent to nothing at all, since all definite contents are for
us so far finite, and since the absence of finitude is for
us the absence of contents. If hereupon the mystic
skilfully points out that this apparent zero is still, by
virtue of the contrast, defined as our goal, as our coming attainment, as our peace, our hope, our heaven, our
God, — then one rightly replies to the mystic that what
makes his Absolute appear thus glorious is precisely its
presented contrast with our imperfection. But a zero
that is contrasted with nothing at all, has so far not
even any contrasting character, and remains thus a genuine and absolute nothing. Hence, if the Absolute of the

Mystic is really different from nothing, it is so by virtue of the fact that it stands in real contrast with our own real but imperfect Being. We too then are. If our life behind the veil is, as the mystic says, our goal, if already, even as we are, we are one with the Knower, then the absolute meaning does not ignore, but so far recognizes as real, even by virtue of the contrast, our present imperfect meaning.

It follows that if Mysticism is to escape from its own finitude, and really is to mean by its absolute Being anything but a Mere Nothing, its account of Being must be so amended as to involve the assertion that our finite life is not mere illusion, that our ideas are not merely false, and that we are already, even as finite, in touch with Reality.

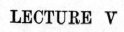
LECTURE V

LECTURE V

MYSTICISM, which our last lecture discussed, has one
great advantage over Realism. The realist, namely, gives
you a conception of Being which pretends to be authoritative; but this authority appears, like the realistic
type of Being itself, something merely external and
therefore opaque. The realist demands, as a matter of
common sense, that you first accept as real his Independent Beings. Hence, if you are to comprehend the
realist's position, you must make your own reflections;
you must do your own critical thinking. Realism is
essentially dogmatic, and gives you no aid in your attempt to sound the inner meaning of the realistic doctrine. But Mysticism, on the contrary, is from the
outset in a way reflective; it is founded upon an explicit appeal to your own experience. It points out to
you first that if any object is real for you, it is you
alone who can find, within yourself, the determining
motive that leads you to call this object real. Hence
Mysticism depends upon making you considerate of these,
your metaphysical motives, aware of your meaning. You
ascribe to this or that object reality. Mysticism is a
practical doctrine. It observes at once that you merely
express your own need as knower when you thus regard
the object as existent. Mysticism asks you hereupon

to define your needs in an absolutely general way. What do you want when you want Being? Mysticism replies to this question, as the sage Yâjnavalkya replies, in the Upanishads, to the questions of his wife Maitreyî: *You want yourself,* — the Self in its completeness, in its fulfilment, in its final expression. In brief, when you talk of reality, you talk of self-possession, of perfection, and of peace. And that is, therefore, all that you mean by the Being of the world or of any type of facts. Being therefore is nothing beyond yourself. You even now hold it within you, in your heart of hearts. Being therefore is just the purely immediate. *To be* means to quench thought in the presence of a final immediacy which completely satisfies all ideas. And by this simple reflection, the mystic undertakes to define the Absolute.

I

The advantage of this mystical method of dealing with the problem of Reality lies in the fact that Mysticism, because it is essentially a self-conscious and reflective doctrine, explicitly states its own defects, and points beyond its own abstractions. Realism actually asserts hopeless contradiction, and then stubbornly declines to take note of the fact that it does so. But philosophical Mysticism always expounds its own paradoxes, and actually glories in them. The process of getting beyond Realism therefore involves a hostile and paradoxical dialectic, whereby one exposes the realistic paradoxes. The realist himself takes as little part in this process as possible, and opposes to his critics merely the authority of sane common sense. Everybody knows, he insists, that the world is independently real. But to ask what independent reality means is, he remarks, mere morbid curiosity. To doubt the independence, would be to doubt the value of sanity. " When Bishop Berkeley said there was no matter, and proved it, 'twas no matter what he said." Such is the spirit of any typically realistic reply to Berkeley. Hence to be realistic is essentially to ignore every fundamental criticism of the ontological predicate. Even Herbart, that most honest and critical of realists, could see no sense in trying to get behind the ultimate fact of what he called the Absolute Position of the real itself. If there is show or seeming, said Herbart, there is what points towards or hints at the real. But the real itself is the finally posited, that hints at nothing beyond itself, and that therefore is independent of the show. That, for such a realism, is the whole story of the ontological predicate, and to inquire further is vain. The rest, even for a man of Herbart's minuteness and caution, consists in inquiring what subjects, what *Wesen*, are worthy to receive this predicate.

The only way to deal with Realism is therefore to insist, with equal obstinacy, that a realist shall explain, not what objects he takes to be real, but what he means by their independence. Such obstinacy is hostile. No realist willingly coöperates in the undertaking. The critical task is accordingly ungracious and abstract. For Realism depends upon not knowing what it does; and to point out to it what it is doing seems to it and to any mere bystander like a carping and unkindly assault.

But the mystic, on the contrary, is in a much larger measure his own critic.   He is essentially dialectical. And his dialectic process is very much that of Elaine in the song of Love and Death that Tennyson puts into her mouth.   Like Elaine, the mystic is reflecting upon the final goal of his life-journey.   That goal for him is the Reality, the Soul, the Self.   It is as such infinitely precious to him.   But what is this absolute goal, just in so far as it is Real at all?   Is it a live Being, or after all is it not rather identical with mere Non-Being, with dreamless sleep, with that "rapture of repose" on the face of the dead that Byron's well-known lines describe. Or, to use Elaine's speech, is it Love or Death that the mystic defines as his Absolute?   Like Elaine, the mystic equally defines both Love and Death, both the Perfect, and the Nothing; or if you like, he leaves both of them, and the whole difference between them, consciously and deliberately undefined, while his entire doctrine consists in saying, exactly as the adorable Elaine says, "I know not which is sweeter, No, not I." That, as we in effect saw at the last time, is the precise technical sense of the

> " Nescio, nescio
> Quae jubilatio,
> Lux tibi qualis."

of Bernard's hymn concerning the *Urbs Sion unica, mansio mystica*.   That is the sense of Yâjnavalkya's *Neti, Neti*.   And Mysticism, curiously enough, has inspired whole nations and generations of mankind by saying essentially nothing whatever but what, in her despair, Tennyson's Elaine so pathetically sings.

Now so easy is it, from a merely external point of view, to see the formal defect of the outcome of this train of thinking, that the great difficulty in expounding the mystic position, is, not to destroy its illusions, but rather first dramatically to create them in the hearer's mind, to the end that he may at least historically appreciate the meaning of the mystical definition of Being. But remember, in any case, that if it is thus easy from without to make naught of the mystic's result, it is also fair to add that this refutation is itself made easy through the mystic's own explicit confession. His doctrine has the honesty of reflective thought about it. He tells you where his own paradoxes are to be found. And the value of dealing with him lies not in refuting him, for in effect he already himself provides the whole refutation; but in comprehending both why he has inspired mankind, and why he creates the illusion that his empty, swept, and garnished dwelling is the very house of God. And yet after our foregoing account, it should not now be hard to see wherein the illusion and the truth of Mysticism are to be found.

The mystic asserts that the real cannot be wholly independent of knowledge. Herein he is right. He asserts that the reality of which you think and speak is first of all a reality meant by you. This is profoundly true. He declares that within yourself lies the sole motive that leads you to distinguish truth from error, reality from unreality, the world from the instant's passing contents. And in all this the mystic, whether Hindoo or Christian, is a representative of the simple facts about Being, — facts which everybody concerned with the subject ought to know merely as a matter of general education.

And the mystic further observes that, despite all this, you have not now won, as finite thinker, the true presence of the very Being which you seek and which you still contain within your very meaning. He points out that, in your present poor form of self-consciousness, just now, you find within you what you do *not* wholly mean, and mean, as if it were beyond you, a truth that, although it is nigh you, even in your heart, you do *not* at present find. He insists that your finite disquietude is due to your restlessness in this essentially intolerable situation. He advises you that, in looking for Being, you are attempting to end this disquietude. Now in all this the mystic is distinctly an empiricist, a reporter of the facts, as you can at any moment see them for yourself if you will. Moreover, he is a decidedly practical thinker.

But as a religious teacher he is inspiring, first of all, just because he appeals to your own individuality. He breathes the common spirit of all the higher religions when he conceives your goal as an inner salvation, and your search for truth as essentially a practical effort to win personal perfection. It is no wonder then that the mystics have been the spiritual counsellors of humanity. Where the realist falsely sunders the *what* and the *that*, the outer world and the individual soul, the theoretical and the practical interests, the mystic sees the unity of life's business, identifies the needful and the true, unites the moral Ought with the theoretical Ideal, teaches that the absolutely Real, by virtue of its very function as the Real, must also be the absolutely Good, gives life a

genuine coherence of meaning, and defines the whole
duty of man as simple fidelity to that meaning. To the
mystics, then, has been historically committed the feed-
ing of the flock of the faithful, the gathering of the
heavenly manna, the saving of humanity from the abyss
into which the mere respectability of dogmatic Realism,
if left to itself, would have infallibly plunged all the
deeper interests of the Spirit.

So much for the obvious positive efficacy of the mystical undertaking. But the undertaking itself takes the
form, as we said, of a search for a certain limiting state
of that finite variable which is called your knowledge,
or your experience, or your insight, and for a definition of what happens when that state is reached. The
mystic also attempts to define how this state is related
to consciousness, and he tries to treat this limiting
state very much as (if he were a mathematician) he might
attempt to define, in a purely quantitative world, the
limit of an infinite series of terms, and to consider how
one series of values can be a function of another. The
mystic ignores the sum of the series. He cares only for
the final term itself, viewed as the limit which the other
terms approach. And he attempts to define this limiting state of the finite variable by a process which is, as
a fact, fallacious. His position is that since, in us mortals, consciousness means ignorance, and since, the less
we observe our ignorance, the nearer we are to unconsciousness, therefore, at the limit, to be possessed of absolute knowledge is to be unconscious.

If you persist in asking how the mystic can thus conceive the zero of consciousness as also the goal of knowl-

edge, then he replies with his endlessly repeated *reductio
ad absurdum*.   If, he says, you stopped anywhere short
of unconsciousness in the series of states of finite consciousness, you would find yourself thinking of something beyond you, desiring another, less troubled, state, —
confessing your imperfection.   You would, therefore, be
confessedly *not* in presence of Being.   If you are to get
into the presence of Being, and know what the Knower
finally knows, you must then finally pass to the limit
itself.[1]   But so to pass is to leave no variety, no external object, no passing moment's ideas, no conscious
content in the field of knowledge.   It is, in short, to
leave nothing present but the Knower alone, and the
Knower as finally immediate datum, too completely immediate to be conscious at all.

If one hereupon replies that this paradox of the mystic, the passing to the limit, and undertaking to define
it in terms of the vanishing series, deprives the Absolute of any value as a Being, by making the whole truth
a mere zero, then the mystic assures you that just *this*
zero has infinite value, because it is the goal of the series
of states of finite consciousness.   Do you not want peace?
he says.   Can anything be of more worth to you than
attainment?   If attainment involves what for finite consciousness means the quenching of desire, of thought, and
of consciousness, does that deprive the search for attainment of meaning?   For now that you are finite, all your
passion is for attainment and for peace.

---

[1] Nevertheless, as one must in any case point out, even this process
might, at the limit, prove discontinuous.   The Knower might possess
some new type of consciousness.   As a fact, he does.

But hereby the final sense of Mysticism, and the final reply to the mystic, once more clearly enough comes to sight. Overlooking the merely formal defect of the argument as to the limiting state of knowledge one can say : It is true, in arithmetic, that zero is a very important member of the number series. But it gets its whole importance by its contrasts and its definite quantitative relations with the other numbers. Just so here, if the Absolute is not only zero, but also real, also the goal, also the valuable, it is so by contrast with the finite search for that goal. But to suppose, as the mystic does, that the finite search has of itself no Being at all, is illusory, is Mâya, is itself nothing, this is also to deprive the Absolute of even its poor value as a contrasting goal. For a nothing that is merely other than another nothing, a goal that is a goal of no real process, a zero that merely differs from another zero, has as little value as it has content, as little Being as it has finitude. What the mystic has positively defined, then, is the law that our consciousness of Being depends upon a contrast whereby we set all our finite experience over against some other that we seek but do not yet possess. As a fact, however, it is not only the goal, but the whole series of stages on the way to this goal that is the Reality. It is the sum, then, or some other function of the terms of the series, that has Being. And, as a fact, Being must be attributed to both the principal members of the relation of contrast, both to the seeking and to the attainment. Else is the attainment the fulfilment of nothing. The finite then also is, even if imperfect. Its imperfection is not the same as any mere failure to be real in any degree. It is real in its own way, if the Absolute is real. And unless the imperfect has Reality, the Absolute has none. We must then abandon the mystic's mere series of gradually vanishing terms for some view that unites these terms into a more connected whole. What is, is not then *merely* immediate, is not merely the limit of the finite series, is not merely the zero of consciousness. The result therefore is that Immediacy is but one aspect of Being. We must afresh begin our effort to define the ontological predicate, by taking account both of finite ideas, and of the sense in which they can be true.

Our result, in case of the mystic, is accordingly very simple. To the realist we formerly said: Your ideas are Independent Beings as surely as their objects are such. Hence your world is rent in twain, and you cannot put it together again. To the mystic we now say: Your Absolute is defined merely as the goal of the finite search. That it is such a goal, this alone, according to your own hypothesis, distinguishes it from mere nothing, for to save the unity of Being, you have deprived it of all other characters than this. Therefore, since your Absolute is only a goal, an attainment, and is naught else, its sole meaning is due to your process of search, in other words to your restless ideas that seek it. Annihilation is something to me only so long as I seek annihilation. Death is a positive ideal only so long as I strive for death. Pure immediacy has a content only so long as it fulfils ideas. In brief, by contrast with and by other relation to finite facts, your zero has its meaning. If, then, your conscious ideas are naught, your Absolute is naught in precisely the same sense, and in precisely the same degree as the ideas and as the finite facts are naught. On the other hand, if your Absolute is real, then, unless it has a distinguishing positive content of its own, unless it is more than mere finality and peace, the finite world of conscious strivings after it, is precisely as real as itself, since your Absolute borrows all its Being from its contrast with those strivings. Precisely, then, as we dealt with the realist by pointing out that his ideas are at least as real as their supposed independent objects, so now we bring the mystic's case to its close, by pointing out that his Absolute, in its abstraction, is precisely as much, and in exactly the same sense of the terms a Nothing, as, by his hypothesis, his own consciousness is.

And herewith we indeed abandon the abstractions of both Realism and Mysticism. What we have learned from those abstractions is that our finite consciousness indeed seeks a meaning that it does not now find presented. We have learned too that this meaning is neither a merely independent Being, nor a merely immediate Datum. What else can it be?

II

Our answer to this question depends upon an effort to amend the extreme statement of Realism. I suppose that no realist, when once confronted with the consequences of the absolute mutual independence of the Real and of the Idea that from without refers to it, will be disposed to admit that he ever really meant such total independence. The Real, he will now admit, is not logically or in its true essence wholly indifferent to whether anybody knows it or not. It is only practically, or relatively, independent. If you still speak of it then as the relatively independent member of the relation, you must indeed, now and henceforth, say that the Real is essentially *such that, under conditions, it would become knowable and known.* This, the essential preparedness of Reality for knowledge, does, therefore, result from the foregoing criticism of Realism. In the light, then, of this consequence, we must proceed. This essential relation of Reality to knowledge already constitutes a part or an aspect of any real Being, even before it becomes known. Even the meteors, wandering there in interplanetary space, unseen, are already such that, if they were to become incandescent by entering our atmosphere, they would become visible to an eye that chanced to look their way. And knowledge comes to pass when things that possess reality apart from knowledge come to influence, as a consequence of the general laws governing interaction, the conscious states of knowing Beings. So at least a Realism, revised in the light of the foregoing, will next be led to maintain.

Such Realism may proceed as follows : " Perception, as a kind of knowledge, results when a real object, in accordance of course with its previous nature, causes impressions in a percipient. But of course no object is wholly indifferent to the effects that it causes. The incandescent meteor changes its physical and chemical properties, even at the moment when it becomes visible. And this change is due to the previous physical and chemical constitution of the meteor, which thereby was always prepared, in one way, to become known to a Being with a power of vision. And this case is a type of the way in which Being and Idea are related. Upon this basis must our metaphysic rest."

I thus merely indicate a general and a well-known popular view as to the *relatively* independent reality of things — a view which usually passes, in the ordinary speech of common sense, for Realism; although, historically speaking, the most thoroughgoing realists have avoided such concessions to popular opinion, just because they really ruin the independence of the Real. Neither the Sânkhya, nor Herbart, regards the independent reality as in truth the genuinely physical cause of knowledge, and, as a fact, one who offers such popular compromises, familiar though they are to us all, must be prepared to go much further, on the way towards Idealism, than he at first imagines. Such a compromise is, in fact, an entire surrender of the realistic thesis.

I will not pause to develope, at any length, the various well-known theories that have been held by modified Realism as to the causation of perception, or as to the evolution of knowledge and of knowing beings, or as to the rest of the natural history, both of ideas and of relations of ideas and "real external things." We are all familiar with such views. They have their important place in psychology and in cosmology. But they are here, in their details, simply not relevant. Our only interest, at present, in such theories, is an interest in seeing what manner of Reality can be ascribed to objects which you call real "apart from" or "externally to" or "in relative independence of" the experience of any particular observer, but which you, meanwhile, regard as, by nature, "sources" or "causes" or "possible causes" of knowledge. When you say, with such a consciously modified Realism, "The Real is not ever wholly independent of whether it is known or not; it is only relatively independent; and it is, in nature, such as to be knowable, or such as, under conditions, to become a cause or source of knowledge," — when you modify Realism in this way, what is the true consequence for your fundamental Theory of Being?

The consequence, I insist, is deeper than you might at first suppose. For it is natural to imagine that you can still keep the convenient part of Realism, — the practically unapproachable indifference, dignity, and compelling authority, of the Independent Beings, while sacrificing so much of the abstractions of pure Realism as it proves to be logically inconvenient to retain. "The world," you perhaps now say, "is there, of course, whether or no this or that man knows it. And a man has practically to submit his knowledge to the Real, just *as if it were* wholly independent of him in every way. Of course no independence is ever really absolute. That has to be admitted. All things are always interrelated. But, practically speaking, the meteors are what they are, whether or no we men see them. And Neptune, when discovered, was not created by the astronomer's computations nor by his telescope nor by his brain. Now this practical independence of any particular knowledge is what we mean by the Being of things. Before, after, and apart from

THE OUTCOME OF MYSTICISM

anybody's knowledge, things remain, *on the whole*, whatever they are. To be and to be known, to be knowable and to be actual, — these are of course ultimately related characters in any being. Yet they are characters that, *on the whole, fall apart*, in the nature of things as they are. Knowledge is, therefore, relatively speaking, an accident in the world. And its business is to conform to the facts, not to create them. Upon so much wo still insist, despite the fate of an extreme and abstract, and of course in so far absurd, Realism."

Yet one must now, in reply, insist upon yet a fresh criticism of the bases even of this modified Realism. And the criticism first takes a very simple form. It asks: Can we, then, divide the Being of things into two parts, as the primary and the secondary qualities of matter have been divided? Can we, then, say of one of these parts of Reality, " *That* is wholly independent of knowledge ; *that* is entirely indifferent to whether anybody knows it or not?" And can we, then, say of the rest of the Being of things (namely, let us suppose, of the secondary qualities of matter), " *That* part is *not* indifferent to knowledge, but alters according to the nature of the particular being who happens to know it?"

The question is momentous for the fate of any modified Realism. It is usually supposed that such a division is easily possible, even if not verifiable in detail. What the meteor is, in so far as it either now flashes or is at least capable of visible incandescence, — that, one may suppose, is an aspect or part of the reality of the meteor which indeed would exist apart from this or that knowledge, but which cannot be expressed ex-

cept by taking account of the actual or possible relation to knowledge. But that the meteor is external
matter, and has mass, extension, or other primary qualities, — this aspect of the meteor would remain real if
there never were any knowledge in the world; and this
aspect is not altered in its character by taking account
of our ideas about it. Some such division of the real
into two parts, one closely and explicitly related to
knowledge, and one independent of knowledge, is very
commonly attempted. One supposes that one is able
to say what the world would still be if knowledge vanished. The rest of the world, the phenomenal aspect
of things, the part of Being that has explicit relation
to knowledge, one supposes to be also capable of definition more or less by itself. Thus Being has two
parts, an independent part, and a dependent part.

But our former analysis of pure Realism, by virtue
of the very abstractness and one-sidedness that made
it at the time so austere, gives us, as it were, a
"razor" wherewith to cut away just the "independent" part of this now divided realistic universe. If
the Real were wholly independent of knowledge, it
would be self-contradictory. Well, just so, if *any part*
of the Reality, if any division of it, if any group of
substances or characters in it, were real in entire independence of knowledge, or were the same whether
known by anybody or not, all of our former analysis
would apply to just that portion of the real universe.
Thus it would be vain to say that the Real is independent of knowledge when or in so far as it causes
no knowledge of itself to exist, or is not a possible

cause of knowledge; and that only when it is an actual or possible cause of knowledge it is in essential relation to the latter. Any such view would be destroyed by our former attack upon the Independent Beings. If no Reality can have entirely independent Being, no part of reality can win such Being. And this consideration ends at once every effort to divide off one section of Being as the independent part.

When we say, then, that the real is in any sense practically or partially independent of knowledge, we do not mean that it has two parts, one in essence independent of whether it is known or not, the other essentially linked to ideas. No, the Real must be through and through, to its very last quality, to its very inmost core, *such as to be fitted to be known*. Its nature is through and through thus tainted, if you please so to say, by adaptation to ideal purposes.

If, then, Being is to keep its practical independence of any particular knowledge, our modified Realism must indeed be not only modified, but transformed. Yet how?

In answer, one has merely to state afresh and more carefully the situation now reached. The Real, for our modified Realism, is to be somehow "outside of any particular knowledge." It is to be "authoritative" over against our "mere ideas." They must "conform" to it. On the other hand, it is such that, under conditions, they may "correspond" to it. If they do so "correspond," they will be true. Independently of this essential relation to knowledge, Being is indefinable. It is there as *that which, if known, is found giving to ideas their validity*, as *that to which ideas ought to correspond*, and as that whose essential relation to ideas is that it is their *model*, and is adapted to their nature as such model. Now independently, I repeat, of this relation, the Real is for us henceforth simply indefinable. Nor can any part, or aspect, or quality of it be defined in logical independence of this relation.

But this new type of Being really involves a new fundamental conception of what it is to be real. To be real now means, primarily, *to be valid, to be true, to be in essence the standard for ideas.* Our transformed theory is now that our ideas have a standard external to themselves, to which they must correspond. If we retain Being in this sense, we still view it as Other than ideas that relate to it, and as outside of our present knowledge. But we do not, in this case, view the real as conceivable, either in whole or in part, in an entire abstraction from knowledge. It may be somehow real *when* knowledge is not. That we shall have to see. But in essence it is always related to the purpose of knowledge, and is altered when these relations alter.

And now let us proceed to define more specifically this new conception of Being. Let us take it first in one of its most recent forms.

III

Is it not indeed plain that, as we ourselves have often heretofore said, when we talk of Being, we are indeed seeking for what, if present, would satisfy or tend to satisfy our conscious needs and meanings? Let us take this very character as the sole basis of our definition of what it is to be. Let us first say that whenever we talk

of Being we mean a definitely Possible Fact of experience, viewed just as something possible for us. Or, again,
let us say that by Being in general we mean precisely
what Kant called *Mögliche Erfahrung*. For is it not also
plain that we are trying to find out, in all our search
for Being, precisely what experience we may hope to
get under given conditions, and what experience we
may not expect to get? Can we not then reduce to
just these terms the whole inquiry after Being in the
province of common sense, in the world of science, and
even in the more mysterious realms of religion? If,
hearing strange sounds in the street, I look out of the
window, am I not trying to define or to confirm some idea
of a possible experience? If an astronomer searches a
star-cluster for variables, or a stellar spectrum for familiar
lines, is he not verifying assertions as to possible contents of experience? If the devout man prays, and
expects an answer, or hopes for immortality, is he not
looking for possible empirical data? What is, is then
for me what, under certain definable conditions, I should
experience. To be is precisely to fulfil or to give warrant to ideas by making possible the experience that
the ideas define.

Well, let us next generalize this notion a little, let us
state it more impersonally, and then let us see what we
get. I have ideas; present experience does not present
to me all that they mean. I look to see how they are
related to Being. What then, apart from my private
and momentary point of view, is Being in general? Is
it not what renders my ideas *Valid or Invalid?* When
I say, *There is a real world*, what do I mean except that

some of my ideas are already, and apart from my private experience, valid, true, well-grounded? When the mystic himself defined his Absolute, what was he defining but the supposed possible goal of a process of finite purification of ideas and of experiences? When the realist spoke of the Independent Beings, what did he himself mean except that certain of our ideas are true or false despite our own desires, or even quite against our wishes? And to set aside as we have done either Mysticism or Realism, what was it but to point out that certain ideal definitions, being contradictory, are necessarily invalid? What is Being then but the Validity of Ideas?

Is not here, then, the true definition of Being? As you may remember, this was, in fact, the third on our list of the historical conceptions of Being. And to consider in detail this Third Conception, which identifies Reality with Validity, the Being of the world with the truth of certain ideas, is our next task.

This new conception of Being, as we shall at once be able to see, is one that, just at the present time, is of exceeding importance in connection with the contemporary discussion of all ultimate problems.

IV

True metaphysical Realism, in all its abstractness, still survives amongst us, and will no doubt, as an opinion, last as long as our race. For man might be defined as an animal who ought to reflect, but who very generally cannot. But you all know a class of persons whom I may as well call, at once, the Critical Rationalists of our own time. These thinkers are not mere empiricists. They are students of science, sometimes too of ethics, and frequently also of religion. They are doubtful, not infrequently quite negative, in their attitude towards Realism. They condemn the notion of things in themselves, and insist either that man's limited insight can never reach the truth about any realistically conceived independent world, or else that there is no such world at all. On the other hand, they are hostile to constructive Idealism, regard the whole recent constructively idealistic movement as a mere dream, and often repeat that, in our philosophy, we must be guided solely by the spirit of Modern Science. In theology they condemn theoretical construction, and if they are positively disposed, prefer a reasonable and chastened moral faith. But the one thing to which they remain steadfastly loyal, is the Validity of some region of decidedly impersonal Truth. As such a realm of impersonal truth they conceive perhaps the moral law, perhaps the realm of natural law revealed to us by science, perhaps the lawful structure of that social order which is now so favorite a topic of study. Their spiritual father is Kant, although they often ignore their parentage. Their philosophical creations are a collection of impersonal principles in whose independent or realistic Being no one altogether believes, but whose value as giving reasonable unity to the realm of phenomena, justifies, to the present age, their validity. These principles are such as Energy; or in the modern sense of the term, Evolution, viewed as the name for a universal tendency in nature; or the Unconscious, taken as a principle for explaining

mental life; or yet other of the frequently great creations of Nineteenth Century thought. These are names
for abstractions, but for abstractions based in some cases
upon a vast experience, and in these cases justified precisely as empirically valid conceptions. The world of
these principles is neither independently real nor yet
illusory, nor yet precisely a spiritual reality. It is said
to be true for us men. In that world the older faiths
may indeed seem endangered. God is, from such a point
of view, no longer a person, not yet is he the mystical
Absolute. The impersonal conception of a Righteous
Order of the universe remains. Theology, one holds,
must reconstruct its notions accordingly. What remain
to us to-day are Virtual Entities, so to speak, — Laws
and Orders of truth, — objects that are to us *as if they
were* finally real. This *as if*, or *as it were*, becomes to
some thinkers, a sort of ultimate category. One no
longer proves that God exists, but only that, *It is as if
he were.* God too, like a logarithm, or like a treaty
of peace between two nations, is to be, to such minds,
a virtual entity or else nothing.

Thinkers of this general type, I say, you all know.
Their spirit, as you read modern books, you have constantly before you. Their characteristic metaphysical
conceptions are founded upon this, our third view of
the ontological predicate. In future this Third Conception may therefore come to be remembered as the typical
ontological idea current in the Nineteenth Century, — in
this age of critical rationalism, and of a cool respect for
truths which do everything but take on the form of
individual life.

A close study of this notion of what it is to be real seems therefore justified by our situation. And so next, during the remainder of the present lecture, I shall illustrate by various cases how objects recognized in one way or another by our thought may suggest this form of the ontological predicate. Then, at the next lecture, I shall follow very briefly some of the earlier stages of the differentiation of this view from Realism in technical philosophy, shall deal very summarily with the history of the conception since Kant (because only since Kant it has come to be fully differentiated from Realism), and finally, I shall show how this conception leads us inevitably beyond itself to a fourth and final view of Being.

V

As one of the purely popular meanings of the ontological predicate we found, in our second lecture, the notion that to be real is to give warrant to ideas, to be genuine. By contrast we found popular speech calling an object whose unreality has been detected, an *appearance*, a *myth*, or even a *lie*. The unreal object thus often gets, by a certain transfer, names which first seem naturally to belong rather to the false opinion, to the idea itself, that has misled the too credulous mind. On the other hand, the real *can be depended upon*. It does not deceive. In a word, it is *true*, and its Being is, somehow or other, more or less the same as its truth.

Such usage is so far only popular. It implies no conscious final definition of Being. But this popular speech has undoubtedly been influenced by a philosophical tradition that dates, in our European thought, back to Plato, and that has been influenced both by theology and by mathematical science. The scholastic theory of Being gave expression to all of these influences together, when, developing a discussion of Aristotle's Metaphysics, it expounded the well-known thesis: *Omne Ens est Verum*, or in another form: "*Ens* and *Verum* are convertible terms."

It is, however, still the case that one who asserts this thesis, or its various popular equivalents, so far does not commit himself to any particular one of our four technical conceptions of what real Being itself fundamentally means. For the scholastics the epithet *verum* was only one of the so-called transcendental predicates of Being, which mentioned an universal character, rather than a defining mark, of Reality. We are now, however, to sketch a theory for which the truth belonging to any real object is to be viewed as the *one essential mark* in terms of which Reality may be defined. And this truth itself is defined in the main as something, external to a mere idea, to which that idea ought to correspond.

We are to begin, before following this theory into its technical philosophical forms, by naming some examples of objects which we ordinarily seem to call real mainly because we first call them true. As a fact, you cannot converse for a quarter of an hour upon topics of common human interest, without speaking of many things that all the company present will tacitly view as in some objective sense real objects, as not "mere ideas" of anybody, as in other words facts, while at the same time, if you look closer, you will find that these ob-

jects are not viewed by anybody present as real in the
same sense in which physical bodies, or the atoms of
Democritus, or the Monads of Leibniz, or Mr. Spencer's Unknowable, have usually been regarded as real
by the realistic metaphysicians who have believed in the
latter entities. Those other objects of common human
interest are viewed, by common sense, namely, not as
Independent Beings, which would retain their reality
unaltered even if nobody ever were able to think of
them, but rather as objects such that, while people can,
and often do think of them, their own sole Being consists in their character as rendering such thoughts about
themselves objectively valid for everybody concerned.
Their whole *esse* then consists in their value as giving
warrant and validity to the thoughts that refer to
them. They are external to any particular ideas, yet
they cannot be defined independently of all ideas.

Do you ask me to name such objects of ordinary
conversation? I answer at once by asking whether
the credit of a commercial house, the debts that a
man owes, the present price of a given stock in the
stock market, yes, the market price current of any
given commodity; or, again, whether the rank of a
given official, the social status of any member of the
community, the marks received by a student at any
examination; or, to pass to another field, whether this
or that commercial partnership, or international treaty,
or still once more, whether the British Constitution, —
whether, I say, any or all of the objects thus named,
will not be regarded, in ordinary conversation, as in
some sense real beings, facts possessed of a genuinely

ontological character? One surely says: The debt exists; the credit is a fact; the constitution has objective Being. Yet none of these facts, prices, credits, debts, ranks, standings, marks, partnerships, Constitutions, are viewed as real independently of any and of all possible ideas that shall refer to them. The objects now under our notice have, moreover, like physical things, very various grades of supposed endurance and of recognized significance. Some vanish hourly. Others may outlast centuries. The prices vary from day to day; the credits may not survive the next panic; the Constitution may very slowly evolve for ages. None of these objects, moreover, can be called mere ideas inside of any man's head. None of them are arbitrary creations of definition. The individual may find them as stubborn facts as are material objects. The prices in the stock market may behave like irresistible physical forces. And yet none of these objects would continue to exist, as they are now supposed to exist, unless somebody frequently thought of them, recognized them, and agreed with his fellows about them. Their fashion of supposed Being is thus ordinarily conceived as at once ideal and extra-ideal. They are not "things in themselves," and they are not mere facts of private consciousness. You have to count upon them as objective. But if ideas vanished from the world, they would vanish also. They then are the objects of the relatively external meanings of ideas. Yet they are not wholly separable from internal meanings.

Well, all of these facts are examples of beings of which it seems easiest to say that they are real mainly in so far as they serve to give truth or validity to a certain group of assertions about each one of them.

I next turn to another region of examples. I have already more than once referred to the sort of Being that, in many minds, attaches to the moral law. What kind of Reality then, in the universe, has justice, or charity, or in general the good? Here indeed we are once more upon ground that the Platonic dialogues have rendered very familiar, — a ground too that the controversies of later forms of Realism and Idealism have caused to appear, to many minds, too much trampled over to be any longer fruitful. I venture only at the moment to insist that in this case familiarity has simply not meant clearness, and that it is far easier to talk of certain questions as hopelessly antiquated, than to give them any precise answer.

Of course it is possible to undertake to regard the moral law, or such objects as justice, in the same light in which we have just been viewing the facts that result from social law and from convention. Every student of Ethics knows, however, the arguments in favor of giving the ethical truths a more permanent type of validity than we assign to prices and to social conventions. In any case, however, the mention of this familiar Platonic group of instances carries us at once over to a form of reality whose formally eternal validity is, to the once awakened metaphysical sense, something both marvellous and unquestionable.

VI

In what way, then, in the next place, is the value
of π, that is, the ratio of diameter and circumference
in the circle, a real fact in the universe? Physically,
one can never verify the existence of any perfect circle in the natural world; empirically, one can never,
by actual measurement, discover in experience the presence of two lengths thus related. But, geometrically and
analytically, one can prove what is often called the
"Existence," as well as certain of what are often called
the real properties of the ratio or quantity π. The
late Professor Cayley, in a noted passage of his Presi-
dential address before the British Association, asserted,
as you may remember, that the mathematical objects,
such as the true circles, are, if anything, more real
than the physical imitations of circles that we can
make, since, as he said, it is only by comparison with
the true circle that the imperfections of the physical
imitation of a circle can be defined. The Platonic
spirit of this assertion is easily recognizable, and at
all events it reminds us that a distinctly modern and
scientific experience can lead a man to assert, without
(as I suppose) any professionally metaphysical bias,
that the most real objects are the ones of which it is
hard to affirm any character except that they have an
Eternal Truth. This case of the geometrical figures
is of old a favorite one in philosophy. In recalling it
here, I may also properly point out that the very latest
discussions about what has been called the reality of
Euclidean and non-Euclidean spaces, have given a wholly

new life to this old story; and the realm of that which
undertakes to be real only in so far as it is true, is a
realm of very distinctly present interest for the philosophy of recent natural science.

As for the purely mathematical instances, in general,
however, they are not at all limited to the geometrical
ones. Modern Analysis, and the Theory of Functions,
contain very many propositions of the class that are
sometimes called "Existence-Theorems." That there
exists a root for any algebraic equation of the nth
degree; that there exists a differential coefficient for
a given function; that, on the other hand, there exist
functions continuous throughout given intervals which
still have within those intervals no differential coefficients; that the limits of this or that variable quantity
(for instance, of convergent infinite series), exist: —
such are examples that may be more or less familiar
even to students who have, like myself, to confine
themselves to decidedly elementary mathematics. Avoid-
ing, however, the mathematical form of expression, one
may here try to make clear the metaphysically important nature of theorems of this sort very much as follows:
In pure mathematics, the student deals with certain objects that, upon their face, are the products of purely
arbitrary definitions. The mathematician builds up these
his objects, as, for instance, the objects of pure Analysis,
very much as he pleases. His ideas are in so far his
facts. So far one would suppose, then, that no questions about existence would trouble the mathematician.
But when one looks closer, one sees that when the
mathematician has once built up such a notion of some

realm of ideal objects, there may then arise the further question whether, *within that realm*, an object that meets certain new requirements, the special requirements, let us say, of a given problem, can be found or not. And this question is one whose answer, for the mathematician, is indeed hereupon not at all a matter of his arbitrary choice. He has, to be sure, created his world of mathematical objects. This world is there, as it were, by his decree, or is real, as ordinary realists would say, only in his head. It is so far like a child's fairyland. But once created, this world, in its own eternal and dignified way, is as stubborn as the rebellious spirits that a magician might have called out of the deep.

Even the poets have told us how their heroes, once created, have often become, as it were, alive after their own fashion, so that the poet could no longer voluntarily control how they should behave. Much more, and for a far more exact reason, are the mathematician's objects, when once created, independent of his private will. Thus then there may indeed arise the question whether, as one may now express the matter, there exists any object, within a given mathematical realm, possessed of certain properties. The *what* of this now sought object is defined, in advance, in terms of these mentioned properties, — properties which, as just said, usually result from the conditions of a special problem. The *that* of the object, its presence as a member of the ideal realm which the mathematician has before defined, is a problem such as may cause almost endless trouble before it is solved. The processes involved in such ontological or existential solutions are, however, very instructive as to the nature of the ideal world; and every student of metaphysics ought to have at least an elementary acquaintance with a few concrete instances of just such investigations in mathematics.

If one hears children disputing over a fairyland of their own invention, and if the question arises whether or no there exists in that fairyland a particular being, say a fairy with six wings, a listener to the dispute easily grows impatient. "Why talk of reality or of unreality?" he says. "The six-winged fairy exists in your fairyland if you make him, and this is true because you are not talking of any real being at all, but only of make believe." Yet in the mathematical realm it is not altogether so. Within limits, you create as you will, but the limits once found, are absolute. Unsubstantial, in one way, as fairyland, the creations of the pure mathematician's ideality still may require of their maker as rigid, and often as baffling a search for a given kind or case of mathematical existence, as if he were an astronomer testing the existence of the fifth satellite of Jupiter, or of the variables of a telescopic star-cluster.

An equation of the nth degree, for instance, is such an ideal mathematical creation. I remember a teacher of mathematics in a far western American town, who used to scoff at the troubles of his historically more famous colleagues regarding the noted theorem as to the existence of a root of such an equation. The equation, as my friend in substance said, was a mathematician's arbitrary creation. There was no use in calling it an equation unless it had a root. And since the mathematician made the equation, and called it such, it had a root if the mathematician said that it had. To discuss the question was thus as useless as to discuss the existence of the six-winged fairy in the fairyland of your own creation. My friend would only admit the significance of inquiring what the value of any of the n roots actually in question might be.

And, as a fact, of course, my friend's argument, despite its quarrel with the labors of Gauss and the other algebraists, had its own relative force. A theory of algebraic quantities is conceivable which should arbitrarily begin one of its sections by defining certain symbols as the roots of algebraic equations, and which should then proceed to demonstrate the properties of these symbols, as well as of the equations in terms of the symbols. Such a method of procedure has indeed been proposed as a formal device in the course of the more recent history of the theory of equations. But as an historical fact, the mathematicians, in the first place, actually proceeded otherwise, defined, apart from the general theory of equations, their realm of algebraic quantities, both of those called "real" and of those called "complex," defined also their general equations, and then, indeed, had upon their hands the problem of proving that within that realm of the algebraic quantities, as thus previously defined, there could be found such as would furnish their general equation with roots. Hereupon, indeed, the resulting problem was one whose solution was no longer, like the creation of the six-winged fairy, a matter of arbitrary choice. The ingenuity of a Gauss was taxed to furnish some of the known solutions. The problem has proved fundamental for algebraic theory. And so my Western friend was wrong.

Of course this is but a single instance. Very many other mathematical cases can be found where problems as to real Being, of the type here at issue, have been the topic not only of inquiry, but of serious and sometimes pretty persistent error on the part of even noted mathematicians themselves. Such was the fortune of the older Theory of Functions with regard to the existence of the differential coefficients of continuous functions. This case cannot be fully explained in non-mathematical language. It is enough here to say that the mathematical world contains countless ideal entities of the type called Functions, and these are beings which have values corresponding to the values of certain quantities called "independent variables." The values of the "functions" therefore, in general, vary when the "independent variables" vary. If the functions vary continuously, whenever the variables vary continuously, the variation of the functions may correspond to such a physical process as a movement, or to such a process as the description of a curve, on a surface, by a continuous motion. Now such an ideally definable process generally has properties corresponding to the rate of the physical motion, or to the instantaneous direction of movement of a point on the curve. And these properties of the functions in question may be investigated by constructing certain other ideal entities, related to the original functions, and derived by a well-known process from them. The new ideal entities are called Derived Functions, or Differential Coefficients, and for a long time it was assumed as almost an axiom that every function continuous within given intervals *must* have, within those intervals, a derived function, or differential coefficient. This seemed as axiomatic as the assertion that every movement must take place at a given, even if constantly altering speed, or that a point moving on a curve must at every instant be moving in a given instantaneous direction. For the derived function, or differential coefficient, was an ideal entity corresponding to such facts as momentary velocity, or instantaneous direction of movement. This assumption, namely the existence of objects called the differential coefficients in question, persisted in the text-books until instances, first few, and then many, were produced, where beings of the type in question, namely continuous functions, were discovered, which had *no* differential coefficients whatever. How this was possible, I cannot pause to define, but I mention this now noted example of a pretty persistent mathematical error, because it exemplifies how, in the world of pure mathematical creations, you can have problems about existence which for a while seem as baffling as similar problems in physics and in natural history. Even mathematical science, then, has had, within the eternal shadowland of its creations, to deal, as it has grown, with sharp contrasts between myth and fact, between false report and real existence,—with contrasts, I once more insist, as striking as those known in the realm of astronomy or of history. The difference between the one science and the others lies in the fact that the mathematician, because of his far more controllable subject-matter, is generally surer of finding his way erelong past these contrasts to the truth that he seeks, while in the physical sciences the ontological errors may persist longer.

As to the method of work used by mathematicians in such cases, where the existence of an object is in question, I again speak quite as a layman in this field; but, so far as I have observed, the mathematicians, in proving the sort of existence of which they speak, proceed very much like students of other types of real Being. To prove the existence of an object whose *what* is already stated, but whose *that* is in question, the mathematician may simply produce, as it were, before your eyes, an object of the desired type, and may then let you observe that it meets the requirement. In such cases he works somewhat as a naturalist might do. He shows you the object and says: "See, it exists." Or again, he may be unable to do this; but instead he may try a sort of experiment with his already accessible ideal objects, and the result of this experiment may give you an indirect but infallible sign that a being of the precise sort here in question must exist, even if it cannot be directly produced. This more indirect method of showing that a being of a given type exists, may roughly be compared to the devices by which the spectroscope reveals the existence of an element in a star, by showing the characteristic lines of the element.

In brief, then, in talking of this his shadowland of ideal beings, the pure mathematician illustrates, in ways often very remarkable, how manifold may be the meanings that can attach to the word *fact*, and how ill those appreciate truth who suppose an object disposed of by relegating it to the world of "pure ideas." An important elementary lesson in metaphysics comes when we liberalize somewhat our notions of what it is to be, not only by examining the various senses in which the word has been used, but by following these senses into the various sorts of examples which make their variety first really appreciated.

Nor are the foregoing the only marks of an ontological, or, so to speak, substantial character about the world of mathematical fact. A very extended, but recently very rapidly growing, series of developments in this mathematical realm tends constantly afresh to show the marvellous character of the world of validity by revealing unexpected unities and connections amongst those of its facts and laws which have been the result of seemingly quite independent definition, and which have been reached in the course of researches that originally had no connection whatever.

VII

By this long series of instances of our third type of real beings, I have meant to show that there are reasons why a philosophical conception, specially planned to meet such cases, should be attempted as a conception of the meaning of the ontological predicate. The obvious contrast between beings of this type and the beings of technical realism proper, in our former sense of that word, is that the entities of the metaphysical realist are supposed to be what they are quite independently of any knowledge, actual, or even possible, which may be supposed, from without, to refer to them, so that if such knowledge vanished from the universe, or if no external knowledge of them had ever come to be, the real beings would remain just what they are. On the other hand, however, the realities of the present type exist explicitly as Objects of Possible Knowledge. Their whole defined Being is exhausted by their validity when regarded from the point of view of such possible knowledge. If nobody had ever recognized the British Constitution, or the prices, credits, debts, marks, and ranks aforesaid, these objects could not be said to be able to retain any being, although now that they are recognized, such objects appear to have a genuine being, and to be relatively independent of this or that individual judgment.

The case of the eternal truths, such as the ethical, or still more obviously the mathematical truths, is more like the case of the atoms or monads of a thoroughgoing realism, since the eternal verities are said to have been valid before any human mathematician or moralist conceived them, and to remain true even if men forget them, or, as in case of the value of π, are physically unable to verify them in concrete circles. Yet, on the other hand, their case has its own peculiar puzzle, in that, when the mathematician himself first conceives of his equations and of his functions, he seems, as we have said, to be engaged in an act of perfectly free construction, as if he were building in fairyland. Yet the familiar miracle of this mathematical realm is that, after one has built, he discovers that the form of his edifice is somehow eternal, and that there are existences which this form has preëstablished, so that he himself looks with wonder to find whether this or that object exists in his new world at all. And meanwhile, despite this eternity and this relative independence of private ideas which characterize the mathematical objects, and give the world of Forms unity, the objects and the forms exist, if at all, not as the atoms and monads of realism exist, nor as the things in themselves of Kant. For nobody, according to Realism, is able to discover the things in themselves, the supposed entities of Realism, by any process of consciously free ideal construction, such as in fact produces the mathematician's ideas. On the other hand, the mathematical beings undertake to be real just as objects of possible thought, as valid truths, and not as independent of all thinking processes, whether actual or possible.

These contrasts and problems may weary. But it is necessary to face them. The world of validity is indeed, in its ultimate constitution, the eternal world. It seems to us so far a very impersonal world and a very cold and unemotional realm, — the very opposite of that of the mystic. Before we are done with it we shall find it in fact the most personal and living of worlds. Just now it appears to us a realm of bodiless universal meanings. Erelong we shall discover that it is a realm of individuals, whose unity is in One Individual, and that theory means, in this eternal world, not mere theory, but Will and Life.

LECTURE VI

LECTURE VI

AFTER having abandoned the abstractions of pure Realism and pure Mysticism, we went on, at the last time, to the study of a Third Conception of Being. We saw at all events how vain it is for any one to assume that, if you doubt metaphysical Realism, if you question whether the world can be real independently of knowledge, of ideas, and of definition, you must necessarily be a mere sceptic, and believe in no authority whatever, and in no world at all. On the contrary, as we saw, even ordinary conversation is full of assertions that objects have genuine Being which are explicitly not objects independent of experience, or of definition, or of ideas. Such supposed genuine beings, which are still not realistic entities, we found exemplified by the prices, debts, and credits of the commercial world, by analogous facts in the world of valid social estimates, and by the moral law. And then, passing from common sense to science, we pointed out the still more marvellous types of existence that people the eternal fairyland of mathematical construction. We saw how the mathematical entities appear to have all the variety, the stubbornness, and the frequently unexpected characters which, in the ordinary world, are said to belong to real beings. The mathematician's realm is in one sense his free creation. In another sense it is a world where that comes to light which he, in his private capacity, had neither intended nor anticipated. In that world he can long go astray, can hold false views as to his own creations, and, just as if he were working in a laboratory, can have these views set right by the outcome of further carefully planned experience, whose instruction he submissively awaits as if he were in no sense the creator of any object present. Like any other student of Real Being, he observes and experiments. The nature with which he deals is at once ideal and eternal, at once rigid and free. The most surprising analogies are often discovered linking together its most widely sundered and seemingly independent regions. The mathematician too has his news of the day, his unexpected events, his fortune, so to speak, even in the realm of a Being that explicitly is only in so far as it is conceived.

Plainly, then, the realm of Validity has a good many persuasively ontological characters. When we enter it, we need not come as sceptics or as mere victims of fantasy. What we there learn is that constructive imagination has its own rigid and objective constitution, precisely in so far as its processes unite freedom with clear consciousness.

And so, as we saw, it is possible, at least by way of trial, to undertake to define Being wholly in terms of validity, to conceive that whoever says, of any object, *It is*, means only that a certain idea, — perhaps an idea suggested by passing experience, perhaps the thought of an empirically discovered law in a natural science, perhaps a free construction of an ideal object in mathematics, — but in any case an idea, *is valid*, has truth, defines an experience that, at least as a mathematical ideal, and perhaps as an empirical event, is determinately *possible*. The truth, validity, or determinate possibility of the experience in question, may be, so far as yet appears, either transient or eternal, either relative or absolute, either something valid for a limited group of people, or something valid for all possible rational beings. But in any case, this third definition of Being attempts to identify the validity of the idea with the true Being of the fact defined by the idea.

I

Our Third Conception of Being has been thus stated and illustrated. It remains here next to follow in the briefest outline its history as an ontological conception, before trying to estimate its final value.

As now repeatedly recognized in these lectures, our Third Conception of Being is, in European thought, partly an indirect result of Plato's doctrine.[1] But it is also probably the historical fact, as we saw in our discussion of Realism, that Plato himself did not, on the whole, conceive his own Ideas in this way. The original Platonic argument about the Ideas amounts in general to saying, on the one hand, that only what

---

[1] That what I here call the Third Conception of Being was in essence Plato's concept, was the thesis, as is well known, of Lotze — a thesis which has often been discussed. Teichmüller and Zeller agree in rejecting Lotze's interpretation of Plato; and, in the main, I here follow their authority.

Plato calls the Ideas are of such nature as to be truly and eternally independent realities, and on the other hand, that the Ideas, while thus independently real, are to be so defined as to explain the universality of knowledge, and the eternal validity of truth. The Platonic Ideas were therefore realistic entities, in the sense of our first conception of what it is to be. They constituted an incorporeal world of independent realities. But the arguments used for their reality, and the relations which they bore to ethical and to other permanent truths, as well as the fact that they corresponded, not to our individual but to our universal conceptions, gave them characters which inevitably led them, in the later Platonic tradition, to assume forms more and more similar, either to beings of the type now in question, or to the sort of Being yet to be defined by our Fourth Conception of Reality, and hereafter to be treated. The Neo-Platonic doctrine identified the Platonic Ideas with the thoughts of the divine Intelligence. St. Augustine, in a proof of God's existence, identified God with Veritas. St. Thomas, in explaining the relation of the Ideas to God, was led to an interesting form of our present or Third Conception of Being; and post-Kantian idealism has remodelled the Platonic Ideas, on the whole, after the plan first suggested by the Neo-Platonic doctrine. In brief, then, Plato's concept of Being, while technically realistic, contains tendencies that inevitably lead to the differentiation of other ontological conceptions. And so our present or Third Conception of Being is, in large part, indirectly due to Plato.

Nearer to our present form of the ontological predicate comes, however, Aristotle's conception of Possible Being, a conception which plays a great part in the whole Aristotelian theory of Nature. The *ens in potentia* of the Aristotelian system occupies a place in a realistic doctrine. Aristotle insists that possibilities are in one sense real beings. Is not an architect a house-builder even when he is not building houses? Is not the sleeper potentially awake? Is not every natural process the realization of possibility?

But the doctrine of course has its obscurities. Where, in the independently real world, which Aristotle all the while assumes, are the mere possibilities when they are not yet realized? If one fairly faces this question, one finds that the possibilities appear to be in some sense ideal. They suggest even to Aristotle his theory of Nature as desiring or willing the yet unfulfilled possibil-ities, — a theory to which he nowhere gives a perfectly rounded expression. And it often seems as if the Possible Being of this Aristotelian doctrine would have to be expressed in terms of validity rather than in terms of the mere realistic entities themselves. It is *true* that the architect can build, the sleeper wake. These truths are valid. They are, for Aristotle, valid about independently real beings; and his doctrine is that there is also an independent or realistic type of Being corresponding to their validity; but this sort of Being, this *ens in potentia*, tends on the whole to assume the essentially ideal form of our present conception of what it is to be. Aristotle, in any case, never really solved the problem of the relation of these two types of being.

A good while later, in the history of thought, the Scholastic Theory of Being, as I a moment since observed, met with still a new instance of our present sort of reality. This instance brings us directly on to theological ground.

St. Augustine, who stands historically on the boundary line between the earlier and later philosophy of the church, proved God's existence by this noted argument: — There must be a *Veritas*, a *Truth*. For if you deny that there is a truth, you assert that it is true that there is no truth; and then you contradict yourself. The sum total of truth, conceived as a unity, is, however, the very essence of God. This argument, in one direction, looks backwards towards Neo-Platonic doctrine. St. Augustine's world of *Veritas* is the Nous of Plotinus. In another direction, the Augustinian proof of God's existence leads on to St. Anselm's Ontological Proof. The representative philosophy of the greater Scholastic period abandoned both St. Augustine's and St. Anselm's proof as invalid, but retained the conception of *Veritas* as part of the definition of the divine nature.

The result is the form of our Third Conception, to which we next mean to call attention. In the classic doctrine of St. Thomas Aquinas, the theory of the nature of God, to which we referred in our second lecture, is a very skilful synthesis of mystical, Platonic, and Aristotelian elements, influenced, of course, by still other traditional motives. According to this doctrine, the divine Essence, the Godhead as it is in itself, is above all, like the Hindoo Atman, simply one and per-

fect; and when we assert a mere plurality of attributes
in God, the variety of these attributes is, as variety, due
to the point of view, and to our imperfect comprehension of the divine unity. One very remarkable apparent
plurality, however, which our understanding finds in God,
is brought to light by the theory of the Divine Knowledge, when viewed in relation to the Creative Will of
God. God as Knower, not only knows all truth, but
he somehow knew in advance of creation, both all things
to be created, and all the possible beings that he has
left or will leave uncreated. This knowledge of many
facts, viewed as a plurality, constitutes for St. Thomas
the realm of the divine Ideas. As the divine ideas, in
the created world, receive discrete and individual embodiments, it seems at first natural to say that God, by
various acts of knowledge, comprehends, and, by various
acts of will, realizes, or leaves unrealized, the beings
whom his wisdom, in advance of creation, conceives.
But this way of stating the case not only would en-
danger the absolute unity of the divine essence, but
also would seem to give the various ideas of the possible created beings a certain independence of one another, and of the divine essence itself; so that it would
seem as if God were, so to speak, forced to know the
essences or natures of the finite facts, and as if these
finite entities, even in advance of creation, had their
own stubborn ideal independence over against God's
unity. Hence arose the scholastic problem whether the
essences of created things, in advance of creation, constituted a true *term*, or, as it were, an eternal limitation
of the divine knowledge.

St. Thomas's way of escaping this consequence involves a theory of Possible Being, as it is in God, in
advance of creation. The theory is to preserve the unity
of the divine essence, is to explain the variety of finite
beings, and is to show the relation of the created beings
to God, in such wise as to avoid the apparent eternity
and relative independence of the essences of finite beings.

In advance of creation, any possible being is known to
God, — but how? God primarily and perfectly knows
himself, and so knows his own absolute fulness of being.
But this nature of God is One and Simple. In knowing
this his own nature, even in its unity, God however views
this nature, by virtue of its very fulness of Being, as
Imitable now in this, now in that aspect, — as imitable
in countless fashions and degrees, and thereby as imitable by various orders of possible beings that God could
create. The divine knowledge of these finite beings
not yet created primarily has, then, God's own nature as
its immediate object. God first knows just himself. But,
secondarily, indeed, this nature can be viewed, not only
as one, and as immediately present to God's insight, but
also, so to speak, as rendering valid countless true possible assertions about possible imperfect imitations of the
Divine nature. The validity of these countless views of
the one divine nature is implied, just as a type of genuine possibility, in the divine perfection, and is accordingly said to be, as it were, known to the divine insight
in one act with the simple self-knowledge of God. And
in this sense are the created beings viewed as possible in
advance of creation. God knows not these beings as
mere data of his knowledge, but as truths valid only

through his own perfection.   After creation, these same
beings assume, with reference to finite knowledge, just
the independent type of reality characteristic of Realism,
and so the Thomistic conception of Real Being employs,
it would seem, all the three types of reality so far in
question in our discussion.   God's reality as directly
viewed by himself is of the mystical type.   The created
world is of the realistic type.   The divine Ideas are, from
our point of view, of the third type.   I need not say
that St. Thomas himself is not to be made responsible for
our definition of these types.

But now at length I pass to the point in the history
of philosophy where this our Third Conception of Real
Being assumes at last its most explicit form.   I refer to
a doctrine remote enough from that of St. Thomas, and
of direct interest for all modern discussions about the
philosophy either of religion or of science.   This is the
doctrine of Kant.

II

To speak of Kant's theory of what he called the realm
of Possible Experience, of *Mögliche Erfahrung*, is to come
at once into the full light of the present, that is, into
the midst of the doctrines that we have inherited from
Kant, and which are current to-day.   Whoever wearies
of Platonic or of Scholastic subtleties, must recognize, if
he knows how to read the meaning of current science,
that the notion of Possible Being, or of Being whose
reality lies in its validity, or in its value as making assertions about it true, is, as I said at the last time, the
favorite type of reality in the writings of a great number

of the recent philosophical expositors of the meaning of natural science. Such writers may or may not recognize their Kantian affiliations; but their position is one whose ontology is almost altogether Kantian, whatever may be their Psychology or their Theory of Knowledge. And such theories are so important for the whole position of religious thought, especially in its relations to scientific thought, that our future fortunes in this research largely depend upon seeing how we are related to this characteristic modern opinion.

Kant was, by early training, a realist. God, nature, the soul, are all in his early works, realities whose independence of even the truest and most certain external thoughts about them is for him obvious. As Kant grew critical, he long pondered over the problems of Time and of Space, and, in 1769, largely in consequence of the discovery of what he took to be fundamentally contradictory characters in space and in time, he came to deny that these so-called forms of our experience can be valid for "Objects as they are in themselves." Later Kant became still more critical, and questioned how, if the Noumena, or objects as they are in themselves, are so remote as his new theory now maintained from our empirical world of time and space phenomena, those real things, independent as they are of our understandings, can be known to us at all. The consequence of this new doubt, and of an interest in nevertheless maintaining the genuine validity of the mathematical and empirical sciences, was the theory expounded in the *Critique of Pure Reason*, in 1781.

In this theory, Kant comes definitely not only to recog-

nize, as every one interested in philosophy knows, a twofold world, — a world of "things in themselves" on the
one side, and of "phenomena" on the other; but also to
define a very important distinction between two sorts of
what he still regarded as genuinely objective reality. For
it is very noteworthy that, for Kant, both regions of his
twofold world are real. That is, both the things in themselves, and the phenomenal facts, are explicitly called by
him objective. Neither is a matter of your private view
or of mine. Neither, so Kant directly says, is subjective.
It is wrong to suppose that Kant viewed his phenomenal
world as a merely inner experience of any one man. The
question whether or no there are inhabitants in the moon
is, for the Kant of the critical philosophy, as much a
question about objective facts as it is for any ordinary
scientific observer of the moon. Yet this question is, in
his opinion, no longer a question about things in themselves; for the moon is a phenomenon in space; and the
unknowable things in themselves have no spatial characters. Precisely so the Newtonian theory of gravitation,
or a problem about the innermost constitution of matter,
is, for the critical Kant, a discussion about real facts, but
not about the things in themselves.

In brief, the former realist, Kant, has now come, not to
resign his Realism, but to add thereto the definition of
another sort of reality. Besides his independent reals,
which he never abandons as unreal, but which he now
regards as wholly unknowable, he asserts as critical philosopher the objective character of beings that are of a
wholly different type from the absolutely independent
realities.

And what are these new objects? Kant tells us in a very explicit way. They are the objects of *Mögliche Erfahrung*, of Possible Experience. The natural sciences are busy with these objects. The latter do not depend upon our will. They are plainly independent of our private individuality. But they are dependent upon the constitution of our experience.

For our experience, — that is, Kant's supposed discovery, — has, quite apart from any things in themselves, its own universal and fixed constitution. It is like a well bounded island in the ocean of mystery. The simile is Kant's. It is like a well ordered state, whose constitution and laws predetermine those facts, such as debts and credits, or such as ranks and social status, — those facts of which we earlier made mention in this discussion. Were it not for this universal constitution of our experience, our momentary opinions would wander like the nomads to whom Kant compares the sceptics in philosophy. As it is, the understanding gives law to nature. Universal assertions are valid. Science is possible.

We have no concern here with the manner in which Kant undertook to define how experience won this, its constitution. Enough, the universality is for him there. And as a result, if you ask whether there are inhabitants in the moon, Kant holds that you are not rightly inquiring about any sort of absolutely independent real beings, for in science you have no business with realistic beings of any sort. The things in themselves exist, but you can never win any sort of idea about them. On the other hand, in thus questioning, you are indeed asking a perfectly fair scientific question, and one in no wise relating to mere states of your own private mind. You are ask-ing, as Kant expresses it, just this, viz., whether, "In the progress of possible experience, you would come to per-ceive the presence of such inhabitants?" An answer to that question is even now true or false. And the objects of the one boundless realm of possible experience, — a realm which the sciences of nature study, are real, pre-cisely in so far as all such propositions, quite apart from your present empirical observation or mine, but not independently of the predetermined constitution of all experience, are even now true or false.

A quotation from Kant's discussion of the second of his so-called Postulates of Empirical Thought (*Kr. d. r. V.* 2d edit., p. 273) will help to bring his thought before you in his own way. "Perception," says Kant, "which gives to a concept its material embodiment, is the only test of actuality. But one can, nevertheless, in advance of the perception of an object, and consequently in a relatively *a priori* fashion, know the existence of this object, in case the thing in question is connected with any of our perceptions according to the principles of the empirical synthesis of phenomena (*i.e.* according to the law of Causality, one of the other fundamental princi-ples). For then the existence of the things is linked with our percepts in a possible experience, and by virtue of our general principles we can pass from our actual perception to the thing in question by a series of possible experiences. Thus we may recognize the existence of a magnetic substance pervading all matter, by virtue of our perception of the magnetic attraction of iron, although an immediate perception of the magnetic matter is impossible to us in consequence of the constitution of our sense organs. For in consequence of the laws of sensation, and of the context of our perceptions, we should come directly to observe the magnetic matter, were our organs fine enough. But the form of our possible experience has no dependence upon the mere coarseness of our actual sense organs. And thus, just so far as perception and its supplementation by virtue of empirical laws together suffice, so far extends our knowledge of the existence of things. But unless we begin with actual experience, and unless we proceed according to the laws of the empirical connection in experience, we vainly seek to guess or to investigate the existence of anything."

So much, then, in general, for Kant's statement of our present conception of the real. The novelty of Kant's account, as against previous approaches to the same philosophical idea, lies in the fact that earlier metaphysic, in trying to define the realm of truth as truth, the realm of the Possible Being of Aristotle or of the Scholastic Theology, had almost always made this conception a mere incident in the account of a world defined either in realistic or in mystical terms, while Kant's region of possible experience is sharply sundered from the realistic universe, and is quite as clearly distinguished from anything resembling that mystical limbo whose *Schwärmerei* Kant himself so much dreaded.

Subtle and difficult as Kant's new ontological conception has been, it has simply dominated the most popularly influential treatments of the philosophy of science ever since. Men who have spoken lightly of Kant have

in this respect followed his footsteps. Mr. Spencer's Unknowable is, on the whole, a realistic conception, although
sometimes spoken of in mystical terms. But Mr. Spencer's world of the Knowable has a reality of the Kantian
type. It is a world of valid empirical truth. John
Stuart Mill elaborated our Third Conception in his
famous chapter on the "Psychological Theory of Our
Belief in an External World," in his *Review of Sir
William Hamilton's Philosophy*. His definition of matter as a permanent possibility of sensation is altogether
of our present type. Several of the writers most prominent in the recent logical movement have used what
is essentially this view of the nature of scientific truth.
So, notably, Wundt, in his discussions of the fundamental ideas of the physical sciences, for example, the ideas
of Substance and of Cause. In a very different spirit,
Avenarius, while rejecting absolute validity, reaches a
view of the real which is much of our present sort.[1]

III

The conception now in question, as you see, is indeed
technical in its character; but it has so many bonds of
connection with popular thinking and with exact science,
that, when once defined, as our century has learned to
define it, it is sure to have a great practical potency in
affairs. In earlier lectures I called the typical realists
the partisans of strict conservatism, the philosophical
defenders of the extreme Right of any social order.

---

[1] The *Reine Erfahrung* of Avenarius constantly strives to become
something merely Immediate, but in vain, just because Avenarius is no
mystic.

The disciples of the new definition I have already called, as they appear at the present day, Critical Rationalists. As a fact, they are critical rather than dogmatic, but they are rather seldom of the extreme Left. Very often they belong to what one might venture to call the left centre of the parliament of thought, — to the moderate Liberals of doctrinal discussion, although the converse of this proposition does not hold true. For there are moderate liberals who are either mystics or constructive idealists.

The characteristics of the ontology of our critical rationalists can now easily be summed up. The Real for the metaphysical Realist, in case he attempts to be thoroughgoing, has to be, if anything, the Independent Individual, for, since it is beyond all our ideal determinations, it has to be in itself absolutely determinate. That the controversy of Aristotle with Plato proved. The Platonic Ideas, as universals, early perished from among the entities of the realistic world, to transmigrate, as it were, to this new realm, or also to reappear, with their own immortal vitality, in that realm of genuine Idealism which we shall later explore. The One Being of the mystic is as One, an Individual, although, as the ineffable goal of all desire, it enjoys all the advantages of a Universal, and is indifferent to all our distinctions. But the present, the Third Conception of Being, has amongst all the four conceptions the unique character that it alone, so far as it has more fully come to understand itself, consciously attempts to define the Real as explicitly and only the Universal.

Those who have imagined that the controversy about the

reality corresponding to our general ideas and about the
universal and the individual (the controversy of Nominal-
ist and of the unhappily so-called Realist), is a wholly
antiquated mediæval absurdity, have curiously failed to
observe the signs of our own times, and the trend of
this characteristic ontology of our present century and
of current science. What are Mill's Permanent Possibilities of Sensation, if you view them as objectively
valid at all, and not as mere private expectations of
our present feeling, — what are they, I ask, but explicit universals? What sort of an individual fact or
being is a mere "possibility"? Kant's empirical objects,
or *Gegenstände der Möglichen Erfahrung*, — his substances, causes, and the rest, what are they but products of the categorizing Understanding, empirically
valid general truths? If one passes from the more
abstract formulas to the concrete cases, glance, if you
please, at that most potent conception, the modern
notion of Energy. I ask not here as to its empirical
basis nor as to its outcome, but solely as to its ontological character as a mere conception. Energy, one may
say, is indeed phenomenally real. Professor Tait's remarkable words as to the objective reality implied by
the permanence of Energy have often been quoted.
But nobody of any authority, I suppose, is yet prepared to maintain in any decisive way that the energy
of the physical world consists of a collection of ultimate individual units or bits of energy, which retain
their individual identity, and as individuals transfer
themselves from one part of matter to another. The
idea has been suggested, but so far not vindicated. In

whatever sense energy is real, in that same sense an unindividuated entity, whose very essence is universal, is real. In vain then does one merely scoff at the early mediæval fashion of speaking of universal principles as if they were real. In a new sense, to be sure, and for new reasons, the ontology of the moment, in the concrete form of the sciences, is constantly recognizing, as in one sense real, objects which, as they are defined, are universals, and which cannot be individuals without altering their definition.

The grounds of this modern recognition of the new universals cannot indeed be judged upon the older scholastic bases. One cannot be fair to these newer concepts without recognizing the changed situation that has resulted from Kant's labors, and from the prominence now given in thought to the conception of Validity as a basis for the interpretation of our Experience. I mention the issue only to show, by a comparison of various problems, in what world we ourselves, at this stage of our study, are moving.

The Real in this sense is furthermore, as we have all along seen, identical with the determinately Possible only in so far as by that term you mean not indeed the fantastically or provisionally possible, such as a golden mountain, but that which would be observed or verified under exactly stateable, even if physically inaccessible, conditions. At the outset of an inquiry, you to be sure define as possible much that you later find to be unreal. Yet so far you have only the provisionally possible. But, for instance, the liquid or solid state of the interior of the earth, or the liquefaction of air, or the melting of

snow, is a possible experience, when you have once proved
that possibility in no provisional sense. For such possibilities, once recognized, are viewed as really valid and
objective physical characters of air or of snow or of the
earth. And now, finally, you may once more see what
we summarized at the outset, namely, how this conception must on the whole stand related to theology and to
religion.

The partisans of our third notion of the real have, indeed, as we have observed, a stately tradition behind them.
They can well assert that they are not mere sceptics or
destroyers of faith. Yet a theology that has been deeply
influenced by this conception will no longer share the
realist's absolute dogmatic assurance, whether positive
or negative, nor yet the mystic's inexpressible communion with his ineffable and immediate truth. Our critical
rationalist lives in a world where nothing in the realistic
sense is real, but where *it is as if there were* independent
realities, which, when more closely examined, prove to
be merely more or less valid and permanent ideas. The
truth, whether transient or eternal, always arouses in
such a world a twofold response or reaction in us who
observe it. It imposes its presence upon us as if it were
an independent reality; and hereupon we submit. But
then it alters its countenance as we consider it critically,
and becomes more and more like a mere product of our
point of view, a mere creation of our experience and our
thought. And hereupon we wonder. This truth seems
to be at first an individual fact. But it transforms itself
as we watch it into an universal principle. After we
have watched such changes awhile, we begin to ques-

tion whether this whole conception is at all capable of finality. The truth is, indeed, valid; but is it *only* valid? The forms are eternal; but are they *only* forms? The universal principles are true; but are they *only* universal? The moral order of the world seems genuine; but is it *only* an order? Is God identical with the world of Forms?

These questions arise in all sorts of ways in our age. They remind us that our problem is here once more a problem about the meaning and the place of individuality in the system of Being, and about the relation of individual and universal in our conceptions.

IV

And now, upon what basis shall we judge the conception at present before us? In one sense it appears to be peculiarly fortified against attack. Unlike Realism, it is from the beginning an essentially reflective and critical conception of Being. It attributes reality to objects only at the very moment of recognizing, as in some sense real, the ideas that relate to these objects. And, unlike Mysticism, it recognizes that to lose sight of the value and positive meaning of finite ideas, is to render naught the very objects which the ideas seek. It observes that when you declare any object to be real, you are in possession of an idea, however exact, or however inexact, however transient and relative, or however universal and eternal, — an idea to which you attribute an essentially teleological significance; since you assert that this idea is true, is valid, or in other words, is adapted to its ideal end. Our present conception regards this adaptation of

the idea to its own end as the primary topic of any ontological assertion, and as the object which any one who
asserts Being first of all inevitably means. And in making this comment upon our universal human relation to
truth, the present conception of Being is indeed insisting upon perfectly obvious and empirical facts.

When the realist says, " The world is first of all independently real, whether or no ideas refer to it, and it only
becomes secondarily and *per accidens* the object of ideas,"
the realist, in his whole view of the nature of Being, begins
by abandoning the realm of experience. He can therefore never empirically verify for you his independent
Beings. He can only presuppose them. You ask him to
show you an Independent Being. He points at the table
or at the stars. But those, for you, and for him alike,
are empirical objects, bound up in the context of experience. Nor could any possible enlargement of experience
ever show anybody a Being wholly independent. The
only way to judge Realism, since experience is thus abandoned by the realist, is to examine the inner consistency
or inconsistency of realistic doctrine. And we have seen
that Realism is wholly inconsistent. But our present
conception begins by observing that an experience of
facts which send you beyond themselves, and to further
possible experience, for their interpretation, is the only
conscious basis for any assertion of a Being that is beyond the flying contents of this very instant. The Third
Conception of Being refuses to ignore this conscious, this
empirical element, present wherever the assertion of
Being is made; for the only possible warrant for any ontological assertion must be found in this element. What

is, fulfils the meaning of the empirically present idea that refers to the Being in question, and except as fulfilling such a meaning, Being can be neither conceived, nor asserted, nor verified. In recognizing this fact of experience, lies the strength of the Third Conception.

In consequence of this reflective considerateness so characteristic of our Third Conception, it frequently appears, in its history, as the immediate outcome of a polemic against Realism. Thus, the negative arguments of Berkeley derive their force from a well-known series of comments upon the nature of the experiences by which we become acquainted with Being. The primary and secondary qualities attributed by many realists to matter, Berkeley analyzes into mere complexes of immediate data and of ideal construction. He then asks the realist the question : — " What do you mean, then, by your independently existing world?" And Berkeley thereupon shows how, primarily, all that Realism consistently means by matter has to be expressed in the form of an assertion that certain empirical ideas of ours are valid, and that their validity is a matter of possible experience. The distant church-tower, for instance, is a hint to the sense of vision of a long series of possible experiences. The assertion that these experiences, of approach to the church, of touch, of entrance to the church, are conditionally possible for any human being, this assertion is valid. And herein lies, for Berkeley, the primary reality of the material world. In order to explain still more exhaustively the validity in question, Berkeley is indeed led to his well-known hypotheses as to the souls, and as to the direct influence of the Divine

Will; and these hypotheses, as Berkeley states them, are once more essentially realistic in their type, since the God of Berkeley appears, in his relation to our valid experience of the natural order, as an independently real creative power, and since the souls, also, in Berkeley's account, get a distinctly realistic sort of Being. But his realistic type of theology is the halting and inconsequent side of Berkeley's doctrine. His critical study of the conception of matter is a contribution to the historical development of our Third Conception of what it is to be. In a similar way, our Third Conception appears in Kant himself, as the result of an attack upon every realistic interpretation of the world of common sense and of physical science, and as a development of the thesis: *Nur in der Erfahrung ist Wahrheit;* only Experience furnishes the ground for truth.

And in fact, if viewed merely as a negative criticism of the realistic conception, the argument for the Third Conception has often been stated, in the history of recent philosophy, in an unanswerable form. How, in fact, shall you maintain that Reality is independent of ideas which refer to it, while at the same time these ideas are other than itself, — how shall you maintain this, when the least reflection shows you that you are using ideas at every step of your discussion of reality, and that whatever you assert of the reality, you can give warrant to the assertion only by first showing reason for regarding your ideas as valid? Suppose, for instance, that you say, as realists have often said: — "Some independent cause for ideas must be assumed. This independent cause has Being. And its being is therefore the same as its independence as a cause." What is this assertion except an insistence that a certain more or less well-known empirical relation, already regarded as valid *within* your realm of experience, namely the relation called causality, has validity *beyond* your present range of experience? And what is this again but merely saying that *if* your senses were improved, *if* your horizon were widened, you would then directly observe how the so-called external facts, which would then be merely contents of your enlarged experience, would appear as empirical causes of what you had formerly called your ideas. Thus restated, however, your Realism turns at once into what Kant called a judgment about the texture of *Mögliche Erfahrung*. Whatever, then, you may attempt to assert, all that your Realism will ever succeed in articulating, is your belief that experience as a whole, that realm of truth of which you regard your present experience as a case and as a fragment, has a certain valid constitution. What Kant says remains then so far the whole outcome of the critical study of Being. You speak of objects, indeed, and these are not the objects of this instant's experience. But they are also not objects merely independent of the ideas that refer to them. For your assertion that the world is, involves a judgment that your present experience is interwoven in the whole context of the realm of valid or of possible experience. This context, however, is not independent of its own fragments. Your ideas are recognized by the whole that they with validity define.

And if you attempt to assert the Being of things in

any more independent sense than this, you struggle in
vain to articulate your meaning. You can then only
take refuge in the dogmatism of the typical realist.
You can, to be sure, call your Realism a "fundamental conviction," or a "wholesome faith," or a "truth
that no man in his sane senses can doubt." But the
strange consequence which then besets your very dogmatism lies in the fact that even in repeating these
confident speeches, you have merely asserted that, in
your opinion, certain ideas now present to you are
valid ideas. You have employed, then, and have admitted as the ultimate standard, your opponent's conception of Being, even in the very act of refuting his
view. You have appealed to the enemy's theory as
your sole warrant for asserting your own. Or perhaps
you may choose, as in an earlier lecture we found
Realism doing, — you may choose to call your opponent's view mere "insanity," and to hurl pathological
epithets at all who doubt Realism. The device is easy.
But this procedure once more is an express appeal to
your adversary's own conception of Being as the standard by which you are to be judged. For the very conception of insanity is an empirical conception, and all
that your assertion means, comes to an expression of
opinion that metaphysical views, other than realistic
ones, when seriously entertained, psychologically tend
to the possible experiences now called insanity. What
you have said is then still nothing but that, in your
opinion, the realm of *Mögliche Erfahrung* has for men
a certain constitution, and that your idea of this constitution appears to you valid. In vain is all your

Realism. Your very speech is in your adversary's tongue. You come to curse his views. Your words are blessings. You are among your opponent's prophets. For you appeal to his standards as your own.

An awakened realist, then, can readily see, if he chooses, that his Realism can get no coherent expression without becoming at once transformed into the very formulas of this our present and Third Conception of Being. In the third lecture of this course, to be sure, I made no attempt to express in this present form the criticism there undertaken of the conception of the Independent Beings. I deliberately refrained from that course in that place, because, as I ventured to say, Realism needs no such external refutation. Merely left to itself, it rends its own world to fragments in the very act of creating that world. I therefore preferred to let Realism first judge itself. We explored its empire under its own guidance, and found absolutely Nothing there. But the reason why the Independent Beings proved to be nothing whatever, now at last explicitly appears. It was because Realism, in defining Being, was actually only defining either Kant's realm of *Mögliche Erfahrung*, or else indeed Nothing at all. As the realm of the Third Conception was not yet in sight, the realist had only the latter alternative. The Being of the third type is however distinctly not an Independent Being. It is objective, but not isolated from the realm of ideas.

Thus well fortified against attack is our Third Conception of Being. In fact, how could one attack it except by undertaking to show that it is invalid? And how could one undertake that task except by first admitting that Being essentially implies the validity of ideas? This reflection is conclusive indeed against a realist, whose Independent Being was first to be real whether or no any ideas were to be found in the universe, and consequently whether or no validity, which is essentially bound up with the Being of ideas, united reality and idea in one context. But this reflection still leaves open one line of possible criticism which may be applied to our Third Conception. Validity or truth may be, as the Scholastic philosophy also would have said, an essential aspect of true Being, without on that account furnishing the final definition of what constitutes the *whole* Being of things. And here is it indeed a fair matter for question. That the Third Conception, as far as it goes, has some degree of validity, is indeed obvious enough. But is it adequate and final? Can the realm of validity remain *merely* a realm of validity? Here is indeed the place where we begin the final stage of our journey towards an adequate view of the meaning of the ontological predicate.

We have now several times insisted upon the empirical basis which the Third Conception of Being, as we have said, inevitably presupposes. But one may here object to our account that, although in many cases our Third Conception rests its assertion that a given idea is valid upon an obviously empirical foundation, this is not always, nor even ever altogether the case. For the mathematician, as we ourselves saw, deals with a world far transcending our actual physical powers of empirical verification. And it is not uncommon to suppose

that the very bases of mathematical science are certain
ultimate necessities of thought, for which no empirical
warrant can be given. The world of validity also often
appears as a world containing an essentially eternal
truth. But, as it may now be asked, does our experience, as such, ever compass eternity? Moreover, one
who asserts the objective validity of an idea, even in
a merely temporal sense, transcends by his very assertion the circle of his present experience. In brief,
every form of Critical Rationalism involves a confi-
dence in a reasoning process. But is reasoning identical with experience?

These considerations may serve to introduce a still
further reflection upon the deeper meaning of our Third
Conception. As a fact, it is far too easy to talk of
validity without analyzing its foundation. But if you
thus analyze, you are led to a view of the nature of
ideas, and of the reasoning process, which indeed shows
that our very conception of validity needs a further
supplement before it can be accepted as at once consistent, and adequate to its own undertaking.

The theory of reasoning has received, in recent logical and scientific thought, an extensive reëxamination,
which students of metaphysics can no longer ignore.
Nowhere has this theory been more carefully revised
than in the history of modern elementary mathematics.
A frequent experience of inconsistencies and of apparent
paradoxes, due to extremely subtle errors in exact
method, has led mathematicians, within the past fifty
years, to a thoroughgoing attempt at a review of the
very bases of Arithmetic, of Geometry, and of Analysis.

The modern study of the Algebra of Logic, founded by
Boole, and continued by Jevons, by Mr. Venn, and by
still others in Great Britain, by Mr. Charles Peirce in
America, and by Schroeder in Germany, has also con-
tributed to set the whole theory of exact reasoning in
a light at once clearer than that of old, and of a nature
to reveal new problems.   No longer can you venture,
in the exact sciences, to make your appeal to dogmatically asserted "ultimate necessities" of reason.   The
mathematician is no longer fond of mere axioms.   And
despite what we have just said about the way in which
the mathematician seems to transcend our present form
of experience, a closer study shows that it is still our
very experience itself that is the mathematician's only
guide to concrete results.   Experience is made better
by no mean, but experience makes that mean.   For in
modern mathematical study, even when you deal with
irrational numbers, like π, and estimate their properties
with an exactness that no physical experience of ours
can hope to follow, — yes, even if you take the wings
of the Calculus, or of the Theory of Functions, and fly
unto the uttermost parts of the realm of the quantitative infinite, even there, in an unexpected, but not the
less compelling sense, actual experience guides you, presented facts sustain you.

For, strangely enough, the logical outcome of this
whole recent review of the bases of mathematical science
can be expressed by saying that the modern mathematician rightly doubts every attempt to prove any proposition in his science unless, in trying to prove, you can
first empirically show him, in a fashion that he can ac-

cept, the actual process of construction belonging to, or creative of, the ideal object of which your proposition undertakes to give an account. Construction actually shown is, then, the test. This actual construction must be also not only shown, but carefully surveyed in present experience, before your proof can be estimated. The object of which you speak may be, like π, or like the total collection of all possible rational numbers, or like the quantitative infinite in any form, an object that nobody amongst us men directly observes. But, nevertheless, the fashion of its construction, the type to which it conforms, the law of its nature, the receipt for manufacturing this object, must be capable of adequate presentation in the inner experience of the mathematician, if any exact result is to be obtained. And as thus presented, the basis of the mathematician's reasoning becomes so far the study of inner experience. The object with which he directly deals is a thing present, seen, given, tested. As our American logician, Mr. Charles Peirce has well said, exact reasoning is a process of experiment performed upon an artificial object, an object made indeed by the mathematician, but observed by him just as truly as a star or as a physiological process is observed by the student of another science, experimented upon just as truly as one experiments in a laboratory.[1] But the marvel is that the present experience of the mathematician with his ideal object somehow warrants him in making assertions about an infinity

[1] A similar view of the nature of the reasoning process is illustrated in the remarkable discussions that fill part of Mr. Bradley's *Principles of Logic*.

of equally ideal objects which are *not* present to him, and which never will be present to any human being.

To illustrate, — suppose that a mathematician wants to prove something about the value of π, or about the universal laws of Arithmetic, or about the properties of a continuous function, or about the sum of an infinite series, or about the mathematical relationships of two infinite collections of ideal objects. What he is concerned to demonstrate, lies in the realm of the infinite, and of the eternally valid. And our direct experience gives us only the passing data and the fragmentary ideas of the moment. Does the mathematician then, like the rationalistic metaphysician of old, hereupon merely appeal to so-called first and fundamental principles? Does he write down axioms, and merely defy you to deny them? Does he assert *a priori* that this or that cannot or shall not be questioned? No, the modern mathematician has no dogmas. He waits for his facts. He asks you to construct, and then to observe these facts with him. What he does is to build up before your eyes something, as Mr. Peirce well says, that either is a diagram or else resembles one, a collection of observable symbols, or of figures in space, arranged in a certain deliberately planned way. In brief, he shows you empirically present inner constructions. He builds up these artificial objects before your eyes, and then he experiments upon them, and asks you to watch the result of the experiment. This result he first reads off, with as much the sense that he is recording present facts of observation, as one would have who should observe, on the street, that yonder horse is in front of yonder cart.

The difference so far is merely that the mathematician makes his empirical objects, and does not wait to see if ordinary natural processes will furnish them to him. His world, therefore, seems at first quite plastic. It is, as we have said, his fairyland. He plays with it. Yet none the less, as he plays, he observes the empirical results of his play. And while he does this, he is as much a student of given facts as is a chemist or a business man. The results of this observation are often unexpected. And once seen (just here lies the mystery of the realm of validity), — once seen, they are also seen to stand for unalterable truth. How this can be, is precisely our present problem. The mathematician, in his own exact way, is thus like Browning's lover. His instant is an eternity. He sees in a transient moment. Every one of his glimpses of fact is like the flash of the moonlight on the water. Yet *what* he sees outlasts the ages of ages. But nothing in all this eternal validity of his outcome makes him less empirical in his actual scrutiny. The validity is to be eternal. But his form of his experience is precisely that of any other human creature of the instant's flight. In examining his diagram, he is as faithful a watcher as the astronomer alone with his star. The mathematician has made his diagram, but he cannot wilfully alter its consequences. And they must first be seen. Then alone can they be believed. Here is the strange antithesis between the empirical form and the eternal content of the realm of mathematical validity.

The valid, then, even the eternally valid, enters our human consciousness through the narrow portals of the instant's experience. Reasoning is an empirical process, whatever else it also is. One who observes the nature of a realm of abstractly possible experience, does so by reading off the structure of a presented experience. Necessity comes home to us men through the medium of a given fact. This is the general result of modern exact Logic. This is the outcome of the recent study of the bases of mathematical science.

And now, in a precisely similar way, the discovery of the more contingent, or, on occasion, of the more transient validity of the non-mathematical truths of the world of possible experience, has the same puzzling and twofold character. You examine, in the field or in the laboratory, a law of the physical world; you assure yourself that yonder ship observed out at sea is a reality; you find out the price of a commodity; you verify the credit of a business man. In any such case, what do you accomplish? What sort of Being do you assert, examine, establish? The answer is, — What you do is to test the validity of an idea about possible experience. You first predict that if you act so or so, if you watch the ship longer, if you make the scientific experiment under given conditions, if you offer the market price for the article, or if you attempt to negotiate the commercial paper, certain empirical results will follow, certain consequences will be experienced by you. This prediction is, for you, merely an assertion about possible perceptions, feelings, ideas. You will, under given conditions, see certain sights, hear certain words, touch certain tangible objects, — in brief, get the presence of certain empirical facts. This is all that you

can find involved in very many of your statements about
the Being of social and of physical realities. Having
defined such ideas of possible experience, you then test
them. If the result conforms to the expectation, you
are so far content. You have then communed with
Being. The Other that was sought appears to have
been found.

But no, it is not wholly right to view the matter
merely thus. For there are countless possible experiences that you never test, and that you still view as belonging to the realm of physical and of social validity.
In fact, just when you express your own contentment
with your tests, you transcend what you have actually
succeeded in getting present to your experience. The
ship has for you, even as a merely valid object in the context of Kant's *Mögliche Erfahrung*, more Being than you
have ever directly verified. If it had not, you would indeed call it a figment of imagination. The prices and
credits of the commercial world involve far more numerous types of valid possible experience than any prudent
merchant cares to test; for, if these facts are valid as
they are conceived, their very Being includes possibilities of unwise investment and of bankruptcy, which the
prudent business man recognizes only to avoid. In fact,
since our whole voluntary life is selective, we all the
time recognize possibilities of experience only to shun the
testing of them.

And so, in sum, the ordinary world of possible experience has this twofold character. We prove that it is
there by testing empirically, from moment to moment, the
validity of our ideas about it; but our very belief in its

Being means that we recognize its possession of far more validity than, in our private capacity, we shall ever test. It is thus with common sense, much as it was with mathematics. The mathematician finds his way in the eternal world by means of experiments upon the transient facts of his inner and ideal experience of this instant's contents. The student of science or the plain man of everyday life believes himself to be dealing with a realm of validity far transcending his personal experience. But his only means of testing any concrete assertion about that world comes to him through the very fragmentary observation of what happens in his inner life from instant to instant.

To generalize, then, the problem so far furnished us by our Third Conception of Reality, we find this as our situation. Ask me how I discover, in a concrete case, the validity of my idea, how I make it out for certain that a given experience is possible; and then I have to answer, " By actual experience alone." When I say then, " A given idea is certainly valid," I primarily mean merely, "A given idea is fulfilled in actual present experience." But if you ask me what I regard as the range of the realm of validity, and what I think to be the extent of possible experience, and of the truth of ideas, then I can only say that the range of valid possible experience is viewed by me as infinitely more extended than my actual human experience. From the mathematical point of view the realm of truth is in fact explicitly infinite. From the point of view of natural science and of common sense, the world of valid possible experience is not only far wider than our concrete human experience, but is interesting to us precisely because we can select from its wealth of possibilities those that we wish, as we say, to realize. Now what our Third Conception so far fails to explain to us is precisely the difference between the reality that is to be attributed to the valid truths that we do not get concretely verified in our own experience, and the reality observed by us when we do verify ideas.

In brief, *What is a valid or a determinately possible experience at the moment when it is supposed to be only possible?* What is a valid truth at the moment when nobody verifies its validity? When we ourselves find the possible experience, it is something living, definite, — yes, individual. When we ourselves verify a valid assertion, it is again something that plays a part in our individual process of living and observing. But when we speak of such truths as barely valid, as merely possible objects of experience, they appear once more as mere universals. Can these universals, not yet verified, consistently be regarded as possessing wholeness of Being?

Or again, we formerly criticised Realism and Mysticism alike because neither of them sufficiently took account of the fact that our ideas of Being and the Being of which we have ideas, must occupy essentially the same ontological position. If, as Realism had said, Being is real independently of ideas, we saw that then ideas are themselves realities independent of Being. And if, as Mysticism had said, ideas are unreal, we saw that the Absolute, which Mysticism undertook to seek, must be unreal in the same sense in which the ideas about it are unreal. Now the former criticism of Realism and of Mysticism must once more be applied to test the adequacy of our present conception. We must see whether validity means the same in our experience as it means when asserted of Being in general. Validity, so far as it has yet appeared in our account, is an ambiguous term. As applied to the ideas that we actually test, it means that they are concretely expressed in experience whenever we test them. As applied to the whole realm of valid truth in general, to the world of nature as not yet observed by us, or of mathematical truth not now present to us, it means that this realm somehow has a character that we still do *not* test, and that never gets exhaustively presented in our human experience. But what is this character?

Or, once more, in our concrete experience, the validity of an idea, once seen, tested, presented, gets what we then regard as an individual life and meaning, since it appears in our individual experience. But in the realm of Being in general this same validity appears universal, formal, — a mere general law. Now can this view be final? Can there be two sorts of Being, both known to us as valid, but the one individual, the other universal, the one empirical, the other merely ideal, the one present, the other barely possible, the one a concrete life, the other a pure form? Is not the world real in the same general sense in which our life in the world is real? Can Critical Rationalism escape the test already applied to its rivals? And if the test is applied, must not all Being prove to be pulsating with the same life of concrete experience?

We shall see. History shows that the rigid world of the Platonic Ideas, when viewed by later speculation, began erelong to glow, like sunset clouds, with the light of the Divine presence; and Neo-Platonism already called the Ideas the thoughts of God. Shall there be possible experience in the realm of validity, and the Lord hath not known its meaning?

This is at present a mere query. Upon the rational answer to this query depends our whole religious philosophy.

LECTURE VII

LECTURE VII

THE INTERNAL AND EXTERNAL MEANING OF IDEAS

WITH the former lecture our inquiry into the conceptions of Being reached a crisis whose lesson we have now merely to record and to estimate. That task, to be sure, is itself no light matter.

I

Experience and Thought are upon our hands; and together they determine for us the problems regarding Being. Realism offered to us the first solution of this problem by attempting to define the Reality of the world as something wholly independent of our ideas. We rejected that solution on the ground that with an Independent Being our ideas could simply have nothing to do. Or, if you please so to interpret our discussion of Realism, we pointed out that our ideas, too, are realities; and that if Realism is true, they are therefore in their whole Being as independent of their supposed realistic objects as the latter are of the ideas. If, then, it makes no difference to the supposed external beings whether the ideas are or are not, it can make no difference to the ideas whether the independent external Beings are or are not. The supposed dependence of knowledge for its success upon its so-called independent object, proves, therefore, to be contradicted by the ontological independence inevitably possessed by the knowing idea, in case Realism is once accepted. For the realistic sort of independence is an essentially mutual relation. The idea can then say to the independent object, in a realistic world: "What care I for you? You are independent of me, but so am I of you. No purpose of mine would be unfulfilled if you simply vanished, so long as I then still remained what I am. And I could, by definition, remain in my whole Being unaltered by your disappearance. Accordingly, since my truth means merely the fulfilment of my own purpose, I should lose no truth if you vanished. In short, I not only do not need you, but observe, upon second thought, that I never meant you at all, never referred to you, never conceived you, and, in truth, am even now not addressing you. In short, you are Nothing."

With such reflections, we woke from the realistic dream, and knew that whatever Being is, it is not independent of the ideas that refer to it.

After our later experience with the fascinating paradoxes of Mysticism had equally shown us that Being cannot be defined as the ineffable immediate fact that quenches ideas, and that makes them all alike illusory, we passed, in the two foregoing lectures, to the realm of Validity, to the ontological conceptions of Critical Rationalism. What is, gives warrant to ideas, makes them true, and enables us to define determinate, or valid, possible experiences. That was the view that we illustrated as our Third Conception of Being. We dwelt upon it so lengthily because, if it is not the final truth, it is, unquestionably, as far as it goes, true.

What we found with regard to this definition of Reality may be summed up briefly thus: In the first place, the conception has an obvious foundation in the popular consciousness. Not only does the ontological vocabulary of ordinary speech illustrate this third conception in several ways; but, amongst the beings known to common sense, there are many that are regarded as real beings, but that are still explicitly defined only in terms of validity. Such beings are the prices and credits of the commercial world, the social standing of individuals, the constitutions of Empires, and the moral law.

In the second place, in science, mathematics deals exclusively with entities that are explicitly conceived by the science in question as of this third type, and of this type only. In the next place, as we found, the Being usually ascribed to the laws and to the objects of physical science, is capable, at least in very large part, of being interpreted in terms of this third conception. Such conceived entities as Energy are typical instances of beings of this sort. And, finally, all the entities of even a metaphysical Realism proved to be such that when one tries not to leave them unintelligibly independent, but to tell what they are, there is no means to define their character which does not first of all declare that their reality involves the validity of certain of our ideas, and the truth of the assertion that, under definable conditions, particular experiences would be possible. What else the Being of such entities would mean, remained for us so far undefinable.

On the other hand, as we concluded our former discussion, considerations crowded upon us, which forced us to observe that in some way this Third Conception of Being, despite all the foregoing, is inadequate.

Valid in its own measure it is, — to say that is to utter the deep commonplace of St. Augustine's form of the ontological proof of the existence of God. For it must indeed be true that there is a *Veritas*. Yet mere *Veritas*, mere validity, still remains to us a conception as unintelligible as it is insistently present to our thought. And our difficulty at the last time came thus to light: In mathematics, you define and prove valid assertions, and deal with entities, such as roots of equations, and properties of functions, whose Being seems to mean only their validity. But how do you prove these propositions about validity? How do you test the existence of your mathematical objects? Merely by experimenting upon your present ideas. What is there before you as you thus experiment? At each step of your procedure, one moment's narrow contents extend to the very horizon of your present finite mathematical experience. Yet if your procedure is, indeed, as it pretends to be, valid, the truth that you define embraces eternity, and predetermines the structure and the valid existence of an infinity of objects that you regard as external to the thought which defines them. Your world of objects then is here boundless; your human grasp of these objects is even pitiably limited. Validity thus implies, in the world of the mathematical entities, a twofold character. As presented, as seen by you, as here realized, the observed validity is apparently given in experience, indeed, but as a mere internal meaning, — the creature of the instant. But as objective, as genuine, the validity is a part of the endless realm of mathematical truth, a realm that is, to use Aristotle's term, the Unmoved Mover of all your finite struggle for insight in this region. How can the one form of Being be thus ambiguous, unless, in constitution, it is also much wealthier in nature than the mere abstraction expressed in our Third Conception makes it seem. Or, to put the case otherwise, the Third Conception of Being, in defining possibilities of experience, tells you only of mere abstract universals. But a mere universal is so far a bare *what*. One wants to make more explicit the *that*, to find something individual.

And, if you pass from mathematics to the physical instances of the third conception, and to the world of moral and social validity, it is of course true that every Being in heaven or in earth exists for you as determining a valid possibility of experience. But countless of these valid possibilities exist for you precisely as possibilities not yet tested by you, and therefore never to be tested. Herein lies the very essence of prudence, of generalizing science, and of moral choice, viz., in the fact that you recognize much experience as possible only to avoid it, and to refrain from verifying in your own person the valid possibility. But what is a mere possibility when not tested? Is it a mere internal meaning? Then where is its Truth? Is it external? Then what is its Being?

These were, in sum, our difficulties in regard to the Third Conception of Being. Their solution, logically speaking, lies now very near. But for us the road must still prove long. Meanwhile, the formulation of all these difficulties may be condensed into the single question, the famous problem of Pontius Pilate, What is Truth? For the Third Conception of Being has reduced Being to

Truth, or Validity. But now we need to make out what constitutes the very essence of Truth itself. It is this which at the last time we left still in obscurity. It is this which lies so near us, and which still, because of manifold misunderstandings, we must long seek as if it were far away.

II

Our course in approaching our final definition of Truth will divide itself into two stages. Truth is very frequently defined, in terms of external meaning, as *that about which we judge*. Now, so far, we have had much to say about Ideas, but we have avoided dwelling upon the nature and forms of Judgment. We must here, despite the technical dreariness of all topics of Formal Logic, say something concerning this so far neglected aspect of Truth, and of our relation to Truth. In the second place, Truth has been defined as the *Correspondence between our Ideas and their Objects*. We shall have, also, to dwell upon this second definition of Truth. Only at the close of both stages of the journey shall we be able to see, and then, I hope, at one glance, whither through the wilderness of this world our steps have been guided. The result will reward the toil.

When we undertake to express the objective validity of any truth, we use Judgments. These judgments, if subjectively regarded, — that is, if viewed merely as processes of our own present thinking, whose objects are external to themselves, — involve, in all their more complex forms, *combinations* of ideas, — devices whereby we weave already present ideas into more manifold structures, thereby enriching our internal meanings. But the act of judgment has always its other — its objective aspect. The ideas, when we judge, are also to possess external meanings. If we try to sunder the external meaning from the internal, as we have so far done, we find then that weaving the ideas into new structures is a mere incident of the process whereby we regard them as *standing for the valid Reality*, as characterizing what their object is. It is true, as Mr. Bradley has well said, that the intended subject of every judgment is Reality itself. The ideas that we combine when we judge about external meanings are to have value for us as truth only in so far as they not only possess internal meaning, but also imitate, by their structure, what is at once Other than themselves, and, in significance, something above themselves. That, at least, is the natural view of our consciousness, just in so far as, in judging, we conceive our thought as essentially other than its external object, and as destined merely to correspond thereto. Now we have by this time come to feel how hard it is to define the Reality to which our ideas are thus to conform, and about which our judgments are said to be made, so long as we thus sunder external and internal meanings.

Yet, for the instant, we must still continue to do so. We must, so to speak, "absent us from felicity awhile," and in this world of merely internal and disappointed meanings, whose true objects are still far beyond, and whose only overt law is so far the law of correspondence to those objects — in this "harsh world," I say, we must "draw our breath in pain," until the real truth shall become manifest, and take the place of these forms which now merely represent it. The Truth that we pursue is no longer, indeed, the Independent Being of Realism; but it still remains something defined as *not* our ideas, and as that to which they ought to correspond, so that their internal meanings, interesting as these may seem, appear the mere by-play, so to speak, of the business of truth-seeking. And that business seems to be the task of submitting our thought to what is not our own mere thought. Well, for the time, we must still accept this situation. And, while we do so, let us examine briefly our processes of judgment, in so far as these consciously refer to external Objects; and let us endeavor to observe how our judgments, as they occur in actual thinking, or are confirmed or refuted by our ordinary experience, seem to view their own relation to Reality. To turn in this direction is to seek help, if you please, from Formal Logic. For Formal Logic is the doctrine that treats of our judgments and of their ordinary meanings as we make and combine them.

Ordinary judgments, all of them, as we have just said, make some sort of reference to Reality. Never do you judge at all, unless you suppose yourself to be asserting something about a real world. You can express doubt as to whether a certain ideal object has its place in Reality. You can deny that some class of ideal objects is real. You can affirm the Being of this or of that object. But never can you judge without some sort of conscious intention to be in significant relation to the Real. The *what* and the *that* are, indeed, easily distinguished, so long as you take the distinction abstractly enough. But never, when you seriously judge in actual thinking, do you avoid reference *both* to the *what* and to the *that* of the universe.

Now, this observation may itself seem questionable. You may object: "Can I not make judgments about fairies and centaurs without asserting whether they are or are not? And if I distinguish between ideas and facts at all, cannot I do so in my judgments also, and make judgments about ideal objects merely as ideal objects, without referring to the Reality in any way?" The answer to all these questions is simply, *No*. To judge is to judge about the Real. It is to consider internal meanings with reference to external meanings. It is to bring the *what* into relation with the *that*. And if you have sundered the external and internal meanings, every attempt to judge, even while it recognizes this sundering as sharpest, is an effort to link afresh what it all the time, also, seems to keep apart. To illustrate the truth of this principle, look over the list of forms of judgment as they appear in the ordinary text-books of Logic. The list in question is, indeed, in many ways, imperfect; but it will serve for our present purpose.

Judgments may be, as the logical tradition says, "Categorical," or "Hypothetical," or "Disjunctive." That is, they may assert, for example, that A *is* B; or they may affirm that *If* A *is* B, *then* C *is* D; or they may declare that *Either* A *is* B, *or else* C *is* D. This ancient classification is no very deep one; but it may aid us to survey how our various sorts of judgment view Reality.

Let us begin with the "hypothetical" judgment, the judgment of the bare "if." This sort of judgment seems, of course, to be capable of becoming as remote as possible from any assertion about Being, and as completely as possible a judgment about "mere ideas." "If wishes were horses, beggars might ride." "If the bowl had been stronger, my tale had been longer." "If a body were left undisturbed by any external cause, it would continue its state of rest, or of uniform motion, in a straight line unchanged." Are not all these judgments about purely ideal objects, and not about Being, or about any real world? Where are wishes horses? When do beggars ride on their own steeds? When were the wise men of Gotham in the bowl? What real body moves undisturbed?

And yet, I answer, these are all of them judgments that, if they are true, do not indeed directly tell us what the world of valid Being actually and concretely contains, but do tell us what that real world does *not* contain. *In*directly, by limiting the range of valid possibilities, they thus throw light upon what the world does contain. Thus the First Law of Motion, as stated, tells us that there are no bodies which, although undisturbed by external causes, still move in lines not straight, and with velocities that vary. Hence, since the physical bodies observed by us turn out to be in motion, in various curves, and with varying velocities, we are directed to look for the causes hereof in the disturbances to which these bodies are subjected. So it is, also, in the other cases mentioned, in so far as these statements are true at all. In general, the judgment, "*If* A *is* B, C *is* D," can be interpreted as meaning that there are, in the world of valid objects, no real cases where, at once, A is B, while at the same time C is nevertheless not D.

A good instance is furnished by any sincere promise, such as a promise to a child, in the form: "*If you do that I will reward you.*" The promise relates to the valid Being of the future. It asserts that this future, when it comes to be present, shall not contain the event of the child's doing that work *un*rewarded by the giver of the promise. So, then, hypothetical judgments tell us that some ideally defined object, often of very complex structure, *finds no place* in Being. Even the fantastic examples of the wishes and the bowl involve the same sort of assertion, true or false, as to a real world.

The judgments of simple assertion, the categorical judgments, are of the two general classes, the "Universal" and the "Particular" judgments, namely those, respectively, that speak of *all* things of a class and those that only tell about *some* things. But here, again, it would seem, at first, as if an universal judgment might concern itself wholly with ideal objects. When a contract is made, universal judgments are, in general, used. "All the property" of a given sort, if ever it comes to exist, is by the terms of the contract "to be delivered," perhaps, to such and such a person. "All payments" under the contract "are to be made," thus and thus. But, perhaps, if ever the contract comes later to be adjudicated, it may be found that no property of the sort in question has ever come into existence, or has ever been delivered at all; and then it may be decided that, by the very terms of the contract, and just by virtue of its legal validity, no obligation exists to make any of the mentioned payments. So all contracts concerning future work, delivery, or compensation are, on their face, about ideal objects, which may never come to be in valid Being at all. In fact, genuinely universal judgments, as Herbart and a good many more recent Logicians have taught, are essentially hypothetical in their true nature. But for that very reason, like the hypothetical judgments, the universal judgments, taken in their strictest sense, apart from special provisos, are judgments that undertake to *exclude* from the valid Reality certain classes of objects. To say that *All* A *is* B, is, in fact, merely to assert that the real world contains no objects that are A's, but that fail to be of the class B. To say that *No* A *is* B is to assert that the real world contains no objects that are *at once* A and B. Neither judgment, strictly interpreted, tells you that A exists, but only that *if* it exists, it is B. Now those mathematical judgments, of whose endless wealth and eternal validity we have heretofore spoken, are very frequently, although by no means always, of the universal type. They refer to Being, — a Being of the third type, — and, when universal, they assert, about a realm of definite or relatively determinate, although still universal validity, or possibility, something that proves to be primarily negative, so far as its relation to its external object is concerned. They accomplish their assertions by means of the very fact that they undertake to exclude from the realm of externally valid Being, certain ideal combinations that, in the first place, would have seemed abstractly possible, if one had not scrutinized one's ideas more closely. Thus, to know that universally $2 + 2 = 4$, is to know that there nowhere exists, in all the realm of external validity, a two and a two that, when added, *fail* to give, as the result, four. In advance of such knowledge, the opposite would seem abstractly possible. But it proves to be only verbally or apparently possible. Determinately viewed, only the "actual sum" is possible.

In general, when we judge in universal ways, we begin, before we attain an insight into the truth of our judgment, by stating, as abstractly possible, *more* ideal alternatives than in the end will prove to be determinately possible, or to be valid possibilities. In the exact sciences, or, again, in case of those practically important realms of Being which we view as subject to our choice, — whenever we win control over a system of ideas, and assert a truth, or decide upon a course of action, and whenever we do this upon the basis of general principles, — our insight is always *destructive of merely abstract possibilities*, and, where our knowledge takes the form of universal judgments, they are always primarily such destructive judgments, so far as they relate to external objects. They tell us, indirectly, what *is*, in the realm of external meanings, but only by first telling us what *is not*.

The consequence is that universal categorical judgments, being always primarily negative in force, enlighten us regarding that realm of the external meanings which is still for us, at this stage, the realm of Being, only by virtue of the junction, overt or implied, of the universal categorical judgments with disjunctive judgments, *i.e.* with judgments of the *either*, *or* type. One who inquires into a matter upon which he believes himself able to decide in universal terms, *e.g.* in mathematics, has present to his mind, at the outset, questions such as admit of alternative answers. "A," he declares, "*in case it exists at all, is either* B *or* C." Further research shows universally, perhaps, that *No* A *is* B. Hereupon the abstract possibilities are in so far reduced, and the world of Being, taken still as a realm of external meanings, is limited to a realm where "*If* A *exists at all, it can only be* C." The purpose of our universal judgments is thus that, by the aid of disjunctive judgments, they enable us to determine the world of Being by cutting off some apparent possibilities as really impossible, and by then taking the remaining alternatives, not in general, as any entirely determinate account of what is, but as a less indeterminate account of Reality than is the one with which we started. To think in universal terms is thus to attempt, as it were, to exhaust the abstractly possible alternatives, and to define what exists in yonder external world as what survives the various stages of ideal destruction through which one passes as one judges. So long as thus, separating ideas from their external meanings, you struggle through universal judgments towards the far-off truth, your principle is the one that Spinoza stated, *Omnis Determinatio est Negatio.* The universal truth is the slayer of what seemingly might have been, but also of what, as a fact, proves to be *not* possible.

As for your disjunctive judgments themselves, even they, too, affirm about external Being only by first denying. "A *is either* B *or* C; *there is no third possibility open,*" — such must be one's assertion when a disjunction is announced. The type of an ideally perfect and evident disjunction is the assertion, "A *is either* B *or not-*B," where B and not-B are the alternative members of a "dichotomy," *i.e.* of an exhaustive and twofold division of the Universe of your Discourse, as at any time you conceive its Reality to be opened to your ideal inspection.

This general situation of our thought in all those branches of inquiry where, as very often in mathematics, we deal with universal truth, and reason out results about Being, while still viewing Reality as Another than thought, is a situation that stimulates us to manifold inquiries. In the first place, as you at once see, the limitations of all our merely abstract and universal reasoning about the world, when taken as a world of external meanings, are, at a stroke, laid bare by virtue of those very considerations. For by mere reasoning, in these universal terms, we never directly and determinately characterize the Being of things as it finally is. We at best, and even if we are quite sure of our universal truths, *tell what external Reality is not*, and add that, of the remaining abstractly possible and definable alternatives, it is doubtless determinately some one, and no other. But, apart from any scepticism, justified or not, regarding the validity of our universal judgments themselves, they at best carry us a certain way only in an undertaking that seems essentially endless, and, in fact, worse than endless. And that is the undertaking of exhausting all the possible alternatives, and so of making the finally valid possibility, that can alone remain, into something absolutely determinate. And where the sole principle is that *Omnis Determinatio est Negatio*, this task is indeed not only endless, but hopeless.

This, in fact, is why mathematical science, especially

in so far as it deals merely with universal truths, can never hope, by any conceivable skill in construction, to replace the more empirical sciences, and merely to define the world in terms of its own sort of universal validity. For every step of the process is a cutting-off indeed of false possibilities, and an assertion of what therefore seems the more precisely and determinately limited range of the valid possibilities. But at every step, also, the range beyond is simply inexhaustible, so far as you take your object as merely external. Unless some other principle than that of mere negation determines the realm of valid Being, then it has no final determination at all. Looking beyond, to that realm of external meanings, we say: A *is never* B. Well then, comes the retort, *What is it?* So far, the answer is, *Whatever else is still possible. Is it* C *then?* A further reasoning process perhaps excludes this, or some other, possibility also. Have we found out the positive contents of Being? No, we have only again excluded. And so we continue indefinitely, not only with an infinite process upon our hands, but with no definite prospect as to positive consequences to be won by exhausting even this infinity. This is the essential defect of "merely reasoning," in abstractly universal terms, about the external nature of things.

But all this has, indeed, another aspect. This negative character of the universal judgments holds true of them, as we have said, just in so far as you sunder the external and the internal meanings, and just in so far as you view the Real as the Beyond, and as merely the Beyond. If you turn your attention once more to the realm of the ideas viewed as internal meanings, you see, indeed, that they are constantly becoming enriched, in their inner life, by all this process. Take your thinking merely as that which is to correspond to an external Other, and then, indeed, your universal judgments tell you only what this Other is not, and leave, as what it is, merely *some* of the possibilities still *un*destroyed. But view the internal meaning of thought as a life for itself, and revel in the beautiful complexities of a mathematical, or other rationally constructed realm of inner expressions of your thoughtful purposes; and then, indeed, you seem to have found a positive constitution of an universe that, alas! is, after all, as contrasted with those "external facts," to be regarded only as a shadowland. "Is it really so yonder?" you say. Is namely the *positive* aspect of all this construction present in that world? Your universal judgments cannot tell. To take, again, the simplest case: To know, by inner demonstration, that $2 + 2 = 4$, and that this is necessarily so, is not yet to know that the so-called "external world," taken *merely* as the Beyond, contains any true or finally valid variety of objects at all, — any two or four objects that can be counted. That you must learn otherwise, namely, of course, by what is usually called "external experience" of that outer world. On the other hand, so far as your internal meaning goes, to have seen for yourself, to have experienced within, that which makes you call this judgment necessary, is, indeed, to have observed a character about your own ideas which rightly seems to you very positive. So, then, universal judgments and reasonings appear to be of positive interest in the realm of internal meanings, but only of negative worth as to the other objects.

All this, however, only brings afresh to light the paradoxical character of all this sundering of external and internal meanings. For at this point arises the ancient question, How can you know at all that your judgment is universally valid, even in this ideal and negative way, about that external realm of validity, in so far as it is external, and is merely your Other, — the Beyond? Must you not just dogmatically say that that world must agree with your negations? This judgment is indeed positive. But how do you prove it? The only answer has to be in terms which already suggest how vain is the very sundering in question. If you can predetermine, even if but thus negatively, what cannot exist in the object, the object then cannot be *merely* foreign to you. It must be somewhat predetermined by your Meaning. But of this matter we shall soon hear more in another connection. The result is so far baffling enough. Yet in this situation most of our ordinary thinking about the world is done.

Let us pass to the "particular affirmative" judgments. As has been repeatedly pointed out in the discussions on recent Logic,[1] the particular judgments, — whose form is *Some* A *is* B, or *Some* A *is not*-B, — are the typical judgments that positively *assert* Being in the object viewed as external. This fact constitutes their essential contrast with the universal judgments. They undertake to cross the chasm that is said to sunder internal and exter-

---

[1] Amongst others by Mr. Charles Peirce, by Schroeder, by Mr. Venn, and, quite independently, by Brentano, in his *Psychologie*.

nal meanings; and the means by which they do so is always what is called "external experience." No "pure thinking" can ever really prove a particular judgment about external objects. You have to appeal to outer experience. On the other hand, all empirical judgments about objects of external meaning, viewed merely as such, are, or should be, in this form of the particular judgments. It is a form at once positive and very unsatisfactorily indeterminate. It expresses the fact that there has been found *some* case where an A that is a B not only *may* exist, in yonder object with which we are to correspond, but *does* exist. The defect of these judgments is that they never tell us, by themselves, precisely *what* object this existent instance of an A that is B really is. In other words, they are particular, but are not individual judgments. Yet, as we shall hereafter more fully see, and have already in a measure observed, what we want our knowledge to show us about the Being of things, is what Reality, taken as an individual whole, or, again, as *this individual*, finally is. Hence, the particular judgments, — those of external experience viewed as external, — are especially instructive as to the nature that our ordinary thinking attributes to Being, and as to what we demand of our Other.[1]

---

[1] The assertion that purely ideal reasoning processes, viewed as mere internal meanings, never result in particular propositions about their external objects, is one extensively discussed by Schroeder and by many others. See Schroeder, *Algebra der Logik*, Bd. II, p. 86, *sqq*. The defence of the assertion in detail, as a matter of formal Logic, would here take us too far afield. Speaking briefly, one can remind the reader, by the use of a familiar example : (1) That *unless* wisdom is conceived necessarily to follow from the nature of man, you cannot, by " mere reason-

Our situation, then, is, in substance, this: We have
our internal meanings. We develop them in inner experience. There they get presented as something of universal value, but always in fragments. They, therefore,
so far dissatisfy. We conceive of the Other wherein these
meanings shall get some sort of final fulfilment. We
view our ideas as shadows or imitations of this Other;
and we make judgments as to how well they represent it.
When we study the universally expressible aspects of
Reality, we get the sense, — no matter at present how, —
that, in such cases as those of the judgment $2 + 2 = 4$,
we can, in idea, predetermine the constitution of the
external object. But if we look closer, we see that no

ing," find out whether or no *any* man is wise, so long as man is taken to
be an external object. You have to turn to "external experience." If,
in experience, you then find somebody say Socrates to be a wise man, the
matter is empirically settled in favor of the judgment: *Some man is wise.*
But, (2) on the other hand, *even in case* wisdom followed, as an ideally
necessary result, from the mere nature of man, then you would know
indeed, by mere reasoning, that *if* any man exists at all, that man is wise.
But apart from the "external experience" itself, you would still fail to
know, through the "pure ideas," whether there exists indeed any man at
all. And you still could not assert, despite your reasoning, the truth of
the proposition that *some man is wise*, until you had *first* found that man
exists in the realm of the external meanings. All this is an inevitable
consequence of the sundering between the internal and the external
meanings; and holds true so long as the sundering is insisted upon. The
traditional Logic of the text-books, when it reasons from universals to
their subalternate particulars, or derives particular conclusions from universal premises, does so by tacitly and, in general, by unjustifiably assuming the external existence of the objects reasoned about, while all the
time still sundering external and internal. Reasoning itself is, to be
sure, experience, but is, by hypothesis, experience of internal meanings,
not of the external meanings which are taken, by this sort of thinking,
to be the Reality.

such predeterminations involve more than the assertion that Being, as thus predetermined, *excludes* and *forbids* certain of the ideal constructions that, at first, seem possible. But what Being, in so far as it is merely Other and external, positively contains, we cannot thus discover.

How else shall we attempt to discover this desired fulfilment of our purpose? The ordinary answer is, *By external experience.* Now this so-called external experience is never what you might call "Pure Experience." For only the mystic looks for Pure Experience wholly apart from ideas. And we already know what he finds. He is the only thoroughgoing Empiricist; and he has his reward. What is usually called "Experience," by common sense or by science, is not purely immediate content, and it is not whatever happens to come to hand. It is carefully and attentively *selected* experience. It is experience lighted up by ideas. They, as our internal meanings, are incomplete, and they therefore take the form of asking questions. They formulate ideal schemes, and then they inquire, Have these schemes any correspondent facts, yonder, in that externally valid object? The very question is full of ideal presuppositions, which one in vain endeavors to renounce by calling himself a pure empiricist. Unless he is a mystic he is no such pure empiricist. And if he is a mystic, he abhors ideas and frames no hypotheses, except for the sake of merely teaching his doctrine in exoteric fashion. But a scientific empiricist has hypotheses, — internal meanings, ideal constructions, — and he deliberately chooses to submit these to the control of what he views as external experience. If you ask why he does

so, he answers, very rightly, that he has no other road
open to the grasping of yonder "external object." But
this answer means more than an empiricist of this type
usually observes. Wholly inconsistent with any abstract
Realism (which is always metempirical in its actual assumptions), the wish of the ordinary empiricist, however
highly trained his scientific judgment, and however
steadfast his assurance that the idea and its valid object
are somehow sundered aspects of Being, is always simply
to enrich his internal meanings by giving them a selective control which, of their own moving, they cannot find.
Or, in the ordinary phraseology, Man thinks in order to
get control of his world, and thereby of himself. What
the bare internal meanings, in their poverty, leave as an
open question, the external experience shall decide. If
you ask, again, What experience? the answer always is,
Not *any* experience that you please, but a sort of experience determined by the question asked, viz., whatever
experience is apt to decide between conflicting ideas, and
to determine them to precise meaning.

It is customary to dwell upon the "crushing character,"
the "overwhelming power" of "stubborn empirical facts."
The character in question is, of course, a valid one. Yet
this crushing force of experience is never a barely immediate fact; it is something relative to the particular ideas
in question. For, as I must repeat, our so-called external
experience, that is, our experience taken as other than
our meanings, and viewed as what confirms or refutes
them here or there, never does more, in any question concerning the truth, than to decide our ideal issues, and to
decide them in particular instances, whose character and

meaning for us are determined solely by what ideas of our own are in question. Or, again, empirical judgments, as such, are always particular. Hence, they never by themselves absolutely confirm, or refute, *all* that our ideas mean. And what they confirm, or refute, depends upon what questions have been asked from the side of our internal meanings.

The empirical facts can, indeed, refute, and they very often do refute, abstractly stated universal judgments, by showing particular cases that contradict these judgments. But they can never show, by themselves, that the ideas in question have *no* application, anywhere, in yonder externally valid world, but only that in some case just these ideas fail. Hence, unless I have ideally chosen to stake my all upon a single throw of the dice of " external experience," I am not logically " crushed " by the particular experience that this time disappoints me. If my internal meaning takes, for instance, the form of a plan of external action, I can, if this time defeated, " try again "; and the human will has in all ages shown its power *not* to be crushed by any particular experience, unless its ideas determine that it ought to accept the defeat. Ideas can be quite as stubborn as any particular facts, can outlast them, and often, in the end, abolish them. Even if the internal meaning is a merely imitative conception, that, like a scientific hypothesis, was solely intended to portray the nature of the external fact, then the empirical failure of the hypothesis, in a given instance, shows, indeed, that it is not universally valid as regards yonder external world of finally valid fact, but does *not* show that it is universally *in*valid.

Experience, taken as external and particular, can never prove any absolute negation.

On the other hand, but for the very same reason, our experience, when taken as in contrast to our internal meanings, can never, in any finite time, completely confirm or demonstrate any universal judgment, such as, upon the basis of our internal meanings, we may have asserted. *Some* A *is* B. That is all that your experience, when viewed as other than your ideas, and as that to which you appeal for the sake of defining your external object, can ever by itself reveal. Herein lies the well-known limitation of the merely " inductive " processes of science. That we all believe universal propositions about yonder external world of valid objects, is due to the fact that we are none of us mere empiricists, even in this modified sense. All of us view *some* of our ideas as predetermining the nature of things, so that we conceive the reality as the fulfilment of distinctly internal meanings, — with what right we have yet to see.

All of these considerations arise in a realm where internal and external meanings, without ever being viewed as abstractly independent of one another, are still taken as actually and rightly sundered. And this, as we have now seen, is the case throughout the world of our Third Conception. All who use this conception, that is, all who once learn rationally to modify their Realism, while still regarding the antithesis of internal and of external as finally valid, employ the two main types of judgment which we have now examined. When the mathematicians use the existential judgments, of which we before have spoken, they, too, employ the particular judgments and appeal to what, for their current ideas, constitutes a relatively external realm of experience. When, believing that their own science, too, has become exact, the students of nature, in their turn, use universal judgments; they just as truly appeal, for their sole warrant, to internal meanings, as do the mathematicians when the latter think about universal truth.

As to these two types of judgment, the universal and the particular, they both, as we have seen, make use of experience. The one type, the universal judgments, arise in the realm where experience and idea have already fused into one whole; and this is precisely the realm of internal meanings. Here one constructs, and observes the consequences of one's construction. But the construction is at once an experience of fact, and an idea; at once an expression of a purpose, and an observation of what happens. Upon the basis of such ideal constructions, one makes universal judgments. These, in a fashion still to us, at this stage, mysterious, undertake to be valid of that other world, — the world of external meanings, the realm that is said to be the Reality of which these ideas are the shadow and imitation. But every assertion of this sort implies that in verity the external and the internal meanings are not sundered, but have some deeper unity, which, in this realm of mere validity, you can never make manifest. Meanwhile, this control of idea over fact is, indeed, here viewed as limited. The ideal necessities only determine what the facts are not, and not what the facts are.

On the other hand, since this realm of internal meanings is, in us men, limited and fragmentary, one indeed seeks to enlarge its realm.   And in doing so one appeals to what is called the external experience; and hereupon one makes those particular judgments which are the typical expression of our human sort of external experience. But this is experience so far as it has not yet fused with the internal meanings; but so far as, nevertheless, through selection and through patient effort, it can gradually be brought to the point where it decides ideal issues.   As other than the ideas, this experience is said to be the evidence and the expression of the external objects themselves.   Yet these objects, for the awakened reason, are no longer "things in themselves." Their contrast with the world of "mere ideas" is, indeed, here insisted upon; but we have plainly, so far, no final account of what the contrast is.

III

Yet there remains one further aspect of this whole situation of our judging thought, — an aspect upon which sufficient stress has not been laid.   We have said, as against this Third Conception of Being, that at best it leaves Reality too much a bare abstract universal, and does not assert the individuality of Being.   We have still to express this objection in a more formal way.   As we have seen, all our universal and particular judgments leave Reality, in a measure, indeterminate.   Can we tolerate this view of Reality as final?

Ideas, as such, take, we have said, the abstractly universal form.   External experience, as such, in this realm where we find it sundered from the internal meanings, confirms or refutes ideas in particular cases.   But do

ideas, in so far as they merely imitate or seek their external Other, ever express what common sense often means
by calling that external object an Individual?   Or, on
the other hand, does the external experience ever, as
such, present to us individuals, and show them to us *as*
individuals?[1]

If this question is put simply as an appeal to common
sense, the answer will be unhesitating.   Who does not
know that our knowledge "begins with individual
facts?"   The child "knows its nurse or its mother or
its own playthings first.   Only later does it learn the
universal characters of things."   The individual, then,
is the well known, the familiar, the *first* in Knowledge
and in Being.

This theory, as usually stated, is simply full of incon-
sequences and inaccuracies that I cannot here undertake
to follow out.   Of course, what a child first knows are
objects that we, with our common-sense metaphysic, call
individual things; but there is every evidence that he
knows them by virtue of their characters, their qualities,
their recognizable, and, for that very reason, abstractly
universal features.   All animals adjust themselves to the
what of their world, and pursue or shun objects because
of their odor, taste, color, form, touch-qualities, fashion
of movement, — in brief, because of features that are common to many objects and experiences and that, in so far
as we can empirically make out, are not, except by accident, confined to an individual being or experience.   A

---

[1] I have discussed this point at length in the " Supplementary Essay "
of the book called *The Conception of God*.   See Part III of that Essay,
pp. 217–271.

child's early vagueness in applying names, his "calling of all men and women fathers and mothers,"[1] as Aristotle already observed, shows that our primary consciousness is of the vaguely universal.

And now, not only is this true as to the genesis of our knowledge, but, to the end, it remains true of us mortals that, *Neither do our internal meanings ever present to us, nor yet do our external experiences ever produce before us, for our inspection, an object whose individuality we ever really know as such.* Neither internal meanings nor external meanings, in their isolation, are in the least adequate to embody individuality.

For an individual is unique. There is no other of its individual kind. If Socrates is an individual, then there is only one Socrates in the universe. If you are an individual, then in Reality there is no other precisely capable of taking your place. If God is an individual, then, as ethical monotheism began by saying, *There is no Other.*

Now, by taking note in thought of this supposed uniqueness, you can, of course, in general, define, as a sort of problem to be solved by real Beings, the ideal and abstract nature of individuality itself. But then, you do not, in that case, tell what constitutes any one individual such as he is. But now change the statement of the problem. Try to define, in idea, some one individual, real or fictitious, *e.g.* Achilles, or Socrates, or the universe. At once, when you define, your idea, as an internal meaning, presents to you a combination of characters such as, according to your definition, some Other, *i.e.* some object external to the idea, might embody. In consequence,

---

[1] Aristotle, *Phys.*, Bk. I, 1.

however, the possibility of characterizing, or portraying, the features that are to make yonder external individual unique, has been surrendered in the very act of trying to define what constitutes him an individual. For your object is another, and you here, by hypothesis, know it merely through ideally imitating it and "corresponding" to it. But as individual, the unique Being is to be precisely something that *has no likeness.* Hence, just so far as you define it, you define of it everything but its individuality. Socrates defined, is no longer the unique external meaning, — the individual Being as such. He has now become a mere conceived type of man. That this type has but one real expression, you may, from the side of your internal meanings, dogmatically assert or inevitably presuppose. But you can never tell what, about that kind of man called Socrates, forbids him to get repeated expression in the universe, unless you have expressed the secret of Being in terms different from those involved in this sundering of the external and the internal meanings. The same is true if you try thus abstractly to define what makes either God or the world One Individual, that has no likeness.

But if ideas, as internal meanings opposed to external objects, cannot express the nature of the individuality of the world or of any one Being in it, whence, then, do we ever get this belief that Being is, in fact, individual? Does perhaps our external experience present to us individuals? The answer is again simply, *No.* If, when you define Socrates in inner idea, you define a type of man, and not an unique Being without any likeness, it is equally true that, if ever you had an experience which

made you say, *Here is Socrates*, you would have present
to yourself but, once more, a *type* of empirically observed
man, — a *kind* of experience. When you daily meet your
family and friends, you constantly confirm your internal
meanings by external experiences; but the confirmation,
read accurately, is always a confirmation of ideal types
by *particular* cases, never by really *individual* Beings
directly known as present and yet as unique. You presuppose that your family and friends are individual
Beings. The presupposition may be, yes, to my mind is,
justifiable in the light of a genuine metaphysic. But it
is an essentially metaphysical presupposition, never verifiable by your external experience. In this presupposition lies the very mystery of Being. The *what* is
abstractly universal. The *that* is individual. You
have an idea of your friend. You go to meet him; and
lo, the idea is verified. Yes; but what is verified? I
answer, this, that you have met a certain type of empirical object. "But my friend is unique. There is no
other who has his voice, manner, behavior." "Yes; but
how should your personal experience verify that? Have
you seen all beings in heaven and earth?" Perhaps you
reply, "Yes; but human experience in general shows
that every man is an individual, unique, and without
any absolute likeness." If such is your reply, you are
appealing to general inductive methods. I admit their
significance. But I deny that they rest solely upon external experience, as such, for their warrant. They
presuppose a metaphysic. They do not prove one.
Besides, you are now talking of general principles, and
not of any one verified individual.

In fact, how should any one individual Being present himself, in this external experience of yours, or of all men taken together, in such wise as to show not only that he is of this or this aspect, but that *no other* is like him in the whole realm of Being. It is this *no-Other*-character that persistently baffles both the merely internal meaning, and the merely external experience, so long as they are human and are sundered.

And, now, just this difficulty gives one further reason why our Third Conception of Being, in conflict with common sense, does, indeed, abandon the concept that Being is individual, and confines itself to forming internal meanings, and to confirming them by external experience. It tries to rest content with abstract universals, more or less determined by particular observations.

Yet, in doing thus, can this conception satisfy even the fragmentary internal meanings that we so far sunder from their external objects, and that we then seek to confirm or to refute by external experience? No; for if we can neither abstractly define within, nor yet empirically find without, the individuals that we seek, there can be no doubt that our whole interest in Being, is an interest in individuality. For the Other that we seek is that which, if found, would *determine our ideas to their final truth*. Now, only what is finally determinate can, in its turn, determine. As a fact, while we never abstractly define individuals as such, we certainly love individuals, believe in individuals, and regard the truth with which we are to correspond as determinate. So much is this the case, that whoever should try, as, in fact, our Third Conception of Being seems to try, to define the world of Being in terms exclusive of individuality, seems forced to say, "The final fact is that there is no individual fact, or, in other words, that there is no unique Being at all, but only a type; so that the Being with which our thoughts are to correspond does not determine the 'mere ideas' to any single and unique correspondence with itself, but leaves them finally indeterminate." But is the *Veritas* that is thus left us any *Veritas* at all? Is not the very expression used self-contradictory? Can the absence of finality be the only final fact?

Our general survey of the world of judgments and of reasoning processes, as well as of the accompanying relations between Thought and Experience, is on one side completed. What have we learned? Our survey has not yet solved the problem as to the whole nature of Truth, but has shown us very important features that must, indeed, belong to the inmost essence of the Other that we seek. For one thing, we have found that every step towards Truth *is a step away from vague possibilities, and towards determinateness of idea and of experience.* Our very ideas themselves, even when expressed as hypotheses, or as universal definitions, or as *a priori* mathematical constructions, or as judgments of hypothetical or of universal type, are from the outset *destructive of vague possibilities*, and involve *Determination by Negation*. That is what every step of our survey has shown. Being, then, viewed as Truth, is to be in any case *something determinate, that excludes as well as includes.*

As to the vastly important relation of Thought to external Experience, we have seen that our thought, indeed, looks to this external experience to decide whether our hypotheses about fact can be confirmed. But, on the other hand, while external experience, in confirming ideas, furnishes a positive content which our human internal meanings never can construct for themselves, still the service of our external experience, in revealing what is Real, has perfectly obvious limitations. It can confirm our hypotheses, but never adequately; for it shows us only particular instances that agree with such of our hypotheses as succeed. It can refute our hasty ideal generalizations, but only when they are stated as universal propositions. It can never by itself prove a determinate negative by excluding from Reality *the whole* of what our hypotheses have defined. Hence, our will has its limitless opportunity to "try again"; and external experience never finally disposes of ideas unless the ideas themselves make, for reasons defensible upon the ground of internal meaning only, their own "reasonable" surrender. And, finally, our experience, whether internal or external, never shows us what we, above all, regard as the Real, namely, the Individual fact. Hence, in consulting experience, we are simply seeking aid in the undertaking to give our ideas a certain positive determination, to *this content and no other*. But never, in our human process of experience, do we reach that determination. It is for us the object of love and of hope, of desire and of will, of faith and of work, but never of present finding.

This Individual Determination itself remains, so far, the principal character of the Real; and is, as an ideal, the Limit towards which we endlessly aim. Now, a Limit, in mathematics, may have either one or both of two characters.[1]   It may be that which a given process so approaches that we ourselves are able to get and to remain *near at will* to, — that is, less than any predesignated distance from, — the limit, although the process in question, by itself, never reaches the limit.   So we can get as near as we choose to 2, by adding terms of the series $1 + \frac{1}{2} + \frac{1}{4}$, etc.   Or, again, in the second place, the limit may be defined as that which, never attained by the process in question, is demonstrably a finality that occupies, in order, *the first place immediately beyond* the whole series of incomplete stages which the endless process in question defines.   Thus, 2 is *the least number that lies beyond,* or that is *greater than all possible fractions,* of the form $1 + \frac{1}{2}$, $1 + \frac{1}{2} + \frac{1}{4}$, $1 + \frac{1}{2} + \frac{1}{4} + \frac{1}{8}$, etc.   Usually, in mathematics, both senses of *limit* are combined (as they are in the example just used).   But not so in the case here before us.   Being is not an object that we men come *near at will* to finally observing, so that while we never get it wholly present in our internal meanings, we can come as near as we like to telling all that it is.   But the Real, as our judgments and empirical investigations seek it, is that determinate object which all our ideas and experiences try to decide upon, and to bring within the range of our internal meanings; while, by the very nature of our fragmentary hypotheses and of our particular experiences, it always lies Beyond.

Yet *if we could* reach that limit of determination which

---

[1] See Georg Cantor, in the *Zeitschrift f. Philosophie und Philosophische Kritik*, Bd. 91, p. 110.   The finite limit of a "convergent series" has both characters.   But the "determinate infinite," viewed as the limit of the whole-number-series, has only the latter of the two characters.

is all the while our goal, if our universal judgments were confirmed by an adequate experience, not of *some* object (still indeterminate), but of *the individual* object, or of *all the individual objects*, so that no other empirical expression of our ideas remained possible, then, indeed, we should stand in the immediate presence of the Real. The Real, then, is, from this point of view, that which is *immediately beyond* the whole of our series of possible efforts to bring, by any process of finite experience and of merely general conception, our own internal meaning to a complete determination.

Abstract as this result is, it is already of great significance. It shows us what the Third Conception lacks, namely, a view of the Real as the finally determinate that permits no other. It also shows that the mere sundering of external and internal meanings is somehow faulty. Their linkage is the deepest fact about the universe.

And thus the *first* of the two closing stages of our journey is done. We have learned how the internal meaning is related to its own Limit, in so far as that is just a limit. But thus to view Being is still not to take account of what seems to common sense the most important of all our relations to the Real. And that is the relation of *Correspondence*, — several times heretofore mentioned, but not yet fathomed. "We must not only seek Being as our goal, but we must correspond to its real constitution if we are to get the truth. And somehow it *has* that constitution. We have to submit. The Real may not be wholly independent of our thinking, but it is at least authoritative." So common sense states the case. But that aspect of the matter, as I repeat, we have not yet fathomed.   To complete our definition of Reality, we must undertake to do so.   And here, at last, the sundering of external from internal meaning receives its final test.   Must not that to which our thought has to conform, whether it will or no, remain wholly external to thought itself?   We shall see.   And when we see this, our goal will at last be attained.

IV

A time-honored definition of Truth declares it to mean the *Correspondence between any Idea and its Object.*   The mystery that everybody feels to lie hidden behind this definition depends upon the fact that two relations, both of a very intangible sort, are implied by this definition, and that the combination of these two relations is required to constitute truth.   If an idea is true, it must, in the first place, *have an object.* ˌBut what constitutes the relation called *having an object?*   When is an object the object of a given idea?   And, secondly, the idea must *correspond* with its object.   But what is the relation called *correspondence?*   Until recently, the whole theory of the nature of correspondence remained an extremely undeveloped, although an obviously fundamental conception of Logic.   And still more neglected has been the conception of the relation that constitutes any supposed object the genuine object of an idea, whether the idea be true or false.   As to the problem about correspondence, how much must an idea resemble its object in order to be true?   A photograph resembles the man whom it pictures.   Must a true idea be even so a sort of photograph of its object?   Or, perhaps, may an idea be very unlike an object, and still so correspond therewith as to be a true idea? Are not the items in a ledger very unlike the commercial transactions that they ideally depict? And yet may not the items in the ledger be true? The nature, then, and the degree of that correspondence between idea and object which is meant when one talks of the truth of an idea, is a doubtful matter, and we shall have to consider it more closely. As to the other one of these two problems about idea and object, it seems plain, and in fact seems to be implied in the very definition of truth, that an idea can have an object without rightly corresponding to its object. For how otherwise should falsity and error be possible? To have an object and to correspond to it are therefore different relations. What, then, is the nature of the relation that makes a given idea such as to have a given object, whether or no the idea truly represents the object? These two problems are, then, the two aspects of the general question, What is Truth? regarded now from the side of the correspondence between internal and external.

Let us next attack the first of these two questions. If an idea is to be correspondent to an object, our first impression is that the idea must always possess some one predestined sort or degree of likeness or similarity to its object. Is this necessary? Is it once for all predetermined that its object, as a finished fact, required the idea to be like it? The relation of correspondence, in general, apart from the special problem about ideas and objects, has been most elaborately studied in mathematics, where correspondence is, in the most various forms, a constant topic of exact inquiry. If you have before you two objects, say two curves, or two variable quantities, or two collections of objects, — one of them a collection of symbols, the other a collection of objects to be symbolized, — a relation of correspondence can be established, or assumed, between these two objects, or collections, in the most manifold and, in one sense, in the most arbitrary fashion. Necessary to the relations of correspondence is only this, that you shall be able to view the two corresponding objects together, in a one-to-one relation, or in some other definite way, and, with some single purpose in mind, shall then be able in some one perhaps very limited aspect to affirm of one of them the same that you, at the same time and in the same limited sense, affirm of the other. In consequence, with reference to this one affirmation, you could in some specified wise substitute one of them for the other, whole for whole, part for part, element for element. Thus, if you have before you a collection of counters, and a collection of other objects, you can make these collections correspond, if you are able to arrange both sets of objects in a definite order, and then to say, that the first of your counters agrees with the first of your other objects precisely, and perhaps solely, in being the first of its series; while the second counter agrees with the second of the objects precisely in being the second of the series, and so on. The result will then be that by counting the counters, you can afterwards, perhaps more conveniently, enumerate the objects to be counted. Ordinary counting depends, in fact, upon making the members of a number series, one, two, three, four, etc., arbitrarily correspond to the distinguishable objects of the collection that you number. The result is, then, that by adding, subtracting, or otherwise operating upon the numbers, you can reach results that will be valid regarding the objects that were to be counted. Again, a given plane curve can be made to correspond, point for point, with its own shadow, or with some other systematic projection of the curve as made upon a given surface. In this case, a great number of relationships between the points of the curve will remain true of the corresponding points of the projected curve. In the very familiar case of a map, the parts of the map correspond to the parts of the object represented, in a manner determined by a particular system of projection or of transformation of object into map.

But in consequence of the very general nature of this relation of correspondence, two complicated objects, or two collections of objects, may be made to correspond to one another, part for part, member for member, in wholly different ways. When you count objects, for instance, it makes no difference in what order you count them, or, in other words, in what order you make them correspond, object for object, to your number series. When you draw maps, you may use either Mercator's projection, or some other plan of map-making. In any case, you can still get a definite correspondence of map and object, part for part, although, by varying the plan of projection followed, you may vary the way in which the correspondence used in any one case will prove useful in measuring distances, or in plotting courses on the map once drawn. Any sort of correspondence thus always fulfils one definite purpose, such as the purpose of counting, of map-drawing upon some special plan, or of constructing projections of curves, or of otherwise systematically transforming one set of relationships into another set. But if this special purpose is fulfilled, the correspondence in question is accomplished, and is said to hold true. But in any case, as you now see, correspondence does not necessarily imply, just as it does not exclude, any such common characters in the two corresponding objects, as makes you say that one of the two objects resembles the other in mere external appearance. A photograph looks like the man; a map may look, in outline, like the land mapped. But numbers and the symbols of an algebra no longer seem to our senses at all like the objects defined by these symbolic devices for establishing correspondence; and the accounts in the ledger, while very systematically corresponding, item for item, to the commercial transactions, are very unlike them in immediate interest and in sensible appearance. There is, then, no degree of unlikeness in appearance between two objects which excludes a correspondence — and even the most exact and instructive sort of correspondence — between one object and the other. What is involved in correspondence is the possession, on the part of the corresponding objects, of some system of ideally definable characters that is common to both of them, that is, for the purposes of our thought, the same in both of them, and that is such as to meet the systematic purpose for which the particular correspondence is established.

So much, then, for the relation of correspondence, viewed by itself. If we apply this consideration to the case of the definition of truth, we see that, for the first, a true idea, in corresponding to its object, need not in the least be confined to any particular sort or degree of general similarity to its object. The similarity may be as close or as remote, as sensuously interesting or as abstractly formal as you please. A scientific idea about colors need not be itself a color, nor yet an image involving colors. Or, to state the case in a very crude instance, a true idea of a dog need not itself bark in order to be true. On the contrary, photographs, and wax images, and toy dogs that bark, may correspond to the imitated objects in fashions that are of very little use in framing such ideas as are at once of scientific grade and of a given desired type of correspondence to their objects. The photographs, to be sure, help one to form scientifically valuable ideas far more frequently than does a wax image. But you cannot photograph the solar system, nor yet the constitution of a molecule. Yet you may have symbolically expressed ideas that correspond much more exactly to certain special truths about the solar system and the molecule than any ordinary photographs ever correspond to even the most important visible features of certain of their objects. The modern X-ray photographs very crudely reveal the internal structure of certain solid objects; but a trained student of anatomy of the brain has largely symbolic ideas of its structure which far exceed, in value of their correspondence to their object, all that can ever be hoped for from the X-ray photographs of a brain. In general, the photograph gives us at its best very one-sided ideas of visible objects. It is the aim of science to win ideas that intimately correspond, in however symbolic a fashion, to certain desired aspects of the structure of their objects; and without systems of such more symbolic ideas to aid in our interpretation of what we at any time merely see, such sensible ideas as photographs suggest remain, in general, very imperfect beginnings of a scientific insight into objects.

But what, then, is the test of the truthful correspondence of an idea to its object, if object and idea can differ so widely? The only answer is in terms of Purpose. The idea is true if it possesses the sort of correspondence to its object that the idea itself wants to possess. Unless that kind of identity in inner structure between idea and object can be found which the specific purpose embodied in a given idea demands, the idea is false. On the other hand, if this particular sort of identity is to be found, the idea is just in so far true. The identity that suffices to establish a sufficient correspondence must, then, be, like the identity found in two correspondent curves (as, for instance, in a given curve and in its projection), or like the identity discoverable when you compare the map with the region to which the map corresponds, — it must be, I say, an identity serving some conscious end, fulfilling an intent, possessing a value for your will. Such identity is, in the more abstract sciences, often confined to an agreement in certain very general relationships. It is, then, usually the sort of identity that the scholastics often called analogy, *i.e.* equivalence merely as to the common possession of certain relationships which permit the idea, for a specific purpose, as in a computation, a calculus, or in any system of ideal constructive processes, to act as a substitute, to take the place of its object. But the identity desired may, indeed, also be of a more sensuous type. If so, then, indeed, the idea must sensuously resemble its object. The desired identity may, as in a case of a photograph, involve visible similarities. So the visual image of your absent friend may, indeed, resemble him in seeming, and the desired identity may, as in the ideas that accompany the actions of people who sing or who play in concert, involve musically interesting agreements and harmonies. Or, again, your idea may be one that, like the sympathetic ideas with which two friends accompany each other's sentiments, intends to involve an identity in emotional attitudes. But however the intention varies, always the test of truth is the same. Is the correspondence reached between idea and object the precise correspondence that the idea itself intended? If it is, the idea is true. If it is not, the idea is in so far false. Thus it is not mere agreement, but intended agreement, that constitutes truth.

Do you want the image to look like its object? If so, your mental image is a true idea when, like the photograph, it looks like its object; and it is a false representative of its object if, like a poor visual image, it is dim, blurred, and, for its representative purpose, consequently deceitful. But do you want your idea, like a series of numbers, or like a statistical diagram, or like a certain mathematical transformation of given curves and surfaces, *not* to look like its object, but to have a wholly different sort of correspondence, member for member, part for part, point for point, relation for relation, to its object? Then, not similarity of sensible seeming, but precisely the fulfilment of whatever intent was in mind, is the test of the truth of the idea. And, then, the idea would be false in case it did look too much like its object. Do you intend

to sing in tune? Then your musical ideas are false if
they lead you to strike what are, then, called false notes.
But do you want to study acoustics? Then your ideas
of sound are false unless they involve correct inner constructions of the physical relations of sound waves, and
that, too, however fine your musical skill, and however
vivid and accurate your musical imagination may be.
In that case mere accurate images of tones would be false
acoustical ideas.

In vain, then, does one stand apart from the internal
meaning, from the conscious inner purpose embodied in a
given idea, and still attempt to estimate whether or no
that idea corresponds with its object. There is no purely
external criterion of truth. You cannot merely look from
without upon an ideal construction and say whether or
no it corresponds to its object. Every finite idea has
to be judged by its own specific purpose. Ideas are like
tools. They are there for an end. They are true, as the
tools are good, precisely by reason of their adjustment to
this end. To ask me which of two ideas is the more
nearly true, is like asking me which of two tools is the
better tool. The question is a sensible one if the purpose
in mind is specific, but not otherwise. One razor can
be superior to another. But let a man ask, Is a razor a
better or worse tool than a hammer? Is a steam-engine
a better mechanism than a loom? Such questions are
obviously vain, just because they suggest that there is
some one purely abstract test of the value of any and all
tools, or some one ideal tool that, if you had it, would
be good apart from any specific use. Yet there are
philosophers who ask, and even suppose themselves to

answer, questions about the truth of ideas that are just as vain as this.

When Mr. Spencer, according to the tradition of the long series of thinkers whom he in this respect follows, speaks, in a well-known passage, of "symbolic" ideas as essentially inferior in the conscious definiteness of their truth to ideas whose relation to their objects we can directly picture, he applies a criterion to the testing of ideas which is as crude as if one should argue that a razor is not as good a tool as a hammer, because, forsooth, the test of a tool shall be its weight, or the amount of noise that you can make when you use it. Many admirable ideas are, indeed, of the type of mental pictures. That is not only obvious, but worth remembering. There is no reason why such images should not be both valid and important. Sensuous experience may show you many sorts of truth that we cannot at present otherwise express. A man who sees a photograph sees truth, if he is intelligent enough to observe it. A man who sings a tune sings truth, if he is thoughtful enough to know what he is doing. And imageless abstractions, or algebraic symbols, are, indeed, not true by reason of their mere poverty of sensuous life. But, on the other hand, algebraic symbols are, for precisely the purposes of algebra, actually superior, as representations of objects, to any pictures of these objects. And this is not because by any chance we cannot picture the objects, but because, for this end, the symbols are truer than the pictures. The constructions of mathematics are oftener like razors, ideal tools that are all the better for their lack of bulk and grossness, and for the almost invisible fineness of their edge. When you count, it is symbols that you want, not pictures. Hence, the numbers are for your purpose superior to photographs; and the entries in the ledger give a better record of their own aspect of the commercial transactions than a legion of phonographs and kinetoscopes, set up in a shop to record transactions, could, by any perfection of literal reproductions, retain. Symbols, then, are not in the least less definitely and, on occasion, less obviously, consciously, empirically true, or correspondent to their objects, than are, for their own purpose, the most vivid of mental pictures. An idea, again, is true, as a chess player is skilful, or as an artist is powerful, or as a practical man is effective. The question always is, Can the player win his chosen game, the artist succeed in his own selected art, the practical man accomplish his own task, and not the task of some other man? And precisely so the question is, Does the idea win in its own deliberately chosen game of correspondence to its object?

And so we conclude that the object does not, as a finished fact, predetermine the sort of likeness that the idea must possess in order to be true. It is the idea that so far decides its own meaning. And I may once more point out that in all this you may see afresh why, from the opening lecture of this course, I have laid such stress upon the essentially teleological inner structure of conscious ideas, and why I defined ideas as I did in our opening lecture, namely, as cases where conscious states more or less completely present the embodiment, the relative fulfilment of a present purpose. Whatever else our ideas are, and however much or little they may be, at any moment, expressed in rich, sensuous imagery, it is certain that they are ideas not because they are masses or series of images, but because they embody present conscious purposes. Every idea is as much a volitional process as it is an intellectual process. It may well or ill represent or correspond to something not itself, but it must, in any case, make more or less clearly articulate its own present purpose. The constructive character of all mathematical ideas, the sense of current control which accompanies all definite thinking processes, the momentary purposes more or less imperfectly fulfilled whenever we conceive anything, — these are evidences of what is essential to processes of ideation. Volition is as manifest in counting objects as in singing tunes, in conceiving physical laws as in directing the destinies of nations, in laboratory experiments as in artistic productions, in contemplating as in fighting. The embodied purpose, the internal meaning, of the instant's act, is thus a *conditio sine qua non* for all external meaning and for all truth. What we are now inquiring is simply how an internal meaning can be linked to an external meaning, how a volition can also possess truth, how the purpose of the instant can express the nature of an object other than the instant's purpose.

V

So much, then, for the relation of correspondence between idea and object. But, now, when has an idea an object at all? This question, as I before observed, has been decidedly more neglected in fundamental discussions about truth than has the question as to the

nature of the desired correspondence to the object. That
which makes an object the object of a given idea has too
frequently been considered from the side of an accepted
and uncriticised ontological, or, possibly, psychological
theory as to the causation and origin of ideas. The object
of any idea is, for many of the older theories of knowledge, that which arouses, awakens, brings to pass, the
idea in question. The old Aristotelian metaphor of the
seal impressing its form upon the wax is here the familiar
means of exemplifying how an object becomes such by
impressing its nature upon the ideas that it arouses.
The sun shines, a light enters a man's eyes, and the man,
looking up, sees the sun. Thereupon the sun becomes
the object of his ideas. One touches and handles objects;
they impress upon him their solidity and their tangible
form. Thereupon they furnish the basis for further ideas.
Or, again, a distant object is dimly seen. It comes
nearer and nearer, and is found to be some particular
object. When it was distant it was already the object of
ideas, because, affecting one's sense of sight, it roused
curiosity. As it approaches, these ideas are confirmed
or refuted by further observation, and, according to the
sort of correspondence with their object that they undertook to have, they then turn out to be true or false.

In all such accounts of the relation of idea and object, the
existence of the object is presupposed as something well
understood. And not only is this presupposition made,
but the whole existence of the so-called external world,
the existence, too, of the relation called the relation of
causality between the object and the perceiving subject,
yes, the very Being of the subject itself, as an entity that

is supposed to be by nature apt to perceive objects when it is awakened through their presence, — all these very important ontological conceptions are assumed in order to define the special conditions under which a given object becomes the object of the ideas of a given person. Now, of course, we are not concerned here either to accept or to refute these presuppositions of so many theories of knowledge. We have only in passing to observe that these theories cannot help us in our present inquiry. We are now asking what is, by the Being of anything whatever, by the very Reality that one attributes to world or to soul, to causality or to sense organs. In pursuing this inquiry we have been led to a point where the reality of things means for us some condition or ground, whatever it be, — whether conscious or extra-conscious we know not yet, — some genuine basis or guarantee which gives to our ideas their truth. We have thus been led to ask directly, What is Truth? Into this question our question, What is Being? has transformed itself. The word "Truth," however, appears, in traditional language, as a name for something called the correspondence of an idea with an object. And thus it is that we have been brought to face the problem, When has an idea an object? Our effort at present is to see whether we cannot define the Being of things by first defining their relation, as objects, to ideas. We cannot, then, hope to define, for our present purpose, the character of our objects, viewed as objects of ideas, by first presupposing their Being, and the Being of the whole physical world. No doubt there is this world, — but in what sense it is, that is precisely our problem.

Moreover, the view that in order to be object of a given idea, the object must be cause of the idea, or that ideas have to look to their own causes as their objects, is refuted, as a general definition, by a glance at the nature of all those temporal objects of which we have ideas, but which are not now present in time. Is anything in the future, say my own death, or an eclipse due next year, or futurity in general, the cause of my present ideas, true or false, that refer to any such object. When I form a plan, or sign a contract, the hypothetical future event defined by the plan or contemplated in the contract is said, in the familiar Aristotelian phraseology, to be the final cause of the present act, but it certainly is not a cause impressing itself upon knowledge as the seal imprints its form upon the wax. Yet Aristotle, to whom final causation meant at bottom everything, also loves far too much the trivial seal and wax metaphor as his customary means for defining the general relations of object and idea; so much deeper was Aristotle's thought than his phraseology! Even the Nous of Aristotle knows through some sort of so-called touching of its intelligible objects.

But if one attempts to escape from these just-mentioned considerations about the future objects of present ideas, by declaring that the future has as yet no real Being at all, and that it therefore is no real, but only an imagined, object of present ideas, I should, indeed, not in the least accept the objection as valid, but I should for the moment only ask the objector what he thinks about the whole realm of past Being. The most noticeable feature of the past is that it is irrevocable. This character of the past, viz., that it is gone beyond recall, is regarded by us all as objectively valid ; and so it is the object of present ideas. But now I ask, in all seriousness, what is the irrevocable past now doing to our ideas that the fact of its irrevocable absence should, as cause, now be viewed as moulding our ideas ? By means of what stamping process is the seal of the past impressing its form upon the wax of the present ideas ? The irrevocable character of the past is a fact that can become object of an idea only by not being any present cause of ideas at all, since to be irrevocable means to be temporally over and done with altogether. If one says, " But past events were the causes that have led to present events, and that is why we now have ideas of the past," then I should reply: " You miss the point altogether ; not in so far as they occurred, and were causes that led up to present events, not in so far as they were real causes at all, but in so far as they can never occur again, are those past events now viewed as irrevocable." Yet to say, " Those past events can never occur again," is to utter an objective truth, unless indeed all our human view of time is false. But how can the mere truth that an event can never occur again be a cause at all ? Still more, how can it cause me to have ideas of itself ? What, once more, does the irrevocableness of the past do to me when I think of it ? Or do you say, " Our idea of the irrevocable character of the past is in truth only a sort of generalization from our many experiences of physically irrevocable happenings, such as the breaking of china, the spilling of milk, the flight of youth, and all the other proverbial instances of the past that return not " ? Then I answer : If our idea that the past is wholly irrevocable were the result of such

empirical instances, — if, I say, this explanation, which I
hold to be false, were correct, all the more would it be
plain that what causes an idea is not, as such, the object
of the idea, for it is not of broken china, nor of spilled
milk, nor even of lost youth that one thinks in announc-
ing the view that the past is irrevocable, — but of what
one supposes to be an universal law of all time, which one
applies as well to the repeated sequence of the monotonous beats of the pendulum, or to the waves that break
over and over upon the beach, as to youth, or even to
death.   For even of the monotonously repeated series of
events, one asserts that each individual case of the repetition is irrevocable when past.   Even if one's view as to
this matter were false, one's object would here be a character of the whole of time, and a character which is certainly no cause of present ideas.

It is hopeless, then, to persist in the hypothesis that the
object of an idea is as such the cause of the idea.   Were one
to persist in such a view, what would he say about all the
mathematical objects?   Does the binomial theorem act
as a seal, or any other sort of cause, impressing its image
on the wax of a mathematician's mind?   Do the properties of equations do anything to the mathematician when
he thinks of them?   Is not all the fresh creative activity
in this case his own?

VI

Nearer to our desired definition we may come if we
next observe the reason for the plausibility of the usual
appeal to the objects of vision and touch as the typical
cases of objects of ideas.   For, in fact, nobody can doubt

that the pen in my hand, or the sun in the heavens, or the sail on the horizon, may be genuine objects of ideas ; and why do these instances seem so typical of the whole relation of idea and object? I answer, because, in case of these objects, a very typical feature of the relation of idea and object is indeed manifest enough. That an idea has an object depends at least in part upon this, that the idea selects its object. And selection is manifested in consciousness by what is usually called attention, while attention to objects of sense is something very obvious and easy to estimate. Into the intricacies of the psychological theory of attention, we have not here to go. Enough, one who attends, whatever the causal explanation of his process, is, as to the nature and trend of his meaning, selective. And the ideas of an attentive consciousness are the embodiments of such selection. Whatever type or correspondence is involved in the purpose of a given idea, it is then not enough, in case you wish to confirm or to refute the idea, that you should point out how the desired correspondence is to be found, or fails to be found, anywhere that you please or anywhere at random in the world. For the idea must be confirmed or refuted by comparison with the object that the idea itself means, selects, views with attentive expectation, determines as its own object. And while this selection is not merely a subjective matter, left to the mere caprice of the idea itself, certain it is, that in order to find out what the truth of a man's ideas is, you must take account not merely of the sort of correspondence that he intends to attain in the presence of his object, but of the selection that he himself has made of the object by which he wishes his idea to be

judged.   Now this selection involves what we have called
the inner meaning of the idea.   Just as truly as the sort
of correspondence by which an idea is to be judged is predetermined by the internal meaning of the idea, just so
truly is the internal meaning of the idea also to be consulted regarding the intended selection of the object.   If
I have meant to make an assertion about Cæsar, you must
not call me to account because my statement does not
correspond, in the intended way, with the object called
Napoleon.   If I have meant to say that space has three
dimensions, you cannot refute me by pointing out that
time has only one.   And nowhere, without a due examination of the internal meaning of my ideas, can you learn
whether it was the object Cæsar or the object Napoleon,
whether it was space or time, that I meant.

Our preference, however, for the objects of sense, for
the pen, and the sun, as typical instances of objects of
ideas, arises from the fact that in case of just these objects, it is especially easy, by observing, from without, the
acts of the person who has these ideas, to form confident
and, for common-sense purposes, relatively exact notions
of the selection to which the internal meaning of the
ideas has bound the maker of any given judgment about
objects.   Moreover, it is easy for us ourselves to follow
our sense-ideas and their objects with continuous scrutiny
and to observe their relations.   For sense-objects are
vivid, and combine relative permanence with the sort of
plasticity that enables us to get what we call nearer or,
in general, novel views of them; so that in passing back
and forth from idea to object, we seem assured of some
definite relation between them.   And our acts in dealing

with the objects of sense are correspondingly definite, so that observers easily judge what object we mean.

Yet precisely what this relation of object and idea is, we are still called upon to explain, even in case of the most obvious object of sense, and still more in case of objects of a more subtle character, such as past events, valid laws, and mathematical constructions.

Plain, so far, are two considerations : First, the object of an idea is in somewise predetermined, is selected from all other objects, through the sort of attentive interest in just that object which the internal meaning of the idea involves. Unless the idea is thus selective, it can never come to be either true or false. For if it means to be true, it intends a sort of correspondence with an object. What correspondence it intends is determined, as we saw, solely by the purpose which the idea embodies, i.e. by the internal meaning of the idea. Furthermore, the idea intends to attain this correspondence to some particular object, — not to any object you please, not to whatever happens to correspond to the ideal construction in question, but to a determined object. The determination of what object is meant, is, therefore, certainly again due, in one aspect, to the internal meaning of the idea. Nobody else can determine for me what object I mean by my idea.

But hereupon we seem to face, indeed, a fatal difficulty, For the second of the two considerations just mentioned remains. And this is that, if the idea predetermines what object it selects as the one that it means, just as it predetermines what sort of correspondence it intends to have to this object, the idea, nevertheless, does not predetermine whether its object is such that the idea, if finite, shall succeed in attaining entire agreement with the object. Otherwise truth would be mere tautology, error would be excluded in advance, and it would be useless even to talk of an object external in any sense to the idea.

VII

Here, then, is the central dilemma as to the nature of truth. I may state it once more, but now in the form of an antinomy; that is, in the familiar shape of the Kantian Antinomies, with thesis and antithesis. To be sure, the antinomy will be imperfect. On one side will stand a stubborn, but no doubt somehow incompletely stated, apparent truth. On the other side will stand an obvious and demonstrable certainty. We shall have to reconcile an opposition that can be but apparent.

The thesis of our antinomy is as follows: There seems to be, in the object of an idea, just in so far as it is the object of that specific idea, no essential character which is not predetermined by the purpose, the internal meaning, the conscious intent, of that idea itself.

For consider: An object, as we have seen, has two relations to an idea. The one is the relation that constitutes it the object meant by that idea. The other is the sort of correspondence that is to obtain between object and idea. As to the first of these two: An object is not the object of a given idea merely because the object causes the idea, or impresses itself upon the idea as the seal impresses the wax. For there are objects of ideas that are not causes of the ideas which refer to these objects, just as there are countless cases where my ideas are supposed to have causes, say physiological or psychological causes, of which I myself never become conscious at all, as my objects. Nor is the object the object of a given idea merely because, from the point of view of an external observer, who looks from without upon idea and object, and compares them, the idea resembles the object. For the sort of correspondence to be demanded of the idea is determined by itself, and this correspondence cannot be judged merely from without. Again, my idea of my own past experiences may resemble your past experiences, in case you have felt as I have felt, or have acted in any way as I have acted. Yet when my ideas, in a moment of reminiscence, refer to my own past, and have that for their object, they do not refer to your past, nor to your deeds and sorrows, however like my own these experiences of yours may have been. One who, merely comparing my ideas and your experiences, said that because of the mere likeness I must be thinking of your past as my object, would, therefore, err, if it was my own past of which I was thinking. Neither such a relation as causal connection nor such a relation as mere similarity is, then, sufficient to identify an object as the object of a given idea.

Nor yet can any other relation, so far as it is merely supposed to be seen from without, by an external observer, suffice to identify any object as the object of a given idea. For suppose that any such relation, merely observed from without, were regarded as finally sufficient to constitute an object the object of a given idea. I care not what this relation may be. Call it what you will.

As soon as you define such a relation from without, and declare that the idea has an object by virtue of that relation to this object, I shall merely ask: Did the idea itself intend and select that relation as the relation in which its purposed object was to stand to the idea? If you answer " No," then I take my stand beside the idea, and shall persist in demanding by what right you thus impose the relation in question upon the idea as the relation rightly characterizing its object. For the idea, in seeking for truth, does not seek for your aims, so far as you are a merely external observer. The idea is selective. It seeks its own. It attends as itself has chosen. It desires in its own way. If you, having somehow first finished and established your own definition of Being, choose to regard the idea and its object as entities in your own supposed world, then, indeed, you can talk, from your own point of view, of the various real relations of these entities, precisely as a psychologist does when he discusses the origin or the results of ideas. But just now we are not first presupposing that we know what the Being of the object is apart from the idea, and what the Being of the idea is apart from the object. We are trying, in advance of a finished conception of the Being of the object, to define the essential relation that makes an object the object of that particular idea. And as the idea, precisely so far as it intends truth at all, is through and through a selection, a choosing of an object, I ask what reason you can have to say that the object is the object of the idea, unless you observe somehow that the idea chooses for itself this object.

But now if you reply, " Yes, the relation of object to

idea, here in question, is the one chosen by the idea,"
then you admit the essential point. The relation to the
object is so far predetermined by the idea. Hence, as
we have now seen, the object of the idea is predetermined,
both as to what object it is, and as to how it is to correspond to the idea, through the choice made by the idea
itself. The object, precisely in so far as it is object of
that idea, seems thus to be altogether predetermined. In
brief, the object and the idea of that object appear to be
related as Hamlet in the play is related to the intent of
Shakespeare, or as creation and creative purpose in general are related. Hamlet is what Shakespeare's idea
intends him to be. The object is what it is because the
idea means it to be the object of just this idea. And so
much may suffice for our thesis.

But the antithesis runs : No finite idea predetermines,
in its object, exactly the character which, when present
in the object, gives the idea the desired truth. For
observe, first, that the object of a true finite idea, such
as our idea of the world or of space, is in any case something other than the mere idea itself. And the truth of
the idea depends upon a confirmation of the idea through
the presence and the characters of this other, — the object.
Now error is certainly possible in finite ideas. For some
finite ideas are false. And that this last assertion itself
is true, is not only a matter of common opinion, but can
be proved by the very counterpart of the Augustinian
argument about *Veritas*. For if there could be no error,
then the customary assertion that ideas can err, *i.e.* our
well-known common-sense conviction that error is possible,
would be itself an error, and this result would involve a

self-contradiction. Or again, were no error possible, there would be no truth, since then the assertion that there is no truth would itself be no error, or would itself be true. This, again, would be a contradiction. Or finally, if error were impossible, any and every account of Being or truth, of ideas and of objects, of the world or of nothing at all, would be equally true, or in other words, no truth would ever be defined. For truth we define by its contrast with the error that it excludes. So some ideas certainly can and do err in as far as they undertake to be ideas of objects. Ideas can then fail of their desired correspondence with their intended objects, just because these objects are indeed other than themselves. But the error of an idea is always a failure to win the intended aim of the idea, precisely in so far as the idea sought truth. Hence, as no purpose can simply and directly consist in willing or intending its own defeat, it is plain that an idea, precisely in so far as it can turn out to be an erroneous idea, can intend what its object forbids it to carry out, and can mean what its object excludes ; while in so far as the object thus refutes the idea, the object contains what the idea did not purpose, and was unable to predetermine. In brief, the very Possibility of Error, the absolutely certain truth that some ideas give false accounts of their own objects, shows that some objects contain what is opposed to the intent of the very ideas that refer to these objects. And so the antithesis is proved.

VIII

In view of this apparent antinomy, how is the idea related to its object? How is error possible? What is truth ? The answer to these questions, — the solution to all our previous difficulties, is in one respect so simple, that I almost fear, after this so elaborate preparation, to state it, lest by its very simplicity it may disappoint. Yet I must first state it, abstractly, and perhaps unconvincingly, and then illustrate it as I close the present discussion, leaving to a later lecture its fuller developement. The idea, I have said, *seeks its own. It can be judged by nothing but what it intends.* Whether I think of God or of yesterday's events, of my own death, or of the destiny of mankind, of mathematical truth, or of physical facts, of affairs of business, or of Being itself, it is first of all what I mean, and not what somebody merely external to myself might desire me to mean, that both gives me an object, and determines for me the standard of correspondence to the object whereby I must be judged. Moreover, my idea is a cognitive process only in so far as it is, at the same time, a voluntary process, an act, the partial fulfilment, so far as the idea consciously extends, of a purpose. The object meant by the idea is the object because it is willed to be such, and the will in question is the will that the idea embodies. And that is why Realism proved to be impossible ; that is why the Independent Beings were self-contradictory concepts ; that, too, is why the resignation of all definite purpose which Mysticism required of our ideas was impossible without a failure to define Being as any but a mere Nothing. And every definition of truth or of Being must depend upon a prior recognition of precisely this aspect of the nature of ideas.

Whoever says, "I am passive ; I merely accept the

world as my object ; I recognize the superior force of this object, and I have no part in willing that it is my object," any such submissive observer is invited merely to state what object he means, and what idea he has of it.   He will at once find his idea arising before him as a conscious construction, and he will regard this idea as intelligible because he follows its construction with his own unity of purpose.   The vaster the world that he then defines as the overwhelming fate of his intelligence, the larger will be the part that his own consciously constructive will has taken in the definition of the idea.   And by his will, I mean here not any abstract psychological power or principle so to be named.   I speak here of will not as of any causally efficacious entity whatever.   I refer only to the mere fact of any one's consciousness, insisted upon in these discussions from the start, namely, the fact that the contents of an idea are present to mind as the actual embodiment and relative fulfilment of a present purpose, such as for instance you find embodied when you count or sing.   Space, time, past, future, things, minds, laws, — all these constituents of the world, our supposed passive spectator of universe indeed recognizes as objects other than the ideal products of his will ; but his ideas of these objects come to him precisely as constructive processes, present to his consciousness as his own act, and understood by him so far as they are his own meaning.   Moreover, the objects, too, to which these ideas relate, can be understood as objects only when the ideas embody the will to mean them as such objects.

But now, in order that we may also take account of our former problem about the determinateness and individuality attributed to Being, let us add yet one further consideration : Whenever an idea of any grade aims at truth, it regards its object as other than itself, and that the object shall be thus other than itself is even a part of what the idea means and consciously intends. But as a will seeking its own fulfilment, the idea so selects the object, that, if the idea has a perfectly definite meaning and truth at all, this object is to be a precisely determinate object, *such that no other object could take its place as the object of this idea.* And in spite of the fact that the object is such solely by the will of the idea, the idea undertakes submissively to be either true or false when compared with that object.

Now the obvious way of stating the whole sense of these facts is to point out that what the idea always aims to find in its object is *nothing whatever but the idea's own conscious purpose or will, embodied in some more determinate form* than the idea by itself alone at this instant consciously possesses. When I have an idea of the world, my idea is a will, *and the world of my idea is simply my own will itself determinately embodied.*

And what this way of stating our problem implies may first be illustrated by any case where, in doing what we often call "making up our minds," we pass from a vague to a definite state of will and of resolution. In such cases we begin with perhaps a very indefinite sort of restlessness, which arouses the question, "What is it that I want? What do I desire? What is my real purpose?" To answer this question may take a long time and much care; and may involve many errors by the way, errors, namely, in understanding our own purpose.

Such search for one's own will often occupies, in the
practical life of youth, some very anxious years.   Idle-
ness, defective modes of conduct, self-defeating struggles
without number, fickle loves that soon die out, may long
accompany what the youth himself all the while regards
as the search for his own will, for the very soul of his
own inner and conscious purposes.   In such cases one may
surely err as to one's intent.   The false or fickle love is
a sort of transient dream of the coming true love itself.
The transient choice is a shadow of the coming true
choice.   But how does one's own real intent, the object
at such times of one's search, stand related to one's present and ill-defined vague restlessness, or imperfectly conscious longing.   I answer, one's true will, one's genuine
purpose, one's object here sought for, can be nothing
whatever but one's present imperfect conscious will in
some more determinate form.   What one has, at such
times, is the will of the passing moment, — an internal
meaning, consciously present as far as it goes.   And now
it is this will and no other that one seeks to bring to
clearer consciousness.   But what other, what external
meaning, what fact beyond, yes, what object, is the goal
of this quest?   I answer, nothing whatever in heaven or
in earth but this present imperfect internal meaning rendered more determinate, less ambiguous in its form, less
a general longing, more a precisely united and determinate life.   And this, once rendered perfectly determinate, would be what the man in question calls " My life
according to my conscious will."

Well, this case of the vague purpose that one seeks,
not to abandon, but to get present to the moment's con-

sciousness in another, that is a more explicit and precise, form, and if possible, in what would finally prove to be an absolutely determinate form, — this case, I insist, is typical of every case where an idea seeks its object. *In seeking its object, any idea whatever seeks absolutely nothing but its own explicit, and, in the end, complete, determination as this conscious purpose, embodied in this one way. The complete content of the idea's own purpose is the only object of which the idea can ever take note. This alone is the Other that is sought.* That such a search as this is a genuine search for an object, that while sought appears as another and as a beyond, the experience of the mathematical sciences will at once illustrate. As we saw, in a previous discussion, the mathematician deals with a world which his own present ideas, as far as they go, explicitly attempt to predetermine ; yet what these ideas do not at present completely and consciously predetermine for the mathematician's private judgment, in advance of proof, is precisely that further determination of their own meaning which they imply and seek. This further determination the mathematician wins through his process of inquiry. His result is, then, actually willed from the start, in so far as his definitions, which are themselves acts of will, determine in advance the outcome of the proofs and computations of which they are already the initial step. But at the instant when the definitions and considerations of his problem alone are present to the mathematician's passing consciousness, the outcome, the fully developed meaning, is an Other, an Object, which the mathematician seeks. At any moment, in his further research, he may attempt to define this Other by a conjectural or hypothetical construction, a tentative idea, which may to a large extent prove not to correspond with the fully developed purpose which the result of the inquiry, when reached, presents to consciousness in as determinate form as is humanly possible. So far as our narrow human consciousness does permit this result of mathematical inquiry ever to appear to us in its complete expression, it is finally observed, however, as a fact of experience, or complex of facts of experience, as a series of properties and relations, embodied in diagrams, symbols, and systems of symbols. This expression, as far as it goes, fulfils the purpose defined from the start, the very outset of the mathematical inquiry. In this case one says, " Yes, I see this to be true, and I see that this is what the initial definitions meant." Such a result of mathematical inquiry, just in so far as it is satisfactory, is a result that sends us no farther, or that defines no object lying yet beyond itself. This then is the answer to the mathematician's initial query.

In just as far as we pause satisfied, we observe that there " is no other " mathematical fact to be sought in the direction of the particular inquiry in hand. Satisfaction of purpose by means of presented fact, and such determinate satisfaction as sends us to no other experience for further light and fulfilment, precisely this outcome is itself the Other that is sought when we begin our inquiry. This Other, this outcome, is at once uniquely determined by the true meaning already imperfectly present at the outset, and it is also not consciously present in the narrow instant's experience with which we begin. A vaguely indeterminate act of will thus begins a process; the object sought is simply the precise determination of this very will itself to unique and unambiguous expression. And in such a case the thesis and antithesis of our antinomy are reconciled. For the object is a true Other, and yet it is object only as the meaning of this idea.

But how is it when facts of experience are sought, — when the astronomer, having computed the planet's place, looks to see whether the determination conforms to the apparently wholly "external empirical object," when the chemist awaits the result of the experiment in the laboratory, when the speculator watches the waverings of the market, or when the vigilant friend by the bedside longs for the favorable turn of the beloved patient's disease? I answer, in all these cases the apparently conflicting objects and ideas in question are indeed far more numerous and complex in their relations than the mathematician's world. And we shall hereafter consider precisely such complications more in detail. But here we are concerned with the most universal aspects of our problem as to idea and object; and so here I can only respond, *Whatever the object, it is still the object for a given idea solely because that idea wills it to be such.* If it is experience, of a given type, and won under determinate conditions, that you seek, then in just that region of inquiry your inquiring interest, your imperfectly determined initial will, seeks its own more precise determination. But this self-determination is even here the only object that the idea seeks. No idea is confirmed or refuted by any experience except by that more determinate type, or instance, of experience which the less determinate and vaguer will of the inquiring idea has first sought as its ideal goal, as its chosen authority, as its accepted standard, and so as its own object. If I will to watch for stars, or to measure places of heavenly bodies, or to be guided in the determination of my will by the appearance of certain chemical precipitates in test-tubes, or to stake my fortune in the stock-market, or to be determined in my acts by the empirical outcome of this patient's disease, — well, in all such cases, it is an experience that I first am to accept as the determination of my purpose. By that choice my development of my ideas is guided. But for that very reason the awaited experience is, in advance, my object precisely, because it is, just by virtue of my own purpose, the desired determiner of my purpose. The same rule holds here also as in the former cases. The idea is a will seeking its own determination. It is nothing else. And herein lies the explanation of the process which we studied, earlier in this lecture, in our account of the relations between judgment and experience. Judgments, taken as universal, already involve a negative determination of the world of internal meanings through an exclusion of bare possibilities. The judgments of experience, the particular judgments, express a positive, but still imperfect, determination of internal meaning through external experience. The limit or goal of this process would be an individual judgment, wherein the will expressed its own final determination.

But if one here retorts, "Ay, but in the empirical world I have no choice, since facts are facts, and the world is once for all there;" then I reply: I do not now question that the world is there. I am asking in what sense it is there. It is, but what Being has it? We have long since seen that the whole world is real as the object that gives validity to ideas. We have inquired as to the sense in which anything can be called object. We have found the sense in which the idea chooses its object. We have found also that the object is nothing but the will of the idea itself in some determinate expression. But now one points out that in giving our ideas of empirical objects determinate expression, there is a sense in which, once having committed ourselves to given ideas, we have no more choice as to how the ideas shall turn out to be determined. Well, is not this an obvious enough result even of our own view? The idea in seeking for its object is seeking for the determination of its own just now consciously indeterminate will. This is, so to speak, the game that the idea undertakes to play. But consistently with itself the idea cannot choose to change capriciously its own choice, to alter the rules of its own game, even while it plays. If its will is to be determined only by experience that it awaits, then just this experience is the determiner of the will. In this sense the mathematician, too, has no choice. He, too, awaits the outcome of his own sort of experience as he computes, as he observes his diagrams and symbols. For his world also is in its own way an empirical world, and he experiments in that world, and wills to accept the result. In this same sense, too, the youth has no choice as to what he shall find his own will to be, since so long as he wills in his own way, his struggles for self-comprehension are in essence predetermined by his accepted, if not yet momentarily conscious selection, of a life plan. The idea having opened the game of its life, cannot withdraw its own moves without failing of its own determination.

Well, precisely so it is with all the facts of experience in their relation to specific ideas. All finite ideas, even the vaguest, are already in one aspect contents of experience, imperfectly fulfilling purpose. In all cases every idea, whether mathematical, practical, or scientific, seeks its own further determination. In every case it is true that such further determination is also to be given only in terms of experience. Sometimes it is a definite group of sense-experiences that we mean in advance; then we are said to be observant of the physical world; and then in physical nature only do we find the desired determination of our will. Sometimes, as in the mathematician's world, we deal with objects that appear more directly under our control than do physical objects. But there are no ideas that have not an aspect in which they are masses of experience, and masses of experience are never objective facts except in so far as they present the answers to specific questions about fact. And the answer to a question is merely the more precise determination of the will that asks the question.

Of course, my private will, when viewed as a mere force in nature, does not create the rest of nature. But my conscious will as expressed in my ideas does logically determine what objects are my objects.

But one may say : "How if the facts of experience altogether refuse to fulfil given ideas in any sense whatever ? Have not such ideas an object that they seek and never find at all ? Is not the object of a defeated purpose, or of an error, still an object, but a purely ideal one ? Yet here the object remains precisely object of an unfulfilled idea." I answer: An error is an error about a specific object, only in case the purpose imperfectly defined by the vague idea at the instant when the error is made, is better defined, is, in fact, better fulfilled, by an object whose determinate character in some wise, although never absolutely, opposes the fragmentary efforts first made to define them. As for failure, or practical defeat of our plans: The practical object that we have not yet won remains for us a Beyond, or Other than our search, precisely so long as we still seek it; and no merely external buffetting of so-called hard facts ever proves to the resolute will that its practical objects are unattainable, or have no existence, until we see an inner reason why just these objects are really excluded by a fuller understanding of our own ideal purposes themselves. I do not will just now to fly, because my purpose in conceiving nature is now relatively fulfilled in a system of ideas which excludes my possession of the power to fly. But were I an inventor trying to perfect flying-machines, I should continue the effort to find the determination of my will present in a flying-machine, until I became convinced that my purpose as defined stood somehow in conflict with itself, or with the whole idea of nature of which it is a portion.

IX

And now as to what results from all this concerning the essential nature of the object of any idea, and as to that determinateness and individuality of Being which has so perplexed us.

Ideas as they come to us, in their finite imperfections, are at first indeterminate, and for that very reason vague, general, or, as technical language often expresses it, abstractly universal. That is precisely why they at once seek and attempt to define another than themselves, and do so in the form of Universal Judgments. For an universal, in the abstract sense of the term, is, as we have fully illustrated, known to us merely as *that of which there might be another instance.* Whoever seeks his meaning in another complex of facts than the one present to him, thereby makes explicit that what he possesses in his idea is merely a *kind of fulfilment* of his purpose, and not a *whole fulfilment.* Whoever thinks merely of man, of triangle, of life, has a general idea So far as he imperfectly defines a purpose that essentially seeks other expression than the present. Whoever longs, loves, hopes, struggles, aspires; whoever experiments, watches for facts, makes hypotheses, — whoever is finite, possesses in his passing idea a general type of relative fulfilment, but seeks precisely to specify, to render more determinate, precisely this general idea. He first looks for specification in further experience. Finding is a more determinate experience of the very contents of one's ideas themselves than is seeking. As more determinate, it takes the form of Particular Judgments.

Well, if every idea is as such a general type of empirical and fragmentary fulfilment of purpose, if in seeking its object, its Other, the idea seeks only its own greater determination, then, *at the desired limit of determination,* the idea, as already pointed out, would face a present content which would imply, seek, and in fact permit, no other than itself to take for this ideal purpose its place. Now an object, such as Socrates, or this world, or as yourself, is called an individual, as we before said, when one conceives that for a particular and determinate purpose no other object could be substituted for this one. It follows that the finally determinate form of the object of any finite idea is that form which *the idea itself would assume whenever it became individuated, or in other words, became a completely determined idea, an idea or will fulfilled by a wholly adequate empirical content, for which no other content need be substituted or, from the point of view of the satisfied idea, could be substituted.*

Now, if this be the result of our analysis, we can at length define truth and Being at one stroke. You have an idea present at this moment. It is a general idea. Why? For no reason, I answer, except this, viz.: that this idea, being but a partial embodiment of your present purpose, could get and desires to get some other embodiment than the present one. This possibility of other embodiment means for you just now simply the incompleteness, or partial non-fulfilment of your present purpose. Mere generality always means practical defect. You think of your own life. Your idea is general, just because your life could be and will be embodied in other moments than this one. The idea of your own life finds, then, just at this instant, an imperfect expression. Your idea of your own whole life is just now vague. This vagueness means for you the possibility of other embodiments.

Or perhaps you think of numbers, and accordingly count one, two, three. Your idea of these numbers is abstract, a mere generality. Why? Because there could be other cases of counting, and other numbers counted than the present counting process shows you. And why so? Because your purpose in counting is not wholly fulfilled by the numbers now counted. Incompleteness here goes with universality. There could be other instances of the idea, just because what is needed to fulfil the purpose in question is not all here. And this you know in the form both of present imperfect satisfaction, and in the form of the idea of other numbers, and of other counting processes than are here present to you.

Well, if in all such cases of your present and imperfect passing ideas, other cases of your idea were also fully present to your consciousness just now, what would you experience? I answer, *You would experience at once a greater fulfilment of your purpose, and a more determinate idea.* But were not only some, but all possible, instances that could illustrate your idea, or that could give it embodiment, now present, even at this very instant, and to your clear consciousness, what would you experience? I answer, first, *the complete fulfilment of your internal meaning*, the final satisfaction of the will embodied in the idea; but secondly, also, *that absolute determination of the embodiment of your idea as this embodiment would then be present, — that absolute determination of your purpose, which would constitute an individual realization of the idea.* For an individual fact is one for which no other can be substituted without some loss of determination, or some vagueness. You seek another so long as your present purpose is unfulfilled. The fulfilment of the internal meaning of the present idea would leave no other object defined by this idea as an object yet to be sought. And where no other was to be sought, the individual life of the whole idea, as a process at once of experience and of purpose, would be present fact.

Now this final embodiment is the ultimate object, and the only genuine object, that any present idea seeks as its Other. But if this be so, when is the idea true? It is true — this instant's idea — if, in its own measure, and on its own plan, it corresponds, even in its vagueness, to its own final and completely individual expression. Its expression would be the very life of fulfilment of purpose which this present idea already fragmentarily begins, as it were, to express. It is with a finite idea as it is with any form of will. Any of its transient expressions may be at any instant more or less abortive. But no finite idea is wholly out of correspondence to its object, as no will is wholly false to itself.

We have thus defined the object and the truth of an idea. But observe that thus we stand upon the threshold of a new definition of Being. Being, as our Third Conception declared, is what gives true ideas their truth; or in other words, to be real is to be the object of a true idea. We are ready, now that we have defined both object and truth, to assert, as our Fourth and final Conception of Being, this, that *What is, or what is real, is as such the complete embodiment, in individual form and in final fulfilment, of the internal meaning of finite ideas.*

To later lectures must be left both the fuller development and the further defence of this conception of Being. But our argument in its favor is, in its foundation, already before you. Being is something Other than themselves which finite ideas seek. They seek Being as that which, if at present known, would end their doubts. Now Being is not something independent of finite ideas, nor yet a merely immediate fact that quenches them. These were our results when we abandoned Realism and Mysticism. Being involves the validity of ideas. That we learned from critical Rationalism. Yet mere validity, mere truth of ideas, cannot be conceived as a bare universal fact. We wanted to find its concreter content, its finally determinate form. We have carefully studied this form. No finite idea can have or conform to any object, save what its own meaning determines, or seek any meaning or truth but its own meaning and truth. Furthermore, a finite idea is as much an instance of will as it is a knowing process. In seeking its own meaning, it seeks then simply the fuller expression of its own will. Its only Other is an Other that would more completely express it. Its object proves therefore to be, as proximate finite object, any fuller determination whatever of its own will and meaning. But as final object, the idea can have only its final embodiment in a complete and individual form. This final form of the idea, this final object sought when we seek Being, is (1) a complete expression of the internal meaning of the finite idea with which, in any case, we start our quest; (2) a complete fulfilment of the will or purpose partially embodied in this idea;

(3) an individual life for which no other can be substituted.

Now in defining this complete life, in which alone the finite idea, as a passing thrill of conscious meaning, can find the genuine object that it means fully embodied, we have so far still used many expressions derived from the conception of mere validity. We have spoken of what this life would be *if* *it* *were* completely present. But, having used these forms of expression as mere scaffolding, at the close we must indeed observe afresh that all validity, as an incomplete universal conception, needs another, to give it final meaning. If there is validity, there is then an object more than merely valid which gives the very conception of validity its own meaning. All that we learned before. It was that very defect of the third conception which sent us looking for the sense in which there can be an object of any idea.

We have now defined what this object is. It is an individual life, present as a whole, *totum simul*, as the scholastics would have said. This life is at once a system of facts, and the fulfilment of whatever purpose any finite idea, in so far as it is true to its own meaning, already fragmentarily embodies. This life is the completed will, as well as the completed experience, corresponding to the will and experience of any one finite idea. In its wholeness the world of Being is the world of individually expressed meanings, — an individual life, consisting of the individual embodiments of the wills represented by all finite ideas. Now *to be*, in the final sense, means to be just such a life, complete, present to experience, and conclusive of the search for perfection which every finite idea in its own measure undertakes whenever it seeks for any object. We may therefore lay aside altogether our *ifs* and *thens*, our *validity* and our other such terms, when we speak of this final concept of Being. What is, is for us no longer a mere Form, but a Life; and in our world of what was before mere truth the light of individuality and of will have finally begun to shine. The sun of true Being has arisen before our eyes.

In finding this world have we not been already led to the very definition of the divine Life? Yet must we leave to the later lectures some portrayal of what objects this world contains, — enough, the way is now open, and we shall enter at last the homeland.

LECTURE VIII

LECTURE VIII

THE FOURTH CONCEPTION OF BEING

ANY doctrine concerning fundamental questions is likely to meet with two different sorts of objections. The objections of the first sort maintain that the theory in question is too abstruse and obscure to be comprehended. The objections of the second sort point out that this same theory is too simple to be true. Every teacher of philosophy becomes accustomed not only to hear both kinds of objections from his more thoughtful pupils, but to urge them, for himself, upon his own notice. No one, in fact, is a philosopher, who has not first profoundly doubted his own system. And it is in presence of objections that philosophical theses best show their merits, if they have merits.

Upon the present occasion I have more fully to develope the conception of Being to which we were led at the close of the last discussion. While I shall do so, in the first place, independently, I shall come before I am done into intimate connection with some of the principal objections that may be urged against our theses regarding the definition of what it is to be. For the objections will help us to make clearer our position.

I

But let us first restate our thesis as to the nature of Being. There is an ancient doctrine that whatever is, is

ultimately something Individual. Realism early came to
that view ; and only Critical Rationalism has ever explicitly maintained that the ultimate realities are universals,
namely, valid possibilities of experience, or mere truths
as such. Now at the close of the last lecture, after analyzing the whole basis of Critical Rationalism, the entire
conception of the Real as merely valid, we reinstated the
Individual as the only ultimate form of Being. In so far
we returned to a view that, in the history of thought,
Realism already asserted. But we gave a new reason of
our own for this view. Our reason was that the very
defect of our finite ideas which sends us seeking for
Being lies in the fact that whether we long for practical
satisfaction, or think of purely theoretical problems, we,
as we now are, are always seeking another object than
what is yet present to our ideas. Now any ultimate reality, for us while as finite thinkers we seek it, is always
such another fact. Yet this other object is always an
object for our thought only in so far as our thought
already means it, defines it, and wills it to be our object.
But what is for us this other ? In its essence it is already
defined even before we undertake to know it. For this
other is precisely the fulfilment of our purpose, the satisfaction of the will now imperfectly embodied in our ideas,
the completion of what we already partially possess in our
finite insight. This completion is for us another, solely
because our ideas, in their present momentary forms, come
to us as general ideas, — ideas of what is now merely a
kind of relative fulfilment and not an entire fulfilment.
Other fulfilment of the same general kind is needed before
we can face the whole Being that we seek. This kind of

fulfilment we want to bring, however, to some integral expression, to its own finality, to its completeness as a whole fact. And this want of ours, so I asserted, not only sets us looking for Being, but gives us our only ground and means for defining Being.

Being itself we should directly face in our own experience only in case we experienced finality, *i.e.* full expression of what our finite ideas both mean and seek. Such expression, however, would be given to us in the form of a life that neither sought nor permitted another to take its own place as the expression of its own purpose. Where no other was yet to be sought, there alone would our ideas define no other, no Being, of the type in question, lying yet beyond themselves, in the direction of their own type of fulfilment. The other would be found, and so would be present. And there alone should we consequently stand in the presence of what is real. Conversely, whoever grasps only the nature of a general concept, whoever merely thinks of light or colors, or gravitation, or of man, whoever lacks, longs, or in any way seeks another, has not in his experience the full expression of his own meaning. Hence it is that he has to seek his object elsewhere. And so he has not yet faced any ultimate Being. He has upon his hands mere fragments, mere aspects of Being. Thus an entire instance of Being must be precisely that which permits your ideas to seek no other than what is present. Such a being is an Individual. Only, for our present conception of Being, an individual being is not a fact independent of any experience, nor yet a merely valid truth, nor yet a merely immediate datum that quenches ideas. For all these alternatives we have already faced and rejected. On the contrary an individual being is a Life of Experience fulfilling Ideas, in an absolutely final form. And this we said is the essential nature of Being. The essence of the Real is to be Individual, or to permit no other of its own kind, and this character it possesses only as the unique fulfilment of purpose.

Or, once more, as Mysticism asserted, so we too assert of your world, *That art thou.* Only the Self which is your world is your completely integrated Self, the totality of the life that at this instant you fragmentarily grasp. Your present defect is a matter of the mere form of your consciousness at this instant. Were your eyes at this instant open to your own meaning, your life as a whole would be spread before you as a single and unique life, for which no other could be substituted without a less determinate expression of just your individual will. Now this complete life of yours, is. Only such completion can be. Being can possess no other nature than this. And this, in outline, is our Fourth Conception of Being.

II

Now I cannot myself conceive any one lightly accepting such a definition as this, — a definition so paradoxical in seeming, so remote from the limits which common sense usually sets to speculation, and so opposed to many dignified historical traditions ; and indeed I wish nobody to accept it lightly. The whole matter is one for the closest scrutiny. The only ground for this definition of Being lies in the fact that every other conception of reality proves, upon analysis, to be self-contradictory, precisely in so far as it does not in essence agree with this one ; while every effort directly to deny the truth of this conception proves, upon analysis, to involve the covert affirmation of this very conception itself. Upon these assertions of the absolute logical necessity of our conception of Being, our whole case in this argument rests. And in order to make this fact clearer, I must briefly review the former argument.

Our argument in the last lecture was based upon the consideration that Being has, at all events, to be that object which makes ideas true or false. The more special features of our analysis of the relation of idea and object were as follows : —

An idea and its real object, in case the idea has any real object, must indeed plainly possess some characters in common. There must thus be general, or abstractly universal, features, belonging to them both. Upon that point all theories of Being to some extent agree. Even the Mystic, at the moment when he calls all ideas vain, identifies your true Self — yes, the very Self that now has your poor ideas — with the Absolute, and says of your object, viz. of the true Being, "That art thou." Even the Realist, despite the independence of his Beings, holds that the ideas either truly represent the nature of these beings, or else, at all events, have in common with even the unknowable object some features whereby the object embodies in reality the same fact which the idea aims to express when it seeks for the reality. The failure of Realism we found to be due to the logical impossibility of reconciling the independent Being of the object of our ideas with this inevitably assumed sameness of nature, which must be possessed, in however slight a measure, by both the knowing idea and the object that it knows. In the world of the Third Conception of Being, that of Validity, the ideas express with more or less precision, and in their own way, precisely that truth which is to be valid beyond them. And, in fact, as we just saw, the most general conditions which determine for us the problem of Being, demand that the purpose which every idea has in seeking its Other, must have some element in common with that which fulfils this very purpose.

Idea and Reality must, then, possess elements that are common to both of them. On the other hand, as we saw, this mere community is wholly inadequate to the tasks of defining what makes the object belong, as object, to a given idea. For, if you view any idea and its supposed object, merely as one might be imagined viewing them from without, it is wholly impossible to determine what degree of correspondence between them is required either to make the reality that precise object sought by the idea, or to render the idea the true representative of the object to which it is said to refer. A true idea, as Spinoza said, must indeed resemble its ideate. But on the other hand, a mere resemblance of idea and ideate is not enough. Nor does the absence of any specific degree of resemblance necessarily involve an error. It is intended resemblance which counts in estimating the truth of ideas. If in fact you suppose, as an ideal case, two human beings, say twins, absolutely to resemble each other, not only in body, but in experience and in thought, so that every idea which one of these beings at any mo-

ment had was precisely duplicated by a thought which
at the same instant, and in the same fashion, arose in
the other being's life, — if, I say, you suppose this perfect
resemblance in the twin minds, you could still, without
inconsistency, suppose these twins separated from infancy,
living apart, although of course under perfectly similar
physical conditions, and in our human sense what we
men call absolute strangers to each other, so that neither
of them, viewed merely as this human being, ever consciously thought of the other, or conceived of the other's
existence.   In that case, the mere resemblance would not
so far constitute the one of these twin minds the object
of which the other mind thought, or the being concerning whom the ideas of the other were true.

   The resemblance of idea and object, viewed as a mere
fact for an external observer, is, therefore, never by itself
enough to constitute the truth of the idea.   Nor is the
absence of any externally predetermined resemblances,
such as you from without may choose to demand of the
idea, enough to constitute any specific sort of error.
Moreover, when you merely assert that in the world of
Being there is to be found an object which resembles
your idea, you have so far only mentioned two beings,
namely, your idea and its object, and have asserted their
resemblance.   But you have not yet in the least defined
wherein the Being of either of these objects consists.
This, then, is the outcome so long as you view idea and
object as sundered facts agreeing or disagreeing with
each other.   Neither truth nor Being is thus to be
defined.   The result so far is conclusive as against
the adequacy, not only of Realism, and of Mysticism,

but also, as we saw, of even the Third Conception of Being.

For if one asserts, as his account of the nature of Being, that certain ideas of possibilities of experience are valid, he is so far left with a world of objects upon his hands whose only character, so far as he yet defines the Being of these objects, is that these objects are in agreement with his ideas. Such a definition of Being constituted the whole outcome of the Third Conception. The mathematician's ideas, as present to himself, take the form of observed symbols and diagrams. These, so far as they are observed, are contents of experience fulfilling purpose. They so far conform to our definition of what constitutes an idea, for they have internal meaning. But the existent objects concerning which the mathematician endeavors to teach us, are, by hypothesis, not the symbols, and not the diagrams, but valid truths to which these diagrams and symbols — these mathematician's ideas — correspond. The existences of the mathematician's realm are other than his mere finite ideas. Now that such objects have their place in reality, I myself thoroughly believe. But I point out that their reality, the true Being of these objects, is in no wise defined when you merely speak of the ideas as nothing but valid, because the assertion of validity is so far merely the assertion of a correspondence between a presupposed idea and its assumed object, without any account as yet either of the object, or of the truth of the idea. And bare correspondence, the mere possession of common characters in idea and in object not only fails to define, but, as we now see, can never lead us to define, the Being of either idea or object, and in no sense shows or explains to us the relation whereby the idea means, selects, and is in just this way true of just this one object.

The relation of correspondence between idea and object is, therefore, wholly subordinate to another and far deeper relation; and so to say, "My idea has reference to a real Being," is to say, "My idea imperfectly expresses, in my present consciousness, an intention, a meaning, a purpose; and just this specific meaning is carried out, is fulfilled, is expressed, by my object." For correspondence to its object, and intentional selection of both the object and the sort of correspondence, constitute the two possible relations of idea and object. If the bare correspondence determines neither Being nor truth, the intention must determine both Being and truth.   In other words, the Being to which any idea refers is simply the will of the idea more determinately, and also more completely, expressed.   Once admit this definition of the nature of Being, and you will accomplish the end which all the various prior definitions of Being actually sought.

For, first, with the realist, you will now assert that the object is not only Other than the finite idea, but is something that is authoritative over against the finite idea.   The realist gave an abstract expression to this authority of the object when he said that the object is independent of the idea.   The abstraction was false; but it was already a suggestion of the true meaning.   The finite idea does seek its own Other.   It consciously means this Other.   And it can seek only what it consciously means to seek.   But it consciously means to seek precisely that determination of its own will to singleness and finality of expression which shall leave it no Other yet beyond, and still to seek. To its own plan, to its own not here fully determined purpose, the idea at this instant must needs submit. Its very present conscious will is its submission. Yet the idea submits to no external meaning that is not the development of its own internal meaning. Moreover, the finite idea is a merely general idea. But what it means, its object, is an Individual. So you will all agree with the realist that whether or no the idea just now embodies its own object of search as nearly with present truth as the narrow limits of our consciousness permit, it must still seek other fulfilment than is now present, and must submissively accept this fulfilment as its own authoritative truth. But you will reject the realistic isolation of the idea from the object, and of the object from the idea.

If one attempts in some way to modify his Realism by declaring the object not wholly, but only partially, independent of the ideas which refer to it, still such a modified realist would only the more have to face, as we ourselves have been trying to face, the problem as to how the idea and its object are positively related. And if idea and object are left in the end in any way as two separate existent facts, isolated from each other, then one can find no further relation between the isolated idea and object except the relation of greater or less correspondence, and by this relation of mere external correspondence, taken alone, one would be able to define neither the Being of any object, nor the truth of any idea. Or, in other words, a world where ideas and objects merely corre-

spond, as isolated facts, and where no other and deeper
relation links knowledge and Being, is a world where
there is so far neither any knowledge nor any Being at
all.

But secondly, if you accept our Fourth Conception, you
will also agree with Mysticism in so far as, identifying
Being with fulfilment of purpose, the mystic says, of the
object of any of your ideas : *That art thou.* For the
mystic means this assertion not of the imperfect self of
the merely finite idea.   He does not mean that this passing thrill of longing is already fully identical with the
Other that this very longing seeks.   For the mystic, as
for the realist, Being is indeed something Other than our
mere search for Being.   The mystical identification of
the world and the Self is meant to be true of the completed, of the fulfilled and final, or Absolute Self.   Now,
starting with any idea, we shall henceforth say to this
idea, regarding its own object, precisely what the mystic
says of the Self and the World : *That art thou.*   Namely,
the object is for us simply the completely embodied will
of the idea.   It is nothing else.   But we shall henceforth differ from the mystic precisely at the point where
the mystic takes refuge in mere negations.   We, too, of
course, shall also confess our finite ignorance.   But the
Neti, Neti of Yâjnavalkya, the *nescio, nescio* of the
mediæval mystic, will express for us, not the essential
nature of true Being, as the mystic declared, but merely
the present inadequacy of your passing idea to its own
present and conscious purpose, — a purpose known precisely so far as it is embodied at this instant.   We shall
say if we follow to its conclusion this our Fourth Con-

ception, " We know in part, and we prophesy in part ;
but when the object meant, namely, precisely when that
which is perfect is truly said to be, it fulfils, and in so far
by supplementing but not otherwise, it takes away that
which is in part." Our final object, the *urbs Sion unica,
mansio mystica,* is for us, as for the mystic, the unique
Being wherein this our finite will is fulfilled. But this
one object meant, this fulfilment of our will, is not merely
" founded in heaven." Its will is done on earth, not yet
in this temporal instant wholly as it is in heaven, but is
still really done, in these ideas that already consciously
attain a fragment of their own meaning. They are ideas
precisely because they do this. The sadness of the mystical longing is now for us lighted by glimpses of the
genuine and eternally present truth of the one real world.
It is not merely in the mystic trance, but in every rational idea, in so far as it is already a partially embodied
purpose, that we now shall in our own way and measure
come upon that which is, and catch the deep pulsations of
the world. Our instant is not yet the whole of eternity ;
but the eternal light, the *lux eterna,* shineth in our every
reasonable moment, and lighteth every idea that cometh
into the world.

And, thirdly, if you follow our Fourth Conception, you
will now agree with the critical rationalist when he asserts
that Being essentially involves what gives the validity to
ideas. But you will have discovered what conditions are
necessary to constitute validity. The valid finite idea
is first, for whoever possess it, an observed and empirical
fulfilment of purpose. But this fulfilment is also observed in this instant as something incomplete. There-

fore it is that a finite idea seeks beyond itself for its own validity. And it is perfectly true to say that if the idea is valid, certain further experience of the fulfilment of the idea is possible. Leave this further experience, however, as something merely possible, and your definition of Being would so far remain fast bound in its own fatal circle. Is the idea valid or not? If it is valid, then, by hypothesis, further experience that would confirm the idea is possible. This further experience, like any object existent in the mathematician's realm, is both known to be something Other than the idea that refers to it, and is also viewed as a fact precisely corresponding to what the idea means to define. Now so long as you call this Other, this possible experience, merely such a bare possibility, you define, as we have said, only those characters of this object which the object has in common with your merely present idea of the object. The object is so far defined as an experience, and as having this or that type or form. That is what you say when you talk of any being in Kant's realm of *Mögliche Erfahrung*, or of any mathematical fact. All that is thus defined about the object is its mere *what*, the characters that it shares with your present ideas and experiences at the moment when you define it. What therefore you have *not* thus defined is precisely the Being of the object as Other than the very finite idea which is to regard it as an Other. If you have once observed this defect of any assertion of a bare possibility of experience, you will have seen why the mere definition of universal types can never reach the expression of the whole nature of real Beings, and why, for that very reason, the realm of Validity is nothing unless it is more than merely valid, nothing too unless it takes an individual form as an unique fulfilment of purpose in a completed life.

But all the three former conceptions are now to be brought into synthesis in this Fourth Conception. What is, is authoritative over against finite ideas, as Realism asserted, is one with the true meaning of the idea, as Mysticism insisted, and is valid as Critical Rationalism demanded. What is, presents the fulfilment of the whole purpose of the very idea that now seeks this Being. And when I announce this as our Fourth Conception of Being, I do not mean to be understood as asserting a mere validity, but as reporting facts. I do not any longer merely say, as we said at the outset of our discussion, Being is that which, if present, would end your finite search, would answer your doubts, would fulfil your purpose. All that was the language of validity. It was a mere preliminary. Since validity has no meaning unless its general types of truth take on individual form, and unless the *what* turns into the *that*, I now say, without any reserve, What is does in itself fulfil your meaning, does express, in the completest logically possible measure, the accomplishment and embodiment of the very will now fragmentarily embodied in your finite ideas. And I say, that this embodiment means in itself precisely what your present embodiment of purpose in your rational experience means, just in so far as your purposes are not mere fragments, but are also, even in their transiency, results known as, relatively speaking, won, as possessed, as accomplished. The accomplishment of your purpose now means that your experience is viewed by you as the present and conscious expression of a plan. Well, what is, precisely in so far as it is, is in the same way a whole experience finally expressing and consciously fulfilling a plan. And the Being of the real object of which you now think means a life that expresses the fulfilment of just your present plan, in the greatest measure in which your plan itself is logically capable of fulfilment.

Into this categorical assertion of a concrete experience embodying a plan, our whole series of hypothetically valid assertions of the realm of Critical Rationalism have now resolved themselves. A will concretely embodied in a life, — and these meanings identical with the very purposes that our poor fleeting finite ideas are even now so fragmentarily seeking, amidst all their flickerings and their conflicts, to express, — this, I say, is the reality. This alone is. All else is either shadow, or else is partial embodiment, *i.e.* is a striving after that ideal which needs for its own expression this very striving. This alone is real, — this complete life of divine fulfilment of whatever finite ideas seek. It is because the finite idea essentially seeks its Other, so long as it remains indeterminate, that the quest can be attained only when the will of the idea is so embodied that no other embodiment is to be sought. It is because no quest can be defined as a quest without defining valid possible experiences such as would fulfil or defeat this quest, and it is because no such valid possible experiences can be defined without presupposing that something more than mere validity is real, — it is because of all these considerations that we define the fulfilment of the finite quests embodied in our present and partial ideas as the essential nature of Being.

III

So far, then, we have restated and developed our Fourth Conception of Being as the only one capable of defining how an idea can correspond to an object which is other than the idea, but which is still the very object consciously meant by the idea.

But now are there not perfectly natural objections to this conception? There are. They appear in both the before mentioned forms, — as assertions that our conception is too complex and abstruse for the plain-minded man, and as assertions that our definition is too simple for the complexities of the actual universe. Both sorts of objections, however, will prove to be welcome aids to the very comprehension of our conception of Being itself. Let me here begin with a very familiar form that an empirical objection to our theory may take.

"After all," one may say, "you in vain endeavor, through your analysis of this or that conception of Being, to escape the conclusion of enlightened common sense that experience, and experience alone, determines what is and what is not. The whole question as to Being comes in the end to this : A man can frame ideas as he will, and as you say, ideas are indeed wilful enough constructions of merely conceived possibilities. But the question about Being always is, Does experience confirm the ideas? That idea expresses Being which is found to be confirmed by experience. Upon this view of Being all sane science is founded. But this view excludes all *a priori* constructions, and all efforts to pierce the mysteries of the Absolute. Constructions of ideas about possibilities of experience are often allowable enough in science, as mere hypotheses, or as assertions about what is probable. But the test is the concrete, present, immediate experience of this or that observer. What has been seen, felt, or otherwise empirically encountered by some body, is in so far real. Nothing else is for us men knowable about the constitution of Being. Now when you talk about Being as a final fulfilment of ideas, and of human experience as a mere fragment of such a final fulfilment, you transcend human experience. Your view is too abstruse and artificial for plain men. We no longer seek, in these days, for any absolute or final Being. We believe what we find. Nothing final is experienced by men. The realm of the empirical is always, as you say, fragmentary. But then this is the only realm known to men. This alone is for us real. Ideas furnish us the *what*. Concrete experience alone can supply the *that*. I conceive in idea a horse. In experience I thereupon see, touch, drive, or buy and sell horses. Other men do the same. Hence horses are real. But I conceive of a fairy. My idea is perhaps vivid. But still I never see fairies, and I find that none but children and ignorant people fancy that they have seen fairies. So fairies remain unobserved, and so far appear to be unreal. The same rule holds in science. Neptune was first ideally conceived, but this idea was verified by astronomical observation ; for the predicted planet was later observed. So Neptune is a reality. But the heavenly spheres of an older astronomy proved to be mere ideas, since advancing experience proved to be inconsistent with the ideas in question. So in science and in life, it is experience which decides that any supposed Being, whose *what* an idea defines, exists. Away, then, with your hope of finality. Experience is fragmentary, growing, and finite. And Being is only known through experience."

So far the objector. I reply, in a way already indicated at the last lecture. I myself doubt not in the least that the realm of experience is, and is decisive of truth. I doubt not this, simply because our Fourth Conception declares that what is real is an experience presenting the fulfilment of the whole purpose of ideas.

Nur in der Erfahrung ist Wahrheit, said Kant. I not only accept this thesis, but insist upon it. I know of no truth that is not an empirical truth, whatever further character it also possesses. An idea, according to our original definition, is already a fragment of experience although partially fulfilling a purpose. The fulfilment of an idea could not possibly take any form that was not also empirical. Neither God nor man faces any fact that has not about it something of the immediacy of a sense datum. That is for my conception a logical necessity. For what finite ideas seek is expression, embodiment, life, presence. Experience then is real. Ay, but what experience? And above all, in what sense is experience real ? What kind of Being has experience ? This question must be answered by any one who glibly asserts that experience is.   Now it seems strange to find that while many a man laughs to hear how some of the earlier scholastics supposed that not dogs and lions and men, but the canine nature, and leoninity in general, and humanity in the abstract are real, — still this same man will appeal to an ideal authority called Experience in general, — a mere universal idea so far, — as decisive of what is real, or as itself the reality.   As a fact, only individual experience is real, be that the experience of man or God.   And whoever asserts : " The reality is experience," has precisely those alternatives to face about the sense in which experience is real which have been discussed in the foregoing general account of the problem of Being.

There are in the world the experiences of men. Granted.   But are these experiences facts whose Being is wholly independent of the ideas whereby we now assert that these experiences are real ?   If we assert this, then, our empiricism becomes simply one form of Realism. It now defines the *what* of our world as experience ; but the *that* it defines, not at all merely in empirical terms, but rather in realistic terms, namely as a form of Being independent of our ideas, in so far as these ideas refer to the reality of this experience.   A realistic empiricist, therefore, if you look closer, explicitly transcends the very finite experience that he declares to be the only test of truth.

For consider : Suppose that you say that the experience of mankind is a real fact, and is what it is, whatever the metaphysical dreamers say about it.   Now as a finite being, confined to this instant, you do not experience my experience, nor in the same finite sense do I now and here experience your experience. If you assert that my experience is real, you in fact mean to transcend what your present finite experience presents to you. And neither your present fragment of experience can be directly used to verify the fact that my experience exists, nor can my fragment of momentary experience itself be used to verify the fact that you are thinking of me at all, or are referring to me, or are even meaning to assert my existence. And, in the same way, it is not a present fact of any man's momentary finite experience that the body of fact called the combined experience of humanity, or of science, or of any group of men, great or small, exists. Whoever asserts, then, that human experience exists, as a body consisting of the many experiences of various human observers, asserts what no finite human observer ever has, at any moment, experienced. For I insist, no man ever yet at any instant himself observed that mankind as a body, or that any man but himself, was observing facts.

Yet more, no man, at any one of our temporal human instants, ever then and there empirically verifies the existence even of his own past experiences. For, by definition, his past experiences are over, and are irrevocably no longer present, at any present empirical moment. No man, then, has ever observed the empirical fact that he himself has in the past observed facts, or has acquired by experience this which he now views as his own personally possessed body and outcome of experience.

Therefore, let no one who says, in a realistic sense, "Human experience, the experience of many men, exists," venture to add that he himself, or that any other man has, merely as man, empirically verified this assertion. It is false, then, to say that for such an assertion ideas furnish the *what*, and our human experience itself, in the form in which any man gets that experience, ever verifies the *that*. The assertion that a body of human experience exists, gets its *that* from some source not to be found in any one man's experience at any time. Our realistic empiricist is, therefore, so far precisely like other realists. He transcends every man's personal experience. He asserts the existence of independent Beings. He transcends all that any man ever has directly verified, or, as mere man, will at any instant ever verify. He is as transcendently metaphysical in his thesis as a Leibnitz or as a Herbart ever was in talking of Monads or of Reals. He can be decisively judged, however, only by the consistency of his ontological predicate. And we already know, in so far as he is a thoroughgoing realist, his fate.

For human experience, in so far as it is existent apart from our ideas which refer to it, is either something consciously meant by these ideas, or it is something not meant by them. If it is meant by them, it is either their whole real fulfilment in the form defined by our Fourth Conception; or else it is a part of just such a real final fulfilment. But, on the other hand, if it is something wholly independent in its existence of whether our private and momentary ideas refer to it or not; in other words, if it is a realm of facts whose type of Being is the realistic type, then in vain do you call it experience. Like any realistic Being, it is one whose existence cannot be referred to at all without the inconsistencies before observed. And in the end, like any other realistic Being, it is nothing at all.

Our empiricist may then take his choice. He is with us, or against us. If he is the latter, we have already dealt with him. For just so, if the experience to which our empiricist refers is the realm of the valid possibilities of experience, we already know its meaning and outcome. Conceive the realm of possible experience consistently, and it becomes the realm of our own conception of Being. But if one means only the sort of pure experience, the bare immediacy, to which the mystic referred, that sort of experience, as we found, is again explicitly nothing at all.

But if this empirical realm in question is the genuine realm of experience to which our ideas refer when, talking of experience with rational definiteness, we mean to see clearly, to observe closely, to know richly, and to live wisely, this is indeed an empirical world, and it is real. But it is real in the sense of our Fourth Conception. It is a life expressing in fulness what every transient moment of human consciousness fragmentarily embodies, and ideally seeks.

And as to finality, what constitution shall that realm of actual experience possess at all unless this constitution, in its wholeness, is indeed final, and final precisely in the sense of our Fourth Conception? For finality means, for us, the individual constitution of the realm of fact, interpreted in the only possible consistent way. You say, "Experience is." If you are an empiricist you also say, "All that is, is, in at least one aspect, experienced fact." Now, so far, all that is precisely

what our Fourth Conception says. So far we agree
with any empiricist. But if you reject our Fourth Conception, you then add, " This experience which is, is, even
when taken in its totality, a fragmentary experience, —
a mere collection of whatever happens to be ; — and this
world of experience possesses no finality." But do you
mean hereby that of two contradictory propositions made
about the existence of a supposed individual fact in this
whole realm of the real experience, both or neither may
now be true? Do you mean that if I say : " There is life
after death," or, " There was the siege of Troy," or,
" There is the observable planet Neptune," or, " There
is happiness in yonder child's heart as he sings," I can
thus assert a proposition that is neither true nor false, or
that is both true and false at once, and in the same sense?
If this were what you asserted, the assertion would indeed
mean nothing. But otherwise, if the world of experience,
as a real world, has even now, while we speak, an actual
constitution, then any definite proposition about the
world is either true or false when it is made. But if
so, any proposition with a definite internal meaning
involves ideas that, when the proposition is made, consciously mean to refer to the existent facts of that world
of real experience. But such reference to objects does
not consist, as we have now sufficiently seen, in mere
correspondence between idea and object. The only
reference that can constitute the meaning of an idea is
one which involves the complete expression of the will
of the idea. But if every issue which ideas can join,
with regard to the constitution of the empirical world, if
every contradictory opposition which the ideas can ex-

press, has its correspondent decision, *yes* or *no*, in the facts of the truly real empirical world, then the fulfilment of the ideas about experience in the facts of experience to which they refer, is once for all a wholly determinate fulfilment. And in this case, whatever constitution the world of experience in its entirety possesses, is as such an individual and final constitution.

And so, we say, the empirical world is a whole, a life fulfilling the purposes of our ideas. It is that or it is nothing. You labor in vain. The net of truth enmeshes your doubts.

"And yet," as you may now interpose, "we have but just seen that no man experiences, for himself, at any moment, this final constitution of our realm of experience." Of course no man experiences that constitution. Now we see through a glass darkly. It is not yet revealed what we shall be. It is not yet known to us what our own whole experience itself in its details contains. But we know that it is. And we observe the constitution of that realm. It is through and through a constitution that answers our questions, embodies our meanings, integrates our purposes. It is then in essence a realm of fact fulfilling purpose, of life embodying idea, of meaning won by means of the experience of its own content. The now present but passing form of our human consciousness is fragmentary. We wait, wonder, pass from fact to fact, from fragment to fragment. What a study of the concept of Being reveals to us is precisely that the whole has a meaning, and is real only as a Meaning Embodied.

IV

" But," our objector next retorts, " your view is still too abstruse for a plain man, — for how can you thus dare to transcend the limits of human consciousness ? It is true that when a man thinks, he just then consciously aims only at a meaning which is present to himself at the instant. But you talk now about the constitution of a realm of Being that is to lie beyond the limits of any merely human experience. For you admit that no man has yet seen at any one instant this which you call the whole of his meaning empirically expressed. Now, how can you have any assurance as to such a realm of transcendent and superhuman finality of experience? Perhaps there is experience beyond our own, perhaps not. At all events, any man actually knows only his own contents of experience, and with more or less probability he guesses at the existence of other contents than his own in other men. But nobody can assert, with real or positive assurance, any Being that transcends his own present experience. Yet you talk of final Being, and of its constitution. *Perhaps there is no final Being.* Perhaps there is only the present fragment of empirical life. Even my own past and future, as you say, are not present to me. How should I myself at this instant know that there exists more than what is now present to me ? Why, then, cannot we be mere sceptics, doubting all reality not now and here given ? "

I reply at once: State your doubt in a more precise form. Tell what it means. What hypothesis, if any, do you oppose to our own thesis as to this complete and individual, this teleological constitution of the realm of Being, which we have asserted as our Fourth Conception. What is it that you doubt? And what alternative would be true if your doubt were well founded? Hesitate not to give your doubt all possible precision. Philosophy lives upon the comprehension of the meaning of its own doubts.

Let one then say, by way of a mere trial at scepticism: "Beyond a given circle of experience, supposed to be at present known to you and to me, or to me alone, there may be *Nothing at all.* Let us then suppose, for argument's sake, that there *is* nothing at all beyond what you or I may just now feel to be present, as our empirical facts, as our passing conscious ideas, desires, hopes, as our so-called memories, and as the problems of the instant. Let that be the realm of Being. Let there be supposed to be naught in the universe but just this. Now this little realm of given fact has no consciously experienced finality about it, no wholeness, no satisfying constitution, no absoluteness. Yet this little realm of passing consciousness somehow exists. How then shall this Fourth Conception of Being refute the purely sceptical hypothesis thus made? And unless such a sceptical hypothesis is refuted, how can any assertions which transcend the instantaneous limits of our human form of consciousness be made in any wise certain?"

So far the doubter's hypothesis. I reply: This doubt, once stated as a possible account of a realm of Being, has all the responsibilities of any ontology. It hypothetically defines as real, a supposed, or given, finite circle of empirical facts, called this instant's contents. It supposes this circle to be conceived, for the moment, as the whole of Being, as all that there is. Well, what does this hypothetical assertion mean? Stripped of its accessories, it means simply : A certain finite momentary collection of empirical facts, ideas, desires, etc., merely called the present moment, is the universe. Now, to simplify the matter, name this finite conscious instant of experience, of thought and of will, A. One supposes that A is all, or that nothing but A exists. Well, this assertion, like any other metaphysical one, involves a *what* and a *that*. Moreover, it asserts the non-being of anything but A. Now an assertion of non-being is subject to the same general conditions as an assertion of Being. Whatever one means by Being, the meaning of the negative of Being, or of the assertion that something does *not* exist, is determined by the sense given to the predicate by which one affirms Being. Premising this, then, let one estimate the consistency of the hypothesis now in question.

If one asserts ; *A is all* or, *There is naught but A*, the assertion involves ideas, and if it means anything these ideas possess some object. Now by hypothesis, the present moment, or A, does not itself contain the direct experience of the fact that it includes the whole universe of Being. For if A were certainly aware that nothing besides itself could exist, it would consciously have present what exhausted, even in the very present consciousness of A, the whole possible meaning of the idea of Being. But A would itself then be a completely embodied meaning, an absolutely self-possessed Whole of experience, fulfilling its own purpose. Or in other words, our own Fourth Conception of Being would directly apply to it. And our doubter would then be no mere sceptic; for his positive account would be ours. But since, by hypothesis, A is a passing moment, a dissatisfied instant of finite human experience, the fact that it comprises all that is real is not itself present to the experience of A. And the non-being of all except A, the exclusion from Being of all not present in A, is supposed to be a fact, but a fact whose *that*, whose very existence as a real fact, must consequently be sought *elsewhere* than in the conscious experience present to A alone. This already contradicts the hypothesis here in question, as we first stated it. For the fact that A is all Being cannot itself be part of the experience of a consciously fragmentary, or dissatisfied A. Yet A was, by hypothesis, to contain all Being. Our sceptic, then, if you suppose him a mere partisan of experience as the only reality, has begun by contradicting himself.

But this is not all. This supposed fact, that *A is all Being*, or that *Naught but A exists*, may indeed next be made formally consistent with itself by an amendment. Let the hypothesis now run, as amended, thus : "*A contains all experience, or all conscious fact, but besides this conscious fact there does exist the unconscious fact, the mere brute reality, unknown to anybody, and present to nobody's experience, the mere fact that A is, not indeed all Being, but all Experience.*" The sceptical hypothesis thus amended leads, however, at once, to precisely our foregoing alternatives as to the sense in which this supposed fact of the loneliness of A can be asserted as a real fact. *That there is no experience in the universe except A*, is now supposed to be itself a fact, but a fact whose reality nobody experiences. But what kind of Being has this fact? It is, by hypothesis, the object to which the sceptical assertion relates. As such object, other than the sceptic's assertion, but really meant by him as a truth, it is in the position that we have now exhaustively discussed. It cannot be a fact whose Being is wholly independent of the sceptic's own assertion, nor yet a being of the mystical type, nor a merely universal valid truth, of the type of our Third Conception of Being. For all these types of Being have been found logically wanting. Nor can it be in any sense an object merely agreeing with our sceptic's assertion, and externally correspondent thereto. For external agreement with an idea that asserts Being, when such agreement is taken alone, constitutes neither the Being of any object, nor the truth of any idea. That A is the only existent experience must, therefore, be a fact which, as an individual fact, fulfils the will embodied in the sceptic's hypothesis, both in so far as this will refers to that fact, and in so far as the sceptic himself inevitably, even in still supposing the non-being of all but A, talks of Being in general and of the universe in its wholeness. The only possible result is that, in asserting that A is all experience, the sceptic's hypothesis, if consistent with itself, asserts that A itself consciously contains, presents, and fulfils the whole meaning involved in the idea of Being; or in other words that A is not a mere passing thrill of human experience, but is an absolute experience, self-determined, self-contained, individual, whole, and therefore final.

The sceptic's hypothesis, therefore, so soon as it is made

explicit, wholly agrees with our own. Nothing can be but such a whole experience.

V

But our empirical objector may finally turn upon us with another version of his parable. "Who," he may say, "could for a day attempt to hold your Fourth Conception of Being, and still face a single one of the most characteristic facts of human experience, a single practical failure, a single case where dear hopes have to be resigned, an hour of darkness and private despair, a public calamity, or even a sleepless night, — who I say could face such commonplace facts and not have the observation thrust, as it were, upon him by the seemingly irresistible powers of this world, — the well-known observation: '*You reason in vain: these hard facts are against you.*' Your view is too simple for this our complex real world. What is, does not in any essential way fulfil ideas. What is real, is once more whatever experience shows to exist. And experience contains all sorts of non-fulfilments and irrationalities. Chaos or order, joy or defeat, tears of despair and shouts of victory, mysteries, storms, north winds, wars, the wreck of hearts, the might of evil, the meteors that wander in interplanetary darkness, the suns that waste their radiant energy in the chill depths of lifeless space, — these all are facts, — these are Beings. Why talk of Being? What Being in itself is, may well remain unknowable. But what is consistent with the existence of facts, you experience whenever you observe just such wretchedly irrational facts as

these.   Whatever they mean, they involve not fulfilment,
but defeat, of purpose.   And that is what you yourself
experience whenever you lose what is dear, and face the
insoluble mysteries of experience."

The practical weight of such objections can escape no
one.   They constitute in one aspect the well-known problem of evil.   With the positive solution of this problem
for its own sake we are not yet directly concerned.   That
belongs later in these discussions.   Our concern at the
moment is less with the pathetic than with the purely
logical aspect of such objections.   What they point out
is that, empirically, there are countless, if essentially
fragmentary, empirical facts to be recognized, which do
not at present come to us human beings as the embodiment of certain specified purposes.   These facts appear
as involving the temporal defeat of these very purposes
in just these passing instants of wavering search for
Being wherein we now are.   We call these facts, — such
facts as storms, as war, as defeat and despair, as north
winds and sleepless nights, — facts belonging somehow to
the realm of Being.   Yet they are facts that, when
spoken of as ills, are so far defined with reference to the
ideas which they just now temporally defeat.   How do
they stand with reference to our definition of Being?

I reply, for the first, by distinguishing two aspects of
any unwelcome facts, such as the empirical observer of
human destiny may find to be present in the world.
These two aspects are indeed not to be sundered, and are
here distinguished only for the sake of present convenience.   Yet we shall profit by taking care not blindly to
confuse them.   Any unwelcome empirical fact has, namely,

its own positive characters, as a fact that in our human experience appears at a point of time, in certain relations in space, and with numerous other positively definable features, all of which the thought of any historian or any student of science who describes the fact, may define as the object of his own ideas. In addition to these, its own relatively internal and positive features, the unwelcome fact also appears as involving the present temporal defeat of a purpose which, but for this fact, might here have been won. Now these two aspects of the unwelcome fact were long ago distinguished by the ancient as well as by the mediæval students of the problem of evil. "Every evil," said such students, "has, as a positive fact in the world of Being, its own internal perfections. Its evil character is due to its relations to other facts that coexist with it in the same world. Even Satan," said such views, "is an angel; and even as a fallen angel he has extraordinary perfections of nature, which so far constitute a good. His diabolical quality is due to the misuse of precisely these perfections. The best in wrong setting becomes the worst." Upon such bases these older accounts of evil undertook to make the presence of evil in the world consistent with the well known thesis, *Omne Ens est bonum,* — a thesis whose historical relation to our own conception of Being I am far from attempting to deny.

Now I indeed have no doubt that these ancient and mediæval students of the problem of evil often made their own task far too light. Nor am I here concerned to accept their special solutions of the problem as to the place of ill in a divinely ordered world. But it does concern us here to point out that an unwelcome fact of human experience has in general these two sorts of characters, namely, the characters which make it a positively definable temporal and spatial fact, — so far like any other fact of experience, — and the characters which make us say, that it defeats this or that human purpose.

Thus physical death appears in our experience as an occurrence resulting from a series of physiological processes. As a natural phenomenon its very prevalence is of a deep rational interest. Meanwhile, it involves chemical and physical changes which are not essentially different from countless other changes going on in the organic world. For science it therefore has the same sort of importance that any other event in the biological realm may come to have. On this side, one can say that death is definable as an objective fact rendering relatively true, in their own fragmentary degree, our ideas about death. And this one can say in the same sense as that in which one can make this assertion about any natural fact whatever. If our theory of Being assigns to every objective fact a character as a relative fulfilment of the ideas which refer to it, death also, in so far as it fulfils ideas about death, is to just this extent no instance against our theory. Or, in case you will to know the facts about death, would your will be fulfilled if you remained ignorant of death? Or, once more, as facts now are, for us human beings, would you prefer to remain as innocent of any knowledge of death as much lower animals than ourselves may be ignorant? If you ask a question about death, is your will yet fulfilled in case experience refuses the answer? Would not many amongst us prefer to know much more than we now do as to when and how we ourselves are to die? Is not the very uncertainty of the time of death one of its ills for every prudent man? So much then for one aspect of the empirical ill called death. So far, to know its Being is relatively and imperfectly to fulfil ideas. And our theory defines its Being in terms of this fulfilment.

But death — and, above all, not our own death nearly so much as the death of our friends — is an evil in so far as it appears in our experience as a temporal defeat of the purposes of human love, and of the need of the human world for its good men. Well, this is the other, and, for our own theory, indeed, the more problematic aspect of death. For here the passing fragment of fact is that a given human purpose is so far defeated. And this fragment of fact, as we admit, is obviously somehow a part of the real, — a fact of finite Being. And yet our theory asserts that what is, as such, fulfils purposes, and fulfils too the very purposes of our ideas.

I have emphasized death as merely one instance, and by no means of course the worst instance, of that inestimably pathetic story of human defeat and misfortune to which our previous examples a moment ago made reference. Now of course I accept to the full the responsibility of our theory to account in the end, not for the mere fact that some finite purposes are defeated, but for the fact that, in human experience, the very purposes which refer, as ideal strivings, to certain objects as their ends, appear, so far as our more direct mortal ken extends, to be for the instant defeated in presence of the very objects to which they have made reference. It is I who fear my friend's death, and hope for his survival. Yet he dies. I have thought beforehand of my object, namely, of my friend's coming destiny. But my object has so far, at least in a measure, entered into my experience, and has overwhelmed me, whose idea defined the object, with the despair of non-fulfilment. Here is a Being in apparently direct conflict with its own idea, and an idea apparently at war with its own object. How is our theory to explain this?

I answer, in the first place, precisely as the mystic would have done in a similar case: By our own definition of Being, you have not empirically found your whole final object, the entire and individual fact of Being that you seek, so long as you seek still for an Other. It is precisely as the Other that Being is not yet empirically present. Loneliness and despair, just because they are dissatisfied, look beyond themselves for Being. And in presence of death you do thus seek for the Other, namely, for the meaning of this fact, for the solution of this mystery, for the beloved object that is gone, for the lost life, for something not here, for the unseen, — yes, for the Eternal. And in this your search for the eternal lies for you the very meaning of death and of finite despair.

As Mary passionately cried, "They have taken away my Lord, and I know not where they have laid him," so every mourner knows precisely this, — that true Being is not finally here where death is, but is elsewhere. The true object, then, the actual Being that you seek, is not found, but merely seems to be lost, at the moment of death. Where, then, is that object? *Not here, Not here*, cries despair. *Aye, Elsewhere*, answers our teaching, *Elsewhere* is precisely the true Being that you seek.

Look, then, elsewhere. Seek not the living among the dead.

But you will reply: Have we not just admitted that death itself is, like any other amongst our countless human disasters, a fact of experience? Is not a fact an object? Is not an object real? Have we not ourselves called it so? Aye, but we have not said that death is by itself a Whole object. Death, as far as it comes into our experience, is indeed a glimpse of fact, but in the moral world it is the most fragmentary of such glimpses of reality. Whoever faces it faces nothing that he finds as an individual and present reality. What he observes is the absence of precisely what he himself defines as the Whole of Being that he seeks,— the very longing of an unfulfilled idea, which defines the Other, and looks elsewhere for the reality.

Now our theory merely consists in asserting that in every such case the reality sought is a life, and a concrete life of fulfilment, and that this reality is, and is in its wholeness, elsewhere than at this fragmentary instant of human experience. Human experience offers, so far as it goes, only a confirmation of this our view. For we have said that true Being is essentially a Whole Individual Fact, that does not send you beyond itself, and that is, therefore, in its wholeness, deathless. Where death is, Being in its wholeness is not.

"But," so one insists, "but my grief, my defeat, my despair; are they not real? And are they real as determined facts?" I reply: Our theory is indeed responsible for an account of how the temporal and empirical defeat of a specific, although always fragmentary, human purpose can be an incident in a deathless life which in its wholeness involves the fulfilment of a purpose, and of a purpose which includes the very fragmentary purpose now temporally defeated. That account, in its more complete statement, belongs elsewhere, as the explicit discussion of the problem of evil. It is enough at present to point out what all the strongest of human souls have observed and reported as a fact of experience; namely, that through the endurance and the conquest over its own internal ills the spirit wins its best conscious fulfilment. What if this moment of despair be but the beginning, or the fragment, of your whole life as this winning of the object that you now seek? Our theory maintains that, in fact, this is the case. That the fulfilment of the whole of a purpose may involve the defeat of a part of this very purpose, every experience of the beauty of tragedy, of the glory of courage, of the nobility of endurance, of the triumph over our own selves, empirically illustrates.

For tragedy wins our interest by making us suffer, and yet consent to endure, not the tragic hero's suffering, but our own, for the sake of the spiritual beauty that we thereby learn to contemplate. Courage is glorious, because it involves a conquest over our own conscious shrinking in the presence of danger. Who fears not knows not conscious courage. Endurance is noble, because it includes a voluntary defeat of our own unwillingness to endure. And, in general, every form of more complex rational life means a triumph over ourselves whereby alone we win ourselves. Whoever has not faced problems as problems, mysteries as mysteries, defeats as defeats, knows not what that completer possession of his own life means which is the outcome and also the present experience of triumph in the midst of finitude and disaster.   For in the victorious warfare with finitude consists the perfection of the spirit.

LECTURE IX

LECTURE IX

THE concept of Being often passes for the most abstract of human ideas. If the first outcome of our quest, as presented in the two foregoing discussions, is sound, the true concept of Being is the most concrete and living of all our ideas.

I

We began these lectures indeed with an abstraction, with the contrast between telling what an ideal object is, and asserting that this object exists. We called this the contrast between the internal and the external meaning of ideas. This abstraction Realism carried to the extreme, asserting that the idea finds the external object merely as its indifferent fate. All relations between the two are, for Realism, additional facts, existent over and above the primary indifference. Hereupon, however, the inner self-destruction of Realism, which we found to be the logical result of these assumptions, drove us, as we sought for truth, into the mystic's realm. There we first learned something of the deeper meaning of the ancient thesis: *Omne Ens est bonum,* — a thesis which indeed appears in Aristotle's doctrine, but which can never be justified on a realistic basis. *To be* appeared in this world of the mystic to mean the same as to fulfil the inner purpose of ideas. What is, is as such the perfect, the absolute, the finality, and in this respect we have indeed found the mystic to be right. But the mystic sought the highest good of his always consciously imperfect ideas in their own simple extinction. And this void proved to be meaningless. Here then was, so far, no positive reality. We therefore abandoned this region for the more concrete world of modern Critical Rationalism. Here the ideas were indeed different from their objects, and corresponded to them. But our difficulty in this realm was to define, after all, how our objects were other than our ideas, while still remaining authorities to which we made valid reference. And so we were still discontent in this world of Critical Rationalism. We waited until it should be transformed into another.

The Fourth Conception of Being has now undertaken to bring into harmony the motives of all the three other conceptions. What is, is other than the mere idea, yet not because it externally corresponds thereto, but because it completely expresses, in a form that is ultimately individual, the very meaning that the finite idea consciously, but partially and abstractly, embodies in its own general form. The idea wills its own complete expression. What is, fulfils the whole intent of the idea. What is, is therefore at once empirical, for it embodies the idea; significant, for it expresses a meaning; an individual, for it gives the idea such an expression as seeks no other beyond. Whatever is less than such a completed life as this, is a fragment of Being, a finite idea still consciously in search of its own wholeness, a mere kind of relative fulfilment such as needs, implies, and looks to another to complete its own purpose.

On the other hand, every such duality of idea and object, or of fragment and whole, is secondary to and subservient to the one will or purpose which the idea partially, and the completed individual life of the object wholly, embodies, and embodies even by including the fragmentary will of every idea. If you want to express the truth in its wholeness, you must not merely say first, *There is an idea*, and secondly, *There is also an object*, and thirdly, *These two correspond*. For when you speak thus, you deal in abstractions; you yourself so far seek as your own Other the very meaning and sense of these abstractions : and merely to speak thus is to define neither truth nor Being. You must rather say : There is an embodied life, a fulfilled meaning, an empirically expressed intent, an individual whole, that attains its own end. This is what we mean when we talk of what is real. To be such a whole life, this alone is to be real. Now of this life my idea, when I speak of an object, is a fragment, as well as, in its relatively present fulfilment, a general type. As a fragment, my idea looks elsewhere for the rest of itself. As a type of imperfect fulfilment, it aims at the complete experience of the whole of this type. But as really one with its object, my idea in thus seeking its Other, seeks only the expression of its own will in an empirical and conscious life. But this life is. For that any idea, true or relatively erroneous, has an object at all, implies such fulfilment.

The *that* thus comes into unity with the *what*. *What*

my object is, my idea at this instant not only imperfectly defines, but fragmentarily presents in its own transient way. *That* my object is, is true in so far as the whole *what* of my object is empirically expressed in an individual life, which is my real world.

Thus, although Realism assured us that the *what* could never predetermine the *that*, the essence never prove the existence, and although this has become a mere commonplace of popular metaphysic, we now have found how the *that*, the very existence of the world, predetermines the *what*, or the essence of things, and the fact of Being has become for us the richest of concrete facts.

For despite the relative failures and errors of our finitude, the real world cannot fail to express the whole genuine intent of our ideas, their completely understood internal meaning. Ideas, in other words, in so far as they are consistent with their own completed ideal purpose, cannot remain unexpressed in a concrete life of individual experience. For if they remained unexpressed, their final meaning could only take the form of hypotheses whose verbal statement would begin with an *if*. The final truth would be that *if* certain empirical expressions took place, certain ideal results would follow. But as we have seen, what is *merely* valid, is not even valid. For the Third Conception of Being failed to express how even itself could be true, just because it left us with a mere general *what*, and never reached the *that*.

Suppose, in fact, that what we have with equal propriety called the meaning and the will of our finite

ideas now partially embodied in this flying instant, is
to remain in the end unexpressed, so that only an *if*-
proposition, valid, but disembodied, contains the truth
of the world when viewed with reference to ideas.
Then still you do not escape from the facts.   For the
fact of this *non*-expression of our ideas, has, by this
very hypothesis, its own real Being.   But what form of
Being shall this fact of the non-expression of the meaning of our ideas, this refusal of the universe concretely
to fulfil our purposes, actually possess?   Shall this brute
fact that our ideas are not expressed possess the reality
of an object independent of all ideas?   But such a
reality, as we now know, is a logical impossibility.
Moreover, an object independent of all ideas, even if
such an object were otherwise possible, could defeat, or
could refuse real expression to no idea whatever.   For
what my idea seeks, and what therefore could conceivably be refused to it, by another, is simply its own expression in just that reality which it means and intends
to possess as its own object.   The reality, therefore,
which shall positively refuse it expression, is *ipso facto*
the reality to which the idea itself appeals, and is not
independent of this appeal.   For you are not put in the
wrong by a reality to which you have made no reference; and error is possible only concerning objects that
we actually mean as our own objects.   The object that
is to defeat my partial and fragmentary will is then *ipso
facto* my whole will, my final purpose, my total meaning determinately and definitively expressed.   Hypotheses never verified, *if*-propositions to which no concrete
expression corresponds, have part in existence of course,

but only as fragments of ideas. They exist only as errors take place. I can be in partial error, but only because at this instant I may imperfectly grasp my own whole meaning as I refer to my object. My will, as it is now transiently embodied, can fail in any partial way of realization, but only because I now fail to be wholly aware of my own will. Therefore hypothetical propositions counter to fact are possible only as fragments. But however far I wander in the wildernesses of my temporal experience, the eternal fulfilment of my own life encompasses me. I escape not from the meshes of the net of my own will. I fail at this instant to observe this fact, merely because of the imperfection of my momentary form of human consciousness. I interpret my facts hypothetically and often falsely, in so far as I fail to grasp just now my own whole purpose.

Schopenhauer defines my world as my own will. If by my will he meant the individual embodiment and expression of the whole meaning of my ideas, he would thus be right. But then he would indeed be no pessimist. For the longing and the misery of finitude that in my present form of human consciousness now so frequently bound the horizon of my darkened instants of fragmentary experience — this longing and misery, when they beset me, I say, involve that very search for Another, that very dissatisfaction with the abstractness and dreary generality of my present ideas, which I express in my own way whenever, out of the depths, I cry after Reality. People often object to Schopenhauer's view of the world as the will, that that doctrine, as Schopenhauer frequently expresses it, is a mere Animism. We know, they say, that the world is real ; but how should we know that its inner Being, so foreign to ours, resembles our own will ? But our own Fourth Conception of Being is not in the older sense animistic. For it does not first say, *The world is known to be real*, and then add, *And we conjecture that this reality resembles that of our own will*. What our view asserts is that the world is and can be real only *as* the object expressing in final, in individual form, the whole meaning which our finite will, imperfectly embodied in fleeting instants, seeks and attempts to define as its own Other, and also as precisely its own ultimate expression. In other words, the world, from our point of view, becomes real only as such an ultimate expression of our ideas. But when the sceptic here retorts, *But perhaps then no world is real at all*, we reply with the now several times repeated observation that the non-being of any specific object is subject to the same conditions as the Being of all things. What is not, is not, merely because our complete object, the complete expression of our whole meaning, when, in this transient moment, we speak of the thing that is not, excludes its presence. The very possibility of our ignorance and error implies the presence of the whole self-conscious truth.

II

Results in philosophy must needs lead to new problems. With this definition in mind of what it is to be, how shall we next undertake to describe that more special constitution of the world which our concept of Being involves ?

The general title of our course called attention to a

certain well-known problem for which we are now at
length fully prepared. The World and the Individual, —
these are now upon our hands. Their Being we have
defined, not only in general, but with an explicit reference to both of them. But what we have so far, for the
greater part of our discussion, deliberately ignored, is an
attempt to describe in any detail their precise mutual relations. It is just to these relations that we shall henceforth devote ourselves, both in the brief remaining space
of this first half of our series, and in all that is to constitute the second half of these lectures. What is, as
we have already asserted, is the *World*. We have also
asserted that it is the *Individual*. Both terms appear
equivocal. The world is real, — ay, but what world?
The world, so our Fourth Conception has answered, — the
world that any idea views as its own wholly expressed
meaning and object. "Yes," you may say, "but are not
our ideas many and various? Is it not one thing to
think of mathematical truth, and quite another to think
of physical truth? Is not the world of the mathematician a different object from the world of the moralist?
Are these not then various worlds adapted to express various meanings? Do these worlds constitute one realm, —
a single universe? And if so, how?" But we have also
said that the individual is real. Here still more naturally
you may ask, "What individual?" Our answer has
been : The whole individual life that expresses and presents the meaning of any single idea. But you will still
properly be dissatisfied. You will say : "Are not the individuals as various as are all our various ideas? And
how are these individuals of which you have so far spoken

to be related to what we mean when we talk of individual men, of souls, of moral personalities, or of one man as different from any other man?"

Now these are precisely the central questions of religion. These, therefore, are the problems most significant for our whole quest. These two are issues which no one who attacks the central concepts of metaphysical doctrine ought to ignore. The unity of the world, the triumph of the divine plan, the supremacy of good in the universe, these are the interests which religion expresses by asserting that God reigns as a rational, self-conscious, world-possessing, and single Being. The freedom of individuals, the deathless meaning of the life of each person, the opportunity for moral action, these are the interests of every form of ethical religion. I have been forced, before approaching these issues, to dwell so elaborately and so long upon the concept of Being, because that concept is no abstraction, but is precisely the richest and most inclusive of all conceptions, and because, until we had grasped its meaning, any speech as to the various beings that may be found in the world, and as to their relations to the whole and to one another, would have altogether lacked metaphysical foundation. But our task having been so far accomplished, we are prepared to pass from the doctrine of what it is to be real, to the consequent theory regarding what are the existent realities. Hereupon, however, we enter upon the true task of a religious theory.

The problems just stated, if one views them in advance, appear to admit of two opposed solutions. Of these the one would lay the emphasis upon the unity of the whole world, while the other would insist both upon the variety, and, in some modified way, upon the relative independence of the individual lives. The one thesis could be briefly summarized thus : This Fourth Conception of Being asserts that what is, expresses, in a complete life of concrete experience, the whole meaning of the ideas that refer to any object. Now, when any one of us rationally speaks of the universe, of the whole of Being, he has an idea, and this idea means precisely the entire world itself. Whatever life pulsates anywhere, whatever meaning is at any time fragmentarily seen embodied in flying moments, — all such lives and meanings form the object of our metaphysical inquiry. Now our very power to make the whole of Being our problem, already implies that the object of our inquiry, whatever it proves to contain, has as the fulfilment of one idea, the constitution of a single life of concrete fulfilment. All varieties of individual expression are thus subordinate to the unity of the whole. All differences amongst various ideas result from and are secondary to the very presence of one universal type of ideal meaning in all the realm of life. All appearance of isolation in finite beings, all the fragmentariness of their finitude, these are indeed but aspects of the whole truth. The One is in all, and all are in the One. All meanings, if completely developed, unite in one meaning, and this it is which the real world expresses. Every idea, if fully developed, is of universal application. Since this one world of expression is a life of experience fulfilling ideas, it possesses precisely the attributes which the ages have most associated with the name of God. For God is the Absolute Being, and the perfect fulness of life. Only

God, when thus viewed, is indeed not other than his world, but is the very life of the world taken in its wholeness as a single conscious and self-possessed life. In God we live and move and have our Being.

The other thesis, at first sight apparently opposed to the foregoing, may be stated as follows : This Fourth Conception of Being appeals, when rightly understood, to the self of each individual thinker. And it appeals to individual thinkers only, whether human or divine. We have often spoken in the foregoing of any idea as if, taken apart from other ideas, it possessed, so to speak, a selfhood of its own, the selfhood imperfectly exemplified, transiently embodied, in your consciousness at this instant while you think and purpose. Now this manner of speech might indeed be said to lay too much stress upon mere fragments. A momentary human idea is indeed not by itself alone a self, although it does fragmentarily contain the partial will of a self. But the meaning that it contains belongs in truth to some individual thinker, to this soul, to this man, to you or to me. Now, however mysterious may be the difference between you and me, we are in such wise different beings, that the unity of Being must find room for our variety. Above all, our ethical freedom, our practical, even if limited, moral independence of one another, must be preserved. The world then is a realm of individuality. Hence it must be a realm of individuals, self-possessed, morally free, and sufficiently independent of one another to make their freedom of action possible and finally significant.

These are the two possible interpretations of our Fourth Conception. It will be our attempt in what immediately follows, in this and in the next lecture, to develope and to reconcile both interpretations. We shall maintain that the unity of the divine life, and the universality of the divine plan, define one aspect, and a most essential aspect of the world of our Fourth Conception. We shall also maintain and try to make in general explicit, how this unity is not only consistent with the ethical meaning of finite individuality, but is also the sole and sufficient basis thereof.

III

The unity of the whole world, and the unversality of the idea of Being, first demand our attention. We have asserted that our Fourth Conception involves the absolute unity of the final knowing process. In precisely what sense and for what reason do we make this assertion?

Our concept of Being implies that whatever is, is consciously known as the fulfilment of some idea, and is so known either by ourselves at this moment, or by a consciousness inclusive of our own. If we address the finite thinker, and consider the implications of his knowledge, we point out to him that what he now experiences is but a fragment of the object that he means. But the object that he means, so we tell him, can have no form of Being that is independent of his meaning. Nor can he be said to have any meaning not now wholly fulfilled in his present experience, unless that very meaning is present to an insight that includes and completes his own conscious insight according to his own real intent. This essentially idealistic account of what it is to be, we have now elaborately justified by an analysis of the very concept of meaning, or of the relation of idea and object. If any fact, not at any instant consciously present to the finite thinker, is really meant by him, then there is something true, *about* his consciousness, which his momentary consciousness of his own meaning at once implies, and nevertheless in its internal meaning does not directly and wholly exhaust for him, here and now. And this relatively external truth which is intended by the finite consciousness, and which is inclusive of all that at any instant this finite consciousness finds present to itself, is a truth whose Being can be neither of the realistic type, nor of the mystical type, nor of the merely valid type of Being, nor of any form except a conscious form, — a form whose existence includes and completes what the finite thinker at any moment undertakes to know. It follows of necessity that in the world as we define it, there can exist no fact except as a known fact, as a fact present to some consciousness, namely, precisely to the consciousness that fulfils the whole meaning of whoever asserts that this fact is real.

In view of this essential feature of our finite situation as thinkers, it follows at once that the whole world of truth and being must exist only as present, in all its variety, its wealth, its relationships, its entire constitution, to the unity of a single consciousness, which includes both our own and all finite conscious meanings in one final eternally present insight. This complete insight is indeed not *merely* one, but is observant of all the real finite varieties, of experience, of meaning, and of life. Nor is the external insight *merely* timeless ; but it is possessed of an inclusive view of the whole of time, and of whatever, when taken in its wholeness, this our time-process means. This final view, for which the realm of Being possesses the unity of a single conscious whole, indeed ignores no fragment of finite consciousness; but it sees all at once, as the realm of truth in its entirety.

This, I say, is the unquestionable and inevitable outcome of our Fourth Conception of Being. And the proof of this outcome is very brief.

For whatever is has its being, once more, only as a fact observed, and exists as the fulfilment of a conscious meaning. That is our definition of Being. But now let one say, There are many facts, ideas, and meanings in the world. Each of these exists only as the object that fulfils the whole meaning of a knowing process. So far, then, there exist many knowing processes, each with its own meaning fulfilled. The world so far contains many knowers, many ideas, or many Selves, if you are pleased to use that word. But our Fourth Conception hereupon continues : Are these many knowers mutually related or not? Answer as you will. Let them be or not be in any specific sort of mutual relation. Then this, the fact about their relations, exists, but exists only as a known fact. For our theory asserts universally that all which has Being exists only as known object. The fact about the true relations of the various knowing beings and processes is, however, a fact unintelligible except as expressing and including their own very existence; and by hypothesis this inclusive fact is a consciously known fact. That the various knowers are, then, and that they are in given relationship or in given relative independence of one another, — all this is a consciously known fact. There is, in consequence, a conscious act or process for which the existence and the relations of all the various knowing processes constitute a present and consciously observed truth. But this assertion, the inevitable consequence of our doctrine, implies that one final knower knows all knowing processes in one inclusive act.

Moreover, let the world of fact, taken in its wholeness, possess any constitution that you please. Assert that any degree of multiplicity, of mutual isolation, of temporal succession, of variety in individual existence, or of other dividing principle, variegates the universe, or keeps finite acts, meanings, and interests asunder. Then, by hypothesis, all this variety and mutual isolation is fact, and by our Fourth Conception of Being it all exists only as a consciously known fact. If the sundered finite forms of consciousness are by hypothesis not mutually inclusive, their very sundering, according to our conception of Being, implies their common presence as facts to a knower who consciously observes their sundering as the fulfilment of his own single meaning.

For otherwise the sundering would exist without being fully and consciously present to anybody; since, in so far as a is sundered from b, there is, neither in a alone nor in b alone, a consciousness of all that the sundering implies for both.

And, finally, the knower of the universe in its wholeness can possess, by our definition, no Being that is unknown to himself. For whatever is, is consciously known. And if the being of a is unknown to a, but is known only to another, namely, to b, there so far exists a fact, namely, the relation of a and b, whose presence to knowledge has not yet been defined. But if whatever exists, exists only as known, the existence of knowledge itself must be a known existence, and can finally be known only to the final knower himself, who, like Aristotle's God, is so far defined in terms of absolute self-knowledge.

Herewith the purely abstract statement of the consequences of our Fourth Conception, so far as it concerns the unity of the world, has been made, in the only form consistent with our conception. What is, is present to the insight of a single Self-conscious Knower, whose life includes all that he knows, whose meaning is wholly fulfilled in his facts, and whose self-consciousness is complete. And our reason for asserting this as the Reality lies in the now thoroughly expounded doctrine that no other conception of Being than this one can be expressed without absolute self-contradiction. Whoever denies this conception covertly, so we affirm, asserts it whenever, expressly or by implication, he talks of Being at all. For to talk of Being is to speak of fact that is either present to a consciousness or else is nothing. And from that one aspect of our definition which is involved in the thesis that whatever is, is consciously known, all the foregoing view of the unity of Being inevitably follows.

Such an abstract general statement of the results of our definition of what it is to be, may well be illustrated, however, through an approach to the whole matter of the unity of Being from another side, namely, from the more empirical side. For in conceiving of all that is as a single whole, as the life, the meaning, and the consciousness of a single Self, we are not limited to merely universal considerations. Human thought has long been conscious of some aspects of the unity of Being. The world of ordinary experience, of common sense, and of science, has already its provisional unity, which our own idealism must view as a genuine, if fragmentary, hint of the final unity. Let us then next briefly study this relative unity of the empirical world. It will help to free from barren abstractions our own insight.

Our Fourth Conception of Being is through and through, in one of its aspects, an empirical conception. We derive the very idea of fulfilment and of purpose from the relative and transient fulfilment of purpose that any one of our more thoughtful conscious moments presents to us. And despite the foregoing use of abstractions, it is no part of our idealistic plan to undertake to deduce *a priori* any of the special facts that may exist anywhere in the universe. For our view of the *that* predetermines indeed the general constitution of the *what*, but not our power to predict, apart from experience, what nature and finite mind, what space and time, are to contain. Accordingly in reviewing the empirical world with reference to the special nature of its unity, we must once more be subject to the control of the facts of the universe as known to common sense and to science. We must frankly recognize the seeming varieties of these facts. We must look for unity only in the midst of their empirical diversity. We must see in what sense just this empirical world is to be interpreted in terms of our Fourth Conception. And, in fact, when we thus turn back to experience as our guide, the knowable universe appears a refractory object to which to apply our theory of the unity of Being.

IV

For, apart from the definition of the ontological predicate, the subjects of which we usually assert Being belong
to certain well-known but sharply contrasted types. In
the first place, we ordinarily ascribe Being to nature, to
the physical world so far as it is contemporaneous with
ourselves. We say this whole present physical world
now is. We regard this world as a peculiarly concrete
instance of what it is to be. And in particular Realism
often prefers present natural objects as its instances of
Being. This natural realm is spread out before us in
space, and appears to be of an infinitely wealthy variety
of constitution. In the second place, we ascribe Being
to our fellow-men, and, in particular, to their conscious
inner lives as beings that possess or that are minds. This
social realm is also one that we may call a second region
of concrete fact. In the third place, and in a very
notable way, we also attribute reality to the whole world
of past events. We may say indeed that the past *is not
now*, or that it *no longer is*. But we may say with equal
assurance that the past has a genuine and irrevocable
constitution, and that assertions now made about the past
are at present true or false. In fact, true and false witness in most practical matters relates in general to the
past. We moreover make the past a region for historical
research ; or, as in the case of geology, we regard past
events as the topics of a strictly inductive and very
elaborate natural science whose work is done in the
present. So the past is for us a very genuine being.
Our knowledge and interpretation of the present world,

whether human or physical, is furthermore based upon our views as to the nature of these past events. For the present world consists for us of observed or assumed facts, defined and interpreted in the light of presupposed happenings. Any given present object, for instance, is seen to be this or this object, because we recognize it as identical in character with a fact supposed to have been known in the past. In the main, present Being is thus for us, so to speak, past Being warmed over. There is nothing that we regard as now real unless by virtue of the express or implied judgment that, since in the past this or that has existed, this or that present existence may in consequence be assumed or accepted as a continuation or as an outcome of the realm of past Being. Leave out the realm of the past from our conception of the real world, and our empirical universe at this instant would shrivel, for us, into a mere collection of almost uninterpreted sensations. The world as it is just now has for us Being as a supplement to the world that has been. We shall still further see, in a moment, how manifold are the illustrations of this truth.

In the next place, however, we ascribe, although with a decidedly different emphasis, a form of Being to the future, and to all that is therein to happen. The future, we indeed say, *is not yet*. But present assertions about the future are, even now, and despite a well-known remark of Aristotle's, either true or false, and that quite apart from any theory as to fate, or chance, or freedom. A coming eclipse in any given year is regarded by an astronomer as reality, when he adjusts himself to its Being by preparing an expedition to observe that eclipse. Again, it is now true either that I shall be alive a year from now or that I shall not be alive. Life insurance is a provision made to meet future facts that are regarded as realities, and that are respected accordingly. Future Being is thus the familiar object of hope and fear, of common sense prudence, as well as of predictive science. Omit the future from your scheme of Being, and your world loses all its practical human interest. To be sure, the future, unlike the past, is not regarded as irrevocable, and a believer in freedom thinks the future partly contingent. But even the contingent future event has its Being. Wait, namely, and you shall find out what that Being is, while even now the principle of contradiction applies to assertions about it. Suppose a judge endowed with free will, and deliberating as to the fate of a prisoner left to his judicial discretion. While the prisoner awaits the judge's decision, the fact awaited is supposed by this hypothesis to be a contingent fact. But is not the prisoner anxiously expecting his own discovery of the Being of that very fact? And while he waits, is he dealing with a mere fancy or dream, or a baseless unreality? No, the dreaded decision, although future, and by this hypothesis contingent, is a fact, and has Being; and that is why one awaits its announcement with such concern.

Present Being of two sorts, namely in nature and in minds, Past and Future Being, these four types of reality we have now enumerated as types recognized by common sense and natural science. Our study of the Third Conception of Being, some time since, made us familiar with the still different sort of reality ordinarily attributed to the realm of moral and of mathematical truth. This realm of eternal validity common sense as well as science recognizes ; and as we further saw, when we dealt with our Third Conception, the more transient world of prices, of credits, of social standing, and of institutional existence, is likewise for common sense a realm of true Being, yet a realm neither identical with nature, nor capable of being reduced to the contents present within any number of individual human minds. We have abandoned the Third Conception. But our new conception must find room for the typical instances of Being of the third type, namely, for the mathematical objects, for the socially and morally valid beings. And now, finally, after surveying all these so various types of beings, we have to recall the comment often already made in these lectures, and to assert that not only these different kinds of realities, but also the concrete experiences whereby we come to observe, and the ideas whereby we ourselves define, describe, and in general undertake to know these very objects, are themselves also in their own measure real, and are as truly real as are the various finite objects of common sense that we know.

Now our Fourth Conception of Being, if it is to be adequate to the demands of common sense, must be adjusted to at least all of these varied types of beings. Nature, and the minds of our fellows, together with the contents of these minds, the past and the future beings and events, the eternally and transiently valid truths, and our own experiences and ideas which have all these different sorts of Being for their objects, — all these apparent facts either must be alike comprehended within our final definition of what it is to be, or else must be deliberately explained away as illusory instances, as mere appearances that have no true Being. But whether accepted or explained away, these sorts of beings must at all events be taken into account in attempting to define reality.

V

If, looking over the broad field suggested by the foregoing list of the sorts of beings recognized by ordinary human belief, we thereupon attempt to reduce to unity the characters possessed by these supposed objects in so far as they are said to be real, our next impression may be once more that, despite our Fourth Conception, the Being which the various classes of facts have in common can only be something extremely abstract and barren. If the past, say yesterday, or the Silurian period, has Being in some irrevocable sense, despite the fact that we also say, *It no longer is*, what has such a past in common with the present, except that each belongs to time? And have both past and present Being any less abstract character than this in common with the future, say with the coming history of Europe five centuries hence? Of that coming history we say, *It is not yet*. If in a sense it still has Being, because it also is even now the object of possible true or false assertions, has this type of Being still anything but the name in common with the past or with the present? Or again, if one compares the existence which the mathematician attributes to the roots of an equation of the nth degree, or to the irrational numbers and differential coefficients, with the existence that you now ascribe to your friend's mind, when you converse with him, — in what but the name do these types of Being resemble each other or the foregoing types. And finally, when you say, both of your own warm present inner experience, and of to-day's price of wheat in Chicago or London, that these two have alike real Being, or when you add that the British Constitution is also a reality, is the ontological predicate applied to these different objects in anything like the same sense? And so does it not seem that, as the scholastics would have said, or as Aristotle himself remarked, Being, despite our Fourth Conception, persists in remaining an essentially equivocal word? Only, to us, at the present point reached in these lectures — to us who are no longer realists and who no longer love barren abstractions, the equivocation seems so great as to be altogether hopeless? We were to find unity. But are not the facts once more against us?

So much then merely for an impression as regards the hopelessness of any one final and still empirical unification of Being. But, on the other hand, if you look closer, does it not soon become afresh evident that all these various forms are indeed but mere variations of a single theme, mere differentiations of one idea, whose unity and universality remain indivisible amidst all its vicissitudes?

For, consider : What did we just observe about past and present? Attempt to abstract from any reference to past Being, and what becomes of any concrete notion of present Being? Where are you now? In this city, in this room, aware of yourself as this person? But if I ask you not merely how you know all this to be really so, but what you mean by these various expressions, you at once refer me to the past, not merely for your warrant, but even for your very meaning. This city exists for you only as the recognized city, that is familiar to you because it has long been here. In itself, apart from just your private recognition, it is what it has become. It is the outcome of former stages of its existence. This University is the living presence, in newly developed and growing form, of its own historic past. That is what the present University means. Its present is inseparable from its past. You too are yourself because at this instant you relate yourself to your own past. The meaning of the past is a necessity, if you are to give to your present any rational meaning. Nor is this true alone of your knowledge about yourself. It is true of the very Being that you attribute to your present facts. However rapidly any Being grows, its very growth means relation to its own earlier Being. And no recondite discussion of the supposed permanence of substance is in the least needed to remind you, even if you wholly abstract from the traditional doctrines of substance, that whatever novelties the present may contain, these very novelties get their character, both for you, and for any one to whom they are real at all, by virtue of their relation to past beings and events, so that if, *per impossibile*, the whole past of temporal Being were absolutely stricken out, the present, which would then involve no historical relations to the foregoing, no entrance of novelty into the old order, no growth, no decay, no endurance, and no continuance of a former process in new forms, would simply lose every element that now gives it rational coherence.

Far then from being merely contrasted with present Reality, past Reality, viewed in general, is a correlated

region of that very whole of temporal existence in which
alone the present itself has any comprehensible place or
even any conceivable Being.   Nor can any fact of nature,
however remote from us it now seems, be viewed by us
as real without being caught in the net of this universal
time-order.

But just so the future, not, indeed, when viewed
as to its unknown details, but when conceived as the
region into which the present is passing away, when
regarded as containing the goal of all our hopes, and the
decision of all our cherished interests and destinies, — is
not this future so bound up in one world of Being with
the present, that, if we could indeed abstract from future
Being, present Being would again lose not only all of its
practical interest, but also a large part of its theoretical
meaning?   Observe any object that you please, in a
world of time and change, and the question, What is it?
is in fact logically and inseparably bound up with the
two questions, What was it? and Whither is it tending?
Consider so abstract an object as the position of a material particle in space, as studied in dynamics.   That
position so studied becomes at once a place in a path,
meaningless except as viewed with reference to the past
and future positions of the particle under the system of
forces acting upon it.   For the theory of heat, the present temperature of a cooling body, is a state in a series
of past and future states, determined by the laws of the
conduction of heat.   And in human affairs, just as present history is an outcome of former ages, precisely so it
is a prelude to a future.   And when we say that a youth,
or a nation, *has a future*, *has a destiny*, we refer to an

aspect of the being in question that we regard as a very real aspect. The assertion, *The soul is immortal*, is again an assertion about the supposed real Being of the soul. It has a reference to the present Being of this soul, yet it is *ipso facto* an assertion about the future. And common sense asks the question, Do you believe that there is a future life? Plainly all such expressions regard future Being as a reality, and inseparable from the present.

Yesterday, to-day, and to-morrow, the past, the present, the future, and all the ages, thus enter the realm of conceived temporal Being together. So surely as time is, they all alike are. Their sequence is the actuality of the temporal order. Ignorant as you are of the detailed facts of any of them, you still have to say that temporal Being, in its wholeness, has to be conceived as logically coherent, and is not without all of them alike. If the future is for you uncertain, much of what you regard as the present is uncertain also, and the same is true of the past. These three sorts of Being, then, are not to be sundered. They are merely distinguishable aspects of one conception. The illusion that they are separable arises only when you neglect both their continuity, and that coherence of meaning which forces you constantly to see in the lines of your friend's face his past reflected, in your own memories your very self expressed, and in your future the continuation and expression of the present Being of your will. And once more this temporal unity applies to the whole of nature. In one time all events are conceived as occurring.

As to possible, or valid, Being,—we already saw, in our former discussion, how impossible it is to separate that type of Being from the concrete present experience in terms of which you define it, or from the past experience, whose laws you expect to find repeated when you define physical possibilities. If you write down an equation, and prove its properties, or demonstrate that it has roots, you actually deal with presented symbols and diagrams, with calculations whose outcome you now observe; in brief, with data of experience here and now. If you somehow extend into infinity the valid meaning of these present experiences, your right to do this involves the unity of your present mathematical experience with the whole realm of reality to which you refer. And if you define a physical possibility, such as the possible freezing of a given body of water, or the possible observations of a coming eclipse, you presuppose that certain laws of past experience and of past Being will hold valid in the future; and by virtue of this relation only can you undertake to say of the possible physical experience, *It is valid.*

Validity then, if one rightly affirms it at all, is a type of Being absolutely bound up with the Being of present, of past, and of future experience. Its Being is even for common sense one with their Being.

Despite all the contrasts of even the world of common sense, we deal so far then with one conceived infinitely complex whole, whose Being is of one inclusive type, though differentiated into various types.

The kind of Being that we ascribe to the minds of our human fellows remains to be here very briefly considered. As a fact, and as we shall later see more in detail, when we come to the problems of the second half of the present course of lectures, the Being of my fellow, in general, is, for me, inseparable from my idea of my own Being. As an essentially social creature, I have no rational and self-conscious life for myself, except by virtue of literal and ideal contrasts, and other social relationships, with men whom I conceive as my fellows. I can indeed change or spare very many present relations to other men without losing myself. I can live in the memory of past social intercourse. I can enjoy rational communion with ideal, or at all events with unseen, comrades, as children, as poets, and as many wise souls do ; but if you suppose me even in memory and in fancy as well as in fact absolutely solitary, I should lose my very consciousness of my own meaning as this person living in this world. My whole Being then is bound up with my ideas of my real and ideal and unseen fellows, — of their esteem or rivalry, of the tasks that they set me to do, of my office as their comrade, opponent, rival, enemy, friend, or servant, — in brief, — of their relations to me.

It follows that their Being also is inseparably bound up, for me, with my notion, not only of my present self, but of the past, present, future, and possible world that I regard as real.

And now, if, with this whole series of considerations in mind, we survey once more the types of objects to which we ascribe Being, we find that the very conception of the various types of Being which we first distinguished, demands, even upon purely empirical grounds, their reunion in one whole conception of what it is to be real. For what we have discovered is not merely that various objects are in physical or in moral ways connected in the real world, although this is universally true, but that the fundamental fashions of Being themselves which we ascribe to objects, such fashions as are exemplified by past, present, future, determinately possible, or mentally real Being, are, just as ways of possessing reality, logically inseparable, so that we cannot abandon one of these fashions of Being as illusory, without at once abandoning them all, and surrendering, like the mystic, all of our finite distinctions as mere dreams. Thus our world, however many and various its objects, possesses what we may call Ontological Unity, in so far as all its types of Being, concrete and abstract, appear as various aspects of one type of Being. Nor can you sunder any single idea of an isolated real object from the network established by ideas of reality in general. The whole of this world stands or falls together.

Considerations of this sort are by no means stated in ultimate form, for they have been based upon a provisional acceptance of the world of common sense, with all of its classes of facts. Yet only by such provisional acceptance can we get before us the facts of the empirical world ready for criticism. What we now see is that all our human ideas of real Beings form portions of a single system. All varieties of individuals and of individual ideas must be subordinate to the unity of this system.

VI

Our criticism of the constitution of this system, as we men conceive it can be made, for present purposes, very summary. We have no right to limit the constitution of universal life by the categories of human experience taken merely as human experience. The very meaning of our own ideas regarding the interpretation of nature will be found, in our later cosmological discussions, to involve the thesis that the realm called our own finite experience is only, so to speak, a very special case of an universal type. When the modern doctrine of evolution regards man as a product and outcome of nature, our own view of the universe will in the end have to accept the extremely subordinate place that this empirical doctrine assigns to the finite being called man amongst the beings that people nature. Our cosmology must not be anthropocentric in any special sense. There is, indeed, a sense, in which, according to our view, any rational idea in the whole universe seeks and in its complete development finds, as the expression of its ultimate meaning, the whole of the universe. But we have no right whatever to regard man as the only finite being whose ideas are rational. On the contrary, as we shall see in the second half of the present course, there is no possibility of giving any unity to the inner meaning of human existence without regarding man as a single group only in a vast society of finite beings, whose relationships, although very faintly hinted to us in our experience of natural phenomena, are as concrete and significant as any rational relationships can be. It is precisely in the history of the process called evolution that we have some indication of the type of these extra-human relationships amongst the finite beings who are present in the world in the same sense in which we are present.

In consequence of such aspects of the natural order, I should accordingly reject as inadequate the fashion of dealing with nature, and with the universal categories of finite experience, which was most characteristic of the forms of Idealism prevalent in Germany in the early part of this century. Our historical indebtedness to those forms of Idealism for our Fourth Conception of Being has been obvious all along, and needs here have no explicit confession. On the other hand, the application of this conception to the theory of nature, both by Schelling and by Hegel, seems to me to have been as far astray as a larger minded modern philosophical doctrine can be. It is not so much that this earlier idealistic philosophy of nature was founded upon *a priori* methods, and disregarded the special sciences ; for as a fact the *Naturphiloso phie* both of the Schellingian and of the Hegelian schools derived many, perhaps most of its special principles, from the text-books of science then current ; and its use of experience, if capricious and fragmentary, was in general intended to be serious. But the essential principles of the application of idealistic conceptions of the unity of Being to the interpretation of nature were, in those systems, false, because a disposition to arrange the sciences in an arbitrarily defined hierarchy, to divide nature into sharply contrasted regions, celestial and terrestrial, inorganic and organic, extra-human and human, predetermined all the speculative interpretations attempted. We now know that the special sciences form no mere hierarchy ; that organic and inorganic nature, however divided they may be, are also very profoundly linked. We know that the ancient contrasts between terrestrial and celestial physical processes and substances appear, the farther we go in the study of nature, the less significant. We know that the unity which the evolutionary processes indicate is one that no simple scheme of the formal classification of natural processes into mechanical, chemical, and organic, or even into those of living and non-living nature, can any longer attempt at all exhaustively to characterize.

So much the more must an idealist to-day be unwilling to talk of nature as coming for the first time to self-consciousness in man, or to limit the categories in terms of which nature is to be interpreted, to those which are found directly serviceable in the human process of cataloguing and describing the natural phenomena which come within our finite ken. The older philosophy of nature was not merely too much disposed to anticipate scientific results in an *a priori* way; it was also too crudely and anthropocentrically empirical in its classifications of natural fact, and in its attempts to unify natural fact. Our doctrine, indeed, invites man to be at home in his universe, but does not make man, in so far as you first separate him from nature, the one finite end that nature seeks.

For us to-day, as I may as well forthwith assert, the conceptions which, from our idealistic point of view, promise to admit of the most plastic adaptation to the varieties of empirical fact, and consequently of the most universal application to the interpretation of the inner life of nature, are our social conceptions. These at once are intensely human, and capable, as Kant's ethical doctrine already showed, of a vast extra-human generalization, in so far as we take account of other possible moral agents. In the form of finite social intercourse, amongst human beings, we find exemplified a type of unity in variety, and of variety recalling us always to the recognition of unity, — a type, I say, which permits us, as I believe, to go further in our hypotheses for the interpretation of the vast finite realm called nature, than we can go by the use of any other types of conception. The social life finds room for the most various sorts of mutual estrangement, conflict, and misunderstanding amongst finite beings; while, on the other hand, every form of social intercourse implies an ultimate unity of meaning, a real connectedness of inner life, which is precisely of the type that you can best hope to explain in terms of our Fourth Conception of Being. When I tell you then, in advance, that in the second series of these lectures I shall try to explain our relations to nature as essentially social, and therefore in their deepest essence ethical relationships; when I predict that, without transcending our legitimate rights as interpreters of the empirical results, we shall undertake to show that nature, in a fashion whose details are still only faintly hinted to us men, constitutes a vast society, in whose transactions finite processes of evolution when viewed, not with reference to the eternal meaning of the whole, but with reference to the temporal series of facts, are presumably mere passing incidents, — when I say this, I indicate in some measure how our Idealism will undertake to explain the unity of the world, without becoming, upon that account, merely anthropocentric in its accounts of nature.

There is a sense, as I have said, in which all the world may be viewed as centred about the fully expressed inner meaning of any finite rational idea. But then human ideas, as in fact is implied in their very conscious sense of their own meaning, are not the only ideas of which this can be asserted. It is not until man views himself as a member of an universal society, whose temporal estrangements are merely incidental to their final unity of meaning, that man rationally appreciates the actual sense of the conscious ideas that express his longing for oneness with an absolute life. We are related to God through our consciousness of our fellows. And our fellows, in the end, prove to be far more various than the mere men. It is one office of philosophy to cultivate this deeper sense of companionship with the world. And precisely in this sense of deeper comradeship with nature will lie the future reconciliation of religion and science.

VII

And so, when we speak of the final unity of the world-life, we have no right to define that unity merely in terms of the special categories of the distinctively human type of consciousness. Our foregoing sketch of the manner in which, for us men, present, past, future, physical, mental, mathematical, and moral reality seem to be linked in a single system, is not therefore by itself a sufficient basis for stating the way in which the whole meaning of reality gets presented to the single unity of the consciousness that we have already called divine.

On the other hand, the very essence of our Idealism lies in asserting that just in so far as you have become conscious, not of a merely abstract form of possible unity, but of a sense in which your experience already unites many in one, you have become acquainted with a fact which the

ultimate nature of the divine plan may, and in general
does, vastly transcend, but simply cannot ignore. Your
truth from the absolute point of view will appear, indeed,
as a partial truth, but not upon that account as untrue.
The interesting doctrine of the "Degrees of Truth and
Reality" which Mr. Bradley has lately developed afresh,
although, as I think, Mr. Bradley has given this doctrine
too negative a form, remains upon its positive side, the
common property of all the synthetic forms of post-
Kantian Idealism. Recognizing, as of course I distinctly
do, the close historical relation of what I am saying to the
whole tradition of recent Idealism, I can only point out
here that our human interpretation of the unity of Being,
however much it may be supplemented, in however different a light it may appear from some higher point of
view, remains, in its own relative degree, true, just in so
far as it is at once an assertion of unity, and a concrete
illustration of that unity by facts found somewhere within
the realm of man's actual experience. An abstractly immediate experience of unity, such as the mystic sought,
may remain either barren, or a mere prophecy of some
more philosophical doctrine. A hasty account of the unity
of nature, such as Aristotle's system founded upon the
optical illusion of the rotation of the outermost heaven
about the earth, is already more concrete in its unification
of many natural phenomena in a single scheme. It has
been superseded, but only by a science whose natural phenomena are seen to be in still more significant and deeper
relations. Our own present largest generalization, which
unites the things and processes of nature and mind in one
in the way just indicated, may need very real correction

from an absolute point of view. Yet this preliminary unification has its truth.

In particular, however, as to the special features of our view of nature, our human experience of space-relations is obviously so special in its type that this our view of the space-world may be frankly regarded, I think, as something of decidedly limited truth. It is fairly inconceivable that from the point of view of experience in general, our space-form should remain as more than a fragmentary perspective effect, so to speak, or in other words, as more than what one might call a relatively valid finite point of view. The facts which we view as related to one another in space must indeed be viewed by a larger experience than ours, as present and as linked. But our way of interpreting the linkage is obviously human, and is probably only a very special case of the experience of the various aspects of coexistent meaning in the world of the final experience.

In another way, while time as the form of ethically significant process has doubtless a far deeper truth, temporal succession is subject to a perfectly arbitrary limitation of what one may call the time-span of our human consciousness. What we regard as a present instant is neither a truly instantaneous mere Now, having no finite length, nor a duration long enough to enable us to survey at a glance anywhere nearly as considerable a whole of successively realized meaning as we desire for any one of our more rational human purposes, whether thoughtful, or artistic, or practical. Our human time-consciousness is essentially ill adapted for observing the whole of any one of even our most familiar meanings. In other words, for us men, "the present instant," so-called, has at once temporal succession, the earlier and the later, included within it, and it has a decidedly, and, in fact, a very inconveniently and arbitrarily, limited length.   What happens so rapidly or so slowly that we fail to accommodate to the events our ability to take note of the succession as a present and given fact, all such too rapid or too slow series of occurrences, we fail directly to note as matters of clear consciousness.   Hence, we constantly lose sight even of our own trains of thought and action, even in instances where we most want to survey them.   Our brief, but still by no means indefinitely small time-span of consciousness, determines in this way our whole human form of experience, and of course limits the ethical meaning of our conduct.   Yet how long a temporal period, how much duration, shall constitute the finite interval viewed by a given form of consciousness as a *now*, is a wholly arbitrary matter, so long as *now* means not the ideal mathematical *now*, — the negation of all duration, the mere point between present and future, but rather a period, a succession of events, a finite duration.   In our consciousness, however, the *now* of experience does mean just such an actual, brief, but still finite, interval or period of time, within which and during which events succeed one after another. Now nobody can for an instant defend the rationality of supposing that every possible form of consciousness must have the precise human limitation of time-span.   Yet a notable alteration of time-span, quite apart from any alteration of the contents that succeed one after another in the minds in question, would constitute a variation of a given type of consciousness whose vast possible meaning, both psychological and ethical, it is almost impossible to estimate. A consciousness for which events that happened within a millionth of a second constituted a definite and observable serial succession of present facts, or, on the other hand, a consciousness for which the events occurring during a thousand years were as much present at once, to a single glance at temporal succession, as are now, to us, the successions that, while not too rapid, occur within a time-span of two seconds, — either one of these types of consciousness would have a profoundly different basis for estimating the significance of any given empirical facts of succession. The acts of moral agents whose consciousness thus differed from ours would have a vastly different meaning from our own.

Our idea of what it is to be conscious is therefore, logically speaking, an extremely variable idea. But for that very reason, our Fourth Conception of Being, while it certainly cannot be applied to the effort to conceive the empirical world in unity, without a full recognition of possible variations of the form of consciousnesss, has all the more freedom in undertaking the general task of viewing, as fragmentary aspects of one whole meaning, the varieties of nature and of finite individuality. For it is precisely the wholeness, and not the mere fragmentariness, the presence, and not the mere absence of unity in our consciousness, the relative attainment, and not the mere postponement of our meanings, which, from this point of view, guides us towards a positive view of how the unity of Being is, in the midst of all the varieties, attained. How in detail the final unity is won, what categories precisely

determine the relations of its various contents, what
contents supplement our own and provide for the final
enrichment of the Absolute Life, — all this we of course
cannot predetermine. Yet what our conception maintains is simply this : —

Survey our life, consider our experience. Look at
nature as we men find it. Take account of our temporal and spatial universe. Review the results of our
science. In all this you will discover manifold meanings relatively obtained, manifold interrelationships binding together facts that at first sight appear sundered,
universality predetermining what had seemed accidental,
and a vast fundamental ontological unity linking in its
deathless embrace past, present, future, and what for
us seem to be the merely possible forms of Being. Man
you shall find dependent for his moral personality upon
his fellows, upon nature as a whole for his evolution,
and upon his own ideas, poor and finite and fleeting
although they are, for his very consciousness of his relation to the universe.

Well, now, in addition to all these glimpses of unity,
you shall see, too, countless signs of fragmentariness,
countless seemingly chaotic varieties. We know the
formula for dealing with all these in the light of our
conception. These are precisely the facts whose fragmentariness sends us to Another for the explanation,
yes, for our very idea of any one of them. But just
such cases show themselves hereby as instances of universal principles, whose concrete meaning is not yet
empirically present to us at this instant. Wherever we
question, we have ideas, but not yet an experience of

their objects. Wherever experience contains the fulfilment of a meaning, the answer to a question, the attainment of an empirical unity, there we have so far present
an objective content, a plan relatively fulfilled; and
precisely such unities, however much they may be supplemented, cannot be ignored in the final unity of the
whole of experience.

And so, recognizing as we do the limitations of our
consciousness, we now see what can guide us towards
a concrete definition of the absolute form of consciousness. Here our general concept of Being gives us our
test of truth, but our experience shows us special ways
in which facts not only can be unified, but are unified.
These ways, as far as they go, are for us valid guides.
Thus, then, our general and relatively *a priori* proof of
the unity of Being, in the early part of this lecture,
has itself been brought into unity with the empirical
view of our real world. We see then how the world
of our Fourth Conception must be One. We catch also
a glimpse of how it is One.

VIII

In sum, then, as to the most general form of the absolute unity, our guide is inevitably the type of empirical
unity present in our own passing consciousness, precisely in so far as it has relative wholeness, and is
rational. If one asks, " How should the many be one,
and how should the whole take on the form of variety?"
I answer, " Look within. You may grasp many facts at
once; and when you have even the most fragmentary
idea, your one purpose is here and now partially em-

bodied in a presented succession of empirical facts."
If you ask, "But how can many different ideal processes
be united in the unity of a single idea?" I answer,
"That is precisely what in your own way you can
observe whenever you think, however fragmentarily, of
the various, and often highly contrasting, ideas that
occur to your mind when you grasp the meaning of
any hypothetical or complex proposition,—such as the
present one." If you ask, "But how can what we men
call present and future Being be unified in a single
present unity of consciousness?" I reply, "In idea
you unify them all, whenever you yourself assert propositions as now true of past, present, and future. In
concrete experience, you find a past, a present, a future,
unified even in your own passing moments of consciousness, despite their brief span. As you listen to my
words, several words come to consciousness at once,
and yet as a succession. The first of three words is
past when the second sounds, the third is yet to come
when the second sounds, yet all are at once for you.
Now this *totum simul* is precisely the character that,
within your brief time-span of human consciousness,
you can and do now verify. An eternal consciousness
is definable as one for which all the facts of the whole
time-stream, just so far as time is a final form of consciousness, have the same type of unity that your present
momentary consciousness, even now within its little span,
surveys. But if for the divine mind, some still more
inclusive form takes up our time-stream into a yet
larger unity of experience, all the more is what we
mean by temporal succession present together for the

Absolute Experience. Nor does this mean that at this, your present human and temporal instant, at this hour of the clock, the divine and final moment of consciousness has just now the future and the past before it at a glance. For your own grasp of the contents of your passing instant of consciousness faces at once a series of successive events, but also does not therefore bring before your insight all the successive contents of any present moment at any one temporal point within that present moment. What your own passing consciousness is to grasp at once, within the range of its own time-span, consists of facts which are successive one to another. Now our assertion is that precisely such a grasp of successive facts in one unity of consciousness is characteristic of the Absolute Consciousness in its relation to the whole of time, precisely in so far as the temporal form of realization is valid at all. And that this temporal form has its place in the final unity we know, just because time is for us the *conditio sine qua non* of all ethical significance.

The case of temporal unity is typical of every instance of the application of our Fourth Conception. In so far as your ideas now possess internal meaning, you grasp Many in One. You do not therefore lose the many in the unity, any more than you lose the notes in the melody. Ethical meanings do not involve the mere blending of details in a single whole. Rational insight wins unity only through variety.

And now what our Fourth Conception asserts is that God's life, for God's life we must now call this absolute fulfilment which our Fourth Conception defines, sees the one plan fulfilled through all the manifold lives, the single consciousness winning its purpose by virtue of all the ideas, of all the individual selves, and of all the lives. No finite view is wholly illusory. Every finite intent taken precisely in its wholeness is fulfilled in the Absolute. The least life is not neglected, the most fleeting act is a recognized part of the world's meaning. You are for the divine view all that you now know yourself at this instant to be. But you are also infinitely more. The preciousness of your present purposes to yourself is only a hint of that preciousness which in the end links their meaning to the entire realm of Being.

And despite the vastness, the variety, the thrilling complexity of the life of the finite world, the ultimate unity is not far from any one of us. All variety of idea and object is subject, as we have seen, to the unity of the purpose wherein we alone live. Even at this moment, yes, even if we transiently forget the fact, we mean the Absolute. We win the presence of God when most we flee. We have no other dwelling-place but the single unity of the divine consciousness. In the light of the eternal we are manifest, and even this very passing instant pulsates with a life that all the worlds are needed to express. In vain would we wander in the darkness ; we are eternally at home in God.

LECTURE X

LECTURE X

INDIVIDUALITY AND FREEDOM

IF we have been right in our foregoing discussions, the first principles of religious doctrine have a foundation as simple as the meaning of those principles is inexhaustible. So long as you first assume that the world of fact is merely given, independent of ideas, is found by us as such an independent reality, then indeed every effort to interpret the world quickly loses its way in the labyrinth of our experience. But remember, before you are thus lost, that the world is real only as the object of true ideas, and then your fundamental problem at once becomes that of the essential relation of idea and object. This relation is then the world-knot. Nor does that knot prove insoluble. At any moment, despite the mysteries of experience, you have in your hands the essential solution. For the relation of idea and object is essentially the relation of a partial meaning to a totally expressed rational meaning. And, as we have already seen, and in the present lecture shall further illustrate, the relation of partial and total meaning is, at the same time, the relation of any finite will to the expression of the complete intent of that same will. Without contradiction, therefore, you are unable to assert the real Being of any world, unless you conceive that world as the expressed will whose partial

431

momentary embodiment you even now observe, whenever you get any rational idea before your mind.

This view of the nature of Being, as we have asserted, is no arbitrary hypothesis, but is what a close examination discovers to be involved in the very presuppositions of common sense. In some respects, in fact, the essence of this view may be brought home to our ordinary consciousness, if we remember how the forms of space and of time are from moment to moment conceived by everybody as limitless and as universal, and as predetermining the constitution of the whole natural universe, while this whole infinity of both space and time is viewed as homogeneous with the space and time present at the instant to our own consciousness. The well-known case of the principle of contradiction again illustrates how the consciousness of the moment regards itself as warranted in predetermining the essential constitution of all possible beings. Our study of the conception of Being has been intended simply to render explicit and definite what kind of relationship it is which thus links the instant of human consciousness to the eternal constitution of the whole. We have seen indeed that our fourth definition of Reality gives us no right capriciously to predetermine any of the empirical contents of the world not now present to ourselves. But, on the other hand, we have undertaken to assert that the general constitution of this universe is known to us not merely in so far as the principle of contradiction, or as the forms of time and space, give warrant for universal assertions about reality or about some portion of it ; but also in so far as the fundamental structure of the universe is essentially both teleological and conscious.

We have also endeavored to state, in concrete form, of what nature this teleological structure of Reality proves to be.

I

In the foregoing lecture the unity of the idealistic world engaged our attention. In the present lecture, we are to consider the other aspect, — the Individuality, the Variety of finite beings, and the relative Freedom of finite acts.

No accusation is more frequent than that an Idealism which has once learned to view the world as a rational whole, present in its actuality to the unity of a single consciousness, has then no room either for finite individuality, or for freedom of ethical action. It was for the sake of preparing the way for a fair treatment of this very problem that we from the beginning defined the nature of ideas in terms at once of experience and of will. As we later passed to the assertion of the unity of the world from the final point of view, we have never lost sight of the fact that this is the unity of a divine Will, or, if you please, of a divine Act, at the same time as it is the unity of the divine Insight. The word "Meaning" has for us, from the outset, itself possessed a twofold implication, — not because we preferred ambiguity, but because, once for all, the facts of consciousness warrant, and in fact demand, this twofold interpretation. Whoever is possessed of any meaning, whoever faces truth, whoever rationally knows, has before his consciousness at once, that which *possesses the unity of a knowing process*, and that which *fulfils a purpose*, or in other words, that which constitutes

what we have from the outset called an act of will as well
as an act of knowledge. It is essential to our entire
understanding of our Fourth Conception of Being, that
we should remember the truth in both of these aspects,
not dividing the aspects themselves, nor confounding their
significance.

A few words of purely psychological analysis may then
be, at this point, useful, to clarify the precise relations between intellectual and voluntary processes in our ordinary
consciousness.

Popular psychology long since far too sharply sundered
the Intellect and the Will in the empirical processes of the
finite human mind. Viewing the intellect as a passive
reception of the truth, defining the will as the power to
alter facts, the popular psychology was forced, almost
from the outset, to make an effort to reunite the powers
that it had thus falsely separated. For a very little consideration shows not only that we can will to know, but
also that we are in general guided, in our intellectual
processes, by the very interests which popular pyschology
refers to the will. On the other hand, our voluntary
processes, if they are conscious, are themselves matters of
knowledge. For our conscious volition implies that we
know what we will. In consequence of these obvious considerations, a more modern psychology has been led to its
well-known doctrine that all such psychological divisions
are rather distinctions between different aspects of the
same process, than means for telling us of naturally sundered or even of separable processes. If we regard the
human subject, in the ordinary psychological way, as a
being whose conscious life runs parallel with the highest

physical processes of his organism, we get a view of the relation between the intellect and the will which is far more just, at once to the natural history of the mind, and to the deeper meaning of the inner life of our consciousness. View man as a natural being, and you find him adjusting himself to his environment, acting, as they say, in response to stimuli. The world influences his senses, only to awaken him to such functions as express his interest in this world. Now the whole life of the organism is precisely the life of adjustment. The physical activities accompanying consciousness so take place that the organism preserves itself, and expresses its natural bearing towards its world. And the whole life of consciousness, accompanying these adjustments, constitutes a more or less accurate knowledge of what the adjustments are. The life of our consciousness is therefore a life of watching our deeds, of estimating our deeds, of predicting our deeds, and of interpreting our whole world in terms of deeds. We observe no outer facts without at the same time more or less clearly observing our attitude towards those facts, our estimate of their value, our response to their presence, our intentions with respect to our future relations with these facts.

But, within the circle of this general unity of our consciousness, various distinctions indeed arise. Sometimes the outer fact, viewed more or less in abstraction from its value to ourselves, more completely fills the field of our consciousness, and then we are likely to talk of a state of relatively pure Knowledge. If our state is one in which an idea explicitly appears as attempting to correspond to the presupposed object of its own External Meaning, or to its own Other, we call the process one of Thought about External Reality. Sometimes, however, our acts themselves, viewed as efforts to alter the outside facts, come more clearly before us either for deliberate estimate, or for impulsive decision; and in such cases we find the narrow field of our consciousness more clearly taken up by what we call Will. But facts are never known except with reference to some value that they possess for our present or intended activities. And on the other hand, our voluntary activities are never known to us except as referring to facts to which we attribute in one way or another an intellectually significant Being, — a reality other than what is present to us at the moment.

It follows that when, for general purposes, we study, not the psychology, but, as at present, the total significance of our conscious life, we are much less interested in the separation between knowledge and will than in that unity which psychology already recognizes, and which philosophy finds of still more organic importance. Consequently, when, at the outset of these discussions, we pointed out the element of will in the constitution of ideas, we were dwelling upon precisely what for the psychologist appears as the intimate connection between the knowing process of the mind and the motor responses of the organism to its environment. When we know, we have in the first place present to our minds certain contents, certain data, certain facts, it may be of the outer senses, it may be of the memory and the imagination. But if rational knowledge takes place, these data are not merely present, but they also take on forms; they constitute ideal structures; they fulfil our own purposes. These purposes consciously correspond either to what an ordinary observer would call our visible responses to our environment, or to what a psychologist, who looks closer than an ordinary observer, would find also to involve memories, or hints, or fragments, of former adjustments. The result is, so far, that, when we know, the facts both of sense and of imagination unite in our minds, into the expression of a Plan of Action. And thus the knowing process is a process partially embodying our own will. Upon such an analysis of the nature of ideas all the foregoing discussion has been founded; and now we deliberately repeat and emphasize this interpretation in order to make way for a final statement of the place of the will in our doctrine of being.

From this point of view, then, the contrast between knowledge and will, *within* our own conscious field, is so far this; viz., that we speak of our conscious process as a Knowing, in so far as all the data are woven into one unity of consciousness; while we speak of this same process as Will, in so far as this unity of consciousness involves a fulfilment or embodiment of a purpose. The word "Meaning" very properly lays stress upon both of these aspects at once. For what we call a Meaning is at once something observed with clearness as an unity of many facts, and something also intended as the result which fulfils a purpose. But when we take account of *External* Meanings, we speak of Thought in so far as we seek correspondence to our presupposed Other, and of Will in so far as we seek to produce the Other that shall correspond to the Internal Meaning.

Yet here the distinction, as we have already seen, is wholly relative to the point of view.

But now it next becomes us to take special note of this latter aspect of the will, — an aspect upon which the popular consciousness lays great stress. For the will is usually regarded as primarily the Cause of something which but for the will would not come into existence. We have already spoken of *acts* of will; and the popular view declares that we are conscious of an activity which *causes states of consciousness to exist within ourselves, and acts to come into existence outside of ourselves*, and which is therefore responsible for the actual production of new Being in the universe. But if, with reference to the scientific value of this popular view, we turn to psychology for advice, we find at the present time, in that science, decidedly opposed interpretations of the sense in which the human will can be regarded as a cause. According to one of these interpretations the word "act" is properly to be applied merely to the physical process by which our organism gets adjusted to its environment. The causes of precisely such physical acts are, from this psychological point of view, themselves physical causes. Our consciousness, according to this same view, is not itself a cause, either of the physical act whereby we express our will, or of the states of mind themselves which constitute our inner intent. Our will merely accompanies our adjustment to the environment, and constitutes our own consciousness of the meaning of a certain portion of this adjustment. Our will is not itself one of the forces or powers of nature.

On the other hand, a traditional doctrine, which has

won for itself no small hearing in psychology, regards the volitional, or active, side of our consciousness, not merely as a fact in itself, but as a cause of other facts, both physical and mental. From this point of view, the distinction between intellect and will acquires a fresh importance, and declines to be reduced to that mere distinction of aspects which we have emphasized in the foregoing account. For, as is often said, man, in so far as he is a mere knower, accomplishes nothing; he merely observes. But as doer, as voluntary agent, he is the source of new being; he is an originator. Will, for this view, is nothing if not efficacious. A process that merely accompanies and reflects, without affecting, the adjustments of my organism to its environment, would be no true will. A sort of consciousness which merely observes that from moment to moment my inner life, for me, seems to have meaning, would, as this view asserts, in the end deprive my life of its most important meaning. For above all, as they say, what I mean to be is an originator of facts, and of facts that but for me would not exist. The true problem regarding the place of the will in the universe arises, according to this view, precisely at the point where one asks, Is the will the cause of any existence other than itself?

The two views about the will as cause thus brought into opposition have justly played a great part, both in the psychological and the metaphysical controversies of all periods, ever since the meaning of life began seriously to be considered. And the relation of this whole controversy to the deepest interest of metaphysics is as unquestionable as it is easy to misinterpret. For the word

" cause " is a term of very various meaning. So ambiguous and obscure, in fact, is the idea of cause as customarily used, that I have deliberately preferred to avoid even defining the issue about the causality of the will until our concept of Being had first assumed in general a definite form. Moreover, even at the present stage of our inquiry, although we must indeed deal with one aspect of the issue upon its own substantial merits, we shall do best to avoid, on the present occasion, any thorough-going discussion of the varieties of meaning of the word " cause." We shall do best merely to state the sense in which we ourselves regard the Being of facts as *due to the will*, be that will human or divine. We shall then postpone, until our second course of lectures, a more precise distinction of the various forms of causation, which we shall learn to recognize as present in nature and in mind. For the concept of cause, properly regarded, is rather a cosmological than a fundamentally metaphysical conception.

To metaphysics in general belongs, above all, the question that we have been considering, — the question what it is to be. To metaphysics also belongs the problem, What fundamentally different kinds of Being are there? And in this connection the relation between God and the individual is indeed of essential importance. From the metaphysician you may also expect the answer to the question, To what principles is the actual constitution of the world of conscious volition, and of ethically significant life, due? But it is within the realm of what we call Nature, — namely, within the realm of finite experience, with its various phenomenal

distinctions of organic and inorganic, of apparently living and apparently lifeless beings, — it is, I say, in case
of Nature, that the diversified processes, present to our
ordinary experience, arouse questions as to the special
kinds of causal linkage that, in any particular case, bind
one fact to another. It is in this world, — the phenomenal
or natural, the essentially fragmentary world, the realm
which cannot contain its whole truth within itself, — it
is in this realm, I say, that the special problems concerning physical and mental causation, concerning active
and inactive beings, concerning the relation of physical
organism and mental phenomena, most properly arise.
And we shall do well to keep separate the study of the
whole constitution of the universe (conceived in accordance with the general principles of our theory of Being),
from a study of the special problems of the phenomenal
world. It is not my present purpose, then, to exhaust
the theory of the sense in which will is, and is not, an
active cause in the natural world. What can at present
be asked from us is a general statement of the sense
in which what exists expresses, on the one hand, the will
of God; and, on the other hand, that individual will
which you find at any moment present in a fragmentary
way in your own finite consciousness. I shall maintain
that both God's will and our own finite will get consciously expressed in the world, and that no contradiction results from this statement.

II

At any moment your ideas, in so far as they are rational, embody a purpose. That we have asserted from

the outset. Our original example, that of the melody sung, for the sake of the mere delight in singing, remains for us typical of the entire life of what one may call consciously free and internally unrestricted finite ideas. Now what we in the first place have asserted in regard to such ideas, is that, precisely in so far as they are whole ideas, they stand before our consciousness as present fulfilments of purpose.

Any mere purpose, so far as it is still relatively fragmentary, or is, so to speak, disembodied, or is a mere striving, begins, in any such empirical case, the little drama that is acted within the momentary limits of a finite consciousness. In saying that this, at first disembodied purpose, becomes expressed, whenever any consciousness of such an act passes from its earlier to its later temporal stages, — I merely report what happens. I make as yet simply no assertion with regard to any psychological or physical causation. I assert as yet, in such a case, no effective force. I mention nothing of the nature of a physical or psychical tendency such that, by the mere necessity of its nature, it must work itself out. What my consciousness finds when I sing or speak is that a certain meaning actually gets expressed. My act of singing takes place. At once, then, there are data present, there are facts of consciousness, and there is this significance which these facts embody. Whether the facts could have come into existence in this way unless a given nervous organism or a given psychical entity, endowed with specific powers, subject to general laws, were already in existence, of all that my finite consciousness in the present moment tells me nothing. To assert any such thing is so far to assert a mere psychological or cosmological theory. The basis of such an assertion, if it has any basis, must be sought outside of any one moment's experience. On the other hand, in vain would any psychologist, in vain would any realistic metaphysician, attempt to rob my finite consciousness of the significance which this my own moment of singing or speaking has, for me, embodied. This significance is a matter of my experience. Whatever your system of metaphysics, the singer can say: Here at least the world has meaning, for lo! *I sing*.

Now, as a metaphysical theory, our idealistic doctrine with regard to Being in its wholeness has simply maintained that, without any regard to a doctrine of causation, without regard in the least to any specific view as to the psychology of mental process, *the whole universe, precisely in so far as it is, is the expression of a meaning, is the conscious fulfilment of significance in life*, precisely as the melody present at a given moment to the singer is for his consciousness the momentary expression of a meaning. And so our theory of Being is not founded upon any prior doctrine of causation. Cause and effect, laws mechanical or laws psychological, fate or freedom, in so far as any of these have Being, are from our point of view subject to the prior conditions of the very concept of Being itself. If nothing can be *except* what embodies a meaning, we are not first required to explain how anything whatever comes into Being, or how anything whatever is caused. For the cause of Being would itself have Being, and could itself exist, if our analysis is correct, only as the actual expression of a meaning.

The unhappy slavery of the metaphysics of the past to the conception of causation has been responsible for some of the most fatal of the misfortunes of religion and of humanity. That the existence of God was to be proved only by the means of the concept of causation, was one of the most characteristic of the presuppositions of an earlier theology, and was often supposed to be maintained on the basis of the authority of Aristotle. As a fact, this method of dealing with the theory of Being was false to the deepest spirit of Aristotle himself. For Aristotle's God is primarily the All-perfect Being, and is only secondarily the subject of which causation could be predicated in any form whatever. But however that may be, the theology which conceives the relation between God and the world, and between the world and the individual, as primarily a causal relation, subordinates the universal to the particular in theory, and the significant to the relatively insignificant in practical doctrine. The inevitable results of any such inversion of the rational order is a world where either fate reigns, or absolute mysteries are the final facts ; or where both these unhappy results are combined. That just because the universe is through and through transparently significant, it may later prove to be worth while to regard my will as in this or that respect a cause of certain special results, is intelligible enough. But the genuine significance of my voluntary process is always an affair of my own consciousness regarding the present meaning of my life. You will in vain endeavor to deduce that meaning from the distinctly lower category of causal efficacy. That lower category of causation always implies a comment which somebody else, viewing my act in a relatively external way, may pass upon me from without.

It is indeed metaphysically just to assert that in certain aspects of my life I must needs be regarded as a cause, because I am already known to possess conscious significance, and because some aspects of this significance turn out to be causal. But you can never, on the other hand, discover wherein consists my significance by merely asserting that I am somehow or other a powerful cause. And precisely so it is in the case of God. You can indeed say that this or that fact in the world must be viewed as a result of laws whose source lies in the divine nature. But in asserting this you merely lay stress upon a result of that conscious significance which first of all attaches to the Being of all things, and to the life of God in its wholeness.

I cannot, then, too strenuously insist upon the thought that our own theory of Being places the very significance, both of the whole world and of the individual life, in the actual conscious fulfilment of meaning. Such fulfilment, from our own point of view, is the only reality. We therefore do not explain the existence of meaning in the world by looking, in the end, beyond any meaning for the cause which has brought the significant world to pass. To view the matter in that way would be of the very essence of Realism, and would involve all the contradictions which have already led us to reject the realistic interpretation of Being. Causation will find its place in our world, but as a mere result, — a partial aspect, — a mere item of the very significance of that world itself. For causal connections have a place only as expressing their own aspect of the meaning of things. On the other hand, the mere part, causation, will never appear in our account as the source of the whole ; nor will this causation, which is but a very special form of Being, or a name for various special forms of Being, ever appear as that to which either the Being, or the wholeness of the meaning of the world, is due. And so much, then, for the mere causal efficacy, either of God or of man.

In consequence of these considerations, our primary question in regard to the finite human individual, in his relation to the divine life, is merely the question, In what sense does the finite Being retain, despite the unity of the whole divine life, any individual significance of his own, and what is the relation of this finite significance to the meaning and plan of the whole ? But for the answer to this, our really important question, we may now be prepared, if we next lay new stress upon certain aspects of the Fourth Conception of Being, to which we have made repeated reference.

III

We have said that a meaning gets wholeness and individuality of expression precisely in so far as it gets, at the same time, conscious determination. An imperfect idea is vague. It is general. But it is so, in our own finite consciousness, in *two* senses. (1) Any finite idea, as we have seen, sends us to some other experience to furnish us yet further instances that are needed for its whole expression. This reference to another for the remainder of itself is characteristic of even the clearest and most precise of our finite ideas, just in so far as they are general. Thus, in counting, the single numbers refer us, further on in the number-series, for the rest of what the counting process implies. If one merely counts the first ten numbers, there are still other numbers to count. A complete consciousness of the whole meaning of the number-series would complete this process of seeking Another by presenting the whole individual meaning of the number concept in a finished form. We have, so far, altogether postponed the discussion of those difficulties about the quantitative Infinite which the conception of a completed knowledge of numbers seems to involve.[1] We have asserted only that the arithmetical or mathematical Being of the number-series cannot be consistently expressed, either in realistic form or in the form of mere valid possibilities of experience. We have consequently asserted that even the realm of mathematical Being involves facts which only our Fourth Conception can adequately express. In what way the whole experience in question gets realized, we have pointed out only in the general fashion indicated in the foregoing lecture. The whole Being in question, as we have said, must be present to the final consciousness in its complete form, or in such wise that no other, beyond, remains to be sought. So much, then, for the first inadequacy of our finite general ideas.

(2) But our finite passing consciousness is incomplete or inadequate to its own purposes not merely by lack of contents adequate to express its wholeness, but by reason of vagueness with regard to its own momentarily conscious purposes. The principal source of actual

[1] See the Supplementary Essay to the present volume.

error, in finite consciousness, we have already found to
be the indetermination of our purposes at any stage in
their realization. Now the presupposition of our whole
view is that the final expression of purpose is not
merely complete as to its contents, *but absolutely determinate as to what meaning these contents fulfil.* Now
the finite process, whereby our own consciousness passes
from an indeterminate to a relatively determinate state
of purpose, of intention, of seeking for contents, is
known to us in its psychological manifestations as a
process of Selective Attention, growing more and more
definite as it proceeds. Precisely in so far as we are
conscious of a definite meaning at any instant, we are
conscious of contents selected, as it were, from the background of our own finite consciousness, selected as the
contents which are such that no other contents would
definitely tend to express our will. Now it is the law
of conscious growth in ourselves, that greater determination of purpose, and greater wealth of presented contents, are the correlative aspects of any gradual fulfilment
of meaning. The more we know and the more richly
we find our will fulfilled, the more exclusive and determinate becomes our purpose. The vague purpose is so
far not at the instant clear as to whether *this or that*
would better fulfil its meaning. The precise purpose
selects this *instead* of that. Precise decision is exclusive as well as inclusive. And when I speak of this
fact, I refer once more directly to our consciousness as
my warrant. I presuppose nothing as to the causal
basis, or as to the psychological or physical origin, of
attention. I say that one who rationally finds a mean-

ing fulfilled, discovers at once a wealth of contents, and a very sharply specific exclusiveness of interest fulfilled by these contents.

A satisfied will, a fully expressed meaning, would involve, then, the twofold consciousness that we may express by the two phrases, (1) I have all that I seek, and need no other ; (2) I need precisely these contents, and so select them as to permit no other to take here and for this purpose their place. As a matter of fact, then, a will satisfied, a precisely determinate meaning expressed in facts, is as selective and exclusive on the one hand, as, on the other hand, it is possessed of an exhaustive wealth of contents which meet its selection.

Now it is this selective character of every rational conscious process, a character as manifest to consciousness as it is ultimately significant for the constitution of all Being, — it is this character, I say, which to my mind is responsible above all for the Individuality which we have already characterized as belonging to the whole of Being, and which we shall now find as equally characistic of every region of finite Being. Strange as it may at first seem, a closer examination of the nature of truth makes easily manifest that what is, quite apart from any causal theory, must be viewed by the consciousness that faces Being as a selection from abstractly possible contents. The nature of these contents in general is recognized, and is so far present, at the very moment when the realization of this nature in the single shape selected from amongst all possible shapes is, at the same time, experienced.

This general view, that what is, is a selection from

possibilities, is in another form as characteristic of Realism, and even in a sense of Mysticism, as it is of our own view of Being.

The discovery that the affirmation of reality is logically based upon the exclusion of the barely possible, is constantly made by common sense, is constantly illustrated by daily experience, and is popularly exemplified by that well-known destruction of possibilities which characterizes the passing of youth, the course of history, the reproduction of every species through relatively chance union of the members of that species, and by countless other instances. The Darwinian theory of the genesis of species by natural selection, is only a single instance of the application of this general concept that the real is a selection from amongst possibilities.

In elementary logic, as we earlier showed, it becomes manifest that all universal judgments are at once, as they say, negatively existential, and involve a destruction of logically possible classes of objects. Thus, let there be what the logicians call an Universe of Discourse, that is, a world of possible beings of which you are discoursing. Into that world let two classes of objects, A and B, be introduced. Then in your universe of discourse it becomes logically possible that there should be four subclasses of beings, namely, the things which are both A and B, the things which are A but not B, the things which are not A but which are B, and finally the things which are neither A nor B. Thus, for example, if your universe of discourse is to contain righteous men and happy men, there are possible the four sub-classes of men who are righteous and happy, who are righteous and unhappy, who are unrighteous but happy, and who are neither righteous nor happy. Now begin to make universal assertions about the relations amongst these classes. Assert that all the righteous are happy. At once, as we saw in our seventh lecture, this assertion appears as a negative existential assertion, and as the destruction of a possibility. For you can express it by saying that in your universe the sub-class, otherwise possible, of righteous men who are unhappy, has vanished from existence. Your universe has now reduced its realized possibilities to the existence of three sub-classes. The example is trivial. It is but one of a countless number. To know facts is to destroy mere possibilities. To know that there is even a single righteous man in your universe of discourse, is to destroy so far the abstractly possible alternative that that individual man is unrighteous. This result so far holds with absolute generality, and without regard to your special definition of the concept of Being. Accordingly every realist regards the real as the selection from the possible. And in this we too agree with him.

Spinoza, in his curious compromise between realistic and mystical motives, undertook indeed to deny this selective function of reality; and asserted that from the divine point of view all that is possible is real. In vain, however, would one attempt to carry out this doctrine, except by expressly substituting for all other conceptions of being the Third Conception, viz., that of the real as the valid. But even this conception itself is obliged to distinguish between the relatively determinate genuine possibilities of experience, and the absolutely unrestricted products of any passing fancy. For one who developes even his most general ideas so that they have any relative wholeness of meaning, some possibilities seem to be at once excluded. Thus we already saw that in the mathematician's realm numerous abstract possibilities are excluded whenever a specific theorem is demonstrated. Our rejection, however, of the Third Conception of Being as inadequate was due in the end to a recognition of the fact that, so long as you define mere universals, mere general natures of things, you define neither the Being of objects nor the truth of ideas.

But now, as a fact, our whole experience with the concept of Being has shown us that this exclusion of bare or abstract possibilities by the presence of determinate facts does *not* tend to impoverish, but rather to enrich, our consciousness of what is real; for it is by exclusion of vain possibilities that we become able at once to define a conscious purpose and to get it fulfilled in a precise way. The life in which anything whatever can consistently happen, and in which any purpose can be fulfilled in any way, has in so far no character as a life. So far the experience of such a life is the experience of nothing in particular, — of no meaning. It is indeed true that an object which we regard as possible in the sense that it is still lacking, but is needed for a specific purpose, is precisely the object which our finite experience seeks, longs to possess, regards as beyond itself, calls therefore the desired Other. The absence of such an object is indeed a lack, a relative defeat of the finite purpose. And from our own point of view, the Fourth Conception of Being does indeed involve the thesis that there are no valid possibilities which are to remain in the end, and for God, merely possible and unfulfilled in *this* sense, namely in the sense that while they are needed for a specific purpose, they are still regarded as absent or as non-existent. But, on the other hand, we have also found that what a given finite purpose desires includes its own specific definition, as this one purpose rather than another, as this specific way of selecting facts. Now the more determinate the consciousness of such a purpose becomes, the more does such consciousness involve a selection of some facts rather than others, or an exclusion from Being of what is now regarded as merely and vainly or abstractly possible.

If you ask what manner of partial Being, from the point of view of our Fourth Conception, such abstractly conceived but concretely excluded facts possess, I answer, precisely the fragmentary sort of Being which the consciousness of a specific purpose, that is the consciousness of a particular attentive selection, consciously assigns to them. They are known *as* the excluded facts. They are defined by consciousness only in relatively general terms. As mere kinds of experience, the facts which attention thus excludes are themselves part of the very consciousness which forbids them to have any richer and more concrete Being than this character of remaining mere aspects of the whole. In this sense, but in this only, are they facts whose nature is experienced. And once more, in saying this, I refer to consciousness and to nothing else as my warrant for the meaning that I intend to convey. When one attends, when one chooses, when one finds a meaning at once specific and fulfilled, one actually observes, as an aspect of one's experience, that which one defines as the exclusion of a generally conceived possibility. One's experience of the general nature of this possibility is itself a part of the contents of one's whole present consciousness. The realization of the whole present meaning is known by virtue of this very consciousness that one is excluding from complete expression facts whose general nature one still experiences.

Now what I assert is that our Fourth Conception of Being, in conceiving the real as the present fulfilment of meaning, experienced as such fulfilment from the absolute point of view, still expressly recognizes that every such fulfilment involves conscious selection and exclusion. The facts which fulfil the meaning are at once such that no other beyond is still needed to supply a lack, while, on the other hand, no other facts could take their place without precisely a failure to fulfil the purpose. And in this twofold sense is the world of the fulfilled meaning an individual world, a world whose place no other could take. A consciousness which faced a collection of mere possibilities, without selection, would face neither wholeness nor determination of life. The very perfection of experience involves then, as an element, the exclusion of another, whose general nature is indeed a part of the very experience in question. Just as formal logic and traditional Realism have already recognized that to be real involves the exclusion of bare possibilities, so our own conception also expressly recognizes that the life which is, in its wholeness, is exclusive as well as inclusive ; and that in this sense, once more, the realm of Being has the character of the complete, but for this very reason of the determinate, Individual. So much then for Exclusion and Selection as aspects of will both in God and in man. We next pass on toward more special comparisons between Absolute and Finite Individuality. For Individuality, as we now begin to see, is, in one aspect, the expression of Selective Interest. Yet for a moment we must still treat of Individuality in general.

IV

The concept of the logical Individual, viewed apart from the question as to the distinctions of the various grades of individuality, finite or infinite, is a problem that frequently has received far too indefinite a treatment in logical discussions. What shall the word "individual" in general mean? As we have often already indicated, the technical answer to this question runs : By an individual being, whatever one's metaphysical doctrine, one means an unique being, that is, a being which is alone of its own type, or is such that no other of its class exists. Now, as we saw in an earlier lecture, our human knowledge begins with immediate data, and with vague ideas. But mere colors and sounds, as such, may indeed indicate individual beings; but they are not yet known as individuals; while our early ideas, in their twofold vagueness, both as ideas needing further determination in order to define their purpose, and as ideas needing further embodiment to complete their expression, are far from being consciously adequate ideas of individual entities. A very little examination of our popular conceptions shows how very general all such conceptions are. A very little study of concrete science reveals how hard it is for any man to get a clear idea of what his science regards as the constitution of any of its individual objects. It is far easier to know something about the circulation of the blood, than to have any adequate knowledge of the medical aspects of the case of an individual man whose circulation is in any way deranged by disease. It is precisely the individual case that constitutes the goal of the physician's knowledge. In general a real knowledge of individual facts is the ideal aim of science, rather than the beginning of any form of human insight ; and this one can observe to be true, quite apart from any metaphysical conception of what constitutes individuality.

Yet it is indeed perfectly true that, long before we have any scientific approach to a knowledge of the individual facts of the natural world, we all of us somehow believe that the world contains individual beings. And the historical prominence of the thesis that whatever is, is individual, the prominence, I say, of this thesis in the metaphysics of all ages, is due to deep reasons which seldom come to the clear consciousness of those who are accustomed to talk glibly about individuality. Only our Fourth Conception of Being is able to make the conception at once rational and explicit. It is, so we have asserted, precisely as the final and satisfactory expression of the whole will of an idea that any object can be regarded as unique. But what makes the presupposition that objects are individual precisely in so far as they are real appear so early in human thought, and exercise such a controlling influence over the development of science, is precisely that demand of the finite idea for wholeness of expression, which we have just analyzed in both of its contrasted aspects.   Long before we can ever say, with even a shadow of plausibility, that we ourselves have known and experienced the unique presence of any single fact, as such, our restless finite will itself has demanded that the real world wherein our will seeks, and logically speaking, ultimately finds, its fulfilment, shall be altogether determinate, both in so far as nothing further is needed to complete it, and in so far as nothing else would meet the needs which constitute finite ideas.

But owing to our finitude, will, in our own case, far anticipates its own fulfilment.   The individual, therefore, as a conceived object of inquiry, of desire, and of knowledge, appears in our finite human thought as something that we early define much more in terms of selective exclusion than of empirically observed completeness.   We presuppose the individual in both the foregoing senses; viz., as selected and as complete.   But, if you look closely at that region of our consciousness where first we come nearest to facing what we take to be an experience of individuality, you find, I think, that it is our selective attention, especially as embodied in what one may call our exclusive affections, which first brings home to us what we mortals require an individual being to be. How in fact should a finite being, whose experience constantly passes from one partial fulfilment to another, from one vague general idea to another instance of the same generality, — how should such a being, I say, come to be so sure as most of us are that he has actually stood in the presence of individuals, and has faced beings that are unique?   Yet every man supposes, to take perfectly ordinary instances, that his own father and mother are real individuals, and that other men, too, even where their individuality has been far less closely scrutinized, are still in themselves somehow individuals.   Every man also early believes that the world as a whole, whether he regards it as one or as many, is at all events an individual collection of individuals.   Yet to make this assertion is in any case far to transcend any man's actual experience, regarded merely as that experience comes to us.   For what we find in our finite wanderings are always cases of types, instances of imperfectly fulfilled meanings.   In observing my father, what I each time experience must necessarily be merely the presence to my mind of a certain kind of experience.   That the object of this experience is unique, that in all the universe there is no other like it, how should I myself ever experience this fact?   That this theorem about individuality is itself true, is precisely what our Fourth Conception of Being has now asserted. For whatever the relation between the finite idea and the whole world may be, this we already know from our Fourth Conception, namely that the world in its unity is an individual whole, such that no other could take its place as an expression of this one purpose.

Our idea of individuality comes to our finite consciousness, therefore, rather on the selective side of this consciousness than upon the side of its present fulfilment.   It is not so much what I already know about an individual as what my affections determine to regard as unique in the value of my object, that first brings home to me, in the case of my father or my mother or my home or my personal possessions, or my own life, and later only in the case of indifferent beings, the uniqueness of the object in question. Affection first says in presence of an object, imperfectly presented in experience, not only that there shall be further experience completing and fulfilling this meaning, but also that there shall be in this further experience such unity as constitutes an unique object. Affection first declares that there shall be no other object capable of fulfilling this meaning, beyond the single object whose Being I now presuppose. It is thus, for instance, that the lover says, There shall be none like my beloved. It is thus, too, that the mother says, There shall be no child like my child. It is thus that the loyal friend says, There shall be no friend like my friend. It is thus that the finite Self says, No life shall have precisely the meaning that my life has. It is thus also that the ethical consciousness says, My duty shall be that which nobody but myself can conceivably do. In brief, in our finite life, the sense of the determinate selection of the single object that we shall regard as the fulfilment of our meaning, comes earlier to our consciousness than any specific hope that, in our finite capacity, we shall ever live to see this specific meaning wholly fulfilled.

Now this disposition of our finite will, this tendency to a selection of our objects as unique, is precisely the character which our Fourth Conception regards as also belonging to that Absolute Will which faces the final meaning and fulfilment of the world. For the world as a whole is, from our point of view, an individual fact, not merely by virtue of the completeness of the contents of the Absolute Experience, but by reason of the definiteness of the selection of that object which shall be permitted to fulfil the final meaning. No significant purpose, no element of meaning that finite ideas demand as necessary for their own fulfilment, could indeed be, according to our thesis, wholly ignored from the absolute point of view. But, on the other hand, the very perfection of the fulfilment would logically require of the divine will the sort of determination of purpose of which we too are conscious when we deal with the objects of the exclusive affection. It is will, then, in God and in man, that logically determines the consciousness of individuality. The individual is, primarily, the object and expression of an exclusive interest, of a determinate selection.

From this point of view, the world in its wholeness might indeed be regarded as, so to speak, an only begotten son of the central purpose, — an unique expression, — unique not merely by reason of its wealth, but of its exclusiveness. And thus the category of individuality would be fulfilled in the whole precisely in the sense in which our finite affection presupposes its fulfilment in individual cases.

V

We have thus gradually prepared ourselves to define the relation between the Finite and the Absolute Will. We have studied as aspects of will, both selective attention and the nature of individuality. We have indicated, too, the sense in which, for our Fourth Conception, the world is the fulfilment of purpose. And now, to sum up so far, we do not say that any purpose, divine or human, first existing as a merely separate power, thereupon *causes* its own fulfilment. On the contrary, we say as to God, that from the absolute point of view, the genuine knowledge of the absolute purpose, as an empirical fact, is its own fulfilment. For, according to our central thesis, except as consciously fulfilling a purpose, nothing can, logically speaking, exist at all. In the second place we have also maintained that the fulfilment of the divine purpose is twofold, involving at once wealth of experience conforming to the one meaning, and selection both of the facts which express the meaning, and of the precise and individual determination of the meaning itself. The world that thus expresses meaning appears, from the absolute point of view, as an unique whole, but as also an unique selected whole, such that neither for the whole nor for any of the parts could any other fact be substituted, without failure in the realization of precisely this totality of determinate meaning. And consequently, quite apart from any causal theory, that selective aspect which common sense already regards as essential to the will does indeed appear in our account as a real and logically required character of the divine or absolute will. In the third place, however, we find a similarly selective character belonging to our own will, and an experience of such selection we find in that sort of exclusive interest whereby, even in advance of knowledge, we undertake to define the individuality which we presuppose in all the objects of our more exclusive affection.

If you ask, from this point of view, in what sense the world is to be called rather the expression of the Divine Will, and in what sense it is rather the expression of the Divine Knowledge, I reply that while we have by no means separated these two aspects of the universe, we can now easily see the convenience from many points of view of distinguishing them. The Divine or Absolute Knowledge this world expresses, by virtue of the unity of consciousness in which all its facts are linked, and by virtue too of that universality of meaning which joins all various ideas, in such wise that every finite idea, in so far as it merely refers to another, or has external reference, is general, while the whole expression of these ideas is unique and individual. In this same sense we can also speak of the world, quite accurately, as the expression, or embodiment, or fulfilment, of the Divine Thought. Will, on the other hand, this world expresses, not as if the Divine Will were an external power causing the world, but in so far as the unity of the whole is teleological, is such as ideas intend; or again, in so far as the world attains wholeness, and needs no fact beyond it for its completion; and finally, in so far as this wholeness and uniqueness of the world is the expression of an ideal selection, whose nature is well exemplified by our own exclusive interests, and whose type of fulfilment we all observe whenever we win a rational ideal goal.

Now all these considerations might seem once more to deprive any finite portion, or aspect, of this conscious universe, of any distinguishable private significance. On the contrary, however, precisely the opposite is the true result. For consider. If the whole world is at once the complete expression of a plan, and also the unique expression of such plan, then every fact in it, precisely in so far as we *distinguish* that fact from other facts, and consider its internal meaning, is also inevitably unique, sharing in so far the uniqueness of the whole. For, to illustrate, if in the ordinary empirical world of space, this

room is unique, so that by hypothesis there shall be no
other room like it in the world, then any definable part of
the unique room, by virtue of the very fact that it is different from all the other parts of this same room, has its
own unique individuality as opposed to any other fact in
the universe.

Or again, let A be any fact. First suppose A to be
merely an abstract universal, a general type. Then suppose A to be an individual. If A is as a whole merely
a case of a type, so that there are other cases like it, then
any part of A is in so far also only a case of a type, and
is not unique. But if A is an individual, unique and
elsewhere unexampled, then every fragment of A has its
part in the individuality of the whole, just as a play of
Shakespeare, as this particular expression of the individuality of the poet, has its own uniqueness by sharing in
his.

Now, by hypothesis, the world exists only as *such* an
expression of the meaning of the divine system of ideas,
that no other life than this of the present world could
express precisely this system. But suppose that you lay
stress upon the facts of any finite life. You have a right
to do so, for these facts exist for the Absolute precisely
as much as for you. Then you have, in the first place,
facts that exist only as an expression of a meaning. If
you ask of what meaning they are the expression, the
answer is, of the meaning of the very ideas and of the
very will, that, in the finite consciousness, accompany these
very facts.

Take, for instance, one of your own acts. In part, it
expresses one of your own purposes. Now our theory

does indeed unite both your act and the idea that your act expresses, along with all other acts and ideas, in the single unity of the absolute consciousness. But this single unity of the absolute consciousness, as we already saw at the last time, is nothing that merely absorbs your individuality, in such wise that you vanish from amongst the facts of the world. You remain from the absolute point of view precisely what you now know yourself to be, namely, the possessor of just this ideal purpose, whose internal meaning is embodied in just so much of conscious life as is yours. Our very theory insists that your internal meanings, your ideas viewed as internally significant, your selections and expressions, are typical instances of facts, and of precisely the facts of whose unity the world consists. Now if the whole world is, as whole, the unique expression of the divine purpose, it follows that every finite purpose, precisely in so far as it is, is a partial expression and attainment of the divine will; and also that every finite fulfilment of purpose, precisely as we finite beings find it, is a partial fulfilment of the divine meaning. For from our point of view, while all finite ideas, in so far as concerns their external meaning, are indeed general, still no fact exists *merely* as a case of a type, or merely as an instance of an universal. The very simplest view of any finite fact already makes it a positive part of the unique divine experience, and therefore, as this part, itself unique. A still deeper view recognizes any finite will, say your own present will, as a stage or case of the expression of the divine purpose at a given point of time; but this expression, too, is once more unique. And this expression is also in one aspect no other than what you find it to be, to wit, your own conscious will and meaning.

Thus the individuality of the whole in such wise dwells in the parts, the individuality of the unique divine purpose is in such wise present in each finite purpose, that no finite purpose, viewed merely as an internal meaning, could have its place taken by another without a genuine alteration of the whole; while, on the other hand, it is equally true that the whole would not be what it is were not precisely this finite purpose left in its own uniqueness to speak precisely its own word — a word which no other purpose can speak in the language of the divine will. In brief, then, our view leaves all the unique meaning of your finite individual life just as rich as you find it to be. You are in God; but you are not lost in God. If every finite pulsation of life, despite its aspect of mere generality, its external meaning, has something unique about it, and if this unique aspect of the finite life expresses an internal meaning, then the meaning of every such fact itself is unique. Or to apply the matter once more to yourself : if every instance of your life expresses a will that is to be found expressed in precisely this way nowhere else in all the world, and if this will is the will of which you are now conscious, then we can say that the verdict of your own consciousness when it regards your life as the expression of your individual will is in no wise refuted, but is only confirmed by our Fourth Conception of Being.

Thus it is then that we deal, in case of the finite will and the divine will, with the problem of the One and the Many. A realistic union of the many different beings in one being we long since found to be impossible. For our present point of view, however, the realistic difficulty of the Many and the One has been wholly set aside. It is not indeed for us a question of how the many *things* could become one *thing*. For us the unity of the world is the unity of consciousness. The variety of the world is the internal, but none the less wealthy and genuine, variety of the purposes and embodiments of purpose present within this unity of the one divine consciousness. Now with regard to the ultimate unity and consequent harmony of all this variety, our Fourth Conception has given us indeed a general formula. The Many must, despite their variety, win harmony and perfection by their coöperation. But this principle, so far, gives us no limit either to the empirical variety of will, or of interest and of experience in the absolute, nor any limit to the relative independence which the uniqueness of the individual elements makes possible. What we see, however, is that every distinguishable portion of the divine life, in addition to all the universal ties which link it to the whole, expresses its own meaning. We see, too, that this meaning is unique, and that this meaning is precisely identical with what each one of us means by his own individual will, so far as that will is at any time determinate, uniquely selected, and empirically expressed. So much then for the general relations of Absolute and of Finite will.

VI

Two expressions, familiar to common sense in speaking of finite will, receive herewith their sufficient and, I believe, their only possible justification. Common sense first asserts that, when my will gets expressed, I individually am *active*. Common sense also, in the second place, asserts that when my will gets inwardly expressed in my choice, I individually am *free*. Now into the endless discussions as to the causal relations of this or that aspect of the human will we have declined in this discussion to go. We have declined, because we have said that all causation, whatever it is, is but a special instance of Being, and never can explain any of the ultimate problems about Being. But when we have asserted, as we have now done, that every moment of every finite consciousness has some unique character, and when we have asserted, as we have also done, that in our rational life our momentary will and its finite expression belong to this very unique aspect of our finite life, we have indeed found, in our finite will, an aspect which *no* causation could ever by any possibility explain. For whatever else causation may be, it implies the explanation of facts by their general character, and by their connections with other facts. Whatever is unique, is as such not causally explicable. The individual as such is never the mere result of law. In consequence, the causal explanation of an object never defines its individual and unique characters as such, but always its general characters. Consequently, *if* the will and the expression of that will in any moment of our finite life possess characters, namely, precisely these individual and uniquely significant characters which no causal explanation can predetermine, then such acts of will, as significant expressions of purpose in our life, constitute precisely what ethical common sense has always meant by free acts. If your finite purpose is now

different from that of any other finite being, and if your
finite purpose now in any sense uniquely expresses, however inadequately, its own determinate meaning, in its
own way, then, you can indeed assert: I alone, amongst
all the different beings of the universe, will this act.
That it is true that God here also wills in me, is
indeed the unquestionable result of the unity of the
divine consciousness.   But it is equally true that this
divine unity is here and now realized by me, and by me
only, through my unique act.   My act, too, is a part of
the divine life that, however fragmentary, is not elsewhere repeated in the divine consciousness.   When I
thus consciously and uniquely will, it is I then who just
here *am* God's will, or who just here consciously act for
the whole.   I then am so far free.

The other popular conception, in addition to the conception of freedom, which belongs in this connection, is
that very conception of Activity which I have just employed.   By the term "activity" I regard our ethical common sense as meaning precisely the very fact that our
present will, as the will of an individual, is unique.   By
our activity, then, I mean just the unique significance of
the present expression of our will.   If a general law, —
a merely universal type, — if our characters or temperaments, or some other such universal nature of things, are
expressed in our present experience, then, in so far, we
are indeed mere cases of types.   In so far we do not act.
But if this my present expression of my meaning is in
such wise unique that, but for this meaning, this expression would have no place in the whole realm of Being,
then indeed I may call my present expression of meaning

my act. As my act this my present will is as unique as
is the whole divine life, as free as is the whole meaning
of which the whole world is an expression. *Not* by virtue then of any supposed causal efficacy is the divine will
as a power the producer of the world. And just so, not
by virtue of its potency as a physical agent is our human
action a free cause.

To our later series of lectures must be altogether left
the discussion of any sort of causation in its real, but
in its extremely subordinate, place in the constitution
of reality. But what we at present say to the finite
being is: You are at once an expression of the divine
will, and by virtue of that very fact the expression here
and now, in your life, of your *own* will, precisely in so
far as you find yourself acting with a definite intent,
and gaining through your act a definite empirical expression. We do not say, Your individuality causes your act.
We do not say, Your free will creates your life. For
Being is everywhere deeper than causation. What you
are is deeper than your mere power as a physical agent.
Nothing whatever besides yourself determines either
causally or otherwise just what constitutes your individuality, for you are just this unique and elsewhere
unexampled expression of the divine meaning. And
here and now your individuality in your act *is* your
freedom. This your freedom is your unique possession.
Nowhere else in the universe is there what here expresses
itself in your conscious being. And this is true of you,
not in spite of the unity of the divine consciousness, but
just because of the very uniqueness of the whole divine
life. For all is divine, all expresses meaning. All

meaning is uniquely expressed. Nothing is vainly repeated; you too, then, as individual are unique. And (here is the central fact) just in so far as you consciously will and choose, you then and there in so far know what this unique meaning of yours is. Therefore are you in action Free and Individual, just because the unity of the divine life, when taken together with the uniqueness of this life, implies in every finite being just such essential originality of meaning as that of which you are conscious. Arise then, freeman, stand forth in thy world. It is God's world. It is also thine.

SUPPLEMENTARY ESSAY

GIFFORD LECTURES

FIRST SERIES

SUPPLEMENTARY ESSAY
THE ONE, THE MANY, AND THE INFINITE

Section I. Mr. Bradley's Problem

The closing lecture of the foregoing series has begun the
statement of the doctrine of the Individual. The reality of
Many within One, and the necessity of the union of the One
and the Many, have been maintained, side by side with some
account of the nature that, as I also maintain, ought to be
attributed to the Individual, whether you consider the Absolute Individual, or the Individuals of our finite world, — the
men whose wills are expressed in our life. Now I should be
glad to allow the general theory to stand, for the present,
simply as stated; and to postpone altogether, until the second
series of these lectures, the further defence of the doctrine, —
were it not that the most thorough, and in very many respects
by far the most important contribution to pure Metaphysics
which has of late years appeared in England, has made known
a Theory of Being with which, in some of its most significant
theses, I heartily agree, while, nevertheless, this very Theory
of Being, as it has been stated by its author, undertakes to
render wholly impossible, for our human minds, as now we
are constituted, any explicit and detailed reconciliation of the
One and the Many, or any positive theory of how Individuals
find their real place in the Absolute. Defining and defending
a conception of the Absolute as "one system," whose contents
are "experience," Mr. Bradley, to whose well-known book,

Appearance and Reality, I am here referring, has, nevertheless, maintained that we are wholly unable to "construe" to
ourselves the way in which the realm of Appearance finds
its unity in the Absolute.   He rejects, in consequence, every
more detailed effort to interpret our own life in its relations to
the Absolute, such as, in the foregoing discussions I have begun,
and, in the second series of these lectures, hope to continue.
The reason for this rejection, in Mr. Bradley's case, is of the
most fundamental kind.   It is founded upon the most central
theses of his Theory of Being.   The proper place to discuss it
is in close connection, therefore, with the general theory in
question.   I have stated my own case; but I feel obliged to
try to do justice to Mr. Bradley's interpretation.   For if he is
right, there is little hope for our further undertaking.

The task is no easy one.   I myself owe a great debt to Mr.
Bradley's book, a debt manifest in my criticism of Realism in
Lecture III, and in many other parts of my discussion.   The
book is itself a very elaborate argumentative structure.   One
ought not to make light of it by chance quotations.   One cannot easily summarize its well-wrought reasonings in a few
sentences.   To discuss it carefully would have been wholly
impossible in my general course of lectures.   On the other
hand, to sunder the discussion of it wholly from the present
discourse, would have made such a critical enterprise as here
follows, seem, for me, a thankless polemical task. For lengthy
polemic regarding so serious a piece of work as Mr. Bradley's
is hardly to be tolerated apart from an attempt at construction.
And so I have resolved to attempt the task in the form of an
essay, supplementary to my own statement of a Theory of
Being in these lectures, and preparatory to the discussion of
Man and Nature in the next series.

Even here, however, I must attempt to construct as well as
to object.   And the effort will lead at once to problems which
I had no time to discuss in the general lectures.   Mr. Bradley,
for instance, has shown that every effort to bring to unity the
manifoldness of our world involves us in what he himself often
calls an "infinite process."   In other words, if, in telling

about the Absolute you try to show *how* the One and the Many are brought into unity, and how the Many develope out of the One, you find that, in attempting to define the Many at all, you have defined an actually infinite number. But an actually infinite multitude, according to Mr. Bradley, is a self-contradictory conception. The problem thus stated is an ancient phase of the general problem as to unity and plurality.

From the very outset of the philosophical study of the diversities of the universe, it has been noticed, that in many cases, where common sense is content to enumerate two, or three, or some other limited number of aspects or constituents of a supposed object, closer analysis shows that the variety contained in this object, if really existent at all, must be boundless, so that the dilemma: "Either no true variety of the supposed type is real, or else this variety involves an infinity of aspects," has often been used as a critical test, to discredit some commonly received view as to the unity and variety of the universe or of some supposed portion thereof. Mr. Bradley has not been wanting in his appeal to this type of critical argument. But to give this argument its due weight, when it comes as a device for discrediting all efforts to define the nature of Individuals, requires one to attack the whole question of the actual Infinite, a question that recent discussions of the Philosophy of Mathematics have set in a decidedly new light, but that these discussions have also made more technical than ever. If I am to be just to this matter, I must therefore needs wander far afield. Nobody, I fear, except a decidedly technical reader, will care to follow. I have, therefore, hesitated long before venturing seriously to entertain the plan of saying, either here or elsewhere, anything about what seems to me the true, and, as I believe, the highly positive implication, of Mr. Bradley's apparently most destructive arguments concerning Individual Being and concerning the meaning of the world of Appearance.

Yet the problem of the reality of infinite variety and multiplicity, — a problem thus made so prominent by Mr. Bradley's whole method of procedure, — is one that no metaphysician can permanently evade. The doctrine that the conception of the actually infinite multitude is a self-contradictory conception is a familiar thesis ever since Aristotle. If this thesis is correct, as Mr. Bradley himself assumes, then Mr. Bradley's results, as regards the limitations of our human knowledge of the Absolute, appear to be inevitable, and the effort of these present lectures to define the essential relations of the world and the individual must fail. On the other hand, however, if, as I believe, the very doctrine of the true nature of Individual Being, which these lectures defend, enables us, for the first time perhaps in the history of the discussion of the Infinite, to give a precise statement of the sense in which an Infinite Multitude can, without contradiction, be viewed as determinately real, — then a discussion of Mr. Bradley's position, and of the whole problem of the One, the Many, and the Infinite, will prove an important supplement to our Theory of Being, and an essential basis for the vindication of our human knowledge of the general constitution of Reality. And so I must feel that, if the present task is extended and technical, the goal is nothing less than the defence of what I take to be a true theory of the whole meaning of life.

And so I am now minded to undertake the task of vindicating the concept of the actual Infinite against the charge of self-contradiction. I am minded, also, to attempt the closely related task of defending the concept of the Self against a like charge. In the same connection I shall undertake to show something of the true relations of the One and the Many in the real world. And in the course of this enterprise I shall found the positive discussion upon a criticism of Mr. Bradley's position.

But now, at this point, let any weary reader whom my lectures may have already disheartened, — but who nevertheless may kindly have proceeded so far, — turn finally back. When you enter the realm of Mr. Bradley's Absolute, it is much as it is at the close of Victor Hugo's *Toilers of the Sea*, after the ship that carries away the lady has sunk below the horizon, and after the tide has just covered the rock where the desolate lover had been watching. "There was nothing," says the poet, in his last words, "there was nothing now visible but the sea." As for me, I love the sea, and am minded to find in it life, and individuality, and explicit law. And I go upon that quest. Whoever is not weary, and is not yet disheartened, and is fond of metaphysical technicality, is welcome to join the quest. But in the sea there are also, as Victor Hugo explained to us, very strange monsters. And Mr. Bradley, too, in his book, has had much to say of the "monsters," philosophic and psychological, that the realm of Appearance contains, even in the immediate neighborhood of the Absolute. We shall meet some such reputed "monsters" in the course of this discussion. Let him who fears such trouble also turn back.

In this essay, I shall first try to state Mr. Bradley's theses as to the problem of the One and the Many. Then I shall try to show how he himself seems to suggest a way by which, if we follow that way far enough, something may be done to solve what he leaves apparently hopeless. And, finally, I shall proceed upon the way thus opened until we have found whither it leads. We shall find it inevitably leading to the conception of the actually Infinite. We shall examine the known difficulties of that conception, and shall at last solve them by means of our own conception of the nature of determinateness and Individuality.

I. *Mr. Bradley's First Illustrations of His Problem*

The general doctrine of the Absolute which Mr. Bradley maintains is the result of a critical analysis of a number of metaphysical conceptions which he opposes. Mr. Bradley's work is divided into two books. The first book, entitled *Appearance*, has a mainly negative result. Beginning with the examination of the traditional distinction between primary and secondary qualities, Mr. Bradley shows that this distinction is incapable of furnishing a consistent account of the relation of the phenomenal to the real. The problem of inherence, attacked next in order, is declared to be, upon the basis of the ordinary conception of things and qualities, and of their relationship, insoluble. The reason given in this case is typical of Mr. Bradley's position throughout the book, and, despite the general familiarity of the argument to readers of the Hegelian and Herbartian discussions of the concept of the *thing*, deserves special mention at this point.

A thing is somehow to be one, and "it has properties, adjectives which qualify it.[1] We say that the thing *is* this or that, predicating of it the adjectives that express its qualities." But it cannot be "all its properties if you take them each severally." "Its reality lies somehow in its unity." "But if, on the other hand, we inquire what there can be in the thing besides its several qualities, we are baffled once more. We can discover no real unity existing outside these qualities, or, again, existing within them." To the hypothesis that the unity of the thing may be sufficiently expressed by asserting that "the qualities are, and are in relation," Mr. Bradley replies that the meaning of *is* remains still doubtful when we say, "One quality, *A is* in relation with another quality, *B*" (p. 20). For still one does not, by here using *is*, intend to reduce *A* to simple *identity with* its relations to *B*, and so one is led to say, "The word to use, when we are pressed, should not be *is*, but only *has*." But the *has* seems metaphorical. "And we seem unable to clear ourselves from the old dilemma, If you predicate what is different, you ascribe to the subject what it is *not;* and if you predicate what is *not* different you say nothing at all." Nor does one better the case (p. 21) if one amends the phraseology here in question by asserting that the relation belongs equally to both *A* and *B*, instead of limiting the assertion in form to *A* alone. If the relation, however, be no mere attribute of *A* or of *B*, or of both of them, but a "more or less independent" fact, namely, the fact that "There is a relation *C* in which *A* and *B* stand," then the problem of the unity of the thing becomes the problem as to

[1] Page 19. I cite throughout from the second edition of *Appearance and Reality*.

the genuine tie that binds both A and B to their now relatively independent relation C. For C is now supposed to possess an existence which is not that of A or B, but something apart from either. This tie which unites A and B, in the thing, to C, hereupon appears as a new fact of relation, D, viz., the fact that A and B are so related to C that C becomes their relation to each other. "But such a makeshift at once leads to the infinite process. The new relation D can be predicated in no way of C, or of A and B; and hence we must have recourse to a fresh relation, E, which comes between D and whatever we had before. But this must lead to another, F; and so on indefinitely." The consequence is that we are not aided by letting the "qualities and their relation fall entirely apart." "There must be a whole embracing what is related, or there would be no differences, and no relation." This remark applies not merely to *things*, and to the relations that are to bind into unity their qualities, but to space, and time, and to every case where varieties are in any way related. But although Mr. Bradley asserts thus early the general principle that variety must always find its basis in unity, he wholly denies that, in the present case, we have yet found or defined what the unity in question can be. He denies, namely, that the relational system offered to us so far by the qualities supposed to be inherent in the one thing, or to be related to one another, contains, or can be made to contain, any principle adequate to accomplish the required task, or to "justify the arrangement" that we try to make in conceiving the thing and its qualities as in relational unity.

II. *The General Problem of " Relational Thought"*

The defect in all these accounts of the nature of the thing is not due, according to Mr. Bradley's view, to any accidental faults of definition. The defect depends upon a dilemma that first fully comes to light when the problem about relations and qualities is considered for itself, and apart from the special issue about the thing. The task of expounding this dilemma

Mr. Bradley undertakes in Chapter III of his first book. Here his thesis is (p. 25), that "The arrangement of given facts into relations and qualities may be necessary in practice, but it is theoretically unintelligible."

The true reason why the concept of the thing involved the foregoing paradoxes is now to become more obvious. It is set forth in three successive theses. First (p. 26): "Qualities are nothing without relations." For qualities are different from one another. "Their plurality depends on relation, and without that relation they are not distinct" (p. 28). Even were qualities conceived as in themselves wholly separated from one another, and only *for us* related, still (p. 29) "Any separateness implies separation, and so relation, and is therefore, when made absolute, a self-discrepancy." "If there is any difference, then that implies a relation." Mr. Bradley enforces this assertion by a reference, made with characteristic skill, to the paradoxes of the Herbartian metaphysic of the *einfache Qualitäten* and the *zufällige Ansichten* (p. 30).

But if it is impossible to conceive qualities without relations, it is equally unintelligible to take qualities together with relations. For the qualities cannot be resolved into the relations. And, if taken with the relations, they "must be, and must *also* be related" (p. 31). But now afresh arises the problem as to how, in this instance, the variety involved in the *also* is reducible to the unity which each quality must by itself possess. For a quality, *A*, is made what it is *both* by its relations (since, as we have seen, these are essential to its being as a quality), and by something else, namely, by its own inner character. *A* has thus two aspects, both of which can be predicated of it. Yet "without the use of a relation it is impossible to predicate this variety of *A*," just as it was impossible, except by the use of a relation, to predicate the various qualities of one thing. We have therefore to say that, within *A*, both its own inner character, as a quality, and its relatedness to other facts, are themselves, as varieties, facts; but such facts as constitute the being of *A*, so that they are united by a new relation, namely, by the very relation which makes them constitutive of A.   Thus, however, "we are led by a principle of fission which conducts us to no end."   "The quality must exchange its unity for an internal relation." This diversity "demands a new relation, and so on without limit."

For similar reasons, a relation without terms being "mere verbiage" (p. 32), it follows that since the terms imply qualities, relation without qualities is nothing.   But, on the other hand, if the relation stands related to the qualities, if it is anything to them, "we shall now require a new connecting relation."   But hereupon an endless process of the same kind as before is set up (p. 33).   "The links are united by a link, and this bond of union is a link which has also two ends; and these require each a fresh link to connect them with the old."

The importance for Mr. Bradley of the negative result thus reached lies in the great generality of the conceptions here in question, and in the consequent range covered by these fundamental considerations.   "The conclusion," says Mr. Bradley, "to which I am brought, is that a relational way of thought — any one that moves by the machinery of terms and relations — must give appearance and not truth.   It is a makeshift, a device, a mere practical compromise, most necessary, but in the end most indefensible.   We have to take reality as many, and to take it as one, and to avoid contradiction.   We want to divide it, or to take it, when we please, as indivisible; to go as far as we desire in either of these directions, and to stop when that suits us. . . .   But when these inconsistencies are forced together . . . the result is an open and staring inconsistency."

In the subsequent chapters of Mr. Bradley's first book, he himself sees, in a great measure, merely an application of the general principle just enunciated to such special problems as are exemplified by Space, by Time, by Causation, by Activity, and by the Self.   For all these metaphysical conceptions are defined in terms of a "relational way" of thinking, and involve the problem of the One and the Many.   To be sure, the discussion of the Self, in Chapters IX and X, brings the problem

into decidedly new and important forms, but does not, in Mr.
Bradley's opinion, furnish any acceptable ground for its positive solution.   "We have found," he says, "puzzles in reality,
besetting every way in which we have taken it."   The solution of these puzzles, if ever discovered, must be "a view not
obnoxious to these mortal attacks, and combining differences
in one so as to turn the edge of criticism" (p. 114).   The mere
appeal, however, to the fact of self-consciousness, does not
furnish this needed explicit harmony of unity and variety.
The Self does, indeed, unite diversity and unity in a profoundly important way; but the mere fact that this is somehow done does not show us *how* it is done.

III.   *The Problem of the One and the Many as Insoluble by Thought, yet solved by the Absolute*

Despite this elaborate exposition of the apparent hopelessness of the problem as to the One and the Many, Mr. Bradley's own theory of the Absolute, proposed in his second book,
turns upon asserting that in Reality unity and diversity are
positively reconciled, and reconciled, moreover, not by a simple abolition of either of the apparently opposed principles,
but in a way that leaves to each its place.   For first (p. 140),
"Reality is one in this sense that it has a positive nature exclusive of discord. . . . Its diversity can be diverse only
so far as not to clash."   Yet, on the other hand, "Appearance
must belong to reality, and it must, therefore, be concordant
and other than it seems.   The bewildering mass of phenomenal diversity must hence somehow be at unity and self-consistent; for it cannot be elsewhere than in reality, and reality
excludes discord.   Or, again, we may put it so: The real is
individual.   It is one in the sense that its positive character
embraces all differences in an inclusive harmony."   Further,
"To be real . . . must be to fall within sentience" (p. 144).
Or, again, to be real (p. 146) is "to be something which comes
as a feature and aspect within one whole of feeling, something which, except as an integral element of such sentience,

has no meaning at all." In consequence, "The Absolute is one system," and "its contents are . . . sentient experience." "It will hence be a single and all-inclusive experience, which embraces every partial diversity in concord" (p. 147). It follows that, in the Absolute, none of the diversities which are to us so perplexing, and which, as exemplified by the cases of thing, quality, relation, Self, and the rest of the appearances, are so contradictory in their seeming, are wholly lost. For the Absolute, on the contrary, these diversities are all preserved; only they are "transmuted" into a whole, which is, in ways of which we have only a most imperfect knowledge, internally harmonious. As to the hints that we possess, regarding the nature of the Absolute, they are summarized as follows: "Immediate presentation" (p. 159) gives us the experience of a "whole" which "contains diversity," but which is, nevertheless, "not parted by relations." On the other hand, "relational form," where known to us, points "everywhere to an unity," — "a substantial totality, beyond relations and above them, a whole endeavoring without success to realize itself in their detail" (p. 160). Such facts and considerations give us "not an experience, but an abstract idea" of a "unity which transcends and yet contains every manifold appearance." "We can form the general idea of an absolute experience in which phenomenal distinctions are merged, a whole becomes immediate at a higher stage without losing any richness." But meanwhile we have "a complete inability to understand this concrete unity in detail."

The ground of this, our inability, is the one already illustrated, namely, the necessary incapacity of a "relational way of thinking" to give us anything definite except Appearance, or to harmonize the One and the Many in concrete fashion, or to free our explicit accounts of the unity from the contradictions and infinite processes heretofore illustrated. A more precise exposition of the general defects of thought in question, Bradley undertakes to furnish in his fifteenth chapter, under the title Thought and Reality. Here the nature of relational thought, its inevitable sundering of the *what* and the

that, and its inevitably infinite process in trying to unite them
again, are two topics discussed, with the result, as Mr. Bradley
states the case, that "Thought desires a consummation in
which it is lost," as "the river" runs "into the sea," and "the
self" loses itself "in love." For every act of thought, in
affirming its predicate of the subject, though all the while
knowing that the quality or adjective is not the existent, explicitly faces its own Other, namely, precisely its object, the
existent of which it thinks, the subject to which it applies its
predicates. This existent, by virtue of its "sensuous infinitude," or vaguely endless wealth of presented features, always
defies our efforts exhaustively to define it in ideal terms
(p. 176); and, by virtue of its "immediacy" (p. 177), possesses "the character of a single self-subsistent being," — a
character apparently inconsistent with the "sensuous infinitude." Our thought, however, endeavoring to characterize
this Other, seeks to make ideally explicit how, despite its
endless wealth of presented features, it can be still a single
individual, — a system of variety in unity. Attempting this
task, thought is obliged to use the "relational form" in characterizing the subject; and this at once makes impossible the
expression, in ideal terms, of either the self-dependence or the
immediacy which the subject claims (p. 178). For, analyzing
the subject, in order to define its wealth of content, thought,
in the fashion before illustrated in the case of things, qualities, etc., is led to an infinite process, since every relation
defined requires new relations to make it comprehensible.
Both the internal and the external relations of the subject and
of its contents, accordingly prove to be inexhaustible. Never,
then, is thought's ideal system of predicates adequate to the
subject. The "sensuous infinitude" or undefined wealth that
the subject at first presents, turns, while we think, into the
explicitly infinite series of relational predicates. Moreover,
even were thought's system ever completed, "that system
would not be the subject." For if it were, "it would wholly
lose the relational form."

The result is that thinking "desires to possess," as its end and goal, a character of "immediate, self-dependent, all-inclusive individuality" (p. 179), while "individuality cannot be gained while we are confined to relations." Thought, however, although not possessing the features of reality here in question, can recognize them as its own Other, can "desire them" (p. 180) "because its content has them already in an incomplete form. And in desire for the completion of what none has there is no contradiction." "But, on the other hand (p. 181), such a completion would prove destructive; such an end would emphatically make an end of mere thought. It would bring the ideal content into a form which would be reality itself, and where mere truth and mere thought would certainly perish." "It is this completion of thought beyond thought which remains forever an Other." "Thought can understand that, to reach its goal, it must get beyond relations. Yet in its nature it can find no other working means of progress."

Hence, "our Absolute," once more, will include the differences of thought and reality, of "what" and "that." "The self-consciousness of the part, its consciousness of itself even in opposition to the whole, — all will be contained within the one absorbing experience. For this will embrace all self-consciousness harmonized, though, as such, transmuted and suppressed." But Mr. Bradley still insists that "we cannot possibly construe such an experience to ourselves."

IV. *Mr. Bradley's Definition of "What would Satisfy the Intellect" as to the One and the Many*

Mr. Bradley's critics have very commonly expressed their disapproval of the extremely delicate position in which, by this theory, our finite thinking is left. We are obliged to define the Real as a system wherein unity and diversity are harmonized. We are to conceive this reality as a "sentient experience." And in the Absolute Experience, nothing of our finite variety is to be wholly lost, but all is to be "transmuted." Yet every instance, selected from our own human experience, where, through a process of thinking, or a type of mediated consciousness, we men seem to have won any sort of explicit synthesis and harmony of the One and the Many, is sternly rejected by Mr. Bradley, as furnishing no satisfactory guide to the final knowledge of the *way* in which, in the Absolute, unity and manifoldness are united. The critics have, accordingly, been sometimes disposed to accuse Mr. Bradley of seeking, in his Absolute, for bare identity without diversity; and sometimes tempted, on the other hand, to ask, complainingly, what sort of harmony would satisfy him, and why he supposes that *any* harmony of the One and the Many is attainable at all, even for the Absolute, when he himself rejects, as mere appearance, every proffered means, whereby harmony is to be defined.

In answer, Mr. Bradley has been led, in his second edition, to discuss, in an appendix, the problem of "Contradiction and the Contrary," with special reference to its bearing upon the matter here at issue. The relation of the theory of the contrary to the problem of the relation of unity and diversity appears in the fundamental thesis of the discussion in question.[1] This thesis is as follows (p. 562): "A thing cannot, without an internal distinction, be (or do) two different things; and differences cannot belong to the same thing, in the same point, unless in that point there is diversity. The appearance of such union may be fact, but is for thought a contradiction." In expounding this statement of the principle of contradiction, Mr. Bradley first explains that the thesis "does not demand mere sameness," which to thought "would be nothing." A mere tautology "is not a truth in any way, in any sense, or at all." The Law of Contradiction, then, does not forbid diversity. If it did, "it would forbid thinking altogether." But the difficulty of the situation arises from the fact that, "Thought cannot do without differences; but, on the other hand, it cannot make them. And, as it cannot make them, so it cannot receive them from the outside, and ready-made."

[1] Note A of the second edition, pp. 562, *sqq.* — a paper reprinted from *Mind* with omission.

Thought demands a reason and ground for diversity. It can neither pass from A to B without a reason, nor accept as final the fact that, external to thought's process, A and B are found conjoined. If thought finds a diversity, it demands that this be "brought to unity" (p. 562). And so, if the mere fact of the conjunction of A and B appears, then thought must "either make or accept an arrangement which to it is wanton and without reason, — or, having no reason for anything else, attempt, against reason, to identify them simply" (p. 563). Nor can one meet this difficulty by merely asserting that there are certain ultimate complexes, given in experience, such that in them unity and variety are presented as obviously conjoined, while thought is to explain the "detail of the world" in terms of these fundamental complexes. No such "bare conjunction" is or possibly can be given; for when we find any kind of unity in diversity, that is, when we find diversities conjoined, we always also find a "background" (p. 564) which is a "condition of the conjunction's existence" so that "the conjunction is not bare, but dependent," and is presented to the intellect as "a connection, the bond of which is at present unknown." "The intellect, therefore, while rejecting whatever is alien to itself, if offered as Absolute, can accept the inconsistent if taken as subject to conditions."

Meanwhile, the "mere conjunction," if taken as such, is "for thought contradictory" (p. 565). For as soon as thought makes the conjunction its object, thought must "hold in unity" the elements of the conjunction. But finding these elements diverse, thought "can of itself supply no internal bond by which to hold them together, nor has it any internal diversity by which to maintain them apart." If one replies that the elements are offered to thought "together and in conjunction," Mr. Bradley retorts that the question is "how thought can think what is offered." If thought were itself possessed of conjoining principles, of "a 'together,' a 'between,' and an 'all at once,'" as its own internal principle, it could use them to explain the conjunction offered. But, as a fact (p. 566), "Thought cannot accept tautology, and yet demands unity in diversity. But your offered conjunctions, on the other side, are for it no connections or ways of union. They are themselves merely other external things to be connected." It is, then, "idle from the outside to say to thought, 'Well, unite, but do not identify.' How can thought unite except so far as in itself it has a mode of union? To unite without an internal ground of connection and distinction, is to strive to bring together barely in the same point, and that is self-contradiction." Things, then, "are not contradictory because they are diverse," but "just in so far as they appear as bare conjunctions." Therefore it is that a mere together, "in space or time, is for thought unsatisfactory and, in the end, impossible." But, on the other hand, every such untrue view must be transcended, and the Real is not self-contradictory, despite its diversities, since their real unity is, in the Absolute, present.

If one now asks what then "would satisfy the intellect, supposing it could be got" (p. 568), Mr. Bradley points out that if the ground of unity is "external to the elements into which the conjunction must be analyzed," then the ground "becomes for the intellect a fresh element, and in itself calls for synthesis in a fresh point of unity." "But hereon," he continues, "because in the intellect no intrinsic connections were found, ensues the infinite process." This being the problem "The remedy might be here. If the diversities were complementary aspects of a process of connection and distinction, the process not being external to the elements, or, again, a foreign compulsion of the intellect, but itself the intellect's own *proprius motus*, the case would be altered. Each aspect would of itself be a transition to the other aspect, a transition intrinsic and natural at once to itself, and to the intellect. And the Whole would be a self-evident analysis and synthesis of the intellect itself by itself. Synthesis here has ceased to be mere synthesis, and has become self-completion; and analysis, no longer mere analysis, is self-explication. And the question how or why the many are one and the one is many here loses its meaning. There is no why or how beside the self-evident process, and towards its own differences this whole is at once their how and their why, their being, substance, and system, their reason, ground, and principle of diversity and unity" (*id*). Here, Mr. Bradley insists, the Law of Contradiction "has nothing to condemn." Such an union or "identity of opposites" would not conflict with the Law of Contradiction, but would rather fulfil the law. If "all that we find were in the end such a self-evident and complete whole," the end of the intellect, and so of philosophy, would have been won. But Mr. Bradley is (p. 569) "unable to verify a solution of this kind." Hence, as he says, "Against my intellectual world the Law of Contradiction has claims nowhere satisfied in full." Therefore "they are met in and by a whole beyond the mere intellect." It is, however, no "abstract identity" that thus satisfies the demands of the intellect. "On the other hand, I cannot say that to me any principle or principles of diversity in unity are self-evident." In consequence, while "self-existence and self-identity are to be found," they are to be looked for neither in "bare identity," nor in a relapse into a "stage before thinking begins," but in "a whole beyond thought, a whole to which thought points and in which it is included." Diversities exist. Therefore (p. 570) "they must somehow be true and real." "Hence, they must be true and real in such a way that from *A* or *B* the intellect can pass to its further qualification without an external denomination of either. But this means that *A* and *B* are united, each from its own nature, in a whole which is the nature of both alike." It is the failure of the intellect to define this whole positively and in detail, which is expressed in all the contradictions of the theory of appearance.

Section II. The One and the Many within the Realm of Thought or of Internal Meanings

So far, then, for a summary of Mr. Bradley's general view regarding the mystery of unity in variety, and so much for the reasons which have led him, on the one hand, to maintain that real identity is never "simple," or abstract, but involves

real differences, and, on the other hand, to insist that the true
ground of this union of identity and difference is always, to
us, and to "thought," something not manifest, but only presupposed as "beyond thought." What are we to hold of this
doctrine?

I. *Thought does Develope its own Varieties of Internal Meaning*

Our first comment must repeat what several of Mr. Bradley's
critics have noticed. This is, that within at least one, perhaps limited, but still in any case for us mortals important
region, Mr. Bradley himself finds and reports the working of
a very "self-evident" principle of "diversity in unity."

This is the region in which thought is itself the object
whose process and movement, whose paradoxes and whose endless series of internal distinctions, we observe, or experience,
while we read Mr. Bradley's book, or any similarly deep examination of the realm of the "intellect." In his *Logic*
Mr. Bradley long since gave us a brilliant account of the
movement of thought, — an account that he here lays at the
basis of his discussion. The truth of a considerable portion
of this earlier analysis of the thinking process, I should
unhesitatingly accept. Now it may be indeed that the processes of thought, as Mr. Bradley examines them, constitute
not only a relatively insignificant aspect of Reality, but also a
portion to be labelled "Appearance." Yet the point here in
question is not, for the moment, the dignity or the extent of
the thinking process in the life of the universe, but solely the
exemplary value of the thinking process as an instance of a
"self-evident," even if extremely abstract union of unity and
variety, of identity and diversity of aspects, in an objective
realm. For thought, too, is a kind of life, and belongs to the
realm of Reality, even if only as other appearances belong.

What we in general mean by this comment may first be very
briefly developed. The special applications will indeed detain
us longer. Mr. Bradley requires us to point out to him a case
where diversities shall be "complementary aspects of a process

of connection and distinction," the process being no "foreign compulsion of the intellect, but itself the intellect's own *proprius motus* . . . a self-evident analysis and synthesis of the intellect itself by itself." He fails to find, as he looks through the World of Appearance, any case of the sort such as is sufficient to furnish any self-evident "principle or principles of diversity in unity." Now we here desire to make a beginning in meeting his demand. We ask whether he has wholly taken account of the case that lies nearest of all to him in his research. This case is directly furnished by the intellect. Now the intellect may indeed not be all Reality. Thought may indeed, in the end, have to look "beyond itself" for its own "Other." Yet Reality owns the intellect, too, along with the other Appearances. By Mr. Bradley's hypothesis, Appearance is *der Gottheit lebendiges Kleid*, if by *Gottheit* we mean, for the moment, his Absolute. We have a right to use any rag torn by our own imperfect knowledge from this garment, to give us, if so may be, a hint of the weaving of the whole. The hint may prove poor. But only the trial can tell. And so, why not see how it is that the intellect, powerless though it be to make explicit the union of unity and diversity in the cases where experience furnishes from without "conjunctions" and their "background," still manages to unite unity and diversity in its own internal processes? Might not this throw some light upon even our ultimate problem?

For the intellect, after all, has indeed its *proprius motus*. If it had not, how should we be thinking? And who has more often considered the *proprius motus* of the intellect, who has more frequently insisted that "thought involves analysis and synthesis," than Mr. Bradley himself? Now the intellect, as Mr. Bradley observes, is discontent with its presented "external" object, the "conjunction" in space or in time, because of the uncomprehended unity in diversity of this presented object. The intellect seeks to define the ground of this unity, in case of the Thing, or of the world of Qualities and Relations, or of Space, or of Time, or in case of any of the other

Appearances that seem external to thought. The intellect fails. Why? "Because it cannot do without differences, but, on the other hand, it cannot make them" (p. 562). But can Mr. Bradley wholly mean this assertion *that the intellect cannot make differences?* In the chapters upon the Thing, and upon the other objects presented, as from without, to the intellect, we are indeed shown, when Mr. Bradley's argument is once accepted, that thought does not make, and does decline to receive ready made, the differences offered as real by these external objects, so long as they are taken in their abstraction.

But how is it possible for thought to discover the very fact that it cannot make, and that it declines to receive, certain differences, without itself making, of its own motion, certain other differences, whose internal unity it knows just in so far as it makes them? For when thought sets out to solve a problem, it has a purpose. This is its own purpose, and is, also, in so far an unity, not furnished as from without, but, in the course of the thinking process, developed as from within. When, after struggling to solve its problem, and to fulfil its purpose, thought finds itself in the presence of a puzzle that is so far ultimate, what, according to Mr. Bradley, does it see as the essence of this puzzle? It sees that a given hypothesis as to the unity of A and B (where A and B are the supposed "external" diversities, but where the hypothesis itself has been reflectively developed into its consequences through the inner movement of thought), — that this hypothesis, I say, either leads to various consequences which directly contradict one another, or else, by an internal and logical necessity, leads to an "infinite process," — in other words, to an infinite variety of consequences. In either case, in addition to what thought so far finds puzzling about A and B, thought further sees a diversity, and a diversity that is now *not* the presented "conjunction" of A and B, but a necessary diversity constructively developed by thought's own movement. Thought learns that its own purpose developes this variety. For the hypothesis about A and B (viz., that they are "in relation" or are "substantive and adjective," or whatever else the hypothe-

sis may be) has developed, within itself, as thought has reflected upon it, a certain internal multiplicity of aspects. That
the hypothesis developes these diversities, is a fact, — but a
fact how discovered? The only answer is, by Reflection.
Thought developes by its own processes the meaning, *i.e.* to
use our own phraseology, the "internal meaning" of this
hypothesis. The hypothesis perhaps leads to a self-contradiction concerning the nature of A and B. In that case, the
hypothesis, taken apart from A and B themselves, as an object
for reflection, is seen to imply that some account of A, or of
B, or of $A B$, is both true and false. Now truth is diverse
from falsity, and whoever observes that a given hypothesis
implies, through the development of its "internal meaning,"
the coëxistent truth and falsity of the same account of a supposed external fact, has observed a fact not now about A and
B as such, but about this internal meaning of the hypothesis,
taken by itself, — a fact lying within the circle of thought's
own movement. This fact is a diversity developed by
thought's *proprius motus*.

Or, again, the hypothesis leads to the "infinite process."
An "endless fission" is sometimes said to "break out" in the
world of conceived relations and qualities. This "principle
of endless fission" "conducts us to no end" (p. 31). "Within
the relation" the plurality of the differences is said to "beget
the infinite process" (p. 180). Now, when thought sees that
all this must be, and is, the necessary outcome of "a relational
way of thought" (p. 33), thought again sees a fact, but a fact
now present in its own world of ideas, and as the "self-evident" outcome of its reflective effort to express its own purpose. But, as we insist, despite the diversity, thought's
purpose is, in each case of this type, consciously One. It is
the purpose to find the ground for the conjunction of A and B.
Reflection sees that this one purpose, left to its own development, becomes diverse, and expresses its own identity in a
variety of aspects. When thought sees this result of its own
efforts, and sees the result as necessary, as universal, as the
consequence of a relational way of thinking, then I persist-

ently ask, Does not thought here at least see in one instance, not only *that* identity and diversity *are* conjoined, but *how* they are this time connected, and how the one of them, here at least, expresses itself in the other?

May we not, then, for the moment, overlook our failures as to the understanding of the world external to thought, and turn to the consideration of our success in discovering something of the internal movement of thought. For, in our ignorance, our first interest is in observing not how little we know (since our ignorance itself is, indeed, brought home to us at every instant of our finitude), but in making a beginning at considering how much we can find out. We wanted to see how any unity could develope a plurality. We have already seen, if but dimly. Shall we not begin to use our insight?

I conclude, then, so far, that, if the argument of Mr. Bradley is sound, in the very sense in which I myself most accept its soundness, a "principle of diversity in unity," in the case of the internal meaning of our ideas, is already, in several concrete cases, "self-evident." It remains for us to become better acquainted with this principle. I must explicitly note that this union of One and Many in thought has to be a fact in the universe if it is self-evident, and has to be self-evident if Mr. Bradley's argument is sound.

II. *The Principle of Thought, which is responsible for the Infinite Processes. Definition of a Recurrent Operation of Thought*

The principle in question can be made more manifest by a further reflection. The most important instances in Mr. Bradley's argument are those wherein the "endless fission" appears; and what has led to this "endless fission" which so far forms our principal instance of the internal development of variety out of unity, appears, when reviewed, as in general, this: A certain "conjunction" was offered to us by sense. This "conjunction" thought undertook, by means of an hypothesis, to explain. The resulting process of "fission" had, however, wholly to do with the internal meaning of this hypothesis, and no longer with the original conjunction. It was a fact within the life of thought. The hypothesis ran thus: "The conjunction is to be explained as a relation, holding its own terms in unity." Hereupon thought undertook so to think this hypothesis as to find its whole meaning. Thought hereupon reflectively observed, "But our relation, as soon as defined, becomes also a term of a new relation." More in particular, the original question ran, "What is the unity of A and B?" The hypothesis said, "Their unity lies in their relation R; for the terms of a relationship are linked and unified by that relationship." The reflective criticism runs, "But in creating R, as the ideal link between A and B, regarded now not as they were externally conjoined, but ideally as terms of a relationship, we have only recreated, in the supposed complex R A, or R B, or A R B, the type of situation originally presented. For A and B were to be objects of thought. They therefore needed a link. Therefore, as we said, they were to be viewed as terms linked by their relation. But the relation R, as soon as it is made an object of thought, becomes a term for the same reason which made us regard A and B as terms. For our implied principle was that objects of thought, if various, and yet united, are to be viewed as terms of a relationship. Our thinking process must therefore proceed to note, that if A and B are terms to be linked, R also, by the same right, is a term to be linked to A or to B, or to both, and so on *ad infinitum*."

But the gist of this reflection may be better generalized thus: A thinking process of the type here in question *re*creates, although in a new instance, the very kind of ideal object that, by means of its process, it proposed to alter into some more acceptable form. The change of situation which it intended, leads, and must lead, to a reinstatement of essentially the same sort of situation as that which was to be changed. Or, again, The proposed solution reiterates the problem in a new shape. Therefore, the operation of thought here in question is what one may call, in the most general terms, an iterative, or, again, a recurrent, operation, — an operation whose result reinstates, in a new instance, the situation which gave rise to the operation, and to which the operation was applied.

Now, quite apart from the special circumstances of the problem about A and B, the observation that reflection makes upon *the general nature of any iterative or recurrent process of thinking*, becomes at once of great interest for the comprehension of the question about the One and the Many. We want to find some case of an unity which developes its own differences out of itself. Well, what more simple and obvious instance could we hope for than is furnished by an operation of thought, such that, when applied to a given situation, this operation necessarily, and in a way that we can directly follow, reinstates, in a new case, the very kind of situation to which it was applied? For this operation is a fact in the world. It begins in unity. It developes diversity. Let us, then, wholly drop, for the time, the problem about A and B, in so far as they were taken as facts of sense or of externality. Their "conjunction," presented "from without," we may leave in its mystery, until we are ready to return to the matter later. We have found something more obvious, viz., an iterative operation of thought, one which, when applied, is actually observed to develope out of one purpose many results, by recreating its own occasion for application. Now let us proceed with our generalization. Let there be found *any* such operation of thought, say C. C is to be *one* ideal operation of our thought just in so far as C expresses a single purpose. But let C be applied on occasion to some material, — no matter what. Let the material be M. Hereupon, as we reflect, let us be supposed to observe that the logical necessary result of applying C to M, the result of expressing the purpose in question in this material, or of ideally weaving the material M into harmony with the purpose C, is the appearance of a new material for thought, viz., M'. Let us be supposed to observe, also, that M', taken as a content to be thought about, gives the same occasion for the application of C that M gave. Let the application of C to M' be next observed to lead to M'', in such wise that in M'' there lies once more the occasion for the application of C. Let this series be observed to be endless, that is, to be such that, consistently with its nature, it can possess no last term. Then, as I assert, we shall see, in a special instance, how the endless series $M, M', M'' \ldots$, just as a series of many ideally constructed facts, is developed by the one purpose, C, when once applied to any suitable material, M; and is developed, moreover, by internal necessity, as the very meaning of the objects M, M', etc., and also as the meaning of the operation C itself, and not as a bare conjunction given from "without the intellect." Now in such a case, I insist, we see how the One produces, out of itself, the Many.

Nor let one, objecting, interpose that since an "operation" is a case of activity, and since activity has been riddled by Mr. Bradley's critical fire, the nature of every operation of thought must always remain mysterious. Let no one insist that since the supposed operation C is one fact, and its material M is another fact, in our world of ideal objects, the relation of C to M is as opaque as any other relation, so that we do not understand how C operates at all, nor yet how it changes M into M', nor how the same operation C can persist, and be applied to M' after it had been applied to M. Let no one further point out that since all the foregoing account of C, and of the endless series M, M', M'', involves Time as a factor in the "operation," and since Time has been shown by Mr. Bradley to be a mysterious conjunction of infinite complexity, and so to be mere Appearance, therefore all the foregoing remains mysterious. For to all such objections I shall reply that I so far pretend to find "self-evident" about the iterative processes of thought, only so much as, in his own chosen instances, Mr. Bradley finds self-evident, namely, so much as constitutes the very meaning and ground of his condemnation of the mysterious and baffling Appearances. That the endless process is implied in a certain way of thinking, namely, in a "relational way," Mr. Bradley reflectively observes. I accept the observation, so far as it goes, in the cases stated. But I ask why this is true. The answer lies in seeing that the endlessness of the process is due to the recurrent character of the operation of thought here in question. This relational way of thinking so operates as to reinstate, in a new case, the very type of situation that the explanation desired — the goal of the operation — was, in the former case, to reduce to some simple unity. The first complexity consequently survives the operation, unreduced to unity; while a new complexity, logically (not psychologically) due to the operation itself, appears as something necessarily implied. The reapplication of the same operation, if supposed accomplished, can but reinstate afresh the former type of situation. Hence the endless process. Now this process I consider not in so far as it is a mere temporal series of events, but in so far as it is the development, in a given case, of what a certain thought means. I do not assert the obvious existence of an Activity, but the logical necessity of a certain series of implications. The true meaning of the purpose C, expressed in the content M, logically gives rise to M', which demands equally to be considered in the light of C, and thereupon implies M'', and so on. Thus our argument does not depend upon a theory about how thought, as an "activity," is a possible part of the world at all. I do not profess now to explain, say from a psychological point of view, the inmost nature of the operation in question, nor yet to find self-evident, in this place, the metaphysics of the time process. Mysteries still surround us; but we see what we see. And my point is that while we do not see all of what thought is, nor yet how it is able to weave its material into harmony with its purposes, nor yet what Time is, we do see that we think, and that this thought has, as it proceeds, its internal meaning, and that this meaning has, as its necessary and self-evident result, the reinstatement, in a new case, of the type of situation which the operation of the thought was intended to explain, or in some other wise to transform. When M is so altered by the operation C as to imply M', M'', and so on, as the endless series of results of the iterative operation of thought, we see not only *that* this is so, but *why* this is so. And unless we see this, we see nothing whatever, whether in

Appearance or in Reality. And here, then, the relation of Unity and Variety is clear to us.

Our generalization, however, of the process upon which Mr. Bradley insists, enables us to make more fruitful and positive our result. There are recurrent operations of thought. Whenever they act, they imply, upon their face, endless processes. Do such processes inevitably lead us to results wholly vain and negative? Is the union of One and Many which they make explicit an insignificant union? Or, on the other hand, is this union typical of the general constitution of Reality?

The first answer is that, at all events in the special science of mathematics, processes of this type are familiar, and lie at the basis of highly and very positively significant researches. If we merely name a few such instances of endless processes, we shall see that iterative thinking, if once made an ideal, — a method of procedure, — and not merely dreaded as a failure to reach finality, becomes a very important part of the life of the exact sciences, and developes results which have a very significant grade of Reality.

The classic instance of the recurrent or iterative operations of thought is furnished, in elementary mathematics, by the Number Series. A recurrent operation first developes the terms of this series; and thereby makes the counting of external objects, and all that, in our human science, follows therefrom, possible. A secondary recurrent operation, based upon the primary operation, appears in the laws governing the process called the "Addition" of whole numbers. A tertiary and once more recurrent operation appears in the laws governing Multiplication.[1] In consequence of this recurrent nature of

---

[1] The precise sense in which the Number Series itself is the outcome of a recurrent operation of thought will be explained, in general accord with Dedekind's theory, further on. Addition and Multiplication, in any particular instance, as in the adding or in the multiplying of 7 and 5, are of course operations terminated by the finding of the particular sum or product, and in so far they are finite and non-recurrent. But the laws of Addition and Multiplication (e.g., the Associative law), and the relation of both these operations to one another and to the number system,

the thinking processes concerned, the number series itself is endless; the results of addition and multiplication, the sums and products of the various numbers, are not only endless, but capable of endless combinations; and, in general, the properties of numbers are themselves infinitely infinite in number. But in this case the mathematician does not mourn over the "endless fission" to which the number concepts are indeed due, but he regards the numbers as a storehouse of positive and often very beautiful novelties, which his science studies for their intrinsic interest.

If mathematical science thus begins, in the simplest construction, with the outcome of a recurrent process, it is no wonder that the later development of the science, as exemplified by the theories of negative and of fractional numbers, of irrational and of complex numbers, of infinite series and of infinite products, and of all that, in Analysis and in the Theory of Functions, depends upon these more elementary theories, is everywhere full of conceptions and methods that result from observing what happens when an operation of thought is recurrent, or is such as to reinstate, in its expressions, the occasion for new expressions. Without such recurrence, and without such infinite processes, mathematical science would be reduced to a very minute fraction of its present range and importance.

But we are here primarily concerned with the metaphysical aspect of the recurrent processes of thought. Important as are the countless mathematical instances of our type of operations, we must so deal with their general theory as to be able to identify the results of recurrent thinking whenever they occur, whether in mathematics or in other regions of our reflection.

I propose here, then, first to illustrate, and then to discuss theoretically, the nature and ideal outcome of any recurrent operation of thought, and to develope, in this connection, what one may call the positive nature of the concept of Infinite

are dependent, in part, upon the fact that the result of every addition or multiplication of whole numbers is itself a whole number, uniquely determined, and, as a number, capable of entering into the formation of new sums and products.

Multitude. We shall here see how there are cases, — and cases, too, of the most fundamental importance for the Theory of Being, where a single purpose, definable as One, demands for its realization a multitude of particulars which could not be a limited multitude without involving the direct defeat of the purpose itself. We shall in vain endeavor to escape from the consequences of this discovery by denouncing the purposes of the type in question as self-contradictory, or the Infinite in question as *das Schlecht-Unendliche*. On the contrary, we shall find these purposes to be the only ones in terms of which we can define any of the fundamental interests of man in the universe, and the only ones whose expression enables us to explain how unity and diversity are harmonized at all, or how Being gets its individuality and finality, or how anything whatever exists. Having made this clear, we shall endeavor to show, positively, that the concept of infinite variety in unity, to which these cases lead us, is consistent in itself, and is able to give our Theory of Being true definition.

SECTION III. THEORY OF THE SOURCES AND CONSEQUENCES OF ANY RECURRENT OPERATION OF THOUGHT. THE NATURE OF SELF-REPRESENTATIVE SYSTEMS

I shall begin the present section with illustrations. I shall make no preliminary assumption as to how our illustrations are related to the ultimate nature of things. For all that we at first know, we may be dealing, each time, with deceptive Appearance. We merely wish to illustrate, however, how a *single* purpose may be so defined, for thought, as to demand, for its full expression, an infinite multitude of cases, so that the alternative is, " Either this purpose fails to get expression, or the system of idealized facts in which it is expressed contains an infinite variety." Whether or no the concept of such infinite variety is itself self-contradictory, remains to be considered later.[1]

[1] The discussion of the instances and conceptions of Multitude and Infinity, contained in what follows, is largely dependent upon various

I. *First Illustration of a Self-Representative System*

The basis for the first illustration of the development of an Infinite Multitude out of the expression of a Single Purpose,

recent contributions to the literature of the subject. Prominent among the later authors who have dealt with our problem from the mathematical side, is George Cantor. For his now famous theory of the *Mächtigkeiten* or grades of infinite multitude, and for his discussions of the purely mathematical aspects of his problem, one may consult his earlier papers, as collected in the *Acta Mathematica*, Vol. II. With this theory of the *Mächtigkeiten* I shall have no space to deal in this paper, but it is of great importance for forming the conception of the determinate Infinite. Upon the more philosophical aspects of the same researches, Cantor wrote a brief series of difficult and fragmentary, but fascinating discussions in the *Zeitschrift für Philosophie und Philosophische Kritik:* Bd. 88, p. 224 ; Bd. 91, p. 81 ; Bd. 92, p. 240. In recent years (1895–97) Cantor has begun a systematic restatement of his mathematical theories in the *Mathematische Annalen:* Bd. 48, p. 481 ; Bd. 49, p. 207. Some of Cantor's results are now the common property of the later text-books, such as Dini's *Theory of Functions*, and Weber's *Algebra*. Upon Cantor's investigations is also based the remarkable and too much neglected posthumous philosophical essay of Benno Kerry : *System einer Theorie der Grenzbegriffe* (Leipzig, 1890) — a fragment, but full of ingenious observations. The general results of Cantor are summarized in a supplementary note to Couturat's *L'Infini Mathematique* (Paris, 1896), on pp. 602–655 of that work. Couturat's is itself the most important recent general treatment of the philosophical problem of the Infinite ; and the Third Book of his Second Part (p. 441, *sqq.*) ought to be carefully pondered by all who wish fairly to estimate the " contradictions " usually attributed to the concept of the Infinite Multitude. A further exposition of Cantor's most definite results is given, in a highly attractive form, by Borel, *Leçons sur la Théorie des Fonctions*, Paris, 1898. Side by side with Cantor, in the analysis of the fundamental problem regarding number, and multitude, stands Dedekind, upon whose now famous essay, *Was Sind und Was Sollen die Zahlen ?* (2te Auflage, Braunschweig, 1893), some of the most important of the recent discussions of the nature of self-representative systems are founded. See also the valuable discussion of the iterative processes of thought by G. F. Lipps, in Wundt's *Studien* (Bd. XIV, Hft. 2, for 1898) ; and the extremely significant remarks of Poincaré on the nature of mathematical reasoning in the *Revue de Metaphysique et de Morale* for 1894, p. 370. Other references are given later in this discussion.

which we shall here consider, may be taken, in a measure, from that world "external to thought" whose variety we still find a matter of "mere conjunction" and so opaque. For, despite the use of such a basis, our illustration will interest us not by reason of this aspect, but by reason of the opportunity thereby furnished for carrying out a certain recurrent process of thought, whose internal meaning we want to follow.

We are familiar with maps, and with similar constructions, such as representative diagrams, in which the elements of which a certain artificial or ideal object is composed, are intended to correspond, one to one, to certain elements in an external object.[1] A map is usually intended to resemble the contour of the region mapped in ways which seem convenient, and which have a decidedly manifold sensuous interest to the user of the map; but, in the nature of the case, there is no limit to the outward diversity of form which would be consistent with a perfectly exact and mathematically definable correspondence between map and region mapped. If our power to draw map contours were conceived as perfectly exact, the ideal map, made in accordance with a given system of projection, could be defined as involving absolutely the aforesaid one to one correspondence, *point for point*, of the surface mapped and the representation. And even if one conceived space or matter as made up of indivisible parts, still an ideally perfect map upon some scale could be conceived, if one supposed it made up of ultimate space units, or of the ultimate material corpuscles, so arranged as to correspond, one by one, to the ultimate parts that a perfect observation would then distinguish in the surface mapped. In general, if A be the object mapped, and A' be the map, the latter could be conceived as perfect if, while always possessing the desired degree of visible similarity of contours, it actually stood in such correspondence to A that for every elementary detail of A, namely, a, b, c, d (be these details conceived as points or merely as physically smallest parts; as relations amongst the

[1] Compare the general discussion of "Correspondence" in the course of Lecture VII.

parts of a *continuum,* or as the relations amongst the units of a mere aggregate of particles), some corresponding detail, a', b', c', d', could be identified in A', in accordance with the system of projection used.

All this being understood, let us undertake to define a map that shall be in this sense perfect, but that shall be drawn subject to one special condition. It would seem as if, in case our map-drawing powers were perfect, we could draw our map wherever we chose to draw it. Let us, then, choose, for once, to *draw it within and upon a part of the surface of the very region that is to be mapped.* What would be the result of trying to carry out this one purpose? To fix our ideas, let us suppose, if you please, that a portion of the surface of England is very perfectly levelled and smoothed, and is then devoted to the production of our precise map of England. That in general, then, should be found upon the surface of England, map constructions which more or less roughly represent the whole of England, — all this has nothing puzzling about it. Any ordinary map of England spread out upon English ground would illustrate, in a way, such possession, by a part of the surface of England, of a resemblance to the whole. But now suppose that this our resemblance is to be made absolutely exact, in the sense previously defined. A map of England, contained within England, is to represent, down to the minutest detail, every contour and marking, natural or artificial, that occurs upon the surface of England. At once our imaginary case involves a new problem. This is now no longer the general problem of map making, but the nature of the internal meaning of our new purpose.

Absolute exactness of the representation of one object by another, with respect to contour, this, indeed, involves, as Mr. Bradley would say to us, the problem of identity in diversity; but it involves that problem only in a general way. Our map of England, contained in a portion of the surface of England, involves, however, a peculiar and infinite development of a special type of diversity within our map. For the map, in order to be complete, according to the rule given, will have to contain, as a part of itself, a representation of its own contour and contents. In order that this representation should be constructed, the representation itself will have to contain once more, as a part of itself, a representation of its own contour and contents; and this representation, in order to be exact, will have once more to contain an image of itself; and so on without limit. We should now, indeed, have to suppose the space occupied by our perfect map to be infinitely divisible, even if not a *continuum*.[1]

One who, with absolute exactness of perception, looked down upon the ideal map thus supposed to be constructed, would see lying upon the surface of England, and at a definite place thereon, a representation of England on as large or small a scale as you please. This representation would agree in contour with the real England, but at a place within this map of England, there would appear, upon a smaller scale, a new representation of the contour of England. This representation, which would repeat in the outer portions the details of the former, but upon a smaller space, would be seen to contain yet another England, and this another, and so on without limit.

That such an endless variety of maps within maps could not physically be constructed by men, and that ideally such a map, if viewed as a finished construction, would involve us in all the problems about the infinite divisibility of matter and of space, I freely recognize. What I point out is that if my supposed exact observer, looking down upon the map, saw anywhere in the series of maps within maps, a last map, such that it contained within itself *no* further representation of the original object, he would know at once that the rule in question had not been carried out, that the resources of the mapmaker had failed, and that the required map of England was imperfect. On the other hand, this endless variety of maps within maps, while its existence as a fact in the world might

[1] In the older discussions of continuity, this concept was very generally confounded with that of infinite divisibility. The confusion is no longer made by mathematicians. Continuity implies infinite divisibility. The converse does not hold true.

be as mysterious as you please, would, in one respect, present to an observer who understood the one purpose of the whole series, no mystery at all. For one who understood the purpose of the making within England a map of England, and the purpose of making this map absolutely accurate, would see precisely why the map must be contained within the map, and why, in the series of maps within maps, there could be no end consistently with the original requirement. Mathematically regarded, the endless series of maps within maps, if made according to such a projection as we have indicated, would cluster about a limiting point whose position could be exactly determined. Logically speaking, their variety would be a mere expression of the *single* plan, " Let us make within England, and upon the surface thereof, a precise map, with all the details of the contour of its surface." Then the One and the Many would become, in one respect, clear as to their relations, even when all else was involved in mystery. We should see, namely, why the one purpose, *if* it could be carried out, would involve the endless series of maps.

But so far we have dealt with our illustration as involving a certain progressive process of map making, occurring in stages. We have seen that this process never could be ended without a confession that the original purpose had failed. But now suppose that we change our manner of speech. Whatever our theory of the meaning of the verb *to be*, suppose that some one, depending upon any authority you please, — say upon the authority of a revelation, — assured us of this as a truth about existence, viz., " Upon and within the surface of England *there exists* somehow (no matter how or when made) an absolutely perfect map of the whole of England." Suppose that, for an instance, we had accepted this assertion as true. Suppose that we then attempted to discover the meaning implied in this one assertion. We should at once observe that in this one assertion, " A part of England perfectly maps all England, on a smaller scale," there would be implied the assertion, not now of a process of trying to draw maps, but of the contemporaneous presence, in England, of an infinite number of maps, of the type just described. The whole infinite series, possessing no last member, would be asserted as a fact of existence. I need not observe that Mr. Bradley would at once reject such an assertion as a self-contradiction. It would be a typical instance of the sort of endlessness of structure that makes him reject Space, Time, and the rest, as mere Appearance. But I am still interested in pointing out that whether we continued faithful to our supposed revelation, or, upon second thought, followed Mr. Bradley in rejecting it as impossible, our faith, or our doubt, would equally involve seeing that the *one* plan of mapping in question necessarily implies just this infinite *variety* of internal constitution. We should, moreover, see how and why the one and the infinitely many are here, at least within thought's realm, conceptually linked. Our map and England, taken as mere physical existences, would indeed belong to that realm of " bare external conjunctions." Yet the one thing *not* externally given, but internally self-evident, would be that the one plan or purpose in question, namely, the plan fulfilled by the perfect map of England, drawn within the limits of England, and upon a part of its surface, would, if really expressed, involve, in its necessary structure, the series of maps within maps such that no one of the maps was the last in the series.

This way of viewing the case suggests that, as a mere matter of definition, we are not obliged to deal solely with processes of construction as successive, in order to define endless series. A recurrent operation of thought can be characterized as one that, *if once finally expressed*, would involve, in the region where it had received expression, an infinite variety of serially arranged facts, corresponding to the purpose in question. This consideration leads us back from our trivial illustration to the realm of general theory.

II. *Definition of a Type of Self-Representative Systems*

Let there be, then, any recurrent operation of thought, or any meaning in mind whose expression, if attempted, involves such a recurrent operation. That is, let there be

any internal meaning such that, if you try to express it
by means of a succession of acts, the ideal data which
begin to express it demand, as a part of their own meaning, new data which, again, are new expressions of the
same meaning, equally demanding further like expression.
Then, *if* you endeavor to express this meaning in a series of
successive acts, you get a series of results, M, M', M'', etc.,
which can never be finished unless the further expression of
the purpose is somewhere abandoned. But such a successive
series of attempts quickly gets associated in our minds with
a sense of disappointment and fruitlessness, and perhaps this
sense more or less blinds us to the true significance of the recurrent thinking processes.[1] Let us try to avoid this mere
feeling by dwelling upon the definition of the whole system
of facts which, *if* present at once, *would* constitute the complete expression and embodiment of this one meaning. The
general nature of the system in question is capable of a positive definition. Instead of saying, "The system, if gradually
constructed by successive stages, has no last member," we can
say, in terms now wholly positive, (1) The system is such
that to *every* ideal element in it, M, M', or, in general, $M^{(r)}$,
there corresponds *one and only one* other element of the system,

---

[1] *Leere Wiederholung* is one of Hegel's often repeated expressions in
regard to such series. There is a certain question-begging involved in
condemning a process because of one's subjective sense of fatigue. Yet
Bosanquet, in his *Logic* (Vol. I, p. 173), begins his subtle discussion of
infinite number and series with an instance intended to illustrate the
merely wearisome vanity of search that seems to be involved in a case of
endless looking beyond for our goal. I wholly agree with Bosanquet when
he demands that the "element of totality" (p. 173) must be present in
the work of our thought, — that is, as the ultimate test of its truth.
Wholeness and finality our object must have, before we can properly rest
in the contemplation of its real nature. But as we shall soon see, the
question is whether a real and objective totality, — a full expression of
meaning, — cannot, at the same time, be the explicit expression of such
an internal meaning as can permit no last term in any series of *successive*
operations whereby we may try to express this meaning. We tire soon
of such "tasks without end." But does the *totum simul* of Reality fail
to express, in detail, the whole of what such processes mean ?

which, taken in its order, is the *next* element of the system. This *next* element may be viewed, if we choose, as derived from its predecessor by means of the recurrent process. But it may also be viewed as in a relation to its predecessor, which is the same as the relation of a map to an object mapped. We shall accordingly call it, henceforth, the Image or Representation of this former element. (2) These images are all *distinct*, so that various elements always have various representatives. For the recurrent process is such that, in the system which should finally express it, one and only one element would be derived from any given element, or would be the *next* element in order after that given element. (3) At least *one* element, *M*, of the system, although imaged by another, is itself the image or representative of no other element, so that only a portion of the system is representative. A system thus defined we may call, for our present purposes, an instance of an internally Self-Representative System, or, more exactly, of a system precisely represented by a proper fraction or portion of itself. Of the whole system thus defined we can at once assert that if we take its elements in the order *M*, *M'*, *M''*, etc., there is indeed no last member in the resulting series. The system is, therefore, defined as endless merely by being defined as *thus* self-representative. But since the self-representation of any system of facts is capable of definition, as a single internal purpose, in advance of the discovery that such purpose involves an endless series of constituents, we may, with Dedekind, use the generalized conception of a self-representation of the type here in question as a means of positively defining what we mean by an infinite system or multitude of elements. In thus proceeding, we further generalize the idea which the perfect map of England has already illustrated.

The positive definition of the concept of the Infinite thus resulting has no small speculative interest. Ordinarily one defines infinity merely by considering some indefinitely prolonged series of successive facts, by observing that the series in question does not, or at least, so far as one sees, need not, end at any given point, and by then saying, "A series taken thus as *without end,* may be called infinite." We ourselves, so far in this discussion, have defined our infinite processes on the whole in a negative way. But the new definition of the infinity of our system uses positive rather than negative terms. The conception of a representation or of an imaging of one object by another, is wholly positive. This conception, if applied to the elements of a system A, with the proviso that A', the image or the representation of A, shall form a constituent portion of A itself, remains still positive. But the system A, if defined as capable of this particular type of self-representation, proves, when examined, to contain, *if* it exists at all, an infinite number of elements. Whatever the metaphysical fate of the ideal object thus defined, the method of definition has a decided advantage over the older ones.[1] It may be well at once to quote Dedekind's original statement and illustration of the conception in question, in the passage cited in the note: —

"A System S is called 'infinite' when it is similar[2] to a

[1] More or less vaguely this positive property of infinite multitudes was observed as a paradox whenever the necessity of conceiving "one infinite as greater than another," or as containing another as a part of itself, was recognized. The paradox was in this sense felt already by Aristotle in the third Book of the Physics, ch. 5 (cf. Spinoza's *Ethics,* Part I, Prop. XV. *Scholium,* where the well-known solution is that the true infinite is essentially indivisible, having no parts and no multitude). Explicitly the property of infinite multitudes here in question was insisted upon by Bolzano in his *Paradoxien des Unendlichen* (1851). Cantor, and, in America, Mr. Charles Peirce, have since made this aspect of the infinite multitudes prominent. Most explicitly, however, Dedekind has built up his entire theory of the number concept upon defining the infinite multitude or system simply in these positive terms, without previous definition of any numbers at all. See his *op. cit.,* § 5, 64, p. 17.

[2] In previous definitions, in Dedekind's text, two systems have been defined as *similar (ähnlich),* when one of them can be made to correspond, element for element, with the other, any two different elements having different representations. And a proper part (*echter Theil*), or constituent portion, of a system, has been defined as one produced by leaving out some elements of the whole.

constituent (or proper) part of itself; in the contrary case *S* is called a 'finite' system.

"*Theorem.* — There exist infinite systems.[1]

"*Proof.* — My own realm of thoughts (*meine Gedankenwelt*), *i.e.* the totality *S*, of all things that can be objects of my thought, is infinite. For if *s* is an element of *S*, it follows that the thought *s'*, viz., the thought, *That s can be object of my thought*, is itself an element of *S*. If one views *s'* as the image (or representative) of the element *s*, the representation *S'* of the system *S*, which is hereby defined, has the character that the representation *S'* is a constituent portion (*echter Theil*) of *S*, since there are elements in *S* (for example, my own Ego) (?) which are different from every such thought *s'*, and which are, therefore, not contained in *S'*. Finally, it is plain that it *a* and *b* are different elements of *S*, their images, *a'* and *b'* are also different, so that the representation of *S* is distinct (*deutlich*) and *similar*. It follows that *S* [by definition], is infinite."

Here, as we observe, the infinity of an ideal system is defined, and in a special case proved, without making any explicit reference to the number of its elements. That this number, negatively viewed, turns out to be no finite number, that is, to be that of a multitude with no last term, is for Dedekind a result to be later proved, — a secondary consequence of the infinity as first defined. The proof that my *Gedankenwelt* is infinite, is thus not my negative powerlessness to find the last term, but my positive power to image each of my thoughts *s*, by a new and reflective thought *s'*. It is the finite, and not the infinite, that here appears as the object negatively definable. For a finite system is one that *cannot* be adequately represented through a one-to-one correspondence with one of its own constituent parts.[2] In any

---

[1] *Es giebt unendliche Systeme. Es giebt*, is of course here used to express existence within the realm of consistent mathematical definitions. The conception of Being in question is the Third Conception of our own list.

[2] That the finite and infinite here quite change places is pointed out in

case, the infinite multitude of the elements of S developes, for thought, out of the single positive purpose stated so sharply in Dedekind's definition.

III. *Further Illustrations of Self-Representative Systems of the Type here Defined*

This conception of a system that can be exactly represented or imaged, element for element, by one of its own constituent parts, has of course to meet the objection that such an idea appears, upon its face, paradoxical, even if it is not out and out self-contradictory. But before judging the conception, it is well to have in mind some illustrations of its range of application. A comparison of these will show that, if self-cor-

---

an interesting way by Professor Franz Meyer, in his *Antrittsrede* at Tübingen entitled *Zur Lehre vom Unendlichen* (Tübingen, 1889). The same observation is made by Kerry in his comments upon Dedekind (in Kerry's before-cited *Theorie der Grenzbegriffe*, p. 49). Bolzano, who, in his *Paradoxien des Unendlichen* had much earlier reached a position in many ways near to that of Dedekind, proves the existence of the infinite in a closely similar, but less exact way. Schroeder, in his very elaborate essay in the *Abhandlungen der Leopold. Carolinischen Akad. d. Naturforscher* for 1898, entitled *Ueber Zwei Definitionem der Endlichkeit*, insists indeed that this whole distinction between positive and negative definitions is, from the point of view of formal Logic, vain, and that Mr. Charles Peirce's definition of *finite* systems, given in the *American Journal of Mathematics*, Vol. 7, p. 202, while it is the polar opposite of Dedekind's definition of the Infinite, is, logically speaking, at once equivalent to Dedekind's definition, and yet as positive as the latter, although Mr. Peirce, in the passage in question, starts from the finite, and not from the infinite. Schroeder seems to me quite right in regarding the distinction between *essentially* positive and essentially negative definitions as one for which a purely formal Logic has no place. But as a fact, the distinction in question, between what is positive and what is negative, has an import wholly metaphysical. Our interest in it here lies in the fact that if you begin, in Dedekind's way, with the positive concept of the Infinite, you need not presuppose the "externally given" Many, but may develope the multitude out of the internal meaning of a single purpose. Mr. Charles Peirce, in his parallel definition of finite systems, has first to presuppose them as given facts of experience. We, however, are seeking to develope the Many out of the One.

respondent systems of the type here in question are mere
Appearance, they are, at all events, Appearance worthy of
study. A list of a few conceptions that are more or less
obviously of the present type may make us pause before we
lightly reject, as absurd, the offered definition.

First, then, the series of whole Numbers, as conceived
objects, forms such a self-representative system. The same is
true of all the secondary number-systems of higher arithmetic
(the negative numbers, the rational numbers, the irrational
numbers, the totality of the real numbers, the complex numbers). And all continuous and discrete mathematical systems
of any infinite type are similarly self-representative. But the
mathematical objects are by no means the most philosophically
interesting of the instances of our concept. For, next, we
have the Self, the concept so elaborately studied by Mr. Bradley, and condemned by him as Appearance. And, indeed, if
the Self is anything final at all, it is certainly in its complete
expression (although of course not in our own psychological
life from instant to instant) a self-representative system; and
its metaphysical fate stands or falls with the possibility of
such systems. Dedekind's really very profound use of *meine
Gedankenwelt* as his typical instance of the infinite, also suggests the interesting relation between the concept of the Self
and that of the mere mathematical form called the number-
series, — a relation to which we shall soon return. Thirdly,
the totality of Being, if conceived as in *any* way defined or
characterized, or even as in any way even definable or charac-
terizable, constitutes, in the present sense, a self-representative
system. Obvious it is that our own Fourth Conception of
Being defines the Absolute as a self-representative system.
And, furthermore, despite his horror of the infinite, and despite his rejection of the Self as a final category, Mr. Bradley
himself perforce has to describe his own Absolute as a self-
representative system of our type, as we soon shall see. And
if he attempted to view it otherwise, it would not be the Absolute or anything real at all. In brief, every system of which
anybody can rationally assert anything is either a self-repre-

sentative system, in the sense here in question, or else, being but a part of the real world, it is a more or less arbitrarily selected, or an empirically given portion or constituent of such a system, — a portion whose reality, apart from that of the whole system, is unintelligible.

Far from *lacking* totality, then, in the way in which the infinite, or rather the indefinite, multitude of such accounts as Mr. Bosanquet's is said to lack totality,[1] those genuinely self-representative systems, whose images are portions of their own objects, are the only ones which can be said to possess any totality whatever. It is they alone that are wholly positive in their definition. Finite systems are either capable only of negative definition, or, at all events, have positive characters only by virtue of their relation to their inclusive infinite, or, in our present sense, self-representative systems.[2] Or, again, as we have already begun to see, only the processes of recurrent thought make explicit the true unity of the One and the Many. But these very processes express themselves in systems of the type now in question.

To make these matters clearer, it will be necessary to consider each of the just-mentioned illustrations more in detail. First, then, as to the simple case of the number-system, whose logical genesis we for the moment leave out of consideration, and whose general constitution we assume as known. The whole numbers first form what Cantor calls a *wohl-definirte Menge*, — or exactly defined multitude. That is, you can precisely distinguish between any conceived or presented object that is *not* a whole number (as, for example, one-half, or the moral law, or the odor of a rose), and an object that *is* a whole number, abstract or concrete (*e.g.* ten, or ten thousand, or the

---

[1] See Bosanquet's *Logic, loc. cit. et sq.*

[2] Mr. Charles Peirce, as noted above, has indeed given a perfectly positive and exact definition of a finite system ; but in order to set that definition to work you have first to suppose your Many externally given, while, in order to define the *Gedankenwelt*, or the *Self*, or, as we shall later see, the *Real World*, you have only to presuppose a single, and unavoidable, internal meaning. The infinity then follows of itself.

number of birds on yonder bough). Taking the whole numbers as the abstract numbers, *i.e.* as the members of a certain ideal series, arithmetically defined, the mathematician can, therefore, view them all as *given* by means of their universal definition, and their consequent clear distinction from all other objects of thought.[1] Taking them thus as given, the numbers become entities of the type contemplated by our Third Conception of Being; and as such entities we can admit them here for the moment, not now asking whether or no they have, or can win, a reality of our Fourth type.

Now the numbers form, in infinitely numerous ways, a self-representative system of the type here in question. That is, as has repeatedly been remarked, by all the recent authors who have dealt with this aspect of the matter, the number-system, taken in its conceived totality, can be put in a one-to-one correspondence with one of its own constituent portions in any one of an endless number of ways. For the numbers, if once regarded as a given whole, form an endless ordered series, having a *first* term, a *second* term, and so on. But just so the even numbers, 2, 4, 6, etc., form an endless ordered series, having a *first*, *second*, *third* term, and so on. In the same way, too, the prime numbers form a demonstrably endless series, whereof there is a *first* member, a *second* member, and so forth. Or, again, the numbers that are perfect squares, those that are perfect cubes, and those, in general, that are of the form a^n, where n is any one whole number, while a takes successively the value of every whole number, all such derived systems of whole numbers, form similarly ordered series, wherein each member of each system has its determined place as first, second, third, or later member of its own system, while the system forms a series without end. Take, then, *any*

---

[1] *How* they are to be defined is of course itself a significant logical problem, whereof we shall soon hear more. Cantor's account of the well-defined multitude, *Menge*, or *ensemble*, is found in French translation in the *Acta Mathematica*, tom. II, p. 363. On the general sense in which any multitude can be viewed as *given* for purposes of mathematical discussion, see Borel's *Leçons* (cited above), p. 2.

whole number r, however large. Then, in the ideal class of objects called whole numbers, there is a determinate even number which occupies the rth place in the series of even numbers, when the latter are arranged according to their sizes, beginning with 2. There is equally a prime number, occupying the rth place in a similarly ordered series of primes; and a square number occupying the rth place in a similarly ordered series of square numbers; and a cube occupying the rth place in a like arrangement of cubes; and an rth member in any particular series of numbers of the form a^n, where n is any determinate whole number, and a is taken, in succession, as 1, 2, 3, etc. As all these things hold true for any r, however large, we can say, in general, that every whole number r has its correspondent rth member in any of the supposed series of systematically selected whole numbers, — even numbers, primes, square numbers, cubes, or what you will. But these various selected systems are such that each of them forms only a portion of the entire series of whole numbers. So that the whole series, taken as given, is in infinitely numerous ways capable of being put in a one-to-one relation to one of its own constituent parts.

I doubt not that this very fact might appear, at first blush, to bring out a manifest "contradiction" in the very conception of the "totality" of the whole numbers taken as "given." But closer examination will show, as Couturat, Cantor, and the other authors here concerned (since Bolzano) have repeatedly pointed out, that the "contradiction" in question is really a contradiction only of the well-known nature of any *finite* collection. It was of such collections that the axiom, "The whole is greater than the part," was first asserted. And of such collections alone is it with absolute generality true. Take any finite collection of whole numbers, however large; and *then* indeed the assertion of any of the foregoing one-to-one correspondences of the whole, with a mere part of itself, breaks down. But let us once see that taking *any* number r, however large, we can find the corresponding rth member in any of the ordered series of primes, squares, etc., and then we shall also see that the absolutely universal proposition, "Every whole has its single and separate correspondent member in any one of the various ordered series of selected whole numbers aforesaid," is not only free from contradiction, but is easily demonstrable, and is a mere expression of the actual nature of the number-series, taken as an object of exact thought.

Highly important it is, however, to observe, that the property of the number-series here in question is most sharply conceived, not when one wearily tries, as Mr. Bosanquet has it, to count "without having anything in particular to count," [1] but when one rather tries to reflect, and then observes that the single feature about the number-system upon which all this conceivable complexity depends, is the simple and positive demand that is determined by the thought which conceives any order whatever. For order, as we shall soon more generally see, is comprehensible most of all in cases of self-representative systems of the present type. The numbers are simply a formally ordered collection of ideal objects. Whoever anywhere orders his own thoughts, either defines just such a self-representative system, or sets in order some empirically selected portion of a world that, in its totality, is such a system. And any system once self-representative, in this particular way, is infinitely self-representative. And if you will count its elements, you shall, then, always find that you can never finish the task.

Yet we are not yet done with showing, in this abstractly simple case of the numbers, what this type of self-representation implies. The numbers, namely, form a system not only self-representative in infinitely numerous ways, but also self-representative according to each of these ways, in a manner that can be *doubly* brought under our notice. Take, namely, the collection of series thus represented: —

---

[1] *Logic*, Vol. I, p. 175. In the Theory of Numbers, the properties of the whole numbers are indeed interesting for themselves "*without anything in particular to count*," just because they form an *ordered* series, whose properties are the properties of all ordered systems.

1	2	3	4	5	6	7	8	9	10, etc.
2	4	6	8	10	12	14	16	18	20, etc.
4	8	12	16	20	24	28	32	36	40, etc.
8	16	24	32	40	48	56	64	72	80, etc.

Each of these series, written in the horizontal rows, is ordered. Each is in such wise endless that to every number r, however large, there corresponds a determinate rth member of that particular series. And so each series illustrates the first point, namely, that the whole number-series may be put in a one-to-one correspondence with a part of itself. But each series is formed from the immediately preceding series by writing down, in order, the second, fourth, sixth, eighth member of that series, and so forth, as respectively the first, second, third, fourth member of the new series, and by proceeding, according to the same law, indefinitely. It is at once easy to illustrate a second principle regarding any such self-representative systems. To do this, let us observe that: —

First, Each new series is contained in the previous series as one of its constituent parts, so that each horizontal series is self-representative; while every one is a part of all of its predecessors.

Secondly, Each series is therefore to be derived from the former series in the same way in which the second series is derived from the first series.

Thirdly, The later series, therefore, bear to the earlier series, a relation parallel to that which characterized the members of the series of maps in our first illustration of the present type of self-representative systems.

For just as, in the former case, the one purpose to draw the exact map of England within England, gave rise to the endless series of maps within maps, just so, the one purpose, To represent the whole number-series (as to the order of its constituents) by a specially selected series of whole numbers, arranged in order as first, second, etc, — just so, I say, this one purpose involves of necessity the result that this second or representative series shall contain, as part of itself, an endless series of *parts within parts*. Each of these contained parts represents a preceding part precisely in the way in which the first representative system represents the original system. The law of the process always is that in a self-representative system of the type here in question, if any part A' can stand in a one-to-one relation to the elements of the whole system, A, then *ipso facto* there exists A'' (a part of this part), such that A'' is the image or representative in A', of A' as it was in A. A'' stands, then, in the same relation to A', as that in which A' stands to A; and A'' is also a part of A'. To derive A' from A, by any such process as the one just exemplified, is therefore at once to define, by recurrence, the derivation of A'' from A', or, if you please, the internal and representative presence of A'' within A', of A''' within A'', and *so on without end*. Nor can any A' be derived from A, in such wise as exactly to represent, while a part of A, the whole of A, without the consequent implied definition of the whole series, also endless, A, A', A'', A''', wherein each term is a representative of the former term. So that not only is A self-representative and endless, but each of the derived series is self-representative and endless, while the whole ordered system of series that one can write in the orderly sequence A, A', A'', A''' is again a self-representative sequence, and so on endlessly, — all this complexity resulting self-evidently from the expressions of a single purpose.

One sees, — self-representation of the present type remains persistently true to its tendency to develope types of variety out of unity. Trivial these types may indeed seem; yet the simplicity and the exactness of the derivation here in question will soon prove of use to us in a wholly different field. But it is now time to suggest, briefly, a still more general view of these self-representative systems.

IV. *Remarks upon the Various Types of Self-Representative Systems*

We have so far spoken, repeatedly, of the "present type" of self-representative systems, meaning the type that, in this paper, will especially interest us. In this type a system is capable of standing in an exact one-to-one correspondence with one of its own constituent portions. We are to be interested throughout this paper in cases of self-representation, such as Self-consciousness, and the relation between thought and Reality, and all the problems of Reflection, bring to our notice. And in all these cases, as we shall see, the system before us will combine the characters of selfhood and internal unity of nature, with the character of being also internally manifold, self-dirempted, Other than Self, and that in most complex and highly antithetic fashion. The relational systems of the type of the number-system especially exemplify — of course in a highly abstract fashion — the sort of unity in contrast, and of exact self-representation, which we are to learn to comprehend. Hence, the stress here to be laid upon one type of self-representative system.

Yet, mathematically regarded, this is indeed only one of several possible types of self-representation.

In the work by Dedekind already cited, the general name, *Kette*, is given to any self-representative system, whether of the present type or any other self-representative type. In the most general terms, a *Kette* is formed when a system is made to correspond, whether exactly, and element for element, or in any other way, either to the whole, *or* to a part of itself. The correspondence might be summary and inexact in type, if to many elements of the original system a single element of the representation or image were made to correspond, as, in a summary account or diagram, a single item or stroke can be made, at pleasure, to correspond to a whole series of facts in the original object which the account or the diagram represents. In this way, for instance, the one word *prime* can be made to correspond, in a given discussion, to all the prime numbers. If, in case of a *Kette*, the correspondence of the whole to the part is of this inexact type, the *Kette* need not be endless, but may even consist of the original object, and a *single* one of its constituent parts. Then all the later members of the *Kette*, the A'', the A''', etc., of the previous account, fuse together in this one part, A'. If the map of England, before discussed, be an inexact and summary map, such as we actually always make, it need contain no part that visibly, or exactly, presents the place or the form of the map itself, as a part of the surface of England. But the *Kette* is constructed in such wise that the part is in exact correspondence to the whole when, as in Dedekind's definition of the Infinite, the correspondence is *ähnlich*, so that any different elements in the object have different elements corresponding to them in the image, while every element has its own uniquely determined corresponding image. It will be observed that in case of inexact or dissimilar self-representation, we have a failure or external limitation of our self-representative purpose. Only exact self-representation is free from such external interference.

Yet even an exact self-correspondence can be brought to pass, within a system, by making it correspond *not* to a true portion of itself, but, member for member, to the *whole* of itself. Thus the system *abcd*, consisting of the already distinguishable elements *a, b*, etc., may be put in exact correspondence to itself by making *b* correspond to *a*, and so represent *a*, while, in similar fashion, *c* corresponds to *b, d* to *c*, and, finally, *a* itself to *d*. In this case the system is, in a particular way, "transformed" into the image *bcda*, in such wise as to be exactly self-representative. But the system *abcd* might also be represented, element for element, by the system *cbda*, where the order of the elements was again different, but where *c* now corresponded to the original *a, b* to itself, *d* to *c*, and *a* to *d*. Such "substitutions," as they are called, give rise to self-representative systems of a type different from the one that we have heretofore had in mind. But in the general mathematical theory of "transformations," and of "groups of operations," self-representation of such types plays a great part. And in cases of such a type, to be sure, exact self-representation, and finitude of the system, are capable of perfect combination. Such self-representations need not be endless, and can be exact. There are many remarkable instances known to

descriptive physical science, where the correspondence used
for scientific purposes is of this type. Such are the instances
which occur in crystallography, where the symmetry of a physical object is studied by considering what group of rotations, or
of internal reflections in one or in another plane, or of both
combined, will bring any ideal crystal form to congruence with
itself. All such operations as the rotations and reflections
that leave the crystal form unaltered are, of course, operations which bring to light an essentially self-representative
character in the crystal form, since by any one such operation the crystal form is made precisely to correspond with
itself, while the operation can at once be followed by a new
operation of the same type, which, again, leaves the form
unaltered.

While, however, self-representative systems of ideal or of
physical objects belonging to the later types play a great part
in exact physical and in mathematical science, their study
does not throw light upon the *primal* way in which the One
and the Many, in the processes directly open to thought's
own internal observation, are genetically combined. For
physical systems which permit these transformations of a
whole into an exact image of itself are given as external
"conjunctions," such as crystal forms. We do not see them
made. We find them. The ideal cases of the same type in
pure mathematics have also a similar defect from the point
of view of Bradley's criticism. A system that is to be made
self-representative through a "group of substitutions," shows,
therefore, the same diversities after we have operated upon
it as before; and, furthermore, that congruence with itself
which the system shows at the end of a self-representative
operation of any type wherein all elements take the place of
all, is not similar to what happens where, in our dealings with
the universe, Thought and Reality, the Idea and its Other,
Self and Not-Self, are brought into self-evident relations, and
are at once contrasted with one another and unified in a single
whole. Hence, we shall indeed continue to insist, in what
follows, upon those self-representations wherein proper part

and whole meet, and become in some wise precisely congruent, element for element.[1] We mention the other types of self-representation only to eliminate them from the present discourse.

In case of these self-representative systems, of the type especially interesting to us, we have already illustrated how their particular kind of self-representation developes infinite variety out of unity in a peculiarly impressive way. The general law of the process in question may now be stated, in a still more precise and technical form.

We may once more use the thoroughly typical case of the number-system. We have seen, in general, the positive nature of its endlessness. We want now to define, in decidedly general terms, the infinite process whereby the numbers can be self-represented, in infinitely numerous ways, by a part of themselves, and to state, abstractly, the implications of any such process. Let, then, $f(n)$ represent any "function" of a whole number, such that n is to take, successively, the value of any whole number from 1 onwards; while $f(n)$ itself is, in value, always a determinate whole number. The values of $f(n)$ shall never be repeated. They shall follow in endless succession, and, as we shall also here suppose, in the order of their magnitude from less to more. Not all the numbers shall appear amongst the values of $f(n)$. In consequence, $f(n)$, by means of its *first, second, third* values, etc., shall represent precisely the whole of the number-series, while forming only a part thereof *Otherwise let* f(n) *be an arbitrary function. Then it will always be true that* f(n) *will contain, as a part of itself, a series* $f_1(n)$, *related to* f(n) *in precisely the same way in which* f(n) *is related to the original series of whole numbers.* It

---

[1] Upon the various types of *Ketten*, finite and infinite, "cyclical" and "open," see the very minute analysis given by Bettazzi, in his papers entitled *Sulla Catena di un Ente in un gruppo*, and *Gruppi finiti ed infiniti di Enti*, in the *Atti* of the Turin Academy of Sciences (for 1895-96), Vol. 31, pp. 447 and 506. Bettazzi, in the second of these papers, expresses some dissatisfaction with Dedekind's definition of the Infinite, but withdraws his objections in a later paper, *Atti*, Vol. 32, p. 353.

will also be true that $f_1(n)$ will contain a second series $f_2(n)$, similarly related to $f_1(n)$; and so on without end.

We have illustrated this truth. We now need to develope it for any and every series of $f(n)$, however arbitrary. Consider, then, the values of $f(n)$ as a part of the original number-series. These values of $f(n)$ form an image or representative of the whole number-series in such wise that if r be a whole number appropriately chosen, some one value of $f(n)$, say the value that corresponds to the number p in the original series, or, in other words, the pth value of $f(n)$, is r. But since $f(n)$ images the *whole* of the original number-series, it must contain, as a part of itself, a representation of its own self as it is in that number-series. In this representation, $f_1(n)$, there is again a *first* member, a *second* member, and so on.

Now we can indeed speak of the series $f_1(n)$ as "derived from" $f(n)$ by a second and relatively new operation. But, as a fact, the very operation which defines the series $f(n)$ already predetermines $f_1(n)$, and no really second, or new operation is needed. For if every whole number has its correspondent, or "image," in $f(n)$, then, for that very reason, every separate "image," being, by hypothesis, a whole number, has again, in $f(n)$, its own image; and this image again its own image, and so on without end. Merely to observe these *images of images*, already present in $f(n)$, is to observe, in succession, the various members of the series $f_1(n)$. The law of the formation of $f_1(n)$ is already determined, then, when $f(n)$ is written, no matter how arbitrary $f(n)$ itself may be.

In particular, let p be any whole number, and suppose that, according to the original self-representation of the numbers, $f(p) = r$. Then r also will have its image in the series $f(n)$. Let that image be called $f(r)$. Then $f(r) = f(f(p))$, is at once defined as $f_1(p)$, that is, as that value which $f_1(n)$ takes when $n = p$, or as the image of the image of p. It is easy to see that $f_1(p)$ is the pth value, in serial order, of the series $f_1(n)$. At the same time, since $f_1(p) = f(r)$, and since $f(r)$ occupies, in the series of values of $f(n)$ the rth place, while $f(p)$, or r, occupies the rth place in the original number-series, one can say, in general, that the successive values of $f_1(n)$ are numbers which occupy in $f(n)$ places precisely corresponding to the places which the successive values of $f(n)$ themselves occupy in the original number-series.   Thus the first member of $f_1(n)$ is that one amongst the members of the series of values of $f(n)$ whose place in that series of values corresponds to the place in the original series of whole numbers which was occupied by $f(1)$.   The second member of $f_1(n)$ is, even so, that one amongst the series of values of $f(n)$ which occupies the place in that series of values which $f(2)$ occupies in the original number-series.   And, in general, if, to the whole number p, in the original number series, there corresponded the number r, as the *image* of that number in the series called $f(n)$, then this pth member of the series called $f(n)$ will have, as its image or representative in $f_1(n)$, the number $f(r)$, *i.e.* the value of $f(n)$ when $n = r$.   This number $f(r)$ will constitute, of course, the pth member of $f_1(n)$, and will occupy, in the series called $f(n)$, the very same relative place which $f(p)$ occupies in the original number-series.

Precisely so, $f_1(n)$ contains, as a part of itself, its own image as it is in $f(n)$ and also as it is in the original series.   And this new image may be called $f_2(n)$; and so on without end.[1]   Hence, one process of self-representation inevitably determines an endless *Kette* altogether parallel to our series of maps within maps of England.   The general structure and development of any self-representative system of the present type have now been not only illustrated, but precisely defined and developed.   Self-representation, of the type here in question, creates, at one stroke, an infinite chain of self-representations within self-representations.

---

[1] On the properties of a *Kette*, see further in addition to Dedekind, Schroeder, in the latter's *Algebra der Relative*, in the 3d Vol. of his *Logik*, pp. 345–404.   Compare Borel, *op. cit.*, pp. 104–106.

V. *The Self and the Relational System of the Ordinal Numbers. The Origin of Number; and the Meaning of Order*

Having considered self-representation so much in the abstract, we may now approach nearer to the other illustrations of self-representative relational systems. To be sure, in beginning to do so, we shall, for the first time in this discussion, be able to state the precise logical source of the good order of the number-system, whose self-representative character, now so wearisomely illustrated, is simply due to the fact that the number-series is a purely abstract image, a bare, dried skeleton, as it were, of the relational system that must characterize an ideally completed Self. This observation, in the present form, cannot be said to be due to Hegel, although both his analysis and Fichte's account of the Self, imply a theory that apparently needs to be developed into this more modern form. But the contempt of the older Idealism for the careful analysis of mathematical forms, — its characteristic unwillingness to dwell upon the dry detail of the seemingly lifeless realm of the mathematically pure abstractions, is responsible for much of the imperfect development and relative vagueness of the idealistic Absolute. It is so easy for the philosopher to put on superior airs when he draws near to the realm of the mathematician. And Hegel, despite his laborious study of the conceptions of the Calculus, in his *Logik*, generally does so. The mathematician, one observes, is a mere "computer." His barren *Calcul*, — what can it do for the deeper comprehension of truth? Truth is concrete. As a fact, however, these superior airs are usually the expression of an unwillingness even to spend as much time as one ought to spend over mathematical reading. And Hegel seems not to have solved the problem of the logic of mathematics. The truth is indeed concrete. But if *alle Theorie* is, after all, *grau*, and *grün des Lebens Goldener Baum*, the philosopher, as himself a thinker, merely shares with his colleague, the mathematician, the fate of having to deal with dead leaves and sections torn or cut from the tree of life, in his toilsome effort to make out what the life is. The mathematician's interests are not the philosopher's. But neither of the two has a monopoly of the abstractions; and in the end each of them — and certainly the philosopher — can learn from the other. The metaphysic of the future will take fresh account of mathematical research.

The foregoing observation as to the parallelism between the structure of the number-series and the bare skeleton of the ideal Self, is due, then, in its present form, rather to Dedekind than to the idealistic philosophers proper.[1] It shall be briefly expounded in the form in which he has suggested it to me, although his discussion seems to have been written wholly without regard to any general philosophical consequences. And the present is the first attempt, so far as I know, to bring Dedekind's research into its proper relation to general metaphysical inquiry.

The numbers have been so far taken as we find them. But how do we men come by our number-series? The usual answer is, by learning to count external objects. We see collections of objects, with distinguishable units, the "bare conjunctions" of Mr. Bradley once more. Their mysterious unity in diversity arouses our curiosity. We form the habit, however,

---

[1] Hegel indeed defines the positive Infinite as *das Fürsichseiende*, and sets it in opposition to the merely negative Infinitive, or *das Schlecht-Unendliche*. See the well-known discussion in the *Logik*, *Werke*, 2te *Auflage*, Bd. III, p. 148, *sqq*. Dr. W. T. Harris, in his *Hegel* (Chicago, 1890), and in other discussions, has ably defended and illustrated the Hegelian statements. They are applied to the problem of the quantitative Infinite by Hegel in the *Logik*, in the volume cited, p. 272 *sqq*. But near as Hegel thus comes to the full definition of the Infinite, his statement of the matter remains rather a postulate that the self-representative system *shall be found*, than a demonstration and exact explanation of its reality. The well-known Hegelian assertions that the only true image of the Infinite is the closed cycle (*Logik*, *loc. cit.*, p. 156), that the quantitative infinite is *a return to quality* (*loc. cit.*, p. 271), and that the rational fraction, taken as the equivalent of the endless decimal, is the one typical example of the completed quantitatively infinite process, — these, all of them valuable as emphasizing various aspects of the concept of the infinite, appear in the present day wholly inadequate to the complexity of our problem, and rather hinder than aid its final expression.

of using certain familiar and easily observed collections (our fingers, for instance) as means for defining the nature of less familiar and more complex collections. The number-names, derived from these elementary processes of finger-counting, come to our aid in the further development of our thought about numbers. The decadic system makes possible, through a simple system of notation, the expression of numbers of any magnitude. And so the number-concept in its generality is born.

This usual summary view of the origin of the numbers has its obvious measure of historical and psychological truth. It leaves wholly unanswered, however, the most interesting problems as to the nature of the number-concept. For numbers have two characters. They are *cardinal* numbers, in so far as they give us an idea of how many constituents a given collection of objects contains. But they have also an *ordinal* character; for by using numbers, as the makers of watches, and bicycles, or as the printers of a series of banknotes, or of tickets, use them, we can give to any one object its place in a determinate series, as the first, the tenth, or the ten thousandth member of that series. Such ordinal use of numbers is a familiar device for identifying objects that, for any reason, we wish to view as individuals. Now, a very little consideration shows that the ordinal value of the numbers is of very fundamental importance for their use in giving us a notion of the cardinal numbers of multitudes of objects. For when we count objects by using either the fingers or the number-names, we always employ an already familiar ordered series of objects as the basis of our work. We put the members of this series in a "one-to-one" relation to the members of the collection of objects which we wish to count. We deal out our numbers, so to speak, in serial order, to the various objects to be counted. We thereby label the various objects as they are numbered, just as the makers of the banknotes stamp an ordinal number on each note of a given issue. Only when this process is completed do we recognize the cardinal number which tells us how many objects there are in the collection of the objects counted.

And we recognize this result of counting by the simple device of giving to the whole collection counted a cardinal number corresponding to the *last* member of the ordinal number-series that we have thus dealt out. If, for instance, the last object labelled is the *tenth* in the series of objects set in order by the ordinal process of labelling, then the counted collection is said to contain *ten* objects.

Unless the numbers were, then, in our minds, already somehow a well-ordered series, they would help us no whit in counting objects. Nor does counting consist in the mere collection of acts of synthesis by which we each time add one more, in mind, to the collection of objects so far counted. For these acts of synthesis, however carefully performed, soon give us, if left to themselves, only the confused sense, "There is another object, — and another, — and another." In such cases we soon "lose count." We can "keep tally" of our objects only if we combine the successive series of acts of observing another, and yet another, object, in our collection of objects with the constant use of the already ordered series of number-names, whose value depends upon the fact that one of them comes *first*, another *second*, etc., and that we well know what this order means.

The ordinal character of the number-series is therefore its most important and fundamental character. But upon what mental process does the conception of any well-ordered series depend? The account of the origin of the number-series by the mere use of fingers or of names, does not yet tell us what we mean by any ordered series at all.

To this question, whose central significance, for the whole understanding of the number-concept, all the later discussions and the modern text-books recognize, various answers have been given.[1] The order of a series of objects, presented or

[1] Couturat, in the work cited, gives an admirable summary of the present phases of the discussion ; only that he fails, I think, to appreciate the importance and originality of Dedekind's method of deducing the ordinal concept. The views of Helmholtz and Kronecker are discussed with especial care by Couturat. Veronese, in the introduction to his

conceived, has been most frequently regarded, in the later discussions, either as a datum of sensuous experience, or else as
an inexplicable and fundamental character of our process of
conception. In either case the problem of the One and the
Many is left unanalyzed. For an ordered series is a collection
taken not only as One, but as a very special sort of unity,
namely, as just this Order. That many things can be taken
by us as in an ordered series, — this is true, but is once more
the "bare conjunction" of Mr. Bradley's discussion. We
want to find out what act first brings to our consciousness
that Many elements constitute One Order. Nearest to the
foundation of the matter Dedekind seems to me to have come,
when, without previously defining any number-series at all,
he sets out with that definition of an infinite system of
ideal objects which we have already stated, and then proceeds,
substantially as follows, to show how this system can come to
be viewed Whole.

Let there be a system N of objects, — a system defined
as capable of the type of self-representation heretofore
illustrated. That such a system is a valid object (of the
type definable through our own Third Conception of Being),
we have already seen by the one example of *meine Gedankenwelt*. For the ideally universal law of *meine Gedankenwelt* is that to every thought of mine, *s*, I can make
correspond the thought, *s'*, viz., the thought, "This, *s*, is one
of my thoughts." Because of this single ideal law of the
equally ideal Self here in question, the *Gedankenwelt* is
already given as a conceptual system of many elements, — a
system capable of exact representation by one of its own con-

Principles of Geometry (known to me in the German translation, *Grundzüge der Geometrie*, übers v. Schepp, Leipzig, 1894) gives a very elaborate
development of the number-concept upon the basis of the view that the
order of a series of conceived objects is an ultimate fact or absolute datum
for thought (*op. cit.*, § 3, 14–28, 46–50). Amongst the recent text-
books, Fine's *Number-System of Arithmetic and Algebra* holds an
important place. See also the opening chapter of Harkness and Morley's
Introduction to the Theory of Analytic Functions.

stituent portions. Now let us suppose our particular system N to be a system such as a particular portion, itself infinite, of the *Gedankenwelt*, would constitute. Namely, let us suppose our system N to be capable of a process of self-representation that first selects a *single* one of the elements of N (to be called *One* or element the *first*), and, that then represents the whole of N by that portion of N which is formed of *all* the elements of N except *One*.[1] The result of this mode of self-representation is that N becomes, in the sense before defined, a *Kette*, represented by a part of itself, N'. This part, N', by hypothesis, contains all of the N *except* the chosen *first* element named *One*. In consequence, and because of the very same sort of reasoning that we carried out in case of the map of England made within England, N' will again contain, by virtue of the one principle of its constitution, a further part, N'', which will be derived from N' by leaving out a single element of N', to be called *Two*, and defined as the *second* element of the system. *Two* will be, in fact, the name of that very element in N' which, in the original mapping of N by N', was the element that was made to represent, or to image, element *One*. But the process of expressing the meaning thus involved is now recurrent. For the one plan of representing N by N', with the omission from N' of the single element called *One*, has involved the representing of N' by N'', with the omission from N'' of the single element now called *Two*, — an element which is merely the image in N' of *One* in N. The same plan, however, not so much applied anew, as simply once fully expressed, implies that within N'' there is an N''', an N^{iv}, and so on without end; just as the one plan of mapping England within England involved the endless series of maps. But each of the series of systems N', N'', N''', etc., differs from the previous one simply by the omission of a

---

[1] In order to accomplish this selection, the concept of an individual content, distinguished, within the system, as *this and no other*, must of course be presupposed as valid. Such a concept already implies an individuating interest or Will which selects. But this will is here presupposed only in the abstract.

single element present in its predecessor. And the series of these successively omitted elements has an order absolutely predetermined by the one original plan. That order consists simply in the fact that each element omitted, when any of the new representations, N'', N''', etc., is considered, is, upon each occasion, itself the *Bild*, the image or map or representative, of the very element that was previously omitted, when N'', or N''', or other representation, was made. The endless series *One, Two, Three,* etc., is consequently the series of names of those objects whereof the *first* was omitted when the first representation or the mapping of N was made; while the *second* element represented, in the first map, N', this first element of N. In the same way, in the second map, N'', the element *Three,* the *third* element of the series, represented or pictured the second element, which latter, present in N', had been omitted in N''.

Thus the *one* plan of mapping or representing N by a part of itself, taken as a single act, accomplished at a stroke, logically involves what one can then express as an endless series of maps or images of the portion or element of N that is omitted from the first of the maps. And this endless ordered series of images of the omitted element of N, can be so carried out as to constitute a derived system that contains, in its turn, any member of N that you please, in a particular place, whose order in the series of successive images is absolutely predetermined by the one original plan. Hence, as Dedekind has it, "we say that the system N is, by this mode of representation, set in order *(geordnet).*" [1] But, let us observe, this *whole* order, in all its infinite serial complexity, is logically accomplished by means of one act.

The series of images, or representations, of the element *One,* thus obtained, has of course, at first sight, a very artificial seeming. But a glance at the concrete case of the *Gedankenwelt* will show the sense of the process more directly. Let my *Gedankenwelt* be viewed in its totality, as a system self-represented in the way first defined. Then the one plan

[1] *Op. cit.,* § 6, 71, p. 20.

of representing any thought of mine, whether itself reflective or direct, by a reflective thought of the form, *This is one of my thoughts*, implies that about any primal thought of mine, say the thought, *To-day is Tuesday*, there ideally clusters an endless system, *N*, of thoughts whereof this thought, *To-day is Tuesday*, may be made the *first* member. These thoughts may follow one after another in time. But, logically, they are all determined at one stroke by the one purpose to reflect. The system *N* consists of the original thought, and then of the series of reflective thoughts of the form, *This is one of my thoughts;* — yes, and *This last reflection is one of my thoughts;* and *This further reflection is one of my thoughts;* and so on without end. Now the system *N* is known to be infinite, not by counting its members until you fail and give up the process in weariness, but by virtue of the universal plan that every one of its members shall have a corresponding reflective thought that shall itself belong to the system. Hereby already *N* is defined as infinite, before you have counted at all. But this very plan determines a fixed order of sequence, whether temporal or logical, amongst the constituent elements of *N;* because each new element, to be taken into account when you follow the order, is defined as that element whereby the last element is to be imaged, or reflectively represented. But this recurrent, or iterative, character of the operation of thought whereby you follow the series of elements, is really only the result of the single plan of self-representation whereby once for all the system *N* is ordered according to its defined first member. For the whole system *N*, once conceived as mapped, or represented by that portion of itself which does not include the element called *One*, is even thereby at one stroke defined as an ordered series of representations within representations, like our series of maps of England. This system of representations within representations of the whole of *N*, is given as a valid truth, *totum simul*, by the definition of the undertaking. The series of temporally successive reflective thoughts, however, is found to be ordered as a result of this constitution of the entire system; and therefore is its iterative meaning clear quite apart from any theory as to whether time and succession are appearance or reality.

Now the system N is, by definition, simply that system of thoughts which, if present at once, would express a complete self-consciousness as to the act of thinking that *To-day is Tuesday*. Were I just now not only to think this thought, but to think all that is directly implied in the mere fact that I think this thought, I should have present to me, at once, the whole system N as an ordered system of thoughts. Precisely so, the whole determined *Gedankenwelt*, if present at once, would be a Self, completely reflective regarding the fact that all of these thoughts were its own thoughts. But this complete reflection would, in all its portions, involve an ordered system of thoughts, whose purely abstract form, taken merely as an order, is everywhere precisely that of the number-system.

Self-representation, then, in the sense now so fully exemplified, is not merely, as it were, the property or accident of the number-system; but is, logically speaking, its genetic principle. When order is not a mere "external conjunction," when we know not merely *that* facts seem in order, but *what* the order is, and *how* it is one order through all of its manifold expressions, we do so by virtue of comprehending the internal meaning of a plan whereby a system of conceived objects comes to be represented through a portion of itself. Dedekind has shown that this view is adequate to the logical development of the various properties of the number-system. What we here observe is that the consequent constitution of the number-system is explicitly defined as, of course in the barest and most abstract outline, the form of a completed Self. Here, then, the Intellect, "of its own movement," "itself by itself," defines what, in our temporal experience, whether sensuous or thoughtful, it of course nowhere finds given, namely, a self-representative system of objects, parallel in structure to what the structure of a *Gedankenwelt* would be if it were the *Welt* of a completely self-conscious Thought, none of whose acts failed to be its own intellectual objects. This concept comes to us as positive, and wholly in advance of counting. It involves, first, the general definition of a *Kette*, of the type here in question, whose properties, taken in their abstraction, are as exactly definable as those of a triangle. Not every such *Kette* is a Self, or a *Gedankenwelt;* for of course the general concept of a system possessing some sort of one-to-one correspondence, can be applied in any region, however abstract; and a *Kette* may therefore be defined where the objects in question are taken to be either dead matter or else mere fiction. Consequently the mathematical world is simply full of *Ketten* of the present and of other types. But the notable facts are, first, that the present type of *Kette* becomes the very model of an ordered system, and, secondly, that it becomes this by virtue of the fact that in structure it is precisely parallel to the structure of an ideal Self. Herein the intellect does indeed, of itself, comprehend its own work, even though this work be but an ideal creation.

But all order in the world of space, of time, of quantity, or of morals, however rich its wealth of life, of meaning, or of beauty may be, is order because it presents to us systems of facts that may be viewed as having a first, a second, a third constituent, or some higher form of order; while the rank, dignity, worth, magnitude, proportion, structure, description, explanation, law, or other reasonableness of any of these objects in our world depends, for us, upon our power to recognize in them what, for a given purpose, comes first, what second, and so on, amongst their elements or their higher constituents. The absolutely universal application of the concept of order wherever the intellect recognizes in any sense its own, in heaven or upon earth, shows us the interest of considering even these barest abstractions regarding simple order. The number-series is indeed the absolutely abstract, but also the absolutely universal and inclusive type of all order, — the one thing that every rational being, however much he may differ in constitution from us men, must, in some shape, possess, just in so far as he knows any complete order or system at all, divine or diabolical, moral or physical, æsthetic or social, formal or concrete. For the deepest essence of the number-series lies not in its power to aid us in finding *how many* units there are in this or that collection, but in its expression of the notion that something is first, and something next, in any type of orderly connection that we may be capable of knowing. It is the relational system of the numbers, taken in their whole-ness as one act, which here interests us. Those degrade arithmetical truth who conceive it merely as the means for estimating the cardinal numbers of collections of objects. The science of arithmetic is rather the abstract science of ordered collections. But all collections, if they have any rational meaning, are ordered and orderly. Hence, it is indeed worth while to know where it is that we first clearly learn what order means.

Now it is not very hard to see, and to say, that I first recog-nize order as a form of unity in multiplicity when I learn, of myself, to put something first, and something next, and self-consciously to know that I do so. That counting my fingers, or learning the names of the numbers, first sets me upon the way to attain this degree of self-consciousness, is true enough. But our question is what the concept of order, as the one transparent form of unity in manifoldness, directly implies. In following the analysis of the number-concept, we have been led to the point where this becomes an answerable question. Given, as "bare conjunction," is what you will. The intellect, however, as Mr. Bradley well says, accepts only what it can make for itself. The first object that it can make for itself, however, is seen, as Mr. Bradley also says, to involve the seeming of an endless process. The single purpose of the intellect, in any effort at self-comprehension, proves to be re-current precisely when it is most obvious and necessary. The infinite task looms up before us; and, in impatient weariness, we talk of "endless fission" breaking out everywhere, and are fain to give up the task; failing, however, to observe that just hereby we have already seen how the One must express itself, by the very self-movement of the intellect, as the Many. If we reflect afresh, however, we observe that what we have seen is due to the fact that the only systems of ideal objects which the intellect can define without taking account of "bare external conjunctions," are systems such that to whatever object we have presupposed, another object, expressing the same intellectual purpose, must correspond, as the *next* object in question. This fact, however, is due to the simple necessity of the reflective process in which we are involved.

Our thought seeks its own work as its object. That is of the very essence of this effort to let the intellect express its self-movement. But making its own work its object, observing afresh what it has done, is merely reinstating, as a fact yet to be known, the very process whose first result is observed when the intellect contemplates its own just accomplished deed. Reflection, then, implies, to be sure, what, in time, must appear to us as an endless process. We are not interested, however, in the mere feeling of weariness which this endless process (in consequence of still another "bare conjunction," of a psychological nature) involves to one of us mortals when he first observes its necessity. What interests us is the positive structure of the whole intellectual world. We have found that structure. It is the structure of a self-representative system of the type that we now have in mind. We frankly define all such systems as endless, so far as concerns the variety of their elements. But hereupon we indeed observe that, as self-representative, they are, in a perfectly transparent way, self-ordered. The trivial illustration of the map within the country mapped, has been followed by the more exact illustrations of the self-representative character of the complete number-system when once its traditional structure is accepted as something given and present in totality. With these examples of self-ordered unity in the midst of infinite diversity, we have returned to the question of the logical genesis of the very conception of order of which the number-system is the first example. We have found the answer to our question in the assertion that since a self-representative system, of the type here in question, once assumed as an ideal object, determines its own order, and assigns to its constituents their place as first, next, and so on, and since only such self-representative systems result from the undisturbed expression of the intellect's internal meanings, therefore, an order that shall be transparent to the intellect, or that shall appear to it as its own deed, must be of the type exemplified in Dedekind's analysis.

And so, as far as we have gone, the circle of our investigation is provisionally completed. The intellect has been studying itself, and, as the abstract and merely formal expression of the orderly aspect of its own ideally conceived complete Self, and of any ideal system that it is to view as its own deed, the intellect finds precisely the Number System, — not, indeed, primarily the cardinal numbers, but the ordinal numbers. Their formal order of first, second, and, in general, of *next*, is an image of the life of sustained, or, in the last analysis, of complete Reflection. Therefore, this order is the natural expression of any recurrent process of thinking, and, above all, is due to the essential nature of the Self when viewed as a totality. Here, then, although we are still merely in the world of forms, we know something about the One and the Many.

VI. *On the Realm of Reality as a Self-Representative System*

We must now proceed to apply our previous considerations to the question of the constitution of any realm of Being, or of any universe.

Suppose, in the first place, for a moment, that one is to conceive the universe in realistic terms, as a realm whose existence is supposed to be independent of the mere accident that any one does or does not know or conceive it. Suppose such a world to be once for all there. Then it is possible to show that this supposed universe has the character of a self-representative system, and that, too, even if you try to define its ultimate constitution as unknowable.

For, in the first place, at the moment when you suppose that any fact exists, independently of whether you know it or not, it is obvious that you must in reality be making, or at least, by hypothesis, trying to make, this supposition. For unless the supposition is really attempted, there is no conception of F in question at all. But if the supposition is itself a fact, then, at that instant, when the supposition is made, the world of Being contains *at least two* facts, namely, F, and your supposition about F. Call the supposition f; and symbolize the universe by U. Then the least possible universe that can exist, at the moment when your hypothesis is made, will be such that $U = F + f$.

Having proceeded so far, however, we cannot stop. As we saw in analyzing the realistic concept, Realism hopelessly endeavors to assert that, although what we now call F and f are alike real, they have no essential relations to each other. For our present purpose, however, we need only note that whether or no the relations of F and f are in the least essential to the being of either F or f, taken in themselves, still, when F and f are once together and related, the relations are at least as real as their terms. Or, even if we confine ourselves strictly to our symbols, it remains obviously true that in order merely to report the supposed facts, we had to write, as the actual constitution of our universe, at least $F + f$. Now this universe, as thus symbolized, has not merely a twofold, but a threefold constitution. It consists of F, and of f, *and* of their $+$, *i.e.* of the relation, as real as both of them, which we try to regard as non-essential to the Being of either of them, but which, for that very reason, has to be something wholly other than themselves, just as they are supposed to be different from each other. A system such as Herbart's depends, indeed, upon trying to reduce this $+$ to a *Zufällige Ansicht*, which is supposed, for that reason, to be no part of the realm of the " reals." But, in answer to any such effort, we must stubbornly insist (and here in entire agreement with Mr. Bradley) upon declaring that either this *Zufällige Ansicht* stands for a real fact, for something which *is*, or else the whole hypothesis falls to the ground. For the essence of the hypothesis is that f *rightly* supposes F to exist, or, in other words, that the relation between F and f is one of genuine reference,

assertion, or truth on the part of f, and of actual expression of
the truth of this assertion by the very existence of F. Therefore, the relation between F and f is supposed to be a real fact.
Since, by hypothesis, it is independent of the mere existence
of F and of f, or since, if you please, F, by hypothesis, might
have been real without f, and f, if false, might have existed,
as a mere opinion, in the absence of any F, the relation which
we have expressed by $+$ has its own place in Being, and is a
third and, by the realistic hypothesis, a separate fact; so that
now U contains at least three facts, all different from one
another.

Hereupon, of course, Mr. Bradley's now familiar form of
argument enters with its full rights. Unquestionably a world
with three facts in it, — facts such that, by definition, either
f or F might have existed wholly alone, and apart from
the third fact, is a world where legitimate questions can be
raised about the ties that bind the third fact to the other two.
These ties are themselves facts. The $+$ is linked to f and to
F, and the "endless fission" unquestionably "breaks out."
The relation itself is seen entering into what seem new relations. The reason why this fission breaks out is now more
obvious to us. It lies not in the impotence of our intellect,
impotent as our poor human wits no doubt are, but in the self-
representative character of any relational system. In our
realistic world the system is such that, to any object, there
corresponds, as another object (belonging to the same system),
the relation between this first object and the rest of the
universe. Or, in general, if in the world there is an object,
F, then there is that relation, R, whereby F is linked to the
rest of the world. But to R, as itself an object, there therefore corresponds, at the very least, R', its own relation to the
rest of the world; and the whole system $F + R + R'$ is as
self-representative, and therefore as endless, as the number-
system, and for precisely the same reason: viz., because it
images, and, by hypothesis, expresses, in the abstract form of
a supposed "independent Being," the very process of the Self
which undertakes to say, "F exists."

Now, it would be wholly useless for a realist to attempt to escape from this consequence by persistently talking, as some realists do, about the defective nature of our poor human thought, and about the Unknowability of the Real. For the question is not as to what we do not know, but merely as to what we do know, about the supposed Independent Beings. And what we do know is, that by definition they form a *Kette* of the type now in question. They cannot escape from this consequence of their own definition by declaring their true Being to be unknowable. For if they attempt thus to escape, we shall very simply point out that, as unknowable, and as thus different from our definition of their Being, they, the realities, have now merely a twofold form of Being, namely, their Unknowable and their Knowable form. For, after all, we are supposed to know that they are, and that they appear to us in the form of a *Kette*. The problem of the "two natures" in one being, is, then, upon the hands of any realist who, like Mr. Spencer, thus divides his world; and this relation, whether knowable or unknowable, between the Knowable and the Unknowable aspects, or regions of Reality, will become something different from either of the two; and the new system will once more be a *Kette*, precisely like its predecessor, and for the same reason.

But, finally, one may attempt to escape from the entire situation by declaring that F, in the foregoing account, is, by hypothesis, a fact that does not need f, since f is, by supposition, a conscious process, — an idea, — and F is F whether or no anybody supposes it to exist, or knows it in any way. "Suppose now," a realist may say, "that there were no knowledge or ideas at all, but only the facts independent of all minds, and totally separate from one another. Then the realistic world would not be an endless *Kette*." Therefore it only becomes one, *per accidens*, when known.

In reply, I should point out, that if the world that contains F contains also any other facts, any diversity whatever, Mr. Bradley's repeated analysis of the "endless fission" will at once apply, and the world will become a self-representative system in the former sense. But *F*, if supposed to be wholly alone, and to be the only Being, and absolutely simple, is still not exempt from the universal self-diremption. *When you think of it*, — now, for instance, it is *not* alone. It is, by hypothesis, just now in the same world with the thoughts that define it. "But it is such that it *need* not be together with the thoughts that think it. It could exist independently." Yes, but *to exist alone*, and *to exist in company with another*, are not the same thing. *F*, then, has two aspects, or potencies: the aspect that enables it to exist independently of *f*, or of any thought, and its power to exist in relation to, and along with *f*, and with the rest of the *Kette* determined by the presence of *f*. *F*, the same *F*, has these two states of being, — its existence alone, and what Herbart called its *Zusammen*. Now just as the *Zusammen* is, by hypothesis, a fact, which nobody gets rid of by calling it a *Zufällige Ansicht*, so to be in *Zusammen* is to be in a state very different from the "Being, alone and without a Second," which *F* has before *f* comes. Call *F*, when taken as alone, F_1, and *F*, when taken as in company, F_2. Then the problem, How are F_1 and F_2 related? gives rise to the same sort of *Kette* with which Mr. Bradley has made us so familiar.

I agree, then, wholly with Mr. Bradley, that every form of realistic Being involves such endless or self-representative constitution. And I agree with him that, in particular, realistic Being breaks down upon the contradictions resulting from this constitution. I do not, however, accept the view that to be self-representative is, as such, to be self-contradictory. But I hold that any world of self-representative Being must be of such nature as to partake of the constitution of a Self, either because it is a Self, or because it is dependent for its form upon the Self whose work or image it is. But the realistic world is not able to accept this constitution. In case of the realistic type of Being, then, the endless fission proves to be an endless corruption and destruction of whatever had appeared to be the fact. Why? For the reason pointed out, but without any mention of the mere infinity of the relational process, in our third lecture. You want from a realist the facts, and all the facts, which are essential to his scheme. He names you the facts. You point out that since he inevitably names you a variety of facts, he must also admit that the connections or relations of these facts are real. And then you rightly add that the system in question must be self-representative and endless. But hereupon first appears the contradiction of Realism, viz., when you see that none of these endlessly numerous connections actually connect, because they are to be connections amongst beings that, by definition, are independent of knowledge, and therefore, as we saw, of one another, in such wise that their ties and links, if ever these ties seem to exist at all, must, upon examination, be found to be other real beings, as independent of the facts that they were to link as these, in their first essence, were of one another. The endlessly many elements of this world turn out, then, to be endlessly sundered. The *Kette* of the realist is a chain of hopelessly parted links. It is *this* aspect of the matter which gives their true cogency to the arguments of Mr. Bradley's first book. We do not see, then, how the real that is in any final sense independent of knowledge can be either One or Many or both One and Many. And we do not see this because we can see and define nothing but what is linked with knowledge. But within knowledge itself we do, indeed, still find the self-representative system.

So much for the realistic conception of Being. But if we turn to another conception of the nature of reality, namely, to our Third Conception of Being, then we once more find that this conception, too, involves a self-representative system of the type here in question. For this result has been already illustrated by the number-system, by the *Gedankenwelt* of Dedekind, and by the other mathematical instances cited; since all of these objects, when mathematically defined, appear primarily as beings of the third type of our list. Whether they possess any deeper form of Being, we have yet to see. In general, however, it is interesting to note that, in the proof of the mathematical possibility or validity of infinite systems given by Bolzano, in the passage of his *Paradoxien des Unendlichen*, already cited, the typical instance chosen to exemplify the infinite is that system of truth, or of *wahre Sätze*, whose validity follows from any primary *Satz*, or from any collection of such *Sätze*. If the proposition A is true, it follows, as Bolzano points out, that the proposition which asserts that "A is true," is also true. Call this proposition A'. Then the proposition "A' is true," is also true; and so on endlessly. While Bolzano has not Dedekind's exact conception of the nature of a *Kette*, and does not expressly use Dedekind's positive definition of the infinite, his example of the series of true propositions, A, A', A'', etc., — each of which is different from its predecessor, since it makes its predecessor the subject of which it asserts the predicate *true*, — is an example chosen wholly in the spirit of Dedekind's later selection of the *Gedankenwelt*, and is an extremely simple instance of a self-representative system.[1]

Realism, and the Third Conception of Being in our list, share alike, then, whatever difficulties may cluster about the conception of an infinitely self-representative system. What conception of Being can escape from this fate? Our own Fourth Conception?

No, as we must now expressly point out, our own conception of what it is to be makes the Real a *Kette* of the present type.

---

[1] The parallel *Kette* of knowledge was observed by Spinoza, *Ethics*, P. II, Prop. 43. In the tract, *De Intell. Emendat.*, however, Spinoza tries to explain away the significance of the endlessness of the resulting series. In the *Ethics* he says that whoever knows, knows that he knows, so that to an adequate idea, an adequate idea of this idea is necessarily joined by God and man. But in the *Tractatus* he asserts that the idea of the idea is not a necessary accompaniment of the adequate idea, but merely *may* follow upon the adequate idea if we choose. The contrast of expression in the two passages is remarkable ; and the question is of the most critical importance for the whole system of Spinoza. For if the idea, when adequate, is actually self-representative, the form of parallelism between extension and thought, asserted by Spinoza, finally breaks down, since, to avoid the troubles about the infinite, Spinoza expressly makes extended substance indivisible, so as to avoid making it a self-representative system. Furthermore, in any case, no precisely parallel process to the *idea of the idea* is to be found in extended substance.

For from our point of view, to be, or to be real, means to express, in final and determinate form, the whole meaning and purpose of a system of ideas. But the fact that a given experience anywhere fulfils a particular purpose, implies that this purpose itself is, in some wise, a fact, and has its place in reality. But if this purpose is real, it must, by our hypothesis, be real as a fulfilment of a purpose not absolutely and simply identical with itself. And so any particular purpose of the Absolute is itself such as it is, because it fulfils a particular purpose other than itself. Hence, for us, the Absolute must be a self-representative ordered system, or *Kette*, of purposes fulfilled; and the ordered system in question must be infinite. I accept this consequence. The Absolute must have the form of a Self. This I have repeatedly maintained in former discussions. Despite that horror of the infinite which Mr. Bradley's counsel would tend to keep alive in me, I still insist upon the necessity of the consequence. But I also insist upon several important aspects of the *Kette* in terms of which the Absolute is for me defined. And these aspects enable me to conceive the Absolute not only as infinite, but also as determinate, and not only as a form, but as a life.

First, the implied internal variety is subject to, and is merely expressive of, the perfectly precise and determinate unity of the single plan whereby, at one stroke, the Absolute is defined, or rather defines itself, as a self-representative system. Secondly, because of the now so wearisomely analyzed character of a *Kette* of the type here in question, the self-possession or self-consciousness of the Absolute does not imply any simple identity of subject and object in the absolute Self. The map of England (the subjective aspect in our original illustration) is not identical with the whole of England. Yet, in the supposed *Kette* of maps, once taken as real, the whole of England is mapped within itself. Order primarily implies a first that is represented by the second, third, and later members of the order, but that, as first, is itself representative of nothing else. The Absolute, in my conception, has this first aspect, which is essential at once to the immediacy of its experience, and to the individuality which, in my agreement with Mr. Bradley, I attribute to the whole. But this first aspect of Being must needs be represented, within itself, by the second, third, and other aspects. In other words, a full possession of the fulfilment of purpose, in final and determinate form, involves, as the first element in the conception of Absolute Being, the fact *that* purpose is fulfilled. But this fact is experienced, is known, is present, is seen. Otherwise it is no fact, and the world has no Being. But the fact that this first fact is known, or experienced, is itself a fact, a second fact. This, too, is known; and so on without end.

Thirdly, as I conceive, this whole series without end — a series which can equally well be expressed in terms of knowledge and in terms of purpose — is for the final view, and in the Absolute, no series of sundered successive states of temporal experience, but a *totum simul*, a single, endlessly wealthy experience. And, fourthly, by the very nature of the type of self-representation here in question, no one fashion of self-representation is required as the only one in such a realm of Being. As the England of our illustration could be self-mapped, if at all, then by countless series of various maps, not found in the same part of England and not in the least inconsistent with one another; and as the number-series, — that abstract image of the bare form of every self-representative system of the type here in question, — can be self-represented in endlessly various ways, — so, too, the self-representation of the Absolute permitted by our view is confined to no one necessary case; but is capable of embodiment in as many and various cases of self-representation, in as many different forms of selfhood, each individual, as the nature of the absolute plan involves. So that our view of the Selfhood of the Absolute, if possible at all, leaves room for various forms of individuality within the one Absolute; and we have a new opening for a possible Many in One, — an opening whose value we shall have to test in another way in our second series of lectures.

Our own view, then, also implies that the Absolute is a

Kette of the type now in question. But if one insists that such a doctrine is inevitably self-contradictory and vain, — where shall one still look for escape from this fate which besets, so far, all of the views as to the Real?

Shall one turn to Mysticism? Mysticism, viewed in its philosophical aspect, as we have viewed it in these lectures, knows of a One that is to be in no sense really Many. Every *Kette* must, then, for the mystic, prove an illusion. But, unfortunately for the mystic, the inevitableness of an infinite process is nowhere more manifest than in the movement of his own thought while, weary of finitude, this thought indulges endlessly its sad luxury of a troubled contemplation of its own defects. For this thought, as finite, is, by hypothesis, nothing real at all. Yet it reveals, in its own negative way, the road to absolute peace and truth. This road, however, is a path in the essentially pathless wilderness. This revelation is explicitly an absolute darkness. While you think, you have not won the truth; for thought is illusion. But if you merely cease to think, you have thereby won nothing at all. The Absolute is really known as such *by contrast with your illusion*. It is so far just the Other. You seek it in thought, and find it not. But perhaps the ineffable experience comes. *Ich bin Gott geworden*, says the Schwester Katrei of the tract usually (and, as the critics now tell us, wrongly) attributed to Meister Eckhart. This experience, whenever it comes, — why is it said to be an experience of Being? Viewed from without, it seems a mere transient state of feeling in somebody's mind. But no; it shall be no mere feeling, for it reveals all that thought had ever sought. The peace that passeth understanding fulfils all the needs of understanding. Hence, in this peace thought finds itself satisfied, and ceases. Therefore is Being here attained. Yet if this be the mystical insight, — what has been gained? Thought the deceiver, thought the illusory, bears witness to its own refutation and to its own fulfilment in the peace of the Absolute; for only when this evidence is given of the final satisfaction of all thought's demands is the truth known. And thus the sole testimony that Being is what the mystic declares it to be, is a witness borne by this self-detected and hopeless liar, thought, — whose words are the speech of one who exists not at all, but only falsely pretends to exist, and whose ideas are merely lies. This liar, at the moment of the mystical vision, declares that he rests content ; and therefore we know, forsooth, that we have come upon "that which is," and have caught the "deep pulsations of the world." We accept, then, the last testimony of the wholly hardened and hopeless deceiver; and this dying word of false thought is our sole proof of the Absolute Truth.

Can this be really the mystic's ultimate wisdom? No; the unconscious silence in which he ought forever to dwell, once broken by his first utterance when he teaches his doctrine, leads him to endless speech, — but to speech all of the same infinitely self-denying kind. The ineffable is ineffable. Therefore it is indeed "hard to frame, in matter-moulded forms of speech," the meaning of what has been won at the instant of the mystical vision. This difficult task is, in fact, a self-representative and infinite task. For it is the task of endless denial even of every previous act of denial. The only word as to the Absolute must be *Neti, Neti,* — It is not so, not so. But this only word needs endless repetition in new forms. The Absolute, if you will, was *not* well reported when we just gave, as the reason for the truth of the mystical insight, the fact that thought found itself at rest in the presence of God. For the thought really finds not *itself,* at all. It finds, as the truth, only its own Other. But in what way does it find its Other as the truth? Answer, By seeing, in the endless process of its own failure, the necessity of its own defeat, — the need of Another. So then — as we afresh observe — thought *does* know itself as a failure. It *does* represent to itself its own defeat. It does, then, learn, by a dialectic process, to comprehend its own lying nature. But herewith we return to our starting-point, and can only continue the same process without end.

In brief, mysticism turns upon a recognition of the failure of all thinking to grasp Reality. But this recognition is itself thought's own work. Thought is, so far, a system which represents to itself its own nature, — as a nature doomed to failure. If you try to express this recognition, however, not as thought's work, but as a direct revelation, in a merely immediate experience, of a final fact, you at once rediscover that this fact is final only if it is known, as in contrast to the failure of thought. The failure of thought must, therefore, once more be known to thought. But such self-knowledge on thought's part can only be won through the ineffable experience; and so you proceed back and forth without end. The reason for this particular endless chain is that mysticism turns upon a process whereby something, namely, thought, is to represent to itself its own negation and defeat. The consequence is a self-representative system of failure, in which every new attempt, based upon the failure of the former attempts to win the truth, itself involves the process of transcending the former failure by means of the very principle whose failure is to be observed.

And now, at last, let us ask, Does Mr. Bradley's Absolute escape the common fate of all of our conceptions of Being? Is Mr. Bradley's Absolute alone exempt from being a self-representative system of the type here in question?

I am obliged to answer this question in the negative. Mr. Bradley's account of the Absolute often comes near to the use of mystical formulations, but Mr. Bradley is of course no mystic; and nobody knows better than he the self-contradictions inherent in the effort to view the real as a simple unity, without real internal multiplicity. As we have seen, Mr. Bradley's Absolute is One, and yet does possess, as its own, all the manifoldness of the world of Appearance. The central difficulty of metaphysics, for Mr. Bradley, lies in the fact that we do not know *how*, in the Absolute, the One and the Many are reconciled. But that they both are in the Real is certain. Reality is explicitly called by Mr. Bradley a System. "We insist that all Reality must keep a certain character. The whole of its contents must be experience; they must come together into one system, and this unity itself must be experience. It must include and must harmonize every possible fragment of appearance" (*op. cit.*, p. 548). "Reality is one experience, self-pervading, and superior to mere relations" (p. 552). Now that Reality, while a "system," is to be viewed as experience, this assertion is due to Mr. Bradley's definition of what it is to be real. "I mean that to be real is to be indissolubly one with sentience. It is to be something which comes as a feature and aspect within one whole of feeling, something which, except as an integral aspect of such sentience, has no meaning at all" (p. 146). "You cannot find fact unless in unity with sentience, and one cannot in the end be divided from the other, either actually or in idea."

Now this account of the Absolute must of course be taken literally. It is not a speech about an Unknowable. It is, indeed, not an effort to tell how the unity is accomplished in detail. But it is a general, and by hypothesis a true account, of what the final unity must accomplish. We have therefore a right to observe that Mr. Bradley's Absolute, however much above our poor relational way of thinking its unity may be, really has two aspects that, although inseparable, are still distinguishable. The varieties of the world are somehow "absorbed," or "rearranged," in the unity of the Absolute Experience. This is one aspect. But the other aspect is that, since this absorption itself is real, — is a fact, — and since to be real is to be one with sentience, the fact *that* the absorption occurs, *that* the One and the Many are harmonized, and *that* the Absolute is what it is, is also a fact presented within the sentient experience of the Absolute. It is not, then, that the rivers of Appearance merely flow into the silent sea of Reality, and are there lost. No; this sentient Absolute, by hypothesis, feels, experiences, is aware, that it thus absorbs its differences. In general, whatever the Absolute is, its experience must make manifest to itself. For either this is true, or else Mr. Bradley's definition of Reality is meaningless. Let A be any character of the Absolute. Then the fact *that* A *is a character of the Absolute*, as such, and not of the mere appearances, is also a genuine fact. As such, it is a fact experienced.

The Absolute therefore must not merely *be A,* but experience itself, as possessing the character of *A.* It is, for instance, "above relations." If this is a fact, and if this statement is true of the Absolute, then the Absolute must experience that it is above relations. For Mr. Bradley's definition of Reality requires this consequence. The Absolute of Mr. Bradley must not, like the mystical Absolute, merely ignore the relations as illusion. It must experience their "transformation" as a fact, —and as its own fact. Or, again, the Absolute is that in which thought has been "taken up" and "transformed," so that it is no longer "mere thought." Well, this too is to be a fact. In consequence of Mr. Bradley's definition of what he means by the word "real," this fact must take its place amongst the totality of fact that is in its wholeness experienced. The Absolute, then, experiences itself as the absorber and transmuter of thought. Or, yet again, the Absolute is so much above "personality" that Mr. Bradley (p. 532) finds "intellectually dishonest" "most of those" who insist upon regarding the Absolute as personal. Well, this transcendence of personality is a fact. But "Reality must be one experience; and to doubt this conclusion is impossible." "Show me your idea of an Other, not a part of experience, and I will show you at once that it is, throughout and wholly, nothing else at all." Hence, the fact that the Absolute transcends personality is a fact that the Absolute itself experiences as its own fact, and is "nothing else at all" except such a fact.

As we have before learned, the category of the Self is far too base, in Mr. Bradley's opinion, to be Reality, and must be mere appearance. The Absolute, then, is above the Self, and above any form of mere selfhood. The fact that it is thus above selfhood is something "not other than experience"; but is wholly experience, and is the Absolute Experience itself. In fine, then, the Absolute, in Mr. Bradley's view, knows itself so well, — experiences so fully its own nature, — that it sees itself to be no Self, but to be a self-absorber, "self-pervading" to be sure (p. 552), and "self-existent,"[1] but aware

[1] "Our standard is Reality in the form of self-existence" (p. 375).

of itself, in the end, as something in which there is no real
Self to be aware of. Or, in other words, the Absolute is
really aware of itself as being not Reality, but Appearance,
just in so far as it is a Self. Meanwhile, of course, this Absolute experiences, also, the fact that it is an "individual"; that
it is a "system"; that it "holds all content in an individual
experience"; that "no feeling or thought of any kind can fall
outside its limits" (p. 147); that it "stands above and not
below its internal distinctions" (p. 533); that "it is not the
indifference, but the concrete identity of all extremes." For
all these statements are said by Mr. Bradley, in various places,
to be accounts of what the Absolute really is. But if the
Absolute is all these things, it can be so only in case it experiences itself as the possessor of these characters. Yet all the
concrete self-possession of the Absolute remains something
above Self; and apparently the Absolute thus knows itself to
be, as a Self, quite out of its own sight!

Now in vain does one endeavor to assert all this, and yet to
add that we know not *how*, in detail, all this can be true of
the Absolute. We know, at all events, that apart from what
is flatly self-contradictory in the foregoing expressions, Mr.
Bradley's Absolute is a self-representative system, which
views itself as the possessor of what, through all the unity,
remains still in one aspect another than itself, namely, the
whole world of Appearance. And we know, therefore, that
the Absolute, despite all Mr. Bradley's objections to the Self,
escapes from selfhood and from all that selfhood implies, or even
transcends selfhood, only by remaining to the end a Self. In
other words, it really escapes from selfhood in no genuine
fashion whatever. For it can escape from selfhood only by
experiencing, as its own, this, its own escape. This consequence is clear. Whatever is in the Absolute is experienced
doubly. Namely, *what* is there is experienced, and *that* this
content is experienced by the Absolute itself, — this final fact
is also experienced. Hence, the whole Absolute must be infinite in precisely Dedekind's positive sense of the term. Mr.
Bradley's Absolute is a *Kette* in the same sense as every other

fundamental metaphysical conception. For it is a self-experiencing and, therefore, self-representative system.

I conclude, then, so far, that by no device can we avoid conceiving the realm of Being as infinite in precisely the positive sense, now so fully illustrated. The Universe, as Subject-Object, contains a complete and perfect image, or view of itself. Hence it is, in structure, at once One, as a single system, and also an endless *Kette*. Its form is that of a Self. To observe this fact is simply to reflect upon the most elementary and fundamental implications of the concept of Being. The Logic of Being has, as a central theorem, the assertion, *Whatever is, is a part of a self-imaged system,* of the type herein discussed. This truth is common property for all, whether realists or idealists, whether sceptics or dogmatists. And hence our trivial illustration of the ideally perfect map of England within England, turns out to be, after all, a type and image of the universal constitution of things. I am obliged to regard this result as of the greatest weight for any metaphysical enterprise.[1] No philosophy that wholly ignores this clo-

---

[1] I was years ago much struck by the remarkable proof, in the first volume of Schroeder's *Algebra der Logik,* of the purely formal proposition that no simply constituted Universe of Discourse could be defined, in terms of the Algebra of Logic, as the absolute whole of Being, without an immediately stateable self-contradiction, resulting from the mere definition of the symbols used in that Algebra. See Schroeder, Vol. I, p. 245. The metaphysical interest of this purely symbolic result is not mentioned by Schroeder himself. The proof given by him turns, however, upon showing that if you regard provisionally, as the " whole of the universe," or as " all that is," any simply defined universe of classes of objects, you are confronted by contradictions as soon as you reflect that the " totality of what is " also contains a realm of secondary objects that you may define by reflecting upon the classes contained in the first universe, and by classifying these classes themselves from new points of view. This realm of secondary objects, however, does not consistently belong to the primary universe that in a purely formal way you first defined. The true totality of Being can therefore only be defined by an endless process, or is an endless reflective system. This proof of Schroeder's first brought home to me the fact that the necessity for defining reality in self-reflecting or endless terms is not dependent upon any one metaphysical interpreta-

mentary fact can be called rational. And hereby we have indeed found a sense in which the "endless fission" of Mr. Bradley's analysis expresses not mere Appearance but Being. Here is a law not only of Thought but also of Reality. Here is the true union of the One and the Many. Here is a multiplicity that is not "absorbed" or "transmuted," but retained by the Absolute. And it is a multiplicity of Individual facts that are still One in the Absolute.

Section IV. Infinity, Determinateness, and Individuality

Despite all the foregoing considerations, however, we have still to face the objection that, even if these constructions be regarded as self-evident products of Thought, they, nevertheless, simply cannot be genuinely true of the final nature of Reality and must somehow be fallacious. For, from Mr. Bradley's side, it would be maintained that however inevitable the seeming of these endless processes, they become self-contradictory precisely when you take them to be real and yet endless. For who knows not the Aristotelian arguments, so often repeated in later thought, against the actual Infinite? Is not the complete Infinite the very type of a logical "monster?" Is not the very conception a self-contradiction? If thought, then, has to conceive Reality as infinite, so much the worse, one may say, for thought. The Real, whatever its appearance, cannot in itself be endless.

I. *The Objections to the Actually Infinite*

It is necessary to consider such arguments by themselves, for the moment, and apart from the foregoing considerations. Let us, then, briefly develope some of these often repeated reasons on account of which so many assert that Reality cannot be an infinite system at all.

tion of the world, whether realistic or idealistic, but is the consequence of a purely abstract account of the formal Logic of the concept of Reality in any of its forms.

One may begin with the case as Aristotle first stated it, in the Third Book of the *Physics*, and elsewhere. There can, indeed, exist a Reality that permits us, if we choose to number its parts, to distinguish within it what we call elements, in such wise that *we* can never end the process of numbering them. So space is for us capable of infinite, that is, of indefinite division, *if* you choose to try to take it to pieces. But such divisibility is a mere possibility. Space, if real, is not endlessly divided. It is only *in potentia* divisible so far as you please to conceive its parts. The limitless exists, therefore, only *in potentia; λείπεται οὖν δυνάμει εἶναι τὸ ἄπειρον.* For were space actually either made up of endless parts, or in such wise real as to be infinitely great, there would result the contradiction of an actually infinite number as the number of the parts of a real collection. But a number actually infinite is contradictory; for it then could not be counted; it would have no determinate size; it would possess no totality; and it would so be formless and meaningless. Again, were any one portion of the world's material substance infinite, how could room be left for the other portions? Were the whole infinite, how could it be a whole at all? For any whole of reality is limited by its own form, and by the fact that, as an actual whole, it is perfectly determinate. The difficulty as to the infinite must be solved, then, by saying that what is real forms a definite and, for that reason, a finite totality; while within this totality there may be aspects which our thought discovers to be, in this or that respect, inexhaustible through any process of counting that follows some abstractly possible line of our own subjective distinctions or syntheses. We can say, of such aspects of the world, that you may go on as long as you please, in counting their special type of conceived complexities, without ever reaching the end. But this endlessness is potential only, and never actual.

These well-known Aristotelian considerations have formed the basis of every argument against the actual infinite in later thought. The special point of attack has, however, often shifted. In general, as the later arguments have repeatedly urged (quite in Aristotle's spirit), the infinitely complex, if real, must be knowable only through some finished synthesis of knowledge. But a finished synthesis is inconsistent (so one affirms) with the endlessness of the series of facts to be synthesized; and hence an infinite collection, if it existed, would be unknowable. On the other hand, an infinite collection, if real apart from knowledge, could be conceived to be altered by depriving it of some, or of a considerable fraction, of its constituent elements. The collection thus reduced (so one has often argued) would be at once finite (since it would have lost some of its members) and infinite, since no finite number would be equal to exhausting the remaining portion. Hence the reduced collection and, therefore, the original collection must be of a contradictory nature, and so impossible. In a variation of this argument often used, one employs, as an image, some such instance as an inextensible rod, one end of which shall be in my hands, while I shall be supposed to believe that the rod, which stretches out of my sight into the heavens, is infinitely long, as well as quite incapable of being anywhere stretched. Suppose the rod hereupon drawn, or, if you please, anyway mysteriously moved, a foot towards me at this end. If I am to believe in the infinity and inextensibility of the rod, I shall believe that the whole of the rod, and every part thereof, is now a foot nearer to me than before. But in that case the furthest portion of the rod must also be a foot nearer than before, or must have been "drawn in out of the infinite," as one writer has stated the case.[1] It can therefore no longer be an infinite rod. Hence, it was not actually infinite before the drawing in of this end.

All such arguments insist, either upon the supposed fact

---

[1] Constantin Gutberlet, *Zeitschrift für Philosophie* (*Ulrici-Falckenberg*), Bd. 92, Hft. II, p. 199. The wording of the example is a little different in the text cited. The force of the argument no longer exists for one who approaches the concept of the Infinite through that of the *Kette*. Cantor observes as much in his answer to Gutberlet in the same journal. The puzzle turns upon falsely identifying the properties of finite and infinite quantities.

that our own conception of an infinite series is necessarily a conception of an indefinite and, therefore, of an essentially incomplete sequence, or else upon the assertion that an infinite collection, if viewed as real, would prove to be in itself of a quantitatively indefinite and changeable character. In the one case, the argument continues by showing that an indefinite and incomplete sequence is incapable of being taken to be a finished reality beyond our thought. In the other case, one insists that the quantitatively indefinite collection, if viewed as real, would stand in conflict with the very notion of reality, since the real is, as such, the determinate. "The essence of number," says Mr. Bosanquet,[1] "is to construct a finite whole out of homogeneous units." "An infinite number would be a number which is no particular number; for every particular number is finite." "An infinite series[2] . . . is not anything which we can represent in the form of number, and therefore cannot be, *quâ* infinite series, a fact in our world. . . . Our constructive judgment requires parts *and* a whole to give it meaning. Parts unrelated to any whole cannot be judged real by our thought. Their significance is gone and they are parts of nothing."

More detailed, in the application of the general charge of indefiniteness thus made against the conception of the infinite collections, are the often used arguments such as exemplify how, if infinite collections are possible at all, one infinite must be greater than another, while yet, as infinite and determinate, all the boundless collections must (so one supposes) be equal. Or, again, in a similar spirit, one has pointed out that, by virtue of the properties which we have deliberately attributed to the *Ketten* of the foregoing discussion, two infinite collections, if they existed, would be, in various senses of the term *equal*, at once equal and unequal to each other, or would

---

[1] *Logic*, I, p. 175. We have already seen how imperfect this view of the number-series is, since the number-series, as a product of thought, is primarily ordinal, and its essence is to express, very abstractly, the orderly development of a reflective purpose.

[2] *Loc. cit.*, p. 177.

contradict the axiom as to the whole and the part.[1] These
arguments can be illustrated by an endless list of examples,
drawn from the realm of discrete collections of objects, as well
as from cases where limitless extended lines, surfaces, or
volumes are in question, and from cases where limitless divisibility is to be exemplified. The variety of the examples, however, need not confuse one as to the main issue. What is
brought out, in every case, is that the infinite collections or
multitudes, if real at all, must be in paradoxical contrast to
all finite multitudes, and must also be in such contrast as to
seem, at first sight, either quite indeterminate or else hopelessly incomplete, and, in either case, incapable of reality.

Upon a somewhat different basis rest a series of arguments
which have more novelty, just because they are due to the experience of the modern exact sciences. In the seventeenth century one of the greatest methodical advances ever made in the
history of descriptive science occurred, when the so-called
Infinitesimal Calculus was invented. The Newtonian name,
Fluxions, used for the objects to whose calculation the new
science was devoted, indicated better than much of the more
recent terminology, that one principal purpose of this advance
in method, was to enable mathematical exactness to be used in
the description of continuously varying quantities. But the
generalization which was made when the Calculus appeared had
been the outcome of a long series of studies of quantity, both
temporal and spatial. And the Calculus brought under one
method of treatment, not only the problems about continuous
processes of actual change, such as motions, or other continuous physical alterations, but also problems regarding the properties, the relations, the lengths, and the areas of curves, and

---

[1] Couturat, in his dialectical discussion between the "finitist" and the
"infinitist," in *L'Infini Mathematique*, p. 443 *sqq.*, gives full room to a
statement of these arguments of his opponents. Our account of the
Ketten has discounted them in advance. Dedekind's Definition of the
Infinite deliberately makes naught of them. If infinite multitudes corresponding to his definition can be proved real, these paradoxes will be
simply obvious properties of such multitudes.

regarding the corresponding features of geometrical surfaces and solids. For, in all these objects alike, either continuous alterations, or else characters that, although matters of spatial coexistence, may be ideally expressed in terms of such continuous alterations, fell within the range of the methods of the Calculus.

The new method, however, seemed to involve, at first, the conception both of "infinitely small" quantities, and of devices whereby an "infinite number" of such quantities could be summed together, or otherwise submitted to computation. The science of the continuous, in the realm of geometrical forms, as well as in the realm of physical changes, thus seemed to depend upon the conception both of the infinitely small and of the infinitely great; and the successful application of the results of such science in the realm of physics, was sometimes used as a proof that nature contains actually infinite and actually infinitesimal collections or magnitudes. But the early methods of the Infinitesimal Calculus were not free from inexactness, and led, upon occasion, to actually false conclusions. Hence, the paradoxes apparently involved in the logical bases of the science attracted more and more critical attention, as time went on; and, as a consequence, within the present century, the whole method of the Calculus has been repeatedly and carefully revised, — with the result, to be sure, that the conceptions of the actually infinite, in the sense here in question, and the actually infinitesimal (in the older sense of the term), have been banished from the principal modern text-books of both the Differential and the Integral Calculus. The terms, "Infinite" and "Infinitesimal," have been, indeed, very generally retained in such text-books for the sake of conciseness of expression; but with a definition that wholly avoids all the problems which our foregoing discussion has raised. The infinite and the infinitesimal of the Calculus can, therefore, no longer be cited in favor of a theory of the "actually Infinite."

In the world of varying quantities, namely, it often happens that, by the terms of definition of a given problem, you have upon your hands a varying quantity (call it X) which, consistently with these terms, you are able to make, or to assume, as large as you please. In such cases, if some one *else* is supposed to have predesignated, as the value of X, any definite magnitude that he pleases, say X_1, then you are at liberty, under the conditions of the problem, to assume the value of X as larger still, *i.e.* as greater than any such *previously assigned* definite value X_1. Now, whenever the variable X has this character, in a given problem, then, according to the fashion of speech used in the Calculus, you may define X either simply as infinite, or as *capable of being increased to infinity;* and in the Calculus you are indeed often enough interested in learning what happens to some quantity whose value depends upon X, when X thus increases without limit, or, as they briefly say, *becomes* infinite. But in all such cases the term *infinite*, as used in the modern text-books of the Calculus, is, by definition, simply an abbreviation for the whole conception just defined. The variable X need not even be, at any moment, actually at all large in order to be, in this sense, infinite. It only so varies that, consistently with the conditions of the problem, it can be made larger than a predesignated value, whatever that value may be. And the Calculus is simply often interested in computing the consequences of such a manner of variation on the part of X.

Now, unquestionably a quantity that is called infinite in this sense is not the actually infinite against which Aristotle argued. It is merely the limitlessly increasing variable or the potentially infinite magnitude which he willingly admitted as a valid conception. A parallel definition of the infinitesimal is even more frequently employed in the modern text-books of the Calculus, just because the infinitesimal is mentioned more frequently than the infinite. In this sense, a variable magnitude is infinitesimal merely *when it can be made and kept as small as we will,* consistently with the conditions of the problem in which it appears. Thus neither the infinite nor the infinitesimal of the modern treatment of the Calculus has any fixed character, as a finished or finally given quantity, nor any character which could be defined as a determinately real somewhat, apart from our defining thought, and apart from the conditions of a given problem. The Calculus is deeply interested in computing results of such variation without limit; but as a branch of mathematics, it is, in fact, not at all directly interested in our present problem about the actually infinite.[1]

Now, this result of the whole experience of the students of the Calculus with the logic of their own science, — this outcome of the modern critical restudy of the bases of the science of the continuously variable quantities, — tends of itself to indicate (as one may say, and as objectors to the actually Infinite have often said) that the conception of the actually Infinite, formerly confounded with the conceptions lying at the bases of the Calculus, is, as a fact, not only in this region, but everywhere, scientifically superfluous; while the conception of the Infinite merely *in potentia*, originally defended by Aristotle, thus triumphs in the very realm where, for a time, its rival seemed to have found a firm foothold.[2]

Yet it has indeed to be observed that, from the mathematical point of view, not the questions of the Calculus, but certain decidedly special problems of the Theory of Numbers, and of the modern Theory of Functions, have given the mathematical basis for these newer efforts towards an exact and positive definition of the Infinite. As a fact, in our foregoing statement of the merely *prima facie* case for the recent definition of the positively Infinite, we have deliberately re-

[1] All this is not only admitted, but insisted upon by Cantor himself, as a preliminary to his own discussion of *das Eigentlich-Unendliche*, which he sharply distinguishes from such *Uneigentlicher* concept of the Infinite as has to be used in the Calculus. See his separately published *Grundzüge einer allgemeinen Mannigfaltigkeitslehre* (Leipzig, 1883), p. 1, *sqq.* Compare the statement in Professor Franz Meyer's lecture, before cited, to the same effect.

[2] This line of argument against the Infinite has often been used, — most recently perhaps by F. Evellin, in his two articles directed against the metaphysical use of Cantor's theories, in the *Revue Philosophique* for February and November, 1898.

frained from making any mention of the special problems about continuity, or of the conceptions of the Calculus. And it has also been noted that Cantor, who has done so much to make specific the positive concept of *das Eigentlich-Unendliche*, and who has also given us one of the very first of the exact definitions of continuous quantity ever discovered, — himself *rejects* the actually infinitesimal quantities as quite impossible; and does so quite as vigorously as he accepts and defends the actually infinite quantities; so that he fully agrees that the infinitesimal must remain where the Calculus leaves it, namely, simply the variable *small at will*.[1] It must therefore be distinctly understood that, in the discussion of the reality of the infinite quantities and multitudes, appeal need no longer be made to the conceptions of quantity peculiar to the Calculus; while, in general, the majority of those concerned in this inquiry expressly admit that the logic of the Calculus is quite independent of the present issue, and that the infinite of the Calculus is simply the variable *large at will*, which therefore need not be at any moment, even notably large at all.[2]

And now, finally, there is also urged against any conception of the actually Infinite the well-known consideration that the conception of such infinity involves an empty and worthless repetition of the same, over and over, — a mere " counting when there is nothing to count," or, in the realm of explicit reflection, a vain observation that *I am I*, and that *I am I*, again, even in saying that *I am I*, — or an equally inane insistence

---

[1] See Cantor's statement in the *Zeitschr f. Philos.*, Bd. 88, p. 230 ; and in the same journal, Bd. 91, p. 112, in a passage there quoted from a letter addressed by Cantor to Weierstrass. I am unable to understand how Mr. Charles Peirce, in his paper in the *Monist* (1892, p. 537 of Vol. 2) is led to attribute to Cantor his own opinion as to the infinitesimals.

[2] Mr. Charles Peirce, as I understand his statements in the *Monist* (*loc. cit.*), appears to stand almost alone amongst recent mathematical logicians outside of Italy, in still regarding the Calculus as properly to be founded upon the conception of the actually infinite and infinitesimal. In Italy, Veronese has used in his Geometry the concept of the actually infinitesimal.

that *I know,* and *know that I know,* and so on. The non-mathematical often dislike numbers, especially the large ones, and therefore easily make light of a wisdom that seems only to count, in monotonous inefficacy. Even the more reflective thinkers often believe, with Spinoza, that *knowing that I know* can imply nothing essentially new, at all events after the reflection has been two or three times repeated. The Hindoo imagination, with its love for large numbers, often strikes the Western mind as childish. And in all such cases, since mere size, as such, rightly seems unworthy of the admiration that it has excited in untrained minds, it has appeared to many to be the more rational thing to say that wisdom involves rather Hegel's *Rückkehr aus der unendlichen Flucht* than any acceptance of the notion that infinite magnitudes or multitudes can be real.

II. *The Infinite as One Aspect only of Being*

All the foregoing objections to the conception of the actually infinite rest, in large measure, upon a true and perfectly relevant principle. As a fact, what is real is *ipso facto* determinate and individual. It is this for the reasons pointed out in the closing lectures of the present series. It is this because it is such that *No Other* can take its place. The Real is the final, the determinate, the totality. And now, not only is this principle valid, but it is indeed supreme in every metaphysical inquiry. And therefore we shall, to be sure, find it true that in case, despite all the foregoing highly important objections, we succeed in reconciling infinity with determinateness, we shall still be unable to assert that the Reality is anything *merely* infinite. For infinity, as such, is at best a character, — a feature having the value of an universal. If the Absolute is in any sense an infinite system, it is certainly also an unique and individual system; and its uniqueness involves something very clearly distinguishable from its mere infinity. The Absolute is, in its determinate Reality, certainly exclusive of an infinity of mere possibilities. In this respect I shall here simply repeat the position taken in the discussion supplementary to the book called the *Conception of God*.[1] It is, then, perfectly true, for me, as for the opponents of the actual Infinite, that much must be viewed as, in the abstract, "possible," which is nowhere determinately presented in any final experience of the fulfilment of truth. The special illustration used, in my former book, to exemplify this fact, namely, the illustration of the points on the continuous line, — points which are "possible" in an infinitely infinite collection of ways, but which, however presented, cannot exhaustively constitute the determinate continuity of the line, — this, I say, is an illustration involving other problems besides those of the actual Infinite. The existence of the line, taken as a geometrical fact, contains more than the possible multitudes of multitudes of the points on the line can ever express. And this *more* includes, also, a something more *determinate* than the multitudes of the points can conceivably present. Hence, as I argued in my former book, and as I still deliberately maintain, the Absolute *cannot* experience the nature of the line by *merely* exhausting any infinitude of the points. But to this illustration I can here devote no further space, since the discussion of continuity, and especially of the geometrical *continuum*, lies outside of the scope of this paper. It is quite consistent, however, to hold, as I do, that while the Absolute indeed, by reason of its determinateness, excludes and must exclude infinitely infinite "bare possibilities," known to mere thought, from presentation in any individual way, except as ideas of excluded objects, the Absolute still finds present, in the individual whole of its Selfhood, an actually infinite, *because self-representative*, system of experienced fact. The points on the line, then, if my former illustration is indeed well chosen, are not exhaustively presented, *as constituting the whole line*, in any experience, whatever, Absolute or relative. But this, as we now have to see, is not because the actually Infinite is, to the Absolute, something unrepresented, but because the determinate geometrical continuity of the individual line is something more, and more determinate, than any infinitude of

[1] New York, 1897, p. 194, *sqq.*

points can express. And this individuality of the line I can and do express by saying that, even to a final view, the essence of the individual continuity of any one line involves the "bare possibility" of systems of ideal points over and above any that are found present in this final experience of the line. *Even if* the Absolute, then, observes infinitely infinite collections of points, it sees that the individual continuity of the line is more than they present. This I still assert.

In general, as we shall see, by virtue of what here follows, a fair account of the completeness of the Absolute must be just to *two* aspects. They are the ultimate aspects of Reality. Their union constitutes, once more, the world-knot. And the reason of their union is the one made explicit in our seventh Lecture. The Real is determinate and individual; and the Real is expressive of all that universal ideas, taken in their wholeness, actually demand, or mean, as their absolutely satisfactory fulfilment. In this twofold thesis, as I understand, I am wholly in agreement with Mr. Bradley. But I differ from him by maintaining that we know more than he admits concerning *how* the Real combines these two aspects. I maintain, then, with a full consciousness of the paradoxes involved, that the Reality is indeed a Self, whatever else it is or is not. For the Absolute, as I insist, would have to be not apparently, but really a Self, even in order to be (as Mr. Bradley seems to imagine his Absolute) a sort of self-absorbing sponge, that endlessly sucked in, and "transformed," its own selfhood, until nothing was left of itself but the mere empty spaces where the absorbent Self had been. For the category of Self is indeed immortal. Deny it, and, in denying, you affirm it. As a fact, however, the Absolute is no sponge. It is not a cryptic or self-ashamed, but an absolutely self-expressive self. And to see how it can be so without contradiction, is simply to see how the concept of the actually Infinite, despite all the foregoing objections, is not self-contradictory, is not indeterminate, is not merely based upon wearisome reflections of the same; but is a positive and concrete conception, quite capable of individual embodiment. This is what we shall see in what here follows. The concept of the actually Infinite once in general vindicated from the charge of self-contradiction, all objection to conceiving the Absolute as a Self will vanish; and the transparent union of the One and the Many, which reflective thought has already shown us within its own realm, will become the universal law of Being.

But, on the other hand, if the Absolute is a Self, and, as such, an Infinite, this does not mean that it is anything you please, or that it is at once all possible things, or that it views its realm of fact as having all possible characters at once, and hence as having no character in particular. This Self, and *no Other*, this world and *no Other*, this totality of experience, and *nothing else*, — such is what has to be presented when the Real is known as the real. The Infinite will have to be *also* a determinate Infinite, a self-selected case of its type. For the world as merely thought, or as merely defined in idea, is the world viewed with an abstract or bare universality, and as that which still demands its Other, and which refers to that Other as valid and possible. The world of thought is, as such, an effort to characterize this Other, to imitate it, to correspond to it, and, of course, if so may be, to find it. Hence the world of mere thought has, as its very life, a principle of dissatisfaction; and when it conceives its object as the Truth, it defines, in the object, only the sense in which there is to be agreement or correspondence between the object and the thought. Consequently, an idea taken merely as an imitation of another, or taken as having an external meaning, expresses the Truth only as a barely universal validity. And one who merely takes thought as thought conceives the shadow land which shall, nevertheless, somehow have the value of a standard. In that realm, — the realm of mere validity, — all is mere character, and type, and possibility. And thought is the endlessly restless definition of another, and yet another. And this is true even when thought conceives an Infinite. Hence, infinity, as merely conceived, is indeed not yet Reality as Reality.

Now, the opponents of the actual Infinite, ever since Aristotle, have always seen, and rightly seen, that, as defined by

mere thinking about external meanings, the world is not finally
defined. The restlessly infinite, as such, they have condemned
as in so far unreal. For whoever sees reality, sees that which
has *no Other* like itself, which seeks no Other to define its
being, which is itself no mere correspondence between one
object and another, and, despite its unquestionable character
as the fulfilment of thought, no mere agreement between a
thought and a fact. The Real, then, has not the character
which bare thought, as such, emphasizes, — the character of
being essentially incomplete. It has wholeness. Its meaning
is internal and not external. Therefore, it is indeed a finished
fact. It cannot, then, be infinite *if* infinity implies incompleteness.

But, once more, is the Real for that reason finite? Because
it excludes the search for another beyond itself, does it therefore contain no infinite wealth of presented content within
itself? This is precisely the question. In emphasizing the
exclusiveness of the Real we must be just to the fact that,
whatever it excludes, it cannot, from our point of view, be
poorer, less wealthy, less manifold in genuine meaning, than
the false Other, which its reality reduces to a bare and unrealized possibility of thought. That the world is what it
determinately is, means, from our point of view, that its being
excludes an infinitely complex system of "barely possible"
other contents, which, just because they are excluded from
Reality, are conceived by a thought such that not all of its
"barely possible" ideal objects could conceivably be actualized
at once. In this sense, for us, just as for the partisans of the
barely possible and unactualized infinite, there are indeed
ideas of infinitely numerous facts which remain, from an
Absolute point of view, hypotheses contrary to fact.[1] We
agree, moreover, with our opponents, that no process expresses
reality in so far as this process *merely* seeks, without end, for
another and another object or fact. Hence, for us, as for our
opponents, the Infinite, when taken merely as an endless

[1] See *Conception of God*, pp. 196, 198, 201, 213–214. See also the
concluding lecture of the present series.

process, is falsely taken. As merely that which you cannot exhaust by counting, the Infinite is, by the hypothesis, never found, presented or completed, so long as you simply count. Hence we wholly agree that the Infinite, just in so far as it is viewed as indeterminate, incomplete, or *merely* endless, is not rightly viewed; and that in so far it is indeed unreal. We also fully agree that Absolute knowledge unquestionably recognizes, as an object for its own relatively abstract thought, a distinctly *un*real Infinite, namely, the Infinite of the excluded ideal "bare possibilities" aforesaid. In all this we quite agree with our opponents, and prize their insistence upon the determinateness of the final truth.

Nevertheless, we shall perforce insist upon these theses:—

(1) The true Infinite, both in multitude and in organization, although in one sense endless, and so incapable *in that sense* of being completely grasped, is in another and precise sense something perfectly determinate. Nor is it a mere monotonous repetition of the same, over and over. Each of its determinations has individuality, uniqueness, and novelty about its own nature.

(2) This determinateness is a character which, indeed, includes and involves the endlessness of an infinite series; but the mere endlessness of the series is not its primary character, being simply a negatively stated result of the self-representative character of the whole system.

(3) The endlessness of the series means that by *no* merely successive process of counting, in God or in man, is its wholeness ever exhausted.

(4) In consequence, the whole endless series, in so far as it is a reality, must be present, as a determinate order, but also *all at once*, to the Absolute Experience. It is the process of successive counting, as such, that remains, to the end, incomplete, so as to imply that its own possibilities are not yet realized. Hence, the recurrent processes of thought reveal eternal truth about the infinite constitution of real Being,— their everlasting pursued Other; but themselves,—as mere processes in time,— they are not that Other. Their true Other

is, therefore, that self-representative System of which they are at once portions, imitations, and expressions.

(5) The Reality is such a self-represented and infinite system. And therein lies the basis of its very union, within itself of the One and the Many. For the one purpose of self-representation demands an infinite multiplicity to express it; while no multiplicity is reducible to unity except through processes involving self-representation.

(6) And, nevertheless, the Real is exclusive as well as inclusive. On the side of its thought the Absolute does conceive a barely possible infinity, other than the real infinity, — a possible world, whose characters, as universal characters, are present to the Absolute, and are known by virtue of the fact that the Absolute also thinks. But these possibilities are excluded by reason of their conflict with the Absolute Will.

(7) Yet, in meaning, the infinite Reality, as present, is richer than the infinity of bare possibilities that are excluded. But for that very reason the Reality presented, in the final and determinate experience of the Absolute, cannot be less than infinitely wealthy, both in its content and in its order. Its unity in its wholeness, and its infinite variety in expression, are both of an individual character. The constituent individuals are not "absorbed" or "transmuted" in the whole. The whole is One Self; but therefore is all its own constitution equally necessary to its Selfhood. Hence it is an Individual of Individuals.

With less of complexity and, if you please, with less of paradox, no theory of Being can be rendered coherent. Our present purpose is to bring these various aspects of the twofold nature of Being, as Infinite Being and as Determinate Being, to light and to definition.

We shall return, therefore, to the consideration of the main points made by our objectors, and, as we meet them shall even thereby justify, without needing formally to repeat, our various theses.

III. *The Infinite as Determinate*

The principal one amongst all the traditional objections to
the Infinite is, as we have seen, the thought that the Infinite,
as such, is merely an endlessly sought or an endlessly incomplete somewhat; while the real, as such, is very rightly to be
viewed as the determinate. Hence, the actually Infinite, one
insists, would be at once determinate and indeterminate, and
so would be contradictory.

Now, whatever may be said about the actually Infinite, we
have already seen that the infinite of the merely conceptual
but valid type, the infinite of the realm of mathematical possibilities, is certainly as determinate a conception as any merely
universal idea can ever be, and, as thus determinate, involves
no contradiction whatever. Cling to our Third Conception of
Reality; and then, indeed, there can be no doubt whatever that
the Infinite is real. For there is no contradiction, there is
only a necessarily valid truth involved in saying that to *any*
whole number r, however large, there inevitably does correspond *one* number, and *only* one, which stands amongst all
numbers as the rth member in the ordered series of whole
numbers that are squares, or in the ordered series of the cubes,
or in the ordered series, if you please, of numbers of the form
of a^{100} or a^{1000}, where the exponent is fixed, but where the
number that is to be raised to the power indicated takes successively the series of values, 1, 2, 3, . , . r. The inevitable
result is that to *every* whole number r, without a possible exception, there corresponds, in the realm of validity, and corresponds uniquely, just that particular whole number which
you get if you raise r to the second, third, or hundredth, or
thousandth power. Moreover, this ideal ordering of all the
whole numbers, without exception, in a one-to-one relation (let
us say) to their own thousandth powers, is in such wise predetermined by the very nature of number that, if you undertake to calculate the thousandth power (let us say) of the
number 80,000,000, your result is in no wise left to you, as a
bare possibility that your private will can capriciously decide.

The result is lawfully fixed beforehand by the very essence of mathematical validity, *i.e.* by the very expression of your own final Will in its wholeness. Your calculation can only bring this result to light in your own private experience of numbers. It is an arithmetically true result quite apart from your instantaneous observation. Its triviality, as a mere matter for computation, is not now in question. Its eternal validity, however, interests us. Every number, then, speaking in terms of mathematical validity, already *has* its own thousandth power, whether you chance to have observed or to have computed that thousandth power or not. Yet, in any *finite* collection of whole numbers, those which are the thousandth powers of the whole numbers constitute at most an incomparably minute part of the whole collection. But, on the other hand, viewed with reference to the logically valid truth about all the numbers, these powers, as a mere *part* of the whole series of whole numbers, still occupy such a logically predetermined place that they are set, by their values, in a one-to-one relation to the members of the whole series; so that *not* a small portion, but absolutely *all* of the whole numbers, have their correspondents among the thousandth powers. Now, all these are facts of thought, just as valid as any conceptual constructions, however simple, and just as true as that $2 + 2 = 4$. And by themselves these truths, trivial if you please, are, in all their wearisomeness, not "monstrous" at all, but simply the necessary consequences of an exact conception of the nature of number.

"Monstrous, however," so one may reply, "would be the assertion that in any *real* world there could be determinate facts corresponding to all this merely ideal complexity." On the contrary, as we might at once retort, it would be monstrous if all these truths were *merely* "valid," in a purely formal way, without any correspondent facts whatever in the real world. Can mere validity hang in the void? Must it not possess a determinate basis?

The issue, then, is at once the issue about the Third Conception of Being in our list. Either the truth, the world of mere forms, can indeed hang in the void, valid, but nowhere concrete, or else, just because the infinite is valid, it has its place, as fact, in the determinate experience of the Absolute. At all events, the Infinite, in such cases as have just been cited, is something quite as determinately valid as any barely universal conception can be. And unless it is true that two and two would make four in a world where no experience ever observed the fact, it is true that the infinitely numerous properties of the numbers need some concrete representation.⤙

I grant, however, that these are but preliminary considerations. Every validity, as a bare universal, must be a reflectively abstract expression of a fact that ultimately exists in individual embodiment in the Absolute. Yet, on the other hand, you cannot predetermine the nature of this individual expression *merely* by pointing out that the possibilities in question appear to us endless. For the endlessness might be one of those matters of bare external conjunction of which Mr. Bradley so often speaks. Thus space appears to us endless. I fully grant that we are not warranted in making any one assertion about the Absolute view of the meaning of our spatial experience, by virtue of the mere fact that going on and on endlessly in space appears to us possible, and that, consequently, we can define propositions that would be valid if this possibility is endlessly realized by the Absolute. In passing from the Third to the Fourth Conception of Being, what we did was to see that nothing can be valid unless a determinate individual experience has present to it all that gives warrant for this validity. Because our fleeting experience never gives such final warrant, we are forced to seek for the ground and the basis of any valid truth once recognized by us, and to seek this basis in a realm that is Other than our own experience as it comes to us. This Other is, finally, the Absolute in its wholeness. But we do not assert that the Absolute realizes our validity merely as we happen to think it.

When we regard any valid truth as implying a variety of valid assertions, all for us matters of conceived possible experience, we often take the Many, thus conceived by us, as a mere fact, an uncomprehended "conjunction." I agree altogether with

Mr. Bradley that such varieties might seem, to a higher experience, artificial, and that, as such, they might be "transmuted" even in coming to their unity in the higher view. For in such cases we never experience that these varieties are self-evidently what they seem to us. And our conception that they are many is associated with a confession of ignorance as to what they are. A good example of all this is furnished by our conception of what our own lives, or the course of human history, would have been, if certain critical events had never taken place.[1] What, in such instances, we have on our hands is an ignorance as to the whole ground and meaning of the critical events themselves. A fuller knowedge of what they meant might render much of our speech about the "possibilities" in question obviously vain.

Determinate decisions of the will involve rendering invalid countless possibilities that, but for this choice, might have been entertained as valid. In such cases the nature of the rejected possibilities is sufficiently expressed, in concrete form, by the will that decides, *if only it knows itself as deciding, and is fully conscious of how and why it decides.* That Absolute insight would mean absolute decision, and so a refusal to get presented in experience endlessly numerous contents that, but for the decision, would have been possible, — this I maintain as a necessary aspect of the whole conception of individuality. Whoever knows not decisions that exclude, knows not Being. For apart from such exclusion of possibilities, one would face barely abstract universals, and would, therefore, still seek for Another. Our whole conception of Being agrees, then, with Mr. Bradley's in insisting that the bare *what*, the idea as a mere thought, still pursuing, and imitatively characterizing its Other, not only does not face Being as Being, but can never, of itself, decide what its own final expression shall be. Thought must win satisfaction not as mere Thought, but also as decisive Will, determining itself to final expression in a way that the abstract universals of

[1] On such possibilities, "counter to fact," see again the discussion in the *Conception of God, loc. cit.*, and in later passages of the same essay.

mere thinking can characterize, but never exhaust. Thus, and thus only, can be found that which admits of no Other. So far, then, it is indeed true that nothing is proved real merely by proving its abstract consistency as a mere idea taken apart from the rest of the world.

Or, again, the realm of validity is not exhausted by presented fact in the way suggested by one of Amadeus Hoffman's most horrible fancies (I believe in the *Elixiere des Teufels*), according to which a hero, persistently beset by a double, always finds that, whenever he, in his relative strength, resists a great temptation, and avoids a crime, this miserable double, whom he all the while vaguely takes to be in a way himself, appears, — pale, wretched, fate-driven, — and does, or at least attempts, in very fact, the deed that the hero had rejected. No; whoever knows Being, finds himself satisfied in the presence of a will fulfilled, and needs no fate-driven other Self, no outcast double, to realize for him the possibilities whose validity he rejects. For in rejecting, he wins. And Being is a destruction as well as an accomplishment of Experience.

Upon all this I have elsewhere insisted. That the very essence of individuality is a Will that permits no Other to take the place of *this* fulfilment, — a Love that finds in *this* wholeness of life its own, — I have pointed out in an argument that the Tenth Lecture of the present course has merely summarized.[1] And therefore I am perfectly prepared to admit that when we define as valid, in the realm of mathematical truth, an infinite wealth of ideal forms, we need not, on that account alone, and apart from other reasons, declare that the Absolute Life realizes these forms in their variety as defined by us. Their true meaning it must somehow get present to itself, — otherwise it would face Another of which it was essentially ignorant. But its realization of their meaning may well imply an exclusion of their variety, just in so far as that variety, when conceived by us, expresses our ignorance of

[1] See the *Conception of God*, Supplementary Essay, Part III, especially pp. 247-270. Compare Part IV, pp. 303-315.

what principle of multiplicity is here at work, of how the One and the Many here concerned are related, and of what decision of Will would give these forms a concrete meaning in the universal life.

It remains, then, returning to the typical case of the numbers, to see in what sense a determinate expression of their whole meaning can be found in the life of a Will that fulfils itself through exclusive decisions, but that does not ignore any genuinely significant aspect of the truth. For our Absolute is not in such wise exclusive of content as to impoverish its wealth of ideal characters; and, on the other hand, it is not in such wise inclusive of bare possibilities as to oppose to whatever fact it chooses as its own, the fatal Other deed of Amadeus Hoffman's double-willed and distracted hero.

And here, of course, an opponent of the actual Infinite will be ready with the very common observation that the numbers are indeed, apart from the concrete objects numbered, of a trivial validity. "In a life," he may say, "in a world of decisions and of concrete values, a barren contemplation of the properties of the numbers can have but a narrow place. Hence, no fulfilment of the hopeless task of wandering from number to number need be expected as a part of the Absolute life."

Moreover, such an objector will insist that all these *Ketten* involve mere repetition of the same sort of experience over and over. "To carry such repetition to the infinite end, — what purpose," he will say, "can such an ideal fulfil?" The individual fulfilment of the meaning of the number-series, in the final view, may well, then, take the form of knowing that there are indeed numbers, that they are made in a certain way, that the plan of their order has a particular type, and that this type is exemplified thus and thus by a comparatively few concretely presented ideas of whole numbers. Otherwise, the numbers may be left as unrealized as are those other excluded possibilities of the Will exemplified.

But against this view one has next to point out that, observed a little more closely, even the numbers have characters not reducible to any limited collection of universal types.

They do not prove to be a monotonous series of contents, involving mere repetition of the same ideas. On the contrary, to know them at all well, is to find in them properties involving the most varied and novel features, as you pass from number to number, or bring into synthesis various selected groups of numbers. Consider, for instance, the prime numbers. Distributed through the number-series in ways that are indeed capable of partial definition through general formulas, they still conform to no single known principle that enables us to determine, *a priori*, and in merely universal terms, exactly what and where each prime shall be. They have been discovered by an essentially empirical process which has now been extended, by the tabulators of the prime numbers, far into the millions. Yet the process much resembles any other empirical process. Its results are reported by the tabulators as the astronomers catalogue the stars. The primes have, as it were, relatively individual characters,[1] which cannot be reduced to any barren repetition of the same thing over and over. One may call them uninteresting. But one must not judge the truth by one's private dislike of mathematics, just as, of course, one must not exaggerate the importance of mere forms. Here, then, is one instance of endless novelty within the number-series.

But the real question is, How shall the genuine meaning of all this series of truths be in any way grasped, *unless* the insight which grasps is adequate to the endless wealth of novel, and relatively individual truth that the various numbers present as one passes on in the series? For the will cannot consciously decide against the further realization of certain types of possibility, unless it clearly knows their value. And this it must know in exhaustive, even if ideal and abstractly universal terms. Nobody can fairly tell what value in life numerical truth may possess, unless he first knows that truth. And the numbers whose ordered rationality is, for us men, the very basis of our exact science, show a wealth of truth

---

[1] Of course they are in no sense true individuals, but taken as members of their series, they have relatively unique features.

that we find more and more baffling the further we go. The "perfect numbers" form a series that may be as full of interest, for all that I know, as the primes. The properties of the "Arithmetical Triangle" are linked in the most unexpected fashion with the laws of our statistical science, and with the nature of certain orderly combinations of vast importance in other branches of mathematical inquiry. Countless other combinations of numbers form topics, not only of numerous well-known plays and puzzles, but of scientific investigations whose character is actually adventurous, — so arduous is their course, and so full of unexpected bearings upon other branches of knowledge has been their outcome. Nobody amongst us can pretend to fathom the value for concrete science, and for life, that has yet to be derived from advances in the Theory of Numbers.

These, then, are mere hints of the inexhaustible properties of the number-series. I speak still as layman; but I am convinced that these significant properties are quite as inexhaustible as the number-series itself. Now, the value of such properties you can never tell until you see what they are. Their meaning in the life of reason can only be estimated when they are present. Hence, you can never wisely decide *not* to know them until you have first known them. But they are not to be known merely as the endless repetitions of the same over and over. Hence it is wholly vain to say, "Numbers come from counting, and counting is vain repetition of the same over and over." Whoever views the numbers merely thus, knows not whereof he speaks. It is not "counting, with nothing to count"; it is finding what Order means, that is the task of a true Theory of Numbers.

As a fact, then, the number-series in its wholeness seems to be a realm not only of inexhaustible truth, but of a truth that possesses an everywhere relatively individual type. And its validity has relations that we, at present, but imperfectly know, and a rational value that appears to be fundamental in every orderly inquiry.

We can, then, neither assert that to all the varieties which

our thought may chance to conceive as possible, there correspond just as many final facts for an Absolute Experience; nor
yet can we, on the other hand, exclude from concrete presentation, as final facts, such wholes as include an infinite series,
merely because, for us, if we do not take due account of mathematical truth, the series seems to involve the empty repetition
of "one more" and "one more." For, as Poincaré has so
finely pointed out, in the article before cited, it is precisely the
"reasoning by recurrence" which is, in mathematics, the endless source of new results. Hereby, in the combination of
his previous results for the sake of new insight, the mathematician is preserved from mere "identities," and gets novelties.
The "reasoning by recurrence," however, is that form of
reasoning whereby one shows that if a given truth holds in n
cases, it holds for the $n + 1$st case, and so for all cases. Such
processes of passing to "one more" instance of a given type,
are processes not of barren repetition, but of genuine progress
to higher stages of knowledge.

Precisely so it is, too, if one takes account of that other
aspect of ordered series which it has been one principal purpose of this paper to emphasize. The numbers have interested
us, not from any Pythagorean bias, but because their Order is
the expression, not only of a profoundly significant aspect of
all law in the world, but of the very essence of Selfhood, when
formally viewed. Now reflective selfhood, taken merely as
the abstract series, *I know*, and *I know that I know*, etc., appears to be a vain repetition of the same over and over. But
this it appears merely if you neglect the concrete content which
every new reflection, when taken in synthesis with previous
reflections, inevitably implies in case of every living subject-
matter. A life that knows not itself differs from the same
life conscious of itself, by lacking precisely the feature that
distinguishes rational morality alike from innocence and from
brutish naïveté. A knowledge that is self-possessed differs
from an unreflective type of consciousness by having all the
marks that separate insight from blind faith.

"Thus we see," says Spinoza, in a most critical passage of

his *Ethics*,[1] "that the infinite essence and the eternity of God
are known to all. . . . That men have not an equally clear
cognition of God as they have of ordinary abstract ideas, is
due to the fact that God cannot be imagined, as bodies are
imagined, and that they have associated the name of God with
the images of things that they are accustomed to see." All
the ignorance and unwisdom whose consequences Spinoza sets
forth in the Third and Fourth Parts of his *Ethics*, are thus
declared, in this passage, to be due to the failure of the ordinary human mind to reflect upon, and to observe, an idea of
the truth, *i. e.* of God, which it still always possesses, and
which not the least of minds can really be without. For God's
essence is "equally in the part and in the whole." Thus vast,
then, is the difference in our whole view of ourselves and of
the universe which is to be the outcome of mere self-consciousness. Yet the same Spinoza, in a passage not long since cited
in our notes, can assert that *whoever has a true idea knows that
he has it*, and in a parallel passage can even make light of all
reflective insight, as a useless addition to one's true ideas.

This really marvellous vacillation of Spinoza, as regards the
central importance of self-consciousness in the whole life of
man and of the universe, is full of lessons as to the fallacy of
ignoring the positive meaning of reflective insight. This
positive meaning once admitted, it is impossible to assert that
any limited series of reflective acts can exhaust the self-representative significance of any concrete life. The properties of
the number-series, the inexhaustible wealth of the concept of
Order, and the fecundity of the mathematical "conclusion
from n to $n + 1$," are mere hints of what a reflective series
implies, and of the infinity of every genuine reflective series.
For, on the one hand, we have now sufficiently seen that the
fecundity in question is due to the essentially reflective character of the process whereby the conclusion from n to $n+1$
is justified.[1] On the other hand, our argument as to the

[1] Part II, Prop. 47, *Scholium*.

[2] Dedekind, *op. cit.*, p. 15, §§ 4, 59, has given a formal proof of the
validity of the "conclusion from n to $n + 1$." His proof, an extraordi-

universal fecundity of reflective processes, as merely illustrated by the wealth of the number-forms, is an argument *a fortiori*.

It is easy, as we have seen, to make light of mere numbers because they are so formal, and beecause one wearies of mathematics. But our present case is simply this: Of course the numbers, taken in abstract divorce from life, are mere forms. But if in the bare skeleton of selfhood, if in the dry bones of that museum of mere orderliness, the arithmetical series, — if, *even here*, we find such an endless wealth of relatively unique results of each new act of reflection, in case that act is taken in synthesis with the foregoing acts, — what may not be, what *must* be, the wealth of meaning involved in a reflective series whose basis is a concrete life, whose reflections give this life at each stage new insight into itself, and whose syntheses with all foregoing acts of reflection are themselves, if temporally viewed, as it were, new acts in the drama of this life? If such a life is to be present *totum simul* to the Absolute, how shall not the results of endless acts of reflection, each of an individual meaning, but all given, at one stroke, as an expression of the single purpose to reflect and to be self-possessed, — how shall all these facts not appear as elements in the unity of the whole, elements neither "transmuted" nor "suppressed," but comprehended in their organic unity ?

Unless the Absolute is a Self, and that concretely and explicitly, it is no Absolute at all. And unless it exhausts an infinity, in its presentations, it cannot be a Self. That even in thus exhausting it also excludes from itself the infinity that it wills to exclude, I equally insist. But I also maintain that this exclusion can only be based upon insight, and that, unless the positive infinity is present, as the self-represented whole that is accepted, the exclusion is blind, and our conception of Being lapses into mere Realism. But even Real-

narily brilliant feat of logical analysis, has been exhaustively analyzed, by Schroeder, in the passage before cited. It involves a peculiarly subtle reflection upon what the process of self-representation implies, — a reflection as easy to ignore as it is important to bring to clear light.

ism, as we have seen, is equally committed to the actually infinite.[1]

IV. *The Infinite as a Totality*

And yet one will persistently retort, " Your idea of the complete exhaustion of what you all the while declare to be, as infinite, an inexhaustible series, is still a plain contradiction."

I reply that I am anxious to report the facts, as one finds them whenever one has to deal with any endless *Kette*. The facts are these: (1) This series, if real, is inexhaustible by any process of successive procedure, whereby one passes from one member to the next. It is then expressly a series with *no last term*. Try to go through it from first to last, and the process can never be completed. Now this negative character of the series, if it is real, is as true for the Absolute as for a boy at school. *In this sense,* namely, viewed as a succession, since the series has no last term, its last term cannot be found by God or man, and does not exist. In this sense, too, any effort to

---

[1] As for my reasons for speaking of an Absolute Will at all, despite Mr. Bradley's repeated objections, I must insist that we have precisely the same reasons for attributing a generalized type of Will to the Absolute that we have for attributing to it Experience. And the grounds for this conclusion have been stated at length in Lecture VII of the foregoing series. My insistence means mere report of the facts, in the best accessible language. To say that the Absolute has or is Will, is simply to say that it knows its object, namely itself in its wholeness, *as this and no other*, despite the fact that the " mere " Thought, which it also possesses, consists, as abstract thought, in defining such an Other, and *because* of the fact that *this and no other* satisfies or fulfils the complete internal meaning of the Absolute itself. That Thought, Will, and Experience are not " transmuted " but concretely present from the Absolute point of view, is a thesis merely equivalent to saying that the Absolute consciously views itself as the *immediately given fulfilment of purpose in this and no other life*. As immediately given fact, the life is Experience. In so far as the purpose is distinguished from its fulfilment, one has an Idea seeking its Other. And this is Thought. In so far as *this and no other life* fulfils purpose, we have Will. All these are concretely distinguished aspects of the fact, if the Absolute is a Self, and views itself as such. If this is not true, the Absolute is less than nothing.

complete the series will fail. In this sense, therefore, the series indeed has no "totality," because it needs none. In this sense, finally, it would indeed be contradictory to speak of it as a totality. And all this is admitted, and need not be further illustrated.

(2) The sense in which the series is a totality is, however, if the series is real, not at all the sense in which it merely has no last member. The series is not to be exhausted in the sense in which it is indeed inexhaustible. But you may and must take it otherwise. The sense in which it is a totality expressly depends upon that concept of *totum simul* which I have everywhere in this discussion emphasized. To grasp this aspect of the case, you must view it in two stages. Take the series then *first* as a purely conceptual entity, as a mere idea, or "bare possibility." The *one purpose* of the perfect internal self-representation of any system of elements in the fashion, and according to the type of self-representation, here in question, defines, for any *Kette* formed upon the basis of that purpose, *all* of the ideal objects that are to belong to the *Kette*. And this purpose defines them *all at once*, as we saw in dealing with f_1 (n), and the rest of those series that are involved in any *Kette*. Now this endless wealth of detail is defined at one stroke, so that it is henceforth eternally predetermined, as a valid truth, precisely what does and what does not belong to that *Kette*. And the various series and this *Kette* are here one and the same thing. To find whether this or that element belongs to the *Kette*, may or may not involve, for you, a long time. It will involve for you succession, processes of counting, and much more of the sort indefinitely. This, however, is due to your fortune as a human observer. But the definition of the series has predetermined at one stroke all the results that you thus, taking them in succession, can never exhaust, and has predetermined these results as a fixed Order, wherein every element has its precise place, next after a previous element, next before a subsequent one. As for the *before* and *after*, in this Order, they, too, are ideally predetermined, not as themselves successions, but as valid and simultaneous relations. That *a*

come first, *b* second, etc., is determined by the definition, all at once. The definition of the *Kette* does not, however, like your acts in counting, *first* determine *a* and *afterwards b*. In the truly valid series it is the *a* and *b* that are simultaneously *first* and *next*. You must not confuse then the eternally valid and simultaneously predetermined aspects of this order with the temporal succession of your verifications of the order.

So far, then, you have taken the series as a valid Order, whose ideal totality lies in the singleness of a plan that it is supposed to express. And now comes the second stage of the process of defining our *Kette* as real. Here is indeed the decisive step. *All* the members of the series are *at once* validly predetermined. That we have seen. Whatever can be precisely defined, however, can be supposed immediately given. So now simply suppose that the members are *all* seen, experienced, presented, *not as they follow one after another, in your successive apperception of a few of them, but precisely as the definition predetermines them, namely, all at once.* Hereupon you define the series as a fact, not merely valid, but presented. And so to define it is to define it as actually infinite.

And now I challenge you: "Where is the contradiction in this conception of the presented infinite totality?" Try to point out the precise place of the contradictory element in the system as defined.

You may reply: "The contradiction lies here: That the series has no last term is admitted; yet if all its terms are present, the series must be completely presented. But a completed and ordered series must have a last term. How otherwise should it be completed?"

I rejoin: There is finality and finality, completion and completion. The sort of finality possessed by the series is expressly of one sort, and not of another. By hypothesis the series is not in *such* wise completely presented that its last term is seen. For it has indeed no last term. But it is, by hypothesis, so presented that *all* the terms, precisely as the single purpose of the definition demands them, are present. The definition was not self-contradictory in demanding them as its ideal fulfilment. How should the presentation become contradictory by merely showing what the consistent definition had called for? And now in *no other* sense is the series, as presented, *complete*, than in the one sense of showing, in the supposed experience, *all* of its own ideally defined members. It is not complete in having any closing term.

Your reply to this statement will doubtless at last appeal to the decisive consideration regarding the nature of any individual fact of Being. You will say: " But the determinate presentation of a series of facts involves precisely that sort of completion of the series which makes it possess a last member. For the series, if given, is an Individual Whole, presented as such a complex individual in experience ; and as an individual, the series needs precise limits. As it has a first, so then, if completely individuated, it must be finished by a last member. Otherwise it would lack the determination necessary to distinguish an Individual Being from a general idea." [1]

If the objection be thus stated, it raises afresh the whole question : What is an individual fact of experience? What is an individual whole in experience? Now I have set forth in the foregoing lectures (see Lectures VII and X), and have still more minutely developed elsewhere,[2] a thesis about individuality whose relative novelty in the discussion of that topic, and whose special importance with regard to the issue about the determinateness of the Infinite, I must here insist upon. That every individual Being is determinate, I fully maintain. But how and upon what basis does such determination rest? When, and upon what ground, could one say : *I have seen an individual whole?* *Never*, I must insist, upon the ground that one has seen a group of facts with a sharply marked boundary, or with a definite localization in space or in time,

---

[1] Here, as I believe, is the deepest ground for that Aristotelian objection to the Infinite as "no totality," which we have now so often met. The whole question, then, is as to the true essence of Individuality.

[2] *Conception of God*, Part III of the *Supplementary Essay* of that work. See also *ibid*, p. 331 : "Chasms do not individuate."

or with any temporal or spatial terminus.[1] A finished series of data simply does not constitute an individual whole merely by becoming finished. It is perfectly true that such a finished whole, with its boundary, its last term, or what limit you will, may be viewed and rightly viewed, as an individual; but only for reasons which lie far deeper than its mere possession of limits, and which, in their turn, might be present if such limits were quite undiscoverable. If you insist that only such limited wholes are ever viewed by us men as individual wholes, I retort that we men have never experienced the direct presence of any individual whole whatever. For us, individuals are primarily the objects presupposed, but never directly observed, by love and by its related passions, — in brief, by the exclusive affections which give life all its truest interests. As we associate these affections with those contents of experience whose empirical limits we also experience as essential to their form, the spatially or numerically boundless comes to seem (as it especially seemed to the Greek), the essentially formless, and hence unindividuated realm, where chaos reigns.

But such mere prejudices of our ordinary apprehension vanish, if we look more closely at what individual wholeness means. Never presented in our human experience, individuality is the most characteristic feature of Being. Its true definition, however, implies three features, no one of which has any necessary connection with *last* terms, or with ends, or with any other such accidents of ordinary sense perception, and of the temporal enumeration of details. These three features are as follows: First, an individual whole *must conform to an ideal definition*, which is precise, and free from ambiguity, so that if you know this individual type, you know in advance precisely what kind of fact belongs to the defined whole, and in what way. Secondly, *the individual whole must embody this type in the form of immediate experience*. And thirdly, *the individual whole must so embody the type that no other embodiment would meet precisely the purpose*, the Will, fulfilled by this embodiment.

---

[1] See, as against the theory of space and time as principles of individuation, the *Conception of God*, p. 250, *sqq.*

It is the third of these features that is the really decisive one. The satisfied Will, as such, is the sole Principle of Individuation. This is our theory of individuality. Here it comes to our aid.

For wherever in the universe these three conditions are together fulfilled, determinate individual wholeness gets presented. In our human experience their union, as a fact, is only postulated, and never found present, in the objects which constitute our empirical world. Hence in vain do you choose empirical series such as have last terms, and say, "Lo! these are typical individual wholes. If the Absolute sees individuality, in any collection of facts, he sees it as of *this* determinate type." On the contrary, as we men observe these things, they appear to us to be individuals, solely because we presuppose our own individuality as Selves, and then, in the light of this presupposition, regard these serial acts of ours as individual wholes, merely because in them we have found a relative satisfaction of a purpose.

That finite series are individual wholes at all, is therefore itself a presupposition — never a datum. I take myself to be an individual Self, whose acts, as my own, are unique with the assumed uniqueness of my own purposes. Any one of the various series of my acts which attains, for the moment, its relative goal, is thereby the more marked as my own, and as one. But it is not directly experienced as any individual fact of Being at all, and that for the reason set forth in our seventh lecture. That we are individuals is true, and that our finite series of acts have their own place in Being is also true. But their finitude has only accidental relations to their individuality.

But now, in case of such a *Kette* as we are supposing real, what is lacking to constitute it a determinate whole? It has ideal totality. For a single ideal purpose defines the type of all facts that shall belong to it, and distinguishes them from facts of all other types, and predetermines their order, assigning to every element its ideal place. We suppose now an experience embodying all these elements in such wise that immediacy and idea completely fuse, so that what is here conceived is also given. We finally suppose this to be such an experience, for the Self whose *Kette* this is, that in possessing this series he views himself as this Being *and no other*. Now this last feature of itself constitutes determinateness. To demand that the series should have its end, temporal or spatial, is to mistake wholly the nature of individuality; is to overlook the primacy of the decisive Will as the sole begetter of individuality; and is to apply to the Absolute a character derived from certain experiences of ours which we merely view as individual experiences in the light of a postulate, while, for this very postulate, only the Absolute itself can furnish the adequate warrant and realization.

Our own definition of individuality then, by freeing us from bondage to mere temporal and spatial limits, leaves us free to regard as determinate and as real an experience that contains, and that does not merely "absorb" a wealth of detail which in itself is endless. In so far as this wealth is endless, it does indeed force every process of successive synthesis to remain unfinished; and therefore, in so far as you merely count the successive steps, you shall never find what makes the whole determinate. There is indeed no infinite number belonging to, or terminating, the series of whole numbers. All whole numbers are finite. It is the totality of the whole numbers that constitutes an infinite multitude. But the determinateness of this infinite whole is given, not when the last whole number is counted (for that indeed would be self-contradictory), but when the completely conscious Self knows itself as this Being, and no other. And this it knows not when it performs its last act, but when it views its whole wealth of life as the determinate satisfaction of its Will.

And thus, having vindicated the conception of the really Infinite, we are free, upon the basis of the general argument of these lectures, to assert that the Absolute is no absorber and transmuter, but an explicit possessor and knower of an infinite wealth of organized individual facts, — the facts, namely, of the Absolute Life and Selfhood. How these facts are One and also Many, we now in general know, precisely in so far as we reflectively grasp the true nature of Thought. For the Other which Thought restlessly seeks is simply *itself* in individual expression, — or, in other words, its own purpose in a determinate and conscious embodiment. Since this embodiment has to assume the form of Selfhood, its detail must be infinite. The world is an endless *Kette,* whatever else it is. Yet this infinite wealth of detail is not opposed to, but is the very expression of the internal meaning of the purpose to be and to comprehend the Self. The infinite wealth is determinate because it fulfils a precisely definable purpose in an unique way, that permits no other to take its place as the embodiment of the Absolute Will. And the One and the Many are so reconciled, in this account, that the Absolute Self, even in order to be a Self at all, has to express itself in an endless series of individual acts, so that it is explicitly an Individual Whole of Individual Elements. And this is the result of considering Individuality, and consequently Being, as above all an expression of Will, and of a Will in which both Thought and Experience reach determinateness of expression.